There Are Two Sexes

FOREWORD BY JEAN-JOSEPH GOUX

antoinette fouque

TRANSLATED BY DAVID MACEY AND CATHERINE PORTER

EDITED BY SYLVINA BOISSONNAS

There Are 2 SEXES

ESSAYS IN FEMINOLOGY

COLUMBIA UNIVERSITY PRESS   New York

COLUMBIA UNIVERSITY PRESS

PUBLISHERS SINCE 1893

NEW YORK CHICHESTER, WEST SUSSEX

cup.columbia.edu

Il y a deux sexes, copyright © 1995, expanded edition copyright © 2004, Gallimard

Copyright © Editions Des femmes:

chapter 23, "Gravida," in *Gravidanza* (2007)

chapter 24, "What Is a Woman," in *Génération MLF* (2008)

chapter 25, "Gestation for Another, Paradigm of the Gift," in *Génésique* (2012)

foreword by Jean-Joseph Goux (2013)

Copyright © 2015 Columbia University Press

All rights reserved

Library of Congress Cataloging-in-Publication Data

Fouque, Antoinette.

[Il y a deux sexes. English]

There are two sexes: essays in feminology / Antoinette Fouque;

foreword by Jean-Joseph Goux; translated by David Macey and Catherine Porter; edited by

Sylvina Boissonnas.

pages cm

Includes bibliographical references and index.

ISBN 978-0-231-16986-8 (cloth : alk. paper) — ISBN 978-0-231-53838-1 (e-book)

1. Women. 2. Feminism. 3. Sex role. I. Title.

HQ1208.F6813 2015

305.4—dc23

2014026340

Columbia University Press books are printed on permanent and durable acid-free paper.

This book is printed on paper with recycled content.

Printed in the United States of America

c 10 9 8 7 6 5 4 3 2 1

BOOK & COVER DESIGN: CHANG JAE LEE

References to websites (URLs) were accurate at the time of writing. Neither the author nor
Columbia University Press is responsible for URLs that may have expired or changed since
the manuscript was prepared.

For Vincente and Ezekiel

Contents

Foreword

Antoinette Fouque's work should have been introduced to English-language readers much earlier. It is highly regrettable that the vigorous American debate over French feminism, or, more broadly, over the question of gender, has not benefited from Fouque's original, coherent, and persistent thinking. For several decades now, American feminists, or, to take a wider view, women's studies programs, have analyzed, debated, supported, or contested, after Simone de Beauvoir's contributions, those of Luce Irigaray, Julia Kristeva, Hélène Cixous, and Monique Wittig. Although it is fair to say that Fouque, through her actions, speeches, and writings, has been the chief inspirational force behind the most original and most combative dimensions of the French women's liberation movement, her name appears very rarely in the Anglophone context. There is an anomaly here that the publication of this book by Columbia University Press will, happily, begin to rectify.

From 1968 on, with the creation of the group known as Psychanalyse et Politique (Psychoanalysis and Politics) and the beginning of the Mouvement de Libération des Femmes (Women's Liberation Movement, or MLF), Antoinette Fouque's actions and theoretical positions have given a decisive impetus to French "feminism." Her orientations have had a determining influence, in various forms, on all women whose thought has been burgeoning since the earliest manifestations of this group and this movement.

In this connection several points stand out as marking the originality of Fouque's theoretical and practical positions—positions that were to have widespread repercussions on what later came to be called French feminism.

Fouque's specific ideas about women's liberation can also be read as a critique of Simone de Beauvoir's feminism. With that form of feminism, in Fouque's view, what was won in terms of emancipation was accompanied by an onerous renunciation. The woman who had to ignore or abandon all ambitions in order to devote herself to procreation (the traditional situation under the patriarchal regime) was succeeded by a woman who had to sacrifice her desire to procreate in order to satisfy her ambitions. Thus women emerged from the age-old maternal slavery—and this was certainly a first major step toward their liberation—but at the price of repressing the desire for a child. In Fouque's view, what was required was not to pretend to be unaware of the strength of that desire, but rather to make a place for it in women's liberation. Beauvoirian feminism thus had to be surpassed by a new phase that would no longer be "feminism" in the limited sense, but a true liberation that would take into account the entire set of factors involved in women's full development, countering any notion that the difference between the sexes should be neutralized. In this sense, for Fouque, the feminist challenge remains internal to the patriarchal enclosure, as a position that seeks to obtain powers, roles, and functions for women that had previously been the monopoly of men, but to the detriment of women's own capacities, among which procreation is the most significant and the most inalienable. It is not true that "a woman is a man like any other," as certain feminist slogans from the early days proclaimed. This is why Fouque can declare that she is not "merely a feminist"—a claim that may be surprising and subject to misunderstanding if it is not resituated in the context of the contemporary debates.

Antoinette Fouque's work is aimed at a more complete liberation of women, beyond the limitations that the first feminism imposed. She locates herself within a postfeminism that requires not only political and institutional advances but also a theoretical and philosophical step forward. This step calls for a new understanding—without regressing to earlier positions—of the female libido that is at work in the desire for a child, in gestation, in childbirth. The Freudian conception, accentuated by Lacan, of a single libido that is the same in men and in women and for which the phallus would be the master signifier ought to be succeeded by a conception that takes into account the libido proper to women. Alongside the phallic libido there is the other one, uterine and matricial: the *libido creandi*. Fouque's relation to Freud stems from this fundamental position: she critiques the ideology of masculinity that prevails in Freud and Lacan, but she does not repeat the gesture of a certain feminism that simply liquidates psychoanalysis, for psychoanalysis still offers the only discourse there is on female sexuality. For Fouque, it is more a matter of amending and expanding psychoanalytic theory by challenging it with what is specific in female desire: above all, the desire to procreate. It is in relation to this partial and critical acceptance of Freudian psychoanalysis within the MLF that the well-known collective Psychanalyse et Politique (often called Psych et Po) was established, with the goal of exploring the connections between the unconscious and the political: the unconscious in the political, and also the powers deployed, the hierarchies created, within the unconscious.

This work of elucidation is accompanied by a reinterpretation of genitality, a libidinal phase that was recognized by Freud but that tends to be conflated with the phallic stage, owing to the supremacy attributed to the latter; in Lacan's case it tends to be forgotten or even contested. Not only is it essential not to ignore the desire for a child specific to the *libido creandi* or reduce it to the phallic, but it is essential that gestation, pregnancy, the obscure metamorphoses that take place within women's bodies, all the organic work that has always seemed to go on at an infrasymbolic level, be brought into language and acknowledged at the symbolic level. Hence metaphoric fertility in cultural and artistic creation is also implied in men and women alike.

Before the "penis envy" so heavily stressed by Freud, there is *uterus envy*, male jealousy of women's creative genitality. Appropriating that genitality for themselves, by all sorts of strategies, has always been one of the major concerns of the male world. It is a wound for men, an infringement on their omnipotence. Antoinette Fouque thus identifies a fourth narcissistic wound to be added to the ones Freud enumerated. Not only does the planet Earth not lie at the center of the universe; not only is man not the ruler of creation but a natural being closely related to other mammals; not only is the ego not the master in its own house, since there is the dimension of the unconscious, which the ego does not control; but there is a fourth blow to add to Freud's list of three: the "*genesic blow*." A very old, very primitive wound that myths and religions have worked hard to deny, a wound that did not need the scientific revolutions brought about by Copernicus, Darwin, and Freud to appear, but that has haunted minds from time immemorial: every girl and boy is born of a woman's body. This material, fleshly birth, so hard for men to accept, cannot be evaded, forgotten, denied, transposed, or sublimated. This truth, which is at once hidden and self-evident, difficult to see and impossible to ignore, is foregrounded by a movement that places female genitality at the center of its ethics. Giving life, welcoming in oneself someone other than oneself— what Fouque calls *hospitality of the flesh*—is the basis for the principle of the gift and altruism. With gestation and the act of childbirth, procreation must be taken as the model of the ethics of the gift, the very *paradigm of ethics*.

In this work of critical elucidation, the forgotten, repressed importance of the mother-daughter genealogy has to emerge, or reemerge. This genealogy has long been hidden away in our societies by the burdensome, structuring tradition—at once legal, economic, symbolic, and religious—of filiation and transmission along the father-son axis.

The place Fouque attributes to the mother-daughter relation leads to an original conception of female homosexuality. Just like a man, a woman has a woman—her mother—as her first love object. Then, in the canonical case of her libidinal development, she has to shift to a male love object, has to deny and reject the first object of attachment after having loved it. There is a hindrance here that may keep the woman from achieving full development of her libido, may prevent her from constituting herself fully as a woman subject. A primary, *native homosexuation*, distinct from lesbianism, has to be experienced with another woman or with other women in order to make access to a female, genital libido possible.

There are two sexes. This central affirmation on which Antoinette Fouque insists might seem trivial. It is at stake today, however, in multiple debates. In the subtle but often unrealistic and sterile controversies that arise around the difference between the sexes and its negation, Fouque takes a clearly delineated position, which she draws from numerous anthropological, philosophical, and political sources and from her deepest personal experience as well. At the opposite pole from a way of thinking aimed at neutralizing—or even completely negating—the difference between the sexes, she proclaims the reality of a difference from which it would be fatal, for women, to seek to free themselves. If it is legitimate to denounce the often repressive stereotypes that confine the "genders" to outdated historical and cultural expressions, this does not imply that the difference between the sexes is nothing but a purely conventional and arbitrary construction, just a matter of playing with signifiers, without any relation to the real. Transposing structuralist formalism, which has proved fertile in linguistics, mythography, and narratology, into the domain of the difference between the sexes cannot be achieved without the risk of a sort of bankruptcy analogous, perhaps, to the ruptures between the virtual economy of finance and the real economy. We can enumerate four models that, for Fouque, stand out in the history of women (or in the history of the relations between women and men) and that now open onto an anthropological revolution. The oldest and most powerful is the historical regime of enslaved maternity. A second model has tried to go beyond the first: this model negates the difference between the sexes and proclaims a unisex or a neutral sex as the solution to the conflicts between men and women. This leads to a third model, the one that prevails today in the neoliberal economic universe: here neutralizing and unisex feminism is combined in an unstable and unsatisfactory way with the inadequately assumed desire for maternity. Ultimately, there will be a *fourth model*, the necessity and horizons of which are beginning to appear: a *new human contract*, in a democratic universe that incorporates, with full parity, the ethical structure that is borne by procreation and creation alike. To hasten the advent of this human contract, Antoinette Fouque calls for the creation of a new science, a science of women, *feminology*, a mode of thought that is materialist and fleshly rather than idealist, political and action-oriented rather than metaphysical.

Through her writings and actions alike, through her theoretical stances as well as through the multiple courageous creations of which she has been the origin and the tireless driving force, Antoinette Fouque is a crucial figure in women's struggle for access to authentic freedom. Not only was she one of the founders of the MLF in 1968, then the founder of the publishing house Des femmes and the editor of several militant journals that played a key role in raising public awareness, but she was also the first woman from the Movement to be elected to the European Parliament, where she did significant work on behalf of women. At the UN World Conference on Human Rights, held in Vienna in 1993, she played a decisive role in securing the adoption of an article stating that "the human rights of women and of the girl-child are an inalienable, integral and indivisible part of universal human rights."[1]

In the unsettled situation that confronts us today, it is fortunate that Antoinette Fouque's thought is becoming accessible to an English-speaking public.

Jean-Joseph Goux
December 2013

Preface to the First Edition

There are two sexes. This is a reality that history will henceforth have to make its fourth principle, beyond liberty, equality, and fraternity, if it is to be consistent with its own ideals. What can intellectual, social, and political recognition of this reality contribute to the democratization process? How can we think and practice a form of citizenship predicated on parity? There are two sexes. The *production of living beings* (*production de vivant*) is tripartite, since one (male) multiplied by one (female) makes a future one (male or female). This tripartition has always been denatured by the Trinity: three that make only One. How can we break out of the infernal circle of the *monos*—monotheism, monarchy, monosexuality, all of which prefigure universalism?

The present volume contains a collection of texts that attempt to think further, and differently. *Feminology* is what I call this epistemological field, newly opened alongside the human sciences: a promise of mutual enrichment.[1] The sciences of women seek to understand our foreclosed knowledge, which is both unconscious and excluded. Grounding the time of procreation in the space of gestation, *feminology* is both a genealogy of knowledge and knowledge of genealogy. Making its way back through the natural and human sciences, it will be moving from *gyneconomy* to ethics.[2]

I have always endeavored to think like a woman of action and to act like a woman of thought. Thus, to illustrate the psychopolitical movement I started over twenty-five years ago, I have chosen to publish a set of texts written between two symbolic dates, March 8, 1989 and March 8, 1995.[3]

Preface to the Second Edition

For Marie-Claude

This collection of texts goes back almost ten years. The first article, from 1989, already bore witness to over twenty years of theoretical and practical work, widely disseminated through meetings, demonstrations, creations, and productions organized by the Mouvement de Libération des Femmes[1] and Psychanalyse et Politique.[2] The essay represents a kind of fugue pattern in which the thought—the *geni(t)ality* of women[3]—that inhabits me, and that may well have inhabited me before I was born, is repeated, differentiated, vaporized, polarized, dispersed, decentered, excentered, exceeded. This latent thought manifested itself consciously at least twice. First through a personal experience: the birth of my daughter in 1964 literally discovered and invented it. Then came a public experience that made the *geni(t)ality* of women both explicit and thinkable: the birth of the MLF in October 1968, when Monique Wittig and Josiane Chanel and I, close friends at the time, joined the crowd of May '68 agitators while engaging with the thinkers of the 1960s—at times reacting against them, more often acting in spite of them, beyond them.[4]

This second edition calls for at least two observations. While only a limited number of copies of the first edition were published, they were all sold, which means that the book found an audience at the time. Yet far from proving out of date today, its contents—women's sufferings and struggles—unfortunately turn out to be more topical than ever. Over the past thirty-five years, not a day has passed without my feeling a need to resist, to understand, and to move forward, along with millions of other women. Although these last three decades have probably seen more decisive progress than the preceding two thousand years of history, the four new texts added to this revised edition, written between 1997 and 2002, confirm that the overall picture remains dismal.[5] All over the planet, and with increasing frequency, women continue to be victims of the unilateral violence of male domination in all its possible manifestations, whether private, public, economic, social, cultural, religious, political, symbolic, real, or imaginary. It is as though just as women are asserting their liberation a macho counterliberation is constraining them, deporting them, imprisoning them, crushing them. Every day the courage and strength of women defy a destiny that is not imposed on them by anatomy but is rather prescribed by tradition and constructed by civilizations and history.

This year, in 2004, in France and elsewhere, we shall be celebrating the thirtieth anniversary of state feminism, that is, institutional programs for the benefit of women.

In 1974, after six years of involvement by women of all backgrounds, six years of intense activism on the part of the MLF along with the older feminist currents it had reinvigorated, the first-ever secretary of state for the condition of women was created in France. The street demonstrations, the culture of revolt, the impassioned demands, the utopias, the "Silk" Revolution of the self that the MLF stood for,[6] the omnipotence of ideals and dreams addicted to the pleasure principle were succeeded—rather too harshly at times—by submission to the reality principle. The time for democracy, for well-behaved organizations (NGOs, as they are now widely known) and democratic reforms, had come. And, indeed, over the past thirty years there has been no shortage of reforms: we have seen legislation providing for the abolition of paternal omnipotence, divorce by mutual consent, equality between men and women in the workplace, equality regarding the matrimonial property regime and parental authority, and new laws on rape and sexual assault. The primary function of laws may not be so much to punish as to raise consciousness. Laws set limits, specify prohibitions, define rights, and call for justice to be done, both legally and symbolically. An antislavery law is a precious tool for defending the freedom to live and to think; a law against a specific injustice is a precious tool for defending the freedom to act. Laws substitute nonviolent compromise and negotiation for bellicose confrontation. Endowed with political wisdom and psychological maturity, far from lapsing into terrorism, women in movements have appealed to the rule of law and set about democratizing democracy. Three major milestones may be distinguished in the transformation of hitherto illegitimate demands into rights: the adoption of laws concerning abortion, parity, and secularism.

Recognition of the right to choose abortion, along with contraception, made control over fertility possible for the first time in human history. In opposition to enslaved motherhood, abortion law acknowledges the right to procreate (or not), and therefore the freedom for each woman to think over and through the experience of gestation. What I have called women's *geni(t) ality* thereby breaks free from obscurantism, from the "miracle" of procreation, from the "mystery" of the dark continent. Without ideology, but with no lack of imagination, a new epistemological field is being invented. A place for exploring the *genius of women*[7] in which Enlightenment obstetrics, the Freudian unconscious, the genesic and psychic creation inherent in pregnancy all mesh together as *feminology* to shed light on feminism, just as sociology has shed light on socialism.

With very few exceptions, every woman in democratic countries may now decide, relying on law and technology, whether she wishes to give life or not; fully entitled to be child free, she asserts her independence. With the abortion law in France, a vital measure of public health, women could hope to have full control over their bodies, their sex organs, their flesh, on all of which, below and even beyond the Freudian unconscious, through an unprecedented power play we had just lifted the censorship for the first time in history.

To put an end to the outrageous underrepresentation of French women in a "uni(sex)versalist" republic, the struggle for parity—a trans-European idea sustained by newly founded, highly active ad hoc organizations, by nationwide debate in the media, and above all by the political will of then Prime Minister Lionel Jospin to end a specific form of discrimination and modernize a republic ossified in its abstract egalitarianism—led to a change in the Constitution passed by the French Parliament on June 28, 1999. Article 3 of the Constitution now includes the following statement: "Statutes shall promote equal access of men and women to electoral mandates and elective offices." Yet the choice of "equality" maintains the old order, the abstract logic of One-Whole applied to both sexes: the female sex is blotted out in its irreducible dissymmetry and so is the generative, fertile sharing entailed in the conjugation of the two sexes. The equality trap hinders the shift from the age-old centered, closed, selfish, individualistic libidinal economy, and from the phallocapitalist political economy based on profit, to a generous, generative libidinal economy that is neither binary nor dual but twofold, manifold, and to a political economy based on sharing or even giving.

Just as the law on abortion came up against the ultra-right, the law on parity has come up against free market ultra-liberalism[8] and ultra-phallo-centrism; sovereign androcentrism hinders the emergence of a parity culture. Reduced to its quantitative, anal dimension, compelled by a fainthearted differentialism to express itself in terms of equality, parity is clearly on the road to failure. Only a change in the very foundations of the Constitution—which has yet to recognize women's rights as "inalienable and sacred"—would have opened the way to qualitative parity.[9]

The opposition to parity, like the opposition to its logical extension, the law on joint surnames,[10] is violent. It is a reaction by those who idolize pater-nal omnipotence and who pretend to confuse primary difference—the inau-gural, absolute, fertile, genital difference that engenders living-speaking beings—with secondary differences—the relative, cultural, ethnic, national, dual, anal, phallic differences that produce war and conflict.

To save secularism, a modest law is to be voted on this year. In the debate on this controversial issue, positions are divided. Taking an unequivocal stance, the magazine Elle has urged President Chirac to protect the endan-gered rights of women.[11]

Some would like to persuade us that parity is responsible for introducing the communitarianism currently threatening the republic, as if women con-stituted a minority.[12] Yet those behind the veil are indeed minor, subjugated citizens being displayed, or displaying themselves, in a gesture of voluntary servitude, however warlike it may be. No one has mentioned the torture in-volved in wearing a veil in the sweltering summer heat, where women are prohibited from going for a swim to cool off. We are not dealing here with a mere epiphenomenon, as some contend, but with a major symptom of the sexual divide running through the republic and the citizenry. The French words voile (veil) and viol (rape) are so similar that they can be switched back and forth ad infinitum. Rape reappears in the veil, and the uninterrupted rape of women returns in veiled form. It is often claimed that everything there is to say for or against the veil has already been said, but here again the last word on the subject is a long way off, considering how rudimentary a reading has been offered of what a veiled woman symbolizes: captive femininity and enslaved fertility, erected womanhood on display. Yet "no-veil" advocates often uphold the image of a phallicized woman—transvestite femininity reduced to an artifact or masculinized and trapped in a sterilizing egalitarianism, she too the eroticized organ of her master. Raped or veiled, covered from head to toe or clad in G-strings, women are held hostage, caught between the rock of enslaving tradition and the hard place of porn-market modernity.

On mainland French territory, and not only on the island of Mayotte—where the Constitution allows for retaining "personal status" as opposed to the civil status defined by French common law[13]—but also in the suburbs of Paris, the veil reflects an alarming reality that includes polygamy, excision, in the future conceivably even stoning; it reflects private and public insecurity in a country that, in violation of its own commitments, has refused to arm women with an antisexism law modeled on the antiracism law strictly for defensive purposes.

The positive aspect of the bill on secularism lies in the fact that it strengthens and renders more explicit a form of secularism that previously paid little attention to women's rights, to the mixing of the sexes in education and public life, or to the heterosexuality of basic rights.[14]

State feminism seems to function on an ad hoc basis, taking back with one hand what it has given with the other; it lacks any overarching project or political will with regard to women. Between reform and counter-reform, it pursues a deadly wait-and-see policy.

The current context is of one of mounting confusion. One woman may be in favor of the Civil Solidarity Pact (PACS),[15] but opposed to the law on parity; another may be for parity, but against the law on secularism; a radical feminist who has violently fought against the idea that there is a difference between the sexes may suddenly espouse a cultural differentialism verging on communitarianism. Still, a clear pattern emerges. The law on abortion is contested by right-wing fundamentalists, the law on parity by "uni(sex)versalists," the law on secularism by fundamentalists of every stripe, from the totalitarian, pseudo-democratic, alterglobalist radical left to part of the mainstream, "plural" left eager to win over additional voters. What do all these reactionaries who react so violently have in common? Under what kinds of unconscious confusion, neurosis, psychosis, or perversion are they laboring? The "Mono Gang,"[16] the "Holy Alliance" of totalitarians or fundamentalists, extends much further than the one involving monotheistic religions; it unites all the fervent supporters of One-Whole, those who are hostile to the open At-Least-Two, to the democratic personality, to parity democracy, to partnership democracy. Over the past thirty years a major transformation has taken place. Exposure of the misogyny intrinsic to all civilizations has not only reinforced an endemic sexual misogyny that is universal, although it targets individuals; it has also added in a massive political misogyny, an antifeminism targeting an ongoing movement of the historical condition that cannot be sidestepped.

The fact is that for close to four decades now the women's movement has been a continuum that cannot be stopped. At every moment, somewhere on the planet, there are women individually or collectively asserting their freedom to act and think, fighting to defend their progress and their newly won rights. Each reform brings forth counter-reforms. Women's liberation, the most protracted of all revolutions, must brace itself for the longest and bloodiest of counter-revolutions. We must arm ourselves with watchful patience and muster all our courage to take lucid risks.

The first and second backlashes,[17] which provided the motivation for writing the essays collected here, had little trouble staging reprisals, because the counteroffensive took place against the backdrop of worldwide economic, political, and symbolic breakdown, starting with the first gesture of reparations toward women (the 1975 United Nations Conference on Women in Mexico City). The resurgence of religion preceded the rise of fundamentalism. As early as the mid-1970s, masculine protest and monotheistic paranoia grounded antifeminism in misogyny; antifeminism served to update the most archaic form of racism, just as today's "new (male) feminists" oversee and promote women's emancipation and, driving a wedge between mothers and daughters in a divide-and-conquer strategy, seek to take over the legacy of the women's movement.

Our bodies still do not belong to us, and we have yet to receive equal pay for equal work. This negative picture looks even grimmer when we consider the litany of murders by close relations, gang rapes (a phenomenon by no means limited to the poorest neighborhoods), teenage pregnancies, and cases of incest and pedophilia in which porn-market modernity merges with the traditions of slavery.

In 1998 Amartya Sen won the Nobel Prize in economics for his work as a whole; much of his research has been devoted to the condition of women. Although his writings have been available in French for over fifteen years, he has not acquired a significant following here. It would appear that most of our learned sociologists pay him no attention whatsoever. None of his books has made the best-seller list, and the *gynocide* he exposes has yet to arouse the indignation of a single one of the leading intellectuals so often featured in the media.[18] On several occasions, most notably in the European Parliament and in this collection of articles, I have referred to his shocking report without getting the slightest reaction.[19] A woman is missing? No, one hundred million women are missing from the world population. That makes a human capital deficit of one hundred million. In 2002 Amartya Sen went back on the offensive, but with equally little impact, stating, "But in dealing with the new form of gender inequality, the injustice relating to natality, there is a need to go beyond the question of the agency of women and to look for a more critical assessment of received values. When anti-female bias in behavior (such as sex-selective abortion) reflects the hold of traditional masculinist values from which mothers themselves may not be immune, what is needed is not just freedom of action but also freedom of thought—the freedom to question and to scrutinize inherited beliefs and traditional priorities. Informed critical agency is important in combating inequality of every kind, and gender inequality is no exception."[20]

The new texts added to the present edition confirm this human disaster. From real violence to symbolic violence, from rape to veil, from marital homicide to Sharia law, the massacre goes on with growing intensity. Every day, "if this is a woman,"[21] the media trivialize the danger of dying.

In the New World, in Ciudad Juarez, on the Mexico-Texas border, over five hundred women have been murdered since 1993—after being mutilated, tortured, and/or raped—with total impunity. The gravity of the situation has alarmed the UN and led it to protest against government inaction and indifference.[22] Here in our old Europe, on October 4, 2002, Sohane, a young woman from a housing project in the Paris suburbs, was burned alive in a garbage storage room by a jilted suitor.[23] None of the politicians who protested that same day against a racist crime and a homophobic attack expressed any indignation over this sexist murder or any compassion for the young martyr.[24] A year later, almost to the day, a fifty-year-old woman teacher in Nice suffered the same fate; this crime was similarly trivialized and met with even greater silence.[25] Lethal torture of this sort has become increasingly widespread in Europe. On July 1, 2003, a young, highly popular actress was beaten to death by her lover, a "politically correct" musician with antiglobalist sympathies. In late December, after a flurry of media attention, a highbrow newspaper included this sober remark in its year-end review: "Marie Trintignant

died following a violent dispute."[26] A few squeamish feminists were out-
raged to see such a scene removed from the private sphere, while others,
showing greater dignity and rigor, viewed the murder in the alarming context of marital insecurity. Although the number of road accident victims has
recently gone down in France, unilateral violence still kills five women every
month, with little media coverage apart from the "human interest" or "man-
bites-dog" sections of the daily paper. In Spain, domestic terrorism kills
more people than the Basque separatist group ETA.

Women, the poorest of the poor, are getting poorer and poorer.[27] When I
entered the European Parliament in 1994, I received a first report entitled "La
pauvreté se féminise en Europe" (Poverty increasingly affects women in
Europe). Others were to follow. The charitable organization Secours
Catholique has recently voiced concern over the issue as well.[28] Yet, since the
1975 Conference in Mexico, NGOs and women's rights activists have been
constantly reiterating this distress call. Whereas women produce two-thirds
of global wealth, they own only 1 percent of it, get a mere 10 percent of dis-
posable income, and constitute 75 percent of the world's poorest inhabitants. In opening the doors wide to market forces, our democracies force
women, often the heads of single-parent families, into a life of informal
work, temporary jobs, and unemployment. In the current desocialization
process, France is threatening its gynecologists, closing down maternity
wards, and cutting back on retirement facilities. Although women have "biological advantages . . . over men in resisting disease,"[29] and although many
of them have contributed several children to society, they are the primary
victims of the current health and social service deficit. Their pensions have
been unjustly reduced. Women also made up the vast majority of the heat
wave victims in the summer of 2003.[30]

Job insecurity or motherhood, unemployment or prostitution—the current headlong slide into free market economic liberalism throws women
back upon the two "natural" occupations inherent in their human and historical condition: the world's most beautiful occupation, procreation, and
its oldest, prostitution. In point of fact, from time immemorial, these have
both been forms of slavery used to provide men with children and pleasure.
Free market forces are turning the Earth and women's bodies into commodities. Trafficking, pornography, prostitution. "The economic horror"[31] has
combined with libertine sadism and barbaric individualism to exploit the
voluntary masochism of a few Harkis of the divine marquis.[32] Yet, instead of
demanding the abolition of sexual slavery, a certain branch of the left and a

certain branch of feminism suggest that it should be institutionalized in the form of regulated prostitution. Fundamentalism, terrorism, imperialism, fanaticism, egotism of every kind: both rich and poor spend their budgets on their urge to kill rather than using it to meet the need for nurturing, caring and educating women and children alike.

West and East are busy setting fire to our planet and to women; the world is in flames. Inside, outside, in the family, in the streets, at school, on the highway, in neighborhoods, housing projects, and rural areas, in societies where the rule of law holds sway and elsewhere, whether rich or poor, traditional or modern, at all possible levels of analysis, women are confronted with a particular kind of war, as if their bodies—endowed with a vital function for our species, the *genesic function*—were the target of primordial hatred. Those who point out this grim reality are accused of "victimizing" women, whereas they are merely calling attention to the slaughter and its perpetrators. Serial killers, rapists, jilted suitors, abusive alcoholic spouses, pedophiles, sex tourists—almost without exception, these are all men. Although adequate statistics are lacking, all reports confirm that males dominate this misogynistic world. There is no war between the sexes, simply because women do not wage war; up to now, they have simply been subjected to it.

Such regressions in democracy after thirty years of state feminism confirm the analyses presented in the first edition of this book and the assumptions underlying them. What is at issue here is not so much women's commitment to the cause as the irrelevance of the political and psychoanalytical analyses that have come to the fore. In the intervening years I have amply stressed the structural deficiencies found in the various models for solving the problem, deficiencies that perpetuate the catastrophic situation of women in history. I am referring in particular to the traditional model of *tota mulier in utero* and to the uni(sex)versalist republican model that arose in the wake of an indifferentialist feminism of the *tota mulier sine utero* variety. In one case exploitation is deliberate; in the other it is denied. As for the democratic model, a recycled, compromise version of the two preceding models, it purports to reconcile family life and work life. The fertility rate, dislodged from the female bodies on which it depends and transposed to "the family" or to the science of demography, denies and exploits what I have been calling for years now the *production of living beings*,[33] which in many cases combines with both domestic labor and salaried labor to form a *triple production*.[34]

The combined drift into libertinage and free market liberalism has taken us far afield from the studious years of practical and theoretical struggle in which one could find leaflets arguing that lifting the censorship on the labor power of proletarians was one of Marx and Engel's most telling moves.[35] In 1884 Engels wrote, "The determining factor in history is, in the last resort, the production and reproduction of immediate life . . . the production of the means of subsistence . . . and the production of human beings themselves, the propagation of the species."[36]

In lifting the existing censorship on the unconscious, Freud came up against "a difficulty on the path of psycho-analysis."[37] He identified three major "blows" to human narcissism in history, all of which met with "emotional" rather than intellectual resistance: the cosmological blow dealt by Copernicus, the biological blow dealt by Darwin, and the psychological blow represented by the discovery of the unconscious. In lifting the existing censorship on women's bodies, women's liberation movements everywhere called forth, most often unwittingly, even greater resistance to a fourth blow to narcissism, the genesic blow.[38] However strongly they may assert themselves, masculine protest and its magic trio—frustration, aggression, and regression—have great difficulty suppressing and foreclosing the liberated strengths of women who are demanding the right to exist.

My reading of Melanie Klein, whose work Envy and Gratitude had just been translated into French in 1968, confirmed my intuition that uterus envy plagues the male unconscious infinitely more than penis envy troubles the female unconscious.[39] Yet the word uterus is absent from Klein's conceptual framework. Two hundred years after Diderot's Éléments de Physiologie and the beautiful engraving in his Encyclopedia,[40] the uterus still has not found its way into any dictionary of psychoanalysis or of ethics. It is not enough to identify uterus envy; we must also think through its political effects, which in all areas take the form of real as well as symbolic violence inflicted on women.[41]

Genesic blow to narcissism, uterus envy, foreclosure of the production of living beings, misogyny.

Genesis, the mythology of the religions of the Book, the great Freudian narratives on the evolution of a human species in progress, from the Overview of the Transference Neuroses to Moses and Monotheism,[42] and the monolithic thinking of free market liberalism that currently holds sway in the field of political economics,[43] all represent variations on the theme of envy—a concept that is both psychoanalytical and political—that boil down to the sacrifice of the living (le vivant) and foreclosure of its production.[44] In the realm of political economics, the production of living beings is neither accounted for nor theorized.[45] In the field of psychoanalysis there is no fertile woman, no theory of genitality. Under phallocapitalist law and the postmodern rule of the politically correct, thinking is prohibited.

This is what the Passion of the One, the pseudosymbolic order, anal phallocentrism, and homogeneous indifferentialism have been striving to control, to dominate, to enslave. My hypothesis is that misogyny, or racism against women, the most radical form of racism in existence, is rooted in the very source of the singular power that arouses the envy of all those—children and adults, women and men—who believe, rightly or wrongly, that they are bereft of it and erect in its place an alternative omnipotence (Freud speaks of a "surrogate phallus") that colonizes it, exploits it, and forecloses its economy in favor of various general equivalents. These include gold, father, phallus, and language,[46] all of which, in the history of *homo sapiens sapiens*, symbolize the omnipotent phallus. One of the two sexes must be assimilated or disappear, must be converted or perish. Thus Gilles Lipovetsky considers procreation "a fundamental obstacle to the homogenization of sex roles."[47] Similarly, Lacan (for whom, it should be recalled, "woman does not exist") declared that procreation "evades the symbolic tapestry"[48]—in his seminar on psychoses, no less—and thus effectively outlawed it. There is only one libido, and it is phallic, as Françoise Dolto, more Lacanian than Lacan himself, stressed repeatedly in the mid-1970s. Far from being a privilege, procreation downgraded in this fashion severely penalizes women in any integration process, whereas, if it were to recover its rightful status, procreation should become the primary motive for subverting an order that is perverse in every respect.

The main enemy of women's liberation has not been adequately designated: male monism, phallocentrism, egocentrism, the One as the sole representative of the entire human species. From monotheism to republican equality, there is only the One. Only one God—male; one libido—phallic; one economy—free market liberalism; one kind of citizenship—neuter; one subject—universal; one sex, one individual—monadic, unconnected. The trouble is that while God needs men, men need "the race of women" to provide them with offspring.[49] This explains the colonization of the "dark continent," enslavement (woman as a living instrument),[50] appropriation of the uterus (the principal means of production), exploitation of uterine production. The libido *dominandi, savandi, sciendi* of philosophers or that of the discourse of masters, analysts, scholars, or academics (Lacan)[51]—that phallic libido knows only too well that although a woman may be converted into a hysterical slave (disciple or bitch), and although she may be dressed in feminist guise like a political Marrano, not only does heterogeneous procreation create disorder in the doxa, but even pinning it down in concrete does not suffice to overpower the libido that escapes the phallic libido's grasp every time a woman expresses her desire, the desire to have a child or the desire for another woman that lies at the source of her most intimate drive.

The oldest and yet still contemporary symbolic order pits men against women, dividing them from each other and dividing each of them in two. Creation, culture, the conceptual realm, legitimacy, privilege, and human genius belong to them; procreation, animal-like conception, nature, guilty genitality, illegitimacy, and discrimination belong to us. All Law belongs to man, One-Whole for both. Freud believed he had succeeded where paranoids failed; he lacked the time, and perhaps the audacity, to develop a theory of genitality. And if, through a sudden eruption of woman,[52] *uterus envy* haunts the philosopher, he assumes the insane right to kill her, to set fire to the world, to her home, and her body; or, if he is too close to her, because he is a poet, failing to kill her, he will commit suicide—altruistic suicide, paranoid murder.

Meanwhile, the *libido creandi* of women (in Latin *creare* means both create and procreate), which I have been referring to for a long time as *libido 2*,[53] rejects binary division and conjugates procreation with creation, as befits the mother tongue.

Controllable, thinkable procreation can no longer be a form of slavery. It would also be madness to consider it a privilege; this would once again single out women as omnipotent, castrating, threatening to men, who would consequently demand its abolition. Procreation is no longer something to be forgotten, repressed, foreclosed, cast in the role of an unconscious threat to the paranoid ego. On the contrary, it must be made the motif of work on difference.

Liberating women's *libido creandi* at its very source means constantly challenging war and the death drive. In the twenty-first century this gives rise to a revolution for the human race and opens the way to the *geni(t)ality* of both sexes.

Survivors and much more, supersurvivors and superalive, far beyond their condition as victims, when carrying a triple burden, given the slightest encouragement, women find the energy to transform themselves into leading agents of change, propositional forces, the beating heart of the *triple dynamics* of demography, development, and democracy,[54] in order to carry out a triple revolution involving the symbolic, the economic, and the political.

Our MLF has always upheld the creative commitment of women and expressed its admiration to "heroines" from around the world. On March 8, 1990, a forum at the Sorbonne celebrated women who have distinguished themselves by their strength and courage.[55] Books, periodicals, publishing houses, and films gave voice and exposure to the achievements of these revolutionaries, including one Nobel Prize winner, from Eva Forest to Aung San Suu Kyi and Taslima Nasrin. In Africa 95 percent of all NGOs are operated by women. In Niger women are working to push back the desert, struggling tirelessly to reclaim and irrigate barren land in order to feed the population and revive village markets.[56] And for once France stands out as a model in Europe, combining a high birthrate with a high level of female participation in the workforce—an extremely rare pattern in democratic countries.[57]

Nowhere, however, is there a political will that guarantees women the slightest security. Nowhere, neither among the poor nor among the rich, can women, *feminae sapientissimae*, enjoy their *libido creandi*, express it, exploit it for the common good. Real political will is required to oppose reactionary and destructive forces so that women will no longer be subject to the emancipatory good will of a philosophical, juridical, and political body that is both fragmented and a source of fragmentation. The inalienable, sacred rights of women must be incorporated into the philosophical foundations of our Constitution. And after ratifying the convention on the elimination of discrimination against women,[58] France must act on its commitments by passing a law against sexism and misogyny like the one adopted in the aftermath of the UN Convention on the Elimination of All Forms of Racial Discrimination.[59] Such a law would clearly identify the war criminals in the unilateral war waged against women. Obviously misogyny cannot be abolished any more than anti-Semitism can be; the point is to keep them both at bay.

When is the president of France going to make the struggle against the marital, familial, urban, job, and symbolic insecurity that massacres women a top priority for the republic, as he did successfully where hazardous conditions on the roads were concerned? When is the national education system going to raise the consciousness of our future citizens, in the republican manual that has been distributed in schools since January 2004, about sexism, i.e., misogyny and homophobia, alongside racism, xenophobia, anti-Semitism, and Islamophobia? When will courses touching on religion show adequate awareness of the androcentric character of the monotheistic religions, as well as of all traditions and cultures, even including the modern republic? When will there be an Observatory for Misogyny to create mass awareness of the crimes committed against women? When will there be a budget for research and support to organizations that will allow a full-fledged Ministry of Parity—an additional Prime Ministry—to announce, as part of a comprehensive policy, the emergence of a parity culture and a parity democracy?

It is urgent for us to conduct a gyneconomic investigation comparable to the investigation of the unconscious, before ectogenesis provides the final solution to the problem procreation represents for the One-Whole enthusiasts. It is urgent for us to develop a theory of genitality, before the difference between the sexes fades away into the "queer" movement and feminist indifferentialism.

The maternal body, the matricial flesh, is still every human being's first environment. Whether we are born male or female, a woman is still our first love object. Every woman is acquainted with this homosexed, primary love, this *native homosexuality*,[60] this most intimate place from which her *libido creandi* is transmitted. It is urgent for us to express its beauty before a unitary line divides women from each other and condemns them to lesbianism and incest.

Far from all the isms, heterogeneous and heterodox in relation to all instituted knowledge, *feminology* represents a leap out of the doxa and a field for research. Let the economists who are concerned with moving away from free market liberalism and the philosophers of ethics who want to do away with selfish individualism expand their work to include *gestation, hospitality of the psyche as well as of the flesh, as a paradigm of ethics*; let them reflect upon how the imperative of responsibility, the decentering of the subject, and the paradigm of the gift combine in this case to give birth;[61] let them promote an ethics of gratitude in place of envy and matricidal hatred.

In thanking "the women who have transmitted their mitochondria to us,"[62] Luca and Francesco Cavalli-Sforza pay tribute to the female *anthropo-cultivators*,[63] archaeologists, archives, and archivists of the human species, the female *genitors, genealogists*, artists, creators, educators, *generation* after generation, of the laughing, speaking species, constantly in the role of other, constantly seeking the other, seeking the men likewise liberated, by them, from their solitary All-Powerfulness. From *genesic function to matricial genealogy*, every woman bestows mitochondrial DNA on humanity—it was the genius Rosalind Franklin who discovered DNA with a kind of knowledge that has never abandoned the question of origins. What grounds do we have for doubting that *feminae sapientissimae* actively contributed to the birth of art, in Lascaux and elsewhere?

Neither subservient nor slaves, with neither god nor master, solidly secular, women are moving away from the genesis of the Book, from whose scriptures they have been foreclosed; they are learning to read by recalling, by thanking, by thinking the place they come from, without turning back but rather forging ahead; women have begun to experience their new historical condition,[64] to write the genesis of late modernity.[65] Upheavals. May the time come for cross-fertilities. Fleshly and spiritual. For a new human *contract*.[66] Together. *Tempus est creandi*. For both sexes, each enriched by the other, with no debt and no bargaining.

The old world and modern history are on their way out. In the beginning . . . Once again. Primary thought and propositional capability. The courage to conceive, to bear, to give birth to what is coming. Neither anchored nor adrift, neither sedentary nor nomadic. Gracious memory. Lasting promise. And finally the life drive, alliance, resistance, deliverance;[67] sex playing, body working, flesh thinking, women, free, in movements, as of right now.

> *Two is not the double but the contrary of one, of its solitude.*
> *Two is an alliance, a double thread, unbroken.*[68]

Acknowledgments

My deepest gratitude to Marie-Claude Grumbach, the very close friend without whom there would have been no "book."

Thanks to my friends in the Mouvement des Femmes, with whom life goes on, born anew every day.

Thanks to Isabelle Huppert for proposing that we meet and for allowing me to publish our dialogue.

Thanks to Geneviève Leclaire for the privilege of paying tribute to Serge Leclaire.

Thanks to Françoise Ducrocq for authorizing me to republish the text that she requested for *Traduire l'Europe*.

Thanks to Emile Malet for inviting me to contribute so regularly to *Passages*.

Thanks to Marcel Gauchet for our dialogue in *Le Débat*.

Thanks to Jean Larose for our dialogue in *Gravida*.

Thanks to Pierre Nora for welcoming me into his collection.

Special thanks to Jacqueline Sag, who was in charge of the second edition, for her affectionate and patient demands.

I thank Anne Berger, who introduced us to Catherine Porter.

And I thank Sylvina Boissonnas, Elisabeth Nicoli, Mathilde Kerdelhué, Michèle Idels, and Marie-Aude Cochez.

Many thanks.

Note on the Translation

This translation was a collaborative undertaking. It was begun by David Macey, who completed a first draft of all but one chapter in *Il y a deux sexes* before his death in 2011. Catherine Porter revised his draft and translated the missing material along with one chapter each from *Gravida* and *Génésique*; she also revised the draft of a second chapter from *Génésique* translated by Eileen Powis. Along the way, Porter supplemented the references and added a number of translator's notes. Research assistant William Burton tracked down numerous references and English-language versions of citations, with support from the editorial staff at Des femmes publishing house. Marie-Aude Cochez read the completed translation carefully for accuracy and fluency. Sylvina Boissonnas oversaw the entire project, serving as coordinator and consultant. Antoinette Fouque was the ultimate arbiter on matters of fact and terminology.

There Are Two Sexes

1. Our Movement Is Irreversible

March 8, 1989

Today, March 8, 1989, we meet in the Sorbonne's great amphitheater to celebrate two events:

—March 8, International Women's Day, now celebrated everywhere in the world;

—1989, the bicentennial of the French Revolution and of the Declaration of the Rights of Man.

On March 8, 1857, in New York, seamstresses went into the streets to denounce the exploitation of which they were victims. They demanded reduced working hours (from sixteen to ten hours a day!) and wages equal to those of men.

In 1910 Clara Zetkin proposed that March 8 should be International Women's Day, in homage to the American women protestors but also so that, every year, a day would be devoted to women's demands. The following year, the Second International Socialist Congress approved that proposal. From then on, March 8 was International Women's Day.

On March 8, 1982, in this space, we held the first Estates General of Women Against Misogyny. Women from Egypt, Bolivia, the United States, Austria, Algeria, Iran, Corsica, the Soviet Union, Ireland, women from all social classes and all political horizons bore witness against misogynist oppression and affirmed the necessity of an independent struggle on the part of women.

We chose the Sorbonne, a definitively subversive institution, so that the conjugation of these two dates should mark, here and now, the relaunching of a dynamics of liberation and democratization that will be fruitful for the largest possible number of women.

It is, in fact, within a dynamics initiated in France twenty-one years ago, by two or three women followed by tens of thousands of others, that the initiative of the Women's Alliance is inscribed, for all the women and men who are prepared to express themselves in today's colloquium, from the podium or from the floor.

Some say that it takes thirty years for a system of thought to assert itself. I do not think it is going too far to suggest that at least as much time will be required for a movement like this one to overcome—if not definitively, then at least durably—the oldest oppression of all, that of women, by what is customarily called the patriarchy. In our modern times I would be more inclined to call it the *filiarchy* or the *fratriarchy*, however, for it is thanks to new brotherhoods that the monotheistic, political, and symbolic leagues continue to exclude us from the law, from the polity, and from language.

So we have another ten years, a final straight run up to the third millennium, to accomplish part of our historic task, that is, to transform the attempts we have made into definitive achievements, but also, and especially, to pass the reins on to our daughters.

While all thinkers today, historians and politicians, biologists and philosophers, may agree that the most important of all the changes affecting our civilization on the eve of the third millennium is the irreversible transformation of the relations between men and women, far fewer are loyal enough to attribute such a mutation, the most radical since decolonization and the fall of the European empire, to the women's movement.

Indeed, if we have managed to use the technological advances of contraception as the lever for our biological independence, it is because we have accompanied these advances with awareness, thought, and political action, because we have articulated them with an authentic psychic, affective, physiological, sexual, and cultural—in a word, human—maturation. Women have transformed a simple technological step forward into a movement of civilization; they have turned a "chaotic" revolution into an ongoing, open-ended evolutionary surge. And not only will the relations between men and women be forever altered, but so will those of the human triad, woman-man-child.

What still remains masked—not to say denied—today, then, is the initial function, the dynamic role of the Women's Movement in this transformation. The MLF,[1] so widely denigrated, disfigured, denatured, misjudged, slandered, has nevertheless been the origin, the driving force responsible for the most positive events that have transformed the human condition in our society over the last twenty-one years.

If historians of the contemporary period are honest, they will recognize that the Women's Movement has not only reinvigorated existing institutions—for example, Planning Familial (Planned parenthood), which was involved well before 1968 in the battle over contraception—but has also nourished and influenced contemporary thought, from psychoanalysis to literature by way of philosophy. In addition, it has given rise to other movements, such as the MLAC,[2] a movement of men and women that has followed the MLF in taking up the struggle to decriminalize abortion, while continuing to provide information about contraception, or Choisir, an association that has taken up one of our earliest themes of reflection and forced our legal system to recognize rape as a crime.[3]

Political parties and the state, seeking either to take over this movement as quickly as possible, to put an end to it, or to divert it for their own benefit, have in effect legitimized it over the last fifteen years by creating and recreating an institutional feminism: from the secretary of state for the condition of women, a position introduced by Valéry Giscard d'Estaing in 1974 and assigned to Françoise Giroud, one of Mitterrand's supporters, to the plenary minister of women's rights, a position assigned by François Mitterrand to the archfeminist Yvette Roudy in 1981. It has also been thanks to the Women's Movement that many women have had access to positions in official policy-making bodies—although often, it must be said, under the auspices of a prince, a party boss, a father, a brother, or a male friend. Finally, it was also owing to the Women's Movement and its vigilant effort to maintain women's newly acquired right to make decisions about their own bodies, after the adoption of the 1974 Veil law,[4] that a traditionally conservative electorate was mobilized for the first time, in 1981, on the side of the party of social progress.

If union leaders and psychoanalysts (among others) are honest, they will recognize the winds of freedom and independence—economic, professional, and political as well as libidinal, sexual, and affective—that the Women's Movement has brought to bear on customs and mentalities. The famous "increase in solitude" about which the right, in particular, has hammered away in recent years, might reflect a much more positive attitude than the right would have us believe. Many women now deem it better to live alone than with an abusive companion. An increase in solitude is an effective response to the increase in various forms of narcissism. A voluntary solitude has in fact replaced an age-old servitude. After Virginia Woolf, every woman has sought to assert her right not only to a "room of her own" but also to a "libido of her own," an "identity of her own," a "language of her own," so history will acknowledge that there are two sexes and that this heterosexuality, this heterogeneity, is the condition of humanity's wealth, of its fertility.

Born in the wake of what I continue to call the revolution of 1968, for the events really did bring us into a new era, the MLF has always had to struggle against the current or against the reactionary or frankly fascist tendencies of that revolution. The era that discovered the notion of fraternity, after those of liberty and equality, in May '68, actually instituted a time of brotherhoods that were fratricidal as well as fraternal, from which women were all the more excluded in that, different, they were still not, and perhaps never will be, equal. From the priapism of the May '68 graffiti to the narcissism of male television stars, the era being inaugurated threatened to be worse for women than capitalism was for workers.

Going against the tide of new directions that were announced in 1968 for the twenty-first century and beyond, the MLF thus struck down Narcissus with a fatal blow, the fourth blow after the three announced by Freud, that is, the Copernican, Darwinian, and psychoanalytic revolutions. This is what I used to call the *revolution of the symbolic*, the destitution of the general equivalents that deny that there are two sexes, deny that the *production of living beings* is tripartite, and deny access to a heterosexed parity in history.

Starting with its very first meetings, by activating the notion of mother, by putting it to work, by trying, as we were already saying in 1968–1970, to "liberate the woman in the mother," by asserting that the mother was "not all for the son," or that "the father doesn't exist," the MLF was attacking the infantile narcissistic omnipotence on which the primacy of the phallus is founded. In this blow struck to the narcissistic omnipotence of the son lay "a difficulty in the path of the MLF," in the sense in which Freud spoke of "a difficulty in the path of psychoanalysis," in connection with the blow struck to the ego by the discovery of the unconscious. It was not only in theory but in practice that we attacked them, Father and Son, by refusing to continue to set ourselves up as supports for their castration—in other words, as hysterics. Just when they thought they had us confined in that space, we had ceased to be there.

The internal difficulties persisted, nevertheless. We women, *excluded and interned* in that civilization (according to the concept elaborated by Jacques Derrida), had to deal with our relation to our own origin and, at the same time, we had to advance, to think, and to act, to produce at every moment several contradictory gestures, to spread ourselves in several directions and on several complex, not to say paradoxical, levels. That was the time—perhaps it is still the time—of struggles for equality and/or for difference. These struggles were real headbangers, real heartbreakers. A few of us were convinced that difference without equality could produce only psychic regression and political reaction, but that equality without difference was producing only a sterilizing assimilation, a psychosexual amputation.

As the Movement gained momentum and grew over time or, on the contrary, ran out of steam or got bogged down, the tendency to foreclose its origin rather than to integrate it became more pronounced. We weren't given enough time to understand, to build; we were intimidated or discouraged, pressed to respond, confined to a ghetto; a movement of civilization was reduced to a vulgar fashion, and the limit of equality was assigned to us as the dead end of our destiny, just as, tomorrow, the uniformity of narcissism will be imposed on us as the only path toward (under-)development.

When have women caused blood to flow in a world that is continually being torn apart? What is their alleged verbal violence in comparison with the violence expressed every day in every newspaper, violence against women in particular? Why is there so little tolerance for sororicidal struggles, when on a daily basis fratricidal struggles within a major political party are viewed as signs of democratic health? It seemed as though we were not allowed to deviate one iota. We were supposed to be paragons of perfection. We had "everything wrong."

It will surprise no one that the Women's Movement as a whole had trouble resisting such a strategy, a concerted strategy of marginalization, so much so that it sometimes appeared antiparliamentarian. Despoiled of all its victories, it was constantly disparaged as being a ghetto populated by hysterics. Women in movement reaped indignity, ridicule, excesses, abuses, violence; legitimate women militants, married to a political party, or noble daughters of a prince, reaped dignity, prestige, power. Today, we can see the extent to which those privileges were deceptive, those powers fragile, and the extent to which one would need, for epistemological and political reasons (as much to write the story of the recent past as to open up new ways forward), to recognize the Women's Movement in its proliferating diversity, in its at once divided and ingathering mass, its inspiring force, its vital dynamism, and its innovating independence.

Today, on top of timeless oppression and misogyny, we are experiencing the repression unleashed by our earliest victories. In France, every day, women are degraded, exploited, excluded, raped, beaten, sometimes to death, and killed supposedly out of passion.

In the South, in the East the destabilizing evolution of countries without a democratic past, wild claims of cultural and cultic identities, competition among all differences in the name of sovereign identities (with the exception of the one that informs them all, the difference between the sexes), the exclusion of women from the zones of power, thus from visibility, sending them back to an underdevelopment of representation, the gap that is deepening every day between doing and appearing to the benefit of the latter—all these are brakes, threats to the advancement of women.

One of the symptoms of the 1968 revolution, the entrance into the "phallist" era, is now appearing in broad daylight. At the extremes, narcissistic omnipotence is expressed by a powerful rise in intolerance presaging a future in which, in this struggle to the death for power, based on pure prestige, intolerance will not be limited to religions alone. After the era of liberty and that of equality, there is talk of the era of fraternity, solidarity, and tolerance. "Hands off my buddy"[5] is heard as a contrasting echo in "Hands off my book!" and "Hands off my Koran!" Regarding religion, in Year One of the Rights of Man, Mirabeau had already found it useful to clarify his position: "I am not here to preach tolerance. The most unlimited freedom of religion is in my eyes such a sacred right that the word tolerance, which attempts to express it, strikes me as, in a way, tyrannical in itself, since the existence of the authority that has the power to tolerate infringes on freedom of thought, by the very fact that it tolerates, and thus by implication it might not tolerate."[6] A century later, in 1882, Renan, speaking of laïcité (secularism), was not afraid to cite Pasteur's peremptory assertion that the secular state is "neutral among religions, tolerant toward all denominations and [forces] the Church to obey it on this crucial point."[7] From fundamentalism to phallaïcité,[8] tolerance and intolerance have sent the law into a tailspin.

Everywhere in the world the situation of women has worsened; the regressions are alarming, as they even include the abolition of laws that had been passed in women's favor. Nevertheless, everywhere in the world women are aware, vigilant, and combative.

We want ordinary, everyday barbarianism to cease. In Thailand, working against the sale and prostitution of young girls, women are building a foundation that will take these girls in and provide training. In India women are struggling against personal laws that reduce the liberties of Muslim girls and women. In China women are setting up associations of democratic women in support of progress in human rights. In Algeria, where a repressive family code is in place,[9] women are mobilizing against the headscarf. In the United States hundreds of thousands of women are about to gather in Washington to reaffirm the right to choose motherhood freely, thus the right to abort.[10] Elsewhere, some women have even won political power. In France women are creating, assuming positions of responsibility, struggling: nurses and midwives in hospitals, childcare workers in day care centers have mobilized, seeking not just higher wages but dignity and respect for their knowledge.

Everywhere, we are continuing to fight. The movement is irreversible.

The 1979 United Nations Convention on the Elimination of All Forms of Discrimination Against Women legitimizes our struggles and our actions. In associations and political parties alike, it attributes value to consciousness-raising as well as to the assumption of power when it notes that "discrimination against women violates the principles of equality of rights and respect for human dignity, is an obstacle to the participation of women, on equal terms with men, in the political, social, economic and cultural life of their countries, hampers the growth of the prosperity of society and the family and makes more difficult the full development of the potentialities of women in the service of their countries and of humanity."[11]

Ratified by France in 1983, this convention must be a relay point for the conquest of new rights, new freedoms.

To get rid of woman's "derived libido," "derived law," and "derived identity" once and for all, we must work from now on to make sure that lawmakers dealing with language, the symbolic, and law take our vital requirements into account. It is essential to

1. inscribe, in the Constitution, the principle that "each human being, without distinction of race, religion or creed, possesses sacred and inalienable rights";

2. draw up framework legislation on the basis of a "Universal Declaration of the Rights of Women";

3. draw upon personal time to ensure political responsibility and presence: new duties correspond to new rights;[12]

4. recognize the specific production of women—which makes all the rest possible. Women assume virtually 100 percent of human procreation, and they find themselves penalized by the fact that this production has to remain neglected, foreclosed. This symbolic production—because women speak and create speaking beings—can be viewed as an *anthropoculture*. Excluded from all social, economic, professional, political, and cultural inscriptions, this work is the last form of slavery, the final expenditure of a labor force absolutely owed to the Master, without retribution or recognition, whereas this force is the most formidable contribution to humanity of wealth in the form of the human: thinking creation itself. Penalized by this foreclusion of procreation as creation-production, women are doubly penalized, in their professional activity and in the activity of creation of which they are deprived, even though procreation is recognized by (male) creators themselves as their model;

5. continue to educate and inform ourselves, to transmit what we know and transform ourselves; to create new fields of knowledge, new sciences, at the point of articulation between the pure sciences and the human sciences; to create an epistemological field: the "sciences of women," going from *gyneconomy* to the development of a specific body of laws.[13]

To work toward democratization is to work toward a rule of law that faces up to this dissymmetry with respect to production, and acknowledges the affirmations that stem from it, instead of programming an ideal equality, summarily anchored in assimilationist universalism, that remains an ever receding vanishing point. Let us be realistic: the reality is that there are two sexes in the human species, and such a principle cannot be evacuated without extremely painful long-term consequences, whatever immediate pleasure may ensue.

More than ever, then, we women shall have to make complex gestures, put to work the notion of equality, construct for ourselves our own heterogeneous identities, adapt without denying ourselves, integrate ourselves while also reintegrating our primary, sexed, original identity, instead of repressing it, foreclosing it, or simply ignoring it in favor of a gender; we shall have to come together and recompose ourselves, rather than amputating a part of ourselves or endlessly splitting ourselves apart; we shall have to conceive of our bodies as unique sites of a work of intercreation of the psychic and the physiological; we shall have to consider that our flesh thinks the living-speaking, that it creates when it procreates, and, finally, that it is not a flaw to be *genital*. Indeed, being *genital* may well be a matter of *genius!* As of today, we are the wealth of tomorrow.

Through this colloquium, on the occasion of March 8, we wanted to try to relaunch the dynamics of a women's movement that has refused to stop moving, despite all the obstacles and all the repressions. The participation of hundreds, even thousands, of men and women today gives concrete form to our hope of success.

For several months now, everywhere in the world, in Argentina, Chile, Brazil, Algeria, China, women have been mobilizing on the front lines of the battle for democracy. It is in the spirit of announcing this hope for the 1990s that we have just created the Women's Alliance for Democratization.

We have twenty-one years of struggle for liberation behind us; we have ten years of work for democratization ahead of us to promulgate our thinking and our action definitively and to approach the history of the twenty-first century and the third millennium as adults. For this work of democratization will not be to the exclusive benefit of women.

We are continuing to move forward and in advancing we shall advance democracy as well.

2. Women in Movements—Yesterday, Today, Tomorrow

April 1990

LE DÉBAT: Unlike many post-'68 political actors and some of your sisters in the Women's Movement, you have kept quiet. We know little about you. You are a legendary figure—a vivid reminder of the most outspoken wing of the MLF, the Psychanalyse et Politique group,[1] and yet a mystery . . .

ANTOINETTE FOUQUE: I wonder whether, even today, anything having to do with origins, which are always mythical, anything that remains of some primordial orality, of the mute word, isn't seen as mysterious. Lacan used to say that to speak is to play the fool (*parler, c'est déconner*).[2] As for writing . . . !

As you know, what came to be called the Women's Liberation Movement, the MLF, was created in the wake of May '68. One could even say on that very ground. May '68 was first and foremost an effervescence, an oral explosion, a cry; for me—and not only for me—it was a birth; perhaps that's why it's still burdened with so many mysteries. The Women's Movement may have been started by intellectuals—Monique Wittig, Josiane Chanel, and myself—but the cry came first, and the body along with it; a body so harshly put down by the society of the 1960s, so violently repressed by the moderns of the era, the masters of contemporary thought.

Monique was already a recognized writer. For my part, I was working with literary journals: *Les Cahiers du Sud, Le Mercure de France, La Quinzaine littéraire.* I was reading manuscripts for a publisher. But our movement did not begin with the written word; it began with what was called at the time *la prise de parole*: taking the floor and speaking out, issuing protests and slogans of revolt, words from the body. I used to say that the revolution that the MLF was going to bring about would consist in lifting censorship on the body, just as in psychoanalytic practice and theory Freud had lifted censorship on the unconscious, and, of course, as a result, it would enrich the text, just as Freud had wanted to enrich the conscious mind.

But when you talk about a mysterious, legendary figure, you are going beyond me, I think, and raising the question of origins. This is a huge question that we could talk about for hours; it would touch not only on our contemporaries' relations to that question but also on the relation that I myself, having been at the origin of the MLF (a moment that certain women historians today call its prehistory), have with my own origins, on several levels: real, fantastic, and symbolic. I used to say, in fact, that women's civilizing development would take us from prehistory to posthistory.

The relations that our contemporaries still maintain with the question of origin is one of fear or rejection that is conflated with the fear of women or of a woman: some analysts have used the term *fantasmère*, "phantas-mother," to speak of that archaic figure, which was then in its heyday—for the early Women's Movement excluded men, so as to re-mark our exclusion from most institutions and achieve status through opposition. It was virtually impossible to do otherwise. Reaching further back in history, some erudite readers might have remembered more or less vaguely, in this particular context, another A. Fouque—Adelaïde and not Antoinette, but nonetheless an Aixoise, a new Eve, bearer of sin and hated by her creator—who is at the origin of Zola's monumental work *Les Rougon-Macquart*.[3]

I have to say that I was ill served by the way in which the Movement tended to close itself up, or off, as I have explained, and also by my own shut-in nature, which had to do, starting in adolescence, with my mobility problems and the pain and effort it cost me to get around, to get where I sometimes ought to have been: demonstrations, dinners, social gatherings. I was cut off from all that because I had to save my strength for my work.

And then what can only be called the unconscious root of misogyny—the foreclosure of the origin or, rather, as I have always insisted on putting

it, *the foreclosure of the body of the mother* as the site of the origin of living beings—was redoubled by my own relation to my origins: my psychic relation to my sexual origins, homosexed vis-à-vis the woman who was my
mother and heterosexed vis-à-vis the man who was my father and my political relation to my historical, social, and cultural origins. Complex,
even composite, relations to a heterogeneous origin—I have on occasion written *une(s) origine(s)*, "an origin(s)," just as I have written *une(s)
femme(s)*, "(a) women." The relation of rupture or alliance with an
origin, including one's own, seems to me to orient each individual's
destiny. This, for me, is the crux of it all; it is the very goal of the work
of the body and the thought of the flesh. And it seems to me that as
long as the investigation of this necessarily ambiguous relation does
not take place, we are stuck in a monosexed and therefore lobotomized
humanism.

As for me, I am trying to set origins in motion through a continual labor of "regression-reintegration" instead of repression or even foreclosure. It is like labor in pregnancy, a kind of intimate dynamic, an elementary movement.

As for what is "mysterious," from the Eleusinian mysteries to Freud
and his "black continent," *mysterious* is the term that man comes up with
wherever there is woman; *mutatis mutandi*, it could even be the certificate
of authenticity that attests to the insistence or even the existence of
woman. One day, the sciences of women, *gyneconomy* in particular, may
well take up this mystery, think it through, reduce it, explain it, bring it to
conscious awareness as much as possible, understand it and interpret it.
What does the Romantic dream have in common with the dream in Freud's
interpretation? More or less what the Eleusinian mysteries have in common with the sciences of women.

LD: What were you doing on the eve of '68?

AF: On the surface, I was an ordinary French teacher on long-term disability
leave; in fact, I was a rebel. I was beginning my third year of doctoral
studies, working with Roland Barthes on my thesis, which I never finished, on the notion of a literary avant-garde. I had come to Paris from
Aix-en-Provence in 1960, was married to an intellectual my age. My daughter was four years old. My husband and I were working for François Wahl
at *Le Seuil*.[4] My work, preparing reader's reports, was an education for me
in difficult disciplines—linguistics, psychoanalysis, antipsychiatry—
and I kept abreast of the most recent contemporary texts: Sanguinetti,

Balestrini, Porta; I even translated these authors. My future seemed clear; everything seemed to point me toward publishing, criticism, writing.

But in fact I was very rebellious. A woman's economic independence, professional equality, and intellectual competence were not really valued. The milieu in which I found myself was very conservative in the way it operated, very repressive and intimidating in its modernist theorizings, and so it was extremely misogynist. I was constantly made aware of the false promise of equality, symmetry, and reciprocity that a university education had held out for so long. To have had a baby was almost shameful. Beyond that spurious equality, I felt other needs arising. I wanted to affirm in a positive way that I was a woman, since society—I might even say civilization—was penalizing me for being one.

LD: And it was in that context that you met Lacan?

AF: Yes. Through François Wahl I participated in the publication of Lacan's Écrits: it was an interminable labor, taking more than two years. I was also attending Lacan's seminar, along with Roland Barthes's.

LD: And the analysis?

AF: I contacted Lacan in October 1968, at the time of our earliest meetings. I began my analysis in January 1969 and continued until 1974.

LD: Did you feel that you were a feminist before '68?

AF: It never occurred to me to use that word. I felt like a woman who badly needed to be free, who was suffering, but every ism seemed like a trap to me.

Ever since I was a small child, I have questioned the lot of women. I was born of the desire of a working-class father, in 1936, which began as a year of many victories for him and ended with bitter defeats. I was conceived on January 1 and born on October 1, on the day Franco came to power in Spain. I come from an extended family, part Corsican and part Calabrian. We were something of a tribe, living close together. There was my father and my mother, my father's brother and my mother's sister— my godfather and godmother—and four children. My mother was one of a kind, but I grew up surrounded by the strength of maternal women. From very early on I was aware of their stamina, their courage, and their determination to integrate themselves—and their children at the same time—without disowning themselves.

My mother didn't know how to read or write, and that was her constant complaint—she spoke of this as though it were her greatest misfortune. My father could read a newspaper. They were very civilized people, of the old school; I could almost call them "cultivated" because of their

Mediterranean roots. That is one of the most paradoxical aspects of my highly problematic relationship with writing. (One of the reasons I went to see Lacan was that he was the author of *Écrits*, as Montaigne was the author of *Essais*, but he had never sought to write a book.)

My mother became French through marriage and was very proud of the fact. She considered it a sign of progress to have traded her father's Italian name for her husband's Corsican name. Yet she never forgot her matrilineal genealogy. Neither have I. Just as my mother named me after her mother, I named my daughter after mine. Over four generations, we seem to have been careful to establish a transmission, to inscribe another lineage. This was well before the MLF, and I used to say that I was a woman who was trying to find herself between mother and daughter, between woman and woman.

My mother was the most intelligent woman I have ever known, as well as the most independent. She had a kind of genius for freedom, for freedom without violence. Her mind was always at work. From a very young age, I could see, in spite of a total absence of the trappings of femininity in her—she didn't wear makeup, she wasn't flirtatious, and she had no interest in being elegant or stylish—that my mother was a woman. My father adored her silently. He would whistle the tunes of love songs to her; she knew the words. They met when she was sixteen, and he eighteen, and right until the end they retained a sort of youthful passion, even though my father had the temperament of a virile patriarch. During the war my father had been banned from the region because, while he was on strike, Pétain's police had found him with his Communist Party card in his possession. Just as, during the First World War, my mother as the eldest child had stood fast with her brothers and sisters, now, under the Occupation, she took the whole tribe under her wing. In the most serious, the most dramatic situations she managed to find escape routes and safe havens. She steered us away from death. She was never inert, always active. She could sense danger ahead, and assess it. When there was a decision to be made, she was decisive: she would make her move, with us in tow. She was in charge twenty-four hours a day, always alert but not authoritarian in the least—sometimes angry, most often serious, yet cheerful. For example, when we were bombed out or had been evacuated because Marseille's Vieux-Port district had been destroyed, she proved to be a real strategist, as subtle and crafty as Ulysses.

LD: When May '68 happened, were you aware of what was going on in American feminism?

AF: Not at all. I had opened *The Second Sex* in the sixties only to read: "Women's struggles are behind us." I had never been politically active. I knew that I was born on the left and would die on the left, that I hated war and colonialism. Until I reached adulthood, I was part of what was still called the working class, but I never felt drawn to Sartrean *engagement*, to the "guilty conscience" of the intellectual.

I was concerned about social and political struggles, but from a distance. I observed them as though through a pane of glass. I could never manage to feel implicated and I felt a kind of disgust for the young women of my generation who got involved in the struggles of their lovers, their brother *normaliens*;[5] I felt the same way about my sister who, when she got engaged, tried to convince herself that she was a soccer fan.

I didn't know what feminism was and I could say, now, that I regret that. It was a sign of my ignorance of the struggles of women in history. But I should emphasize that my distrust of ideologies—which I considered to be illusions as dangerous as religions, at the time—was such that I never defined myself as a feminist. Later, I fought against the Women's Movement becoming the "Feminist Movement." It seemed to me, perhaps wrongly, that with the word *woman* we might be able to reach perhaps not all women but at least the greatest possible number.

LD: But wasn't the name Psychanalyse et Politique rather elitist?

AF: I didn't choose that name; one usually doesn't get to choose the name one is given at birth. In fact, Psychanalyse et Politique was what used to be called a consciousness-raising group, but one that did not ignore the dimension of the unconscious, at the level of what Freud called the psychopathology of everyday life, wit, or parapraxis. And at that time, you'll recall, everyone was talking about desire, antipsychiatry, anti-Oedipus, and at Vincennes psychoanalysis was taught outdoors.[6] Our claim that we were articulating psychoanalysis and politics felt more like a luxury than elitism.

One of the things I wanted, at the time, was to bring to as many people as possible what was then the cutting edge of contemporary thought—in other words, to transcend the stereotypes of petit bourgeois culture. I wanted to share with any woman who came to the Movement, just as I had done with the women in my family, with my mother in particular. I wanted to find a common language without bowing to class stereotypes or academic ideals. But the road to hell is paved with good intentions, and just the opposite often happened: I was accused of being a theorizing terrorist; only my accusers weren't workers, they were sociologists, academics who were very hostile to psychoanalysis.

LD: What were you doing during the events of May '68?

AF: Monique Wittig and I were at the Sorbonne. We formed a cultural action committee that drew filmmakers, actors, writers, intellectuals: Bulle Ogier, Michèle Moretti, André Téchiné, Danièle Delorme, Marguerite Duras—these are just a few of the names that come to mind.

LD: You were thirty-two years old then. You found yourselves in the position of elder sister to the generation of '68 properly speaking, with the influence that naturally comes from seniority . . .

AF: You mean in the MLF? Age distinctions were even less important there than at the Sorbonne in May. We were all young and beautiful. For most of us it was our first involvement in politics. We felt as though we had grown fifteen years younger. We all felt, in '68, as though we had come down with a healthy case of adolescence. Later we fought systematically against age distinctions. At our meetings high school girls rubbed shoulders exuberantly with Christiane Rochefort,[7] as women workers did with women engineers, and daughters with mothers.

LD: Did you feel at ease right away in the political environment?

AF: The truth is that if Monique hadn't dragged me by the scruff of the neck I would never have gone to the Sorbonne. I was very intimidated. I had never spoken in public except in class. That probably explains, in my own case, but not only mine, a tone and manner that was simultaneously vibrant and excessive—it was a clumsy revolt; it had been held in check too long.

LD: And from there to the Women's Movement as such?

AF: Monique and I quickly learned from our experience at the Sorbonne that if we did not ask our own questions, on our own terms, we would be overpowered or excluded. For the first time in my life it was necessary and urgent for me to anchor myself in a decisive historical moment in which my personal history began to come into play. It was a need to intervene, to give something to others and also to give something to myself, to act out of gratitude as well as out of egotism. That's what made it different from a commitment of the leftist sort. During the summer of '68, over the holidays, we decided to begin holding meetings in October. We then set about to read and critique the works of Marx, Engels, and Lenin, with whatever means we had at our disposal, but we found nothing that suited us in their doctrines. We were bent on freeing ourselves from the constraints of our domestic, professional, and emotional lives. We wanted to expand the field of our subjectivity. We wanted to embark on the discovery of women through the discovery of each woman, beginning with ourselves. We had thrown ourselves into Maoist-Leninist-Marxist causes, but we were rowing against the tide.

LD: When did you make the further leap and choose the Psychanalyse et Politique orientation?

AF: Almost immediately, since we were reading Freud, too, but I must admit that, though not uncritical, I let myself be dazzled by Freud's undertaking. The masculine ideology that weighed on the psychoanalytic revolution wasn't enough to make me reject such a tool of knowledge, especially if that meant erecting a feminist counterideology. I couldn't see myself, in this high seas adventure, trading Freud's submarine for the scooter of some feminist, even a famous one. Especially since both vehicles seemed to me to be headed in the same direction, straight for the Phallus—but with the feminists you weren't allowed to be aware of it or to point out the shoals. It seemed to me that if we didn't take the unconscious into account, we would soon be drifting straight into delirium. Psych et Po reflected my desire to understand the unconscious aspects of the political engagements of the time, as well as to bring the power of psychoanalysis out into the open not only in institutions and schools but also in the discovery and theorization of the unconscious. I thought it vital that politics should know and question the unconscious, and vice versa. Simply put, there was politics in the unconscious and there was the unconscious in politics. Since then I have often thought of it as a sort of parental couple that brought me into the world of time and space: psychoanalysis is my mother, with her inquisitive intimacy and watchful anguish, and politics is my father, with his proletarian revolt, his commitment to resistance. A couple continually coupling and uncoupling so that both might affirm the uniqueness of their individual fields and the identity of their separate bodies, so that he might give to her, the woman, a political existence, so that she might make him, the man, conscious of his dreams.

LD: There was a period of gestation before the movement went public . . .

AF: Yes. For two years, we worked intensively among ourselves: we met, wrote leaflets, put out information . . . Our first public appearance—there were thirty of us—took place in the spring of 1970, at Vincennes. For me, that was the public debut. Because there were two launchings: one at Vincennes, in the university context, and another at the Arc de Triomphe, staged to commemorate "the unknown soldier's unknown wife." I wasn't there, and that was no accident. This was a media event with three celebrities and almost no one else. Those two events, at Vincennes and at the Arc de Triomphe, pointed up the divergent paths that lay before the Movement.

After we went public, I was offered a lectureship at Vincennes, which I accepted on a collective basis. With the start of the school year in 1970 we began meeting in this broader setting. The Movement started to snowball. Other small groups joined ours.

LD: You met with Simone de Beauvoir?

AF: For a long time she was suspicious of the Movement, even hostile. The impetus for our meeting came from the feminists, but it was she who convened those who were, in her words, its "leaders." I really had to be coaxed, because I couldn't understand this way of going about things. She asked us to explain to her our conception of a women's movement.

Sartre, at the time, was taking up leftist causes. Perhaps there was a desire for symmetry. Perhaps he had explained to her the stakes and the importance of an uprising like this, just as he had incited her to write *The Second Sex* after his *Anti-Semite and Jew*. Ingenuously, we presented our hopes and our dreams. I spoke of my daughter, I spoke of Lacan, of Barthes, and especially of Derrida. I admired his ideas, and most of the time I admired the texts of those about whom he wrote, from Leroi-Gourhan to Blanchot. I did not go over very well, to say the least. Even though I felt a kind of deference toward de Beauvoir's intellectual persona, for her stubborn desire to be at Sartre's side, the couple's life that she was living struck me as hardly exemplary and enviable. I had admired *The Mandarins*; I found it painful to see her turned systematically into the laughing stock of a clan of misogynist intellectuals. But I couldn't understand, then, why this intransigent moralist, this lofty conscience, hadn't joined the Resistance during the war; why, during the Occupation, between her bicycle trips and her climbing excursions around Marseilles, she spent her time getting her manuscripts published at Gallimard, which was controlled by the Nazis at the time. Ultimately, nothing was said, but my plea that our Movement take psychoanalysis into account as the only rigorous discourse on sexuality clearly placed me in the wrong camp. Not long afterward, at our general meeting, the feminists were shouting for heads—

mine on the end of a pike and Simone de Beauvoir's to grace their journal *Les femmes s'entêtent*.[8]

Many of us experienced it as a hostile takeover bid, as an occupation or, if you prefer, a colonization, but we managed to resist the label "Revolutionary Feminist Movement" by insisting on "women" and "liberation."[9] Actually, I don't like talking about Simone de Beauvoir. Just as it is often said that the greatness of an enemy in a fair fight does us honor, I have often said to myself that the unfairness of her attacks made me feel ashamed.

LD: What exactly lay behind the rift over the word *feminist*?

AF: It has been said in recent years that the Movement had two orientations, one toward equality, the other toward identity. I want to make it clear, right from the start, that identity in this context must be understood as the uniqueness of the other and not as sameness.

For many, the best way of fighting oppression and the discrimination that comes from the difference and the dissymmetry between the sexes was to abolish difference, to deny dissymmetry. To my mind, that was like throwing the baby out with the bathwater. The rallying cry "One of every two men is a woman" then became "A woman is a man like any other." It seemed that the only alternative to exclusion was assimilation. This return to an absolute universalism, this militancy in favor of indifference, seemed to me preanalytic and archaic, given how far contemporary thinking had come.

The notion of equality is still quite sketchy. It has to be put to work, set in motion. Those who favored integration exclusively now know its limits. I could say, for example, that equality is the basis for difference or, rather, its impetus: it is the motor of future differences. Difference keeps it in check. It's something like the relation between consciousness and the unconscious. Consciousness is the tip of the iceberg, the part we can see, just as equality is the visible part of differences. Consciousness without the unconscious is only an illusion of intelligence, and equality without difference is only an intellectual construct, a ruinous theoretical delusion.

But I avoided the word "identity", which lent itself to misinterpretation at a time when the human subject was on trial; the word might have been confused with the identical, with sameness, whereas what we had to do was get away from identity and find a decentered position, each one of us, woman and man, according to her or his own uniqueness. Individualist feminism seemed to me to be saying: "The same model for everyone, and everyone for herself." As for us, ours were the desire and the utopia of "each according to her own uniqueness, together."

LD: How do you remember those divisive and controversial years?

AF: As truly frightful. And quite cruel . . . Most of the time, my adversaries wouldn't engage in discussion with me, on the pretext that I would always end up being right. I never went outside the MLF to respond to those attacks except when we were accused later on—our publishing house was the pretext—of being a sect of thieves and criminals. And even then I refused to make a personal issue out of it and left it up to the courts, with Georges Kiejman as intermediary. It was very destructive, but no more so than any political confrontation can be. I suffered as much as I would have had bombs been falling, I lost the last of my motor capabilities, but I learned a lot.

My psychoanalytic work helped me to keep from drowning in hate or in terror; it helped me to symbolize, to swim, to live. The name *feminist*, some women have said, gave them a sense of unity, a dynamic feeling of belonging, a strong ego, and our approach to the issues was like a wet blanket on all that. Our questions were destabilizing, and that's why the disputes were so bitter. But why should women do away with aggressivity, violence, and hatred, and settle a priori into the most disturbing kind of monochromatic Stalinist pacifism?

LD: All of this became intertwined with your analysis with Lacan.

AF: As I have said, my analysis helped me to "roam" instead of foundering in leftist-feminist impasses. It freed me from my adherence to all kinds of illusions that were as perverse for me as they were innocent for others. My analysis kept me decentered, unquestionably a painful state; it kept me withdrawn and silent for the most part, moored in a dissymmetry that was fruitful for me but disturbing for everyone who felt that it didn't fit, that it somehow clashed with Psych et Po. Weren't they dealing with a new sect? Well, that's because they represented the reigning dogma . . .

LD: And yet the École Freudienne[10] itself began to function like a sect of particularly blind followers . . .

AF: In my analysis with Lacan I was always very free with my criticism. I believe he appreciated it, that it helped advance his work, and that, without the MLF, he wouldn't have written *Encore*. I used to go to all his seminars. I also attended his closed clinical seminars at Sainte-Anne,[11] where he presented his patients and for which he himself had offered to register me. But just as I had never wanted to belong to a political party, I never wanted to join the École Freudienne. I had enough to do coping with my inhibitions, my symptoms, my anxieties, without having to deal with institutional constraints, without casting my lot with a group of major intimidators.

We had so much to do to establish our own laws within the law, to get away from the outlaw status to which women are confined, to escape our foreclosure, even more than our exclusion, and we felt so small, so inexperienced, so clumsy . . . It seemed too easy to drive us to the point where we would start to kill each other. We would have preferred to keep up the fight, if debate over ideas was impossible. But many different clans were invested in seeing the fight turn into a death struggle for pure prestige, a fight over power that we lacked and are not about to acquire any time soon. The exception was Simone de Beauvoir: after being a figure of ridicule in the 1960s, she became in her turn an unsurpassable intellectual master, as some of her journalist groupies have written . . . At the same time, it was like riding a great Ferris wheel, experiencing a moment of destabilizing but also joyous giddiness, a chaotic and productive education, an exhausting and exalting apprenticeship to life and history.

LD: Let's not dwell on the most familiar aspects of the Movement: the series of publications beginning with Le torchon brûle in 1970,[12] and especially, of course, the struggle for abortion rights. But just a word or two on that subject. Didn't a media strategy, the kind that you don't like, ultimately pay off in the famous "Manifesto of the 343" in April 1971?[13]

AF: I recognize that, and I acknowledged it immediately. I wouldn't have approached things that way at the time. It was the feminists who had the idea of including celebrities in the manifesto, following the leftist model. That was very positive, but it hasn't made me any less distrustful of the media; they've made me pay dearly. My approach was a bit idealistic. It wasn't a desire to hide, but rather a need not to go on display. My dream was that thought and action could go forward hand in hand, at a slow and confident pace, that we were going to narrow the gap between those who slaved away in obscurity and the stars who stole the spotlight and put on the show. I'm always delighted when a famous personality joins in a struggle, provided that she brings to it more than she takes away; what worries me is the way famous names can capitalize on a cause to which they are not committed. It was that kind of narcissistic speculation that we were confronting; first we had bank credit cards and now we have media credit cards, via various associations and groupings. Watch out for inflation, rollovers, and the market crash of narcissism! It's not that I refused to acknowledge the importance and the validity of the media, but that was the time when they were starting to want to dictate to us, to foist new stereotypes on us, and I saw no shame in not rushing to accept their terms. I not only signed the manifesto but I also actively led the fight for legal and free abortion.

LD: And was it after such a victory, the passage of the law legalizing abortion, that you wanted to further the Movement by creating the publishing house Des femmes?

AF: It was a dream I had had since the Movement began. The negative battles that had to be fought, the struggles to resist and defeat oppression, gave me only very limited and ambivalent satisfaction. I signed the abortion manifesto out of solidarity and conviction; the Veil law was vital for us all,[14] but I could never have had an abortion. From the beginning I wanted to build, to bring into being, to lay out positive paths. I wanted to emphasize women's creative power, to show that women enrich civilization and that they are not merely the keepers of hearth and home, shut up in a community of the oppressed. I wanted to open the Movement up to the public: to publish. My dream was not only a publishing house but also a bookstore, a public place open to men as well as women. I knew that even the most scrupulous publishers chose manuscripts according to criteria that penalized women. The first text we published had been rejected by other publishers. As you know, the experience brought us more envy than either thanks from women or admiration from men. I believe that during those dark years only François Maspero suffered as much as we did.[15] But to be circumspect about it, I think that things could not have gone otherwise.

LD: How would you assess this enterprise? At the time there was much talk about promoting a feminine writing, écriture féminine. What are your thoughts on the project and its outcome today?

AF: To put the best face on things, I suppose that the smart thing to do with the business would be to fold . . . The last ten years have been hard on publishers. As for "écriture féminine," once again, we weren't the ones to come up with the expression. I think it's a French translation of the English expression "female writing." But in French, la femelle hasn't been a human category for several centuries now; in other words, the woman, in French, has lost the integrity of her sex. After having been completely sequestered in her uterus for thousands of years, it now turns out that she doesn't have one, that she is merely gender, the other metaphor for phallic monism. The human female is foreclosed from our language, a phallic language if ever there was one. Thus the feminine is a gender that many men— from the transvestite to the poet, that imaginary transsexual—feel they can assume. We can read femininity in Rilke's writing, or in Rimbaud's. It's not simple . . . A human being is born with a sex, as a girl or a boy, but also as a speaking being. Our experiences, our actions are constantly informed by this physiological determinism. For the man as well as for the woman, physiology is destiny. But at every moment also, what we say or what we write either accepts or rejects the constraint that the body imposes on language and on the fantasies that language produces in its speakers.

One is born a girl or a boy and then becomes a woman or a man, masculine or feminine; writing will therefore never be a neutral act. Anatomical destiny is always being marked or re-marked. The differences between genders come along and validate or invalidate the differences between the sexes. How can writing, as the experience of a sexually differentiated subject, be neutral? We did not want to put the cart before the horse. We accepted the challenge, took the risk of proposing that texts written by women might put language to work in ways that perhaps could bring out—why not?—a difference between the sexes. We never set out to declare as a foregone conclusion that there was such a thing as female writing. When Milan Kundera, in *The Art of the Novel*, speculates on how he might use the word *contraband* to smuggle into Czech the French word for having an erection, *bander*, what is he talking about, what is he doing? Lacan, too, said that language has only that on its mind. What is "that"? Having a hard-on? And in the meantime, how do women find their pleasure? For millennia, men have worked at symbolizing and inscribing their phallic libidos. I remember a wonderful text by Pierre Guyotat, "L'autre main branle" (The other hand jerks off). They could certainly wait a few decades, give us a few centuries, before they decide whether equivalent work by women is possible . . .

Moreover, "l'écriture féminine" has been used as an ultimate weapon, a cream pie to be thrown in the face of first-rate writers who didn't wait either for the MLF or Des femmes to come into being before setting forth their poetics. I'm thinking specifically of Hélène Cixous: her *Dedans*, which won her the Prix Médicis in 1969, carried within it the seeds of everything she would write later.[16]

LD: What about the Women's Movement today? It seems to have been caught up in the general ebbing of the spirit of May '68.

AF: The Movement was a creature of May '68. It made its stand against the tide of extreme leftism and now is going to go far beyond it, just as it is now moving beyond the symbolic restoration that has come with the eighties. You don't need me to tell you that upheavals of such scope don't play themselves out in ten or twenty years. It is not about change, in the sense of a changeover; it is about the species' growing pains. We are at the heart of civilization's famous discontent, the passage from one stage to another, in which women find themselves involved against their will, taken hostage and made to serve as symptoms of the Other's madness. This is what is happening to Salman Rushdie as well. You go as far as you can at any given moment, given the array of forces and what history can handle. It may later seem like an ebbing, but this is deceptive. New paths are opening up, there is groundwater yet from which new inspiration can be drawn. There will be new ways of transcribing what seems illegible to us today. Through progressive regressions, sometimes, perhaps, women are still advancing. After ten or fifteen years of state feminism (Françoise Giroud was named secretary of state for the condition of women in 1974), the founding militants could very well demobilize; it was even vital for them not to repeat themselves and to head in new directions. Most of them have indeed done so.

The many levels of resistance—subjective and objective, psychic, emotional, political and narcissistic—to this movement of civilization are now obvious. Resistance, in politics as in analysis, functions in complex and polyvalent ways and is part of a healthy maturation process.

Clearing pathways to symbolization—a term I prefer to "sublimation"—is a complex undertaking. Creation and invention are necessarily paradoxical. Freud, who for half a century theorized the talking cure, spent the last several years of his life with a cancer of the jaw that prevented him from speaking. His daughter Anna, his Antigone, delivered his lectures for him.

You asked me for a personal example. I could say that my movement, which I have never confused with my mobility, is certainly not unrelated to my paralysis. I am afflicted with one of those forgotten illnesses for which there is still no cure. I've probably had it, latently, since birth or before, and it manifested itself after a vaccination that I had after I finished school. The neurologists warned me that one day very soon I'd be confined to a wheelchair. I've managed to put off that day for more than thirty years, with a lot of effort to adapt to a "normal" life. Analysis has, of course, helped me in this. But perhaps at times it has over-immobilized me. And the Movement that has taken so much of my strength has also given me a great deal. And, finally, perhaps I can say that, just as thirst teaches us what water is, immobility has taught me movement.

The destructive forces came from without. Dialogue among ourselves may have been difficult, but it was made destructive by outsiders in whose self-interest it was to publicize the conflict. Everyone knows that fraternity can breed fratricide. But no one—except the right wing—thinks of using the internal struggles among the various tendencies of the Socialist Party to destroy one member or another. That wasn't the case where we were concerned. Our differences, which after all were quite normal, were used to discredit us. It seemed that everything we did or said had to be held against us. The misogynists were right to defend themselves; the stakes were very real. We simply didn't think that there would be so many misogynists or that they would find so many women to be their accomplices. Every little group, every party, every clique, tried to manipulate and control us, tried to take advantage of us. Each organization yielded up its own version of feminism. Perhaps it was a sign that that ideology was politically and symbolically dependent on the phallic structure. On the horizon was the mirage of equality that, since 1789, has offered the illusion of a Promised Land attainable through a class struggle that no one believed in any longer.

LD: According to a certain logic, one might in good faith consider universality to be more liberating than an identity that imprisons women in their biological determinacy.

AF: Why should biological determinacies continue to be a prison for women? Shouldn't it be just the opposite, from the moment that one has control over one's own fertility? After all, if anatomy is destiny, this also holds true for men. The reality principle cannot ignore these determinacies, and a just society would not exploit them. Equality and difference must go hand in hand; one cannot be sacrificed for the other. Sacrificing equality for difference takes us back to the reactionary positions of traditional societies, and sacrificing the difference between the sexes—and along with it the richness of life that this difference brings—in favor of equality sterilizes women and impoverishes humanity as a whole. It makes it impossible to reach the stage of symbolic genitality. This should be understood as a metaphor and not as some kind of organic reductionism. Genius and *geni(t)ality*: it's the same thing, isn't it? When we recognize the genius of scientists or artists, we admire their ability to produce some living signifier, to bring into the world a form, an element, a unique flesh that didn't exist before they created it. These "geniuses" have always used procreative metaphors in talking about their work. It seems to me that to this day the notion of equality has never been adequately articulated. Once I would have called it an idealistic concept. We never found the model to be of much relevance when we fought alongside women in Latin America or in the Maghreb except on the level of labor issues; even so, women who enjoy the benefits of equal rights in their professional lives are penalized de facto because of the dissymmetry inherent in procreation, a dissymmetry that at first no one wanted to take into account. One day procreation will be seen as *creation of the living-speaking (création du vivant-parlant)*; it will be recognized as a major contribution of riches brought by women to the human community, and, for themselves, not only as physiological-psychosexual maturity but as a possibility of free fulfillment of desire. That is reality for the majority of women, and if some of us, without having to give anything up, also write books or become prime minister, so much the better.

LD: Couldn't it simply have been the considerable success of the Women's Movement in society at large that led to the demobilization of its activists?

AF: You may well be right. Even if it has, today, lost some of its momentum, it's a movement that history will say was a success. And yet the official documents (the UNESCO report), surveys, media analyses,[17] everything indicates setbacks, exclusion, threats, and the repression of women. More than acts of resistance, what we see just about everywhere are counter-movements. Basic misogynistic oppression has been succeeded by an anti-emancipatory repression. The normative prohibitions on which our societies are founded are turning perversely against women's new freedoms. I'm thinking not only of what is a totally political alliance of the three monotheisms, but also of the return of Oedipus, the demanding, abusive parricide son, served up to us by the media in some new guise every day: so-and-so, thirty-eight years old, rapes his sixty-eight-year-old mother; someone else, thirty-six years old, brings a suit against his mother for having abandoned him; another man, younger, kills his girlfriend because she was more successful than he; and so on and so forth. Criminality has a sex. Men who want to remain in their protracted state of infantile omnipotence are afraid of women. Women are afraid because they are in mortal danger. From Louis Althusser[18] to Thierry Paulin, who killed old women, to Karlin's hero,[19] crimes are constantly being justified or excused through powerful identification fantasies. Whether they're delusional or passionate, criminals or artists, sons "identify" sons with utter brutality and complete impunity.

It will no doubt be more difficult for women to free themselves from the Son than from the Father, who, to my mind, does not exist as such; it's hard to cast off the role of Jocasta, to escape the passion according to St. Oedipus. The temptation to redeem the murderer will be great—that's a very feminine way of escaping castration. Have a child and keep him for herself, raving mad or autistic, as a phallus with whom to shut herself up outside herself and in an exile of the self, rather than producing a child and letting him set off toward his own destiny as a man.

LD: Let's return to May '68. In retrospect, how do you understand that movement, and where do you situate the Women's Movement within it?

AF: I experienced May '68 as a real revolution and, as time goes by, I'm more and more convinced of this: it was the great leap out of the capitalist era, which has little left to do today but come to fruition or, better yet, come to an end worldwide. May '68 was the end of the era of economics as the ultimate determinant, both for free market liberalism and for Marxism. And along with that end we saw the end of de Gaulle, the father and founder-president of the most monarchical of republics; almost two hundred years after the regicide, it suddenly became clear that de Gaulle was only a Son. There is no Father. May '68 was the first time the Sons came together as such; after liberty and equality, we entered the era of fraternity. The demands of phallo-narcissism were written everywhere, on all the walls. Remember those two posters—"Power comes from the barrel of a gun," one of them went; the other said "Power comes from the barrel of the phallus"—and those graffiti of erect penises that joyously covered the walls of the Sorbonne, the Latin Quarter, and then Vincennes? All of them self-portraits of the extreme leftist as young Narcissus or old Priapus. I firmly believe that the priapism of the extreme left is something that's been overlooked.

Linked to the narcissistic valorization of the penis, the so-called phallic phase establishes a logic according to which, for the boy, only those like himself, possessing the same prestigious organ, are worthy of respect: the double, the reflection, the twin, the brother, or, these days, the buddy. A chain of identifications among all those that glitter: the golden boys have the gold and the phallus. The former doesn't come without the latter, but it's the latter that manufactures and attracts the former. The phallus presides over the gold. That's what is new.

What is at stake in what Freud called the "primacy of the phallus," for both sexes, is essentially narcissistic in nature. This logic can thus be termed phallo-narcissistic. The omnipotence and omnipresence of the phallus can also be represented by the fetish, which, as Freud says, is erected as a "memorial" before the horror of the supposedly female or maternal castration; it is a pure denial, upheld today by universal commodification, the generalized exhibition of "nomadic objects," the ownership of gadgets, of prostheses—pure denial because how can this mother-woman have lost a penis that she never had except in his, the son-man's, perverse imagination?

The phallus is the emblem, the image, the master signifier, the general equivalent of narcissistic wholeness. A woman, when she finds herself deprived of a "libido of one's own," is subjected to its imperialism, to its mode of economic development. If she is not satisfied with acting as Echo, then she has no choice for self-expression other than to take the phallic path, but at the expense of her psychic and physiological integrity; she commits her body to it or, rather, she is given notice that she must surrender her body as a hostage and succumb to a pathology in which she will be seen by herself and by others as the phallus—body and soul, the erect obelisk body that one still sees today in many movie actresses and models, the Father-God souls that many women writers and government ministers seem to have. And that's how women, with or without the chador, get caught in the trap of a phallic narcissism that has little to do with them and become its most perfect symptom.

Christianity is a *filiarchy*, a religion of the son, a filial monotheism, one might say. Socialism is perhaps its secular version. As you can imagine, in such a climate women have not had an easily defined place, given that nothing excludes girls more than brotherhoods do. By identifying with the sons, girls can always dress themselves up as *filses*, "girl-sons,"[20] but, here again, symmetry is an illusion and a trap. If you've ever experienced the atmosphere of condescension towards women in extreme left-wing groups, you understand this. Their women militants came to the MLF to complain about this, seeking to escape dangerous identifications. Women in France who have sided with violent groups or supported terrorism are rare indeed. The feminists from Action Directe[21] came by once or twice to wreck the Des femmes Bookstore, but the analysis of ambient violence, an analysis to which the Movement as a whole and not only Psych et Po was committed, served as a powerful brake on the all-too-human death drive—though without repressing or denying it.

I never thought the principal enemy was patriarchy, but I have thought and still do think that the main adversary is filiarchy. The coming together of sons and brothers after the parricide to establish democracy excludes women radically and a priori. Society is doubly hommosexed if,[22] moreover, its emblem of power is no longer mere gold. The phallus may turn out to be an even more destructive standard. That was the challenge our movement wanted to take up.

LD: Have subsequent events confirmed this diagnosis?

AF: Absolutely. And beyond my worst fears. The fraternal project has been strengthened. Though forestalled for a time by the Women's Movement, thanks to socialist unity that played a pivotal role, the brothers were quick to take their revenge, and the reprisals are far from over. With May '68 we entered into the pregenital stage. This narcissistic era is very important because it holds the promise of progress, of a civilization that privileges the image—it is part and parcel of the media age, but it represents a mortal danger if it is abused through isolation or massive identification. The image reigns supreme. "The Mirror Stage," an essay Lacan wrote in 1936, foresaw this.[23] In 1968 we shifted into a new libidinal structure that Freud had introduced as narcissism fifty years earlier. After the age of passions and interests that Hirschman has written about,[24] we have the age of powers, identities, sovereignties, the age of the narcissistic democratization of absolute monarchy: first the Sun King and then star wars, which Roberto Rossellini's *The Rise to Power of Louis XIV* heralded in such a subtle way. This is the age of "self-": beings who self-produce, self-exhibit, and self-promote like so many self-made goods. We are going to be living through years of pomp and ceremony, the staging of the ego, a period of generalized false selves rather than self-building. Activities that up until now have been undertaken most discreetly, from mountain climbing to writing, now have to be exhibited and shown on television. For the last fifteen years any writer short on fame has had to pivot around a heliocentric master word and get up on a stage where the ideal substitute for any standard whatsoever sucks in those with the ambition of shining when their turn comes. There is no hint of hegemonic ambition in

Bernard Pivot's personality, the accusations of this or that wounded Narcissus notwithstanding; nonetheless, an important part of Pivot's fame is unquestionably a pure signifying effect.[25]

LD: You have a somber, not to say pessimistic, view of what the future holds for us.

AF: In fact, I think that the twenty-first century world of images and sons that lies ahead of us will be one that excludes women and all differences, even as integration will be the only thing anyone will talk about. After all, for all its promotion of equality, wasn't the nineteenth century nevertheless the century of the bitterest struggles?

LD: Didn't Freud translate a common prejudice into the language of psychoanalysis and make women the locus of narcissism?

AF: Yes, but wrongly, in my opinion . . . Freud simply didn't know that a woman could be anything other than either the son's mother, phallicized by her offspring, or else the father's daughter, "the girl as phallus."[26] The French ethnopsychiatrist Georges Devereux goes even further: speaking of Baubo, he claims that by showing her sex, she immediately situates it on the side of the Phallus.[27] Thus, with women, whatever is not kept hidden is to be considered as something exhibited, as belonging to phallic territory in a narcissistic naturalization. The only way women can avoid phallic exhibition is to put on the chador, the ritual foreskin of this "phallic age" from which it is clearly impossible to escape. So we go from Scylla to Charybdis. But this is a question about which much more needs to be said than I can say here.

LD: In concrete terms, today's proliferation of images is associated with a transformation of the image of men, a transformation that is generally interpreted as a feminization.

AF: Masculine and feminine are twins in a way, monozygotic twins who admire each other, trade places with each other in a perverse mode and play on genders, without real sexual intercourse. Femininity is a disguise. Homosexual men—fashion designers, for example—dream of an ideal femininity and project themselves onto it. Along with the feminization you mention, this is the very heart of a false difference between the sexes that is so constricting for so many women: one has to look like a man dressing up as a woman. We have not gotten out of the category of the double: A and A' rather than A and B.

LD: Could you expand more specifically on the connection you make between "phallic" and "narcissistic"?

AF: At this stage of an erotics that is very remote from its phallic economy, the nature of display, exhibition, the subject's complacency before the mirror, the body's syncope, it's hard to distinguish between a phallus—a symbolic object standing in for every visual object of desire—and a representation of an erect penis. As with capitalism, what we're dealing with is a primitive phallicism, a kind of obscene priapism, an apt figure for extremism. Poles apart, on the *Bébête Show* we have Marchy for Marchais and Pencassine for Le Pen.[28] Still no women there, just their defigurations. Women are exhibited in places where they are not present, and where they are present they are prevented from speaking. It's the historical scene of the oldest kind of theater. Women—symptoms of a castration that has nothing to do with them, but which sons resist with all their might because they are its prey—are made invisible. There are practically no more women to fill the superstar anchor position on the evening news.

The rallying cry of American therapists and academics is *be visible*. Lacan had already advised his disciples: "Make yourself known." And so we are witnessing the emergence of a new type of persons who take on the task of manufacturing themselves through the practice, along with body building, of what might be called "self-building." This could well be an obligation that will, as time goes by, become difficult to shirk without succumbing to more and more drastic episodes of manic-depressive delirium.

LD: So what is to be done, given this new world? It's hard to imagine you settling for simply observing the phenomenon . . .

AF: We must be able, through speculation as well as through analytic regression, to get out in front of what's happening, to fly ahead when we can no longer hobble along, because, as usual, history will not speak in a single voice. Besides, this narcissistic trend wasn't born yesterday. It corresponds to an enduring tendency, but there comes a time when a latent and diffuse phenomenon manifests itself, takes its place in history, and takes over. That, in particular, I think, is what May '68 revealed straightforwardly, and it is in this respect that May '68 was a revolution. The historicization of the narcissistic trend we are facing might not be a bad thing. We could also be seeing the advent of a higher humanism, a civilization in which it might be possible to begin to think. And while we are at it, perhaps we can develop a theory of genitality and think about how to get beyond self-creationism. The *production of living beings* is tripartite: one (male) multiplied by one (female) makes one (male or female). That tripartition is denatured by the Trinity: One alone in Three, Three that make only

One. If we succeed in dismantling such devices, if one day we learn what makes them exclude all heterogeneity, we will then be able to think through genitality, to have done with the fantasy of the dark continent. A well-tempered narcissism must be invented. It's possible to contain the star-cancer of phallic erotics (by star-cancer I mean the flip side of disaster), the narcissistic inflation as well as the ossified phallic disposition that over-compensates for it, by putting the libidinal economy of the phallus to work and by creating the epistemological field of a libidinal economy specific to women. This way we shall begin to conceive of a heterosexed civilization.

There are two sexes. This is a reality that history, if it wants to remain worthy of its ideals, should make its fourth principle, after liberty, equality, and fraternity. The Women's Movement has carried with it, from the beginning, this fourth revolution that I used to call the "revolution of the symbolic."

It's possible to imagine the creation of an epistemological field that will take its place alongside the social sciences, the sciences of men: it would be the sciences of women, which would proceed from *gyneconomy* and *feminology* to the articulation of a body of specific rights. The women's movement has been and remains one of the most powerfully federative movements of civilization. It is that federative aspect that makes me pre-fer the expression "movement of civilization" to "social movement." This movement is continuing to unfold throughout the world. It's a transna-tional rather than international movement—it raises specific issues in each country, but the principles are universal and general. Women's po-litical choices are thus registered at the planetary level. It is within such a framework that we must come to terms with a modern conception of wom-en's rights, the status of women and their demands for identity. With this should come solutions to some of the major problems that currently threaten democracy.

First of all, there are the great problems of the East, the South, and the Maghreb—nationalisms and fundamentalisms but also religious archa-isms and traditionalist stereotypes. I could speak once again of the re-turn of the sons: Isaac, Ishmael, Oedipus, Jesus, all of them figures of a "narcissistic fundamentalism," of a symbolic stereotype. In the rise of Fra-ternity, in the fratricidal duels, partition or rupture still too often takes place via the bodies of women, which become the symptoms through which the madness and depressive megalomania of the Sons is expressed. In India Moslem women are taking a stand against the enactment of laws regulating personal behavior, against Sharia law, and they are allying themselves with women in the secular and democratic Indian state. In Algeria women are mobilizing around the same principles and against the same oppression. Sometimes even risking their lives in the process, they are going to advance not just their own demands but also the cause of Algerian democracy in general.

And then there are the problems of inequality in the work force, of so-called unemployment, of a two-or-three-speed European society, all problems that concern women directly. Unequal employment is compounded by unequal visibility. In this society the dominant males appropriate for their exclusive enjoyment not only creative work but wealth, power, and the media. There is not a single woman among those "at the helm," not a single woman among the thinkers who claim to be leading the century. Narcissism at the end of the twentieth century no longer has anything to do with wildflowers or poetry. We have not only to share the labor but also to grant recognition and value to new kinds of production. By taking into account the kinds of production that belong specifically to women, the value of new tasks will be recognized, and a better balance of power will be achieved. Naturally, I have in mind women's creation of children. Today knowledge of the fertility process is bringing to light the dissymmetry between the sexes in the matter of procreation, a dissymmetry in women's favor. This gap, this inequality with respect to biological roles, this procreative power henceforth can overturn the order of inequalities and transform itself into demographic power. Between 1975 and 1988 the number of single mothers doubled.

In the end only permanent democratization can guarantee the expansion of democracy. Along with the social contract, today we can speak of a contract with nature and of a "contract with life." It's not simply a question of protecting what is human, but of choosing one's identity, one's life. This is the question of any integration that is harmonized with the power to decide. Along with rights, we have desires and duties. Women will have to overcome their repugnance and their inhibitions with respect to power. They will have to agree to assume responsibility, to consider that they have a right to be present and a duty to democratize the polity. The Alliance des Femmes pour la Démocratisation seeks to encourage and promote further thought and new commitments in these directions.[29]

3. There Are Two Sexes

1990

For Antonia, my maternal grandmother
For Vincente, my mother
For Vincente, my daughter

If we could divest ourselves of our corporeal existence, and could view the things of this earth from a fresh eye as purely thinking beings, from another planet for instance, nothing perhaps would strike our attention more forcibly than the fact of the existence of two sexes among human beings.

—Sigmund Freud, "The Sexual Theories of Children,"
in *The Standard Edition of the Complete Psychological Works of Sigmund Freud,*
ed. James Strachey (London: Hogarth, 1959), 9:211–12

GESTATION OF A THOUGHT, THOUGHT OF A GESTATION

One is born a girl or a boy. I was born a girl, on October 1, 1936, to a brilliant, illiterate mother and to an active militant in the Popular Front. The day of my birth the flames went out: Franco seized power in Spain.

My mother: I occupied her from the moment of conception, January 1, 1936 (for the Chinese, conception has the value of birth); hence I experienced the Popular Front in her, through her, and also through her anger over this third pregnancy, imposed on her as she neared her fortieth year. She had been a tomboy, and I was a drag on her freedom. Early on she told me her dreams, the nightmares she had had during her pregnancy: her child had no feet.

I was born a girl, into a culture with a great oral and written tradition, the great Mediterranean South, cradle of monotheisms and democracy, where only God and man had the right to reside. I have known this since my birth, my childhood, my adolescence: in the streets of Marseille there is the brutal presence of boys and the raping aggressiveness of men. Elementary school and later high school confirmed this, as well as the Catholic religion to which I "belong," with its God-in-three-persons or three persons as a single man. The masculine precedes absolutely . . .

Below the surface my mother's incredible strength existed only for me. My mother was French by marriage, not well naturalized; as for me, I was acknowledged as a high school graduate and then qualified as a professor by our democracy. In the legal code my identity was diverted far from my natural ground toward a cultural internment that had to be relentlessly reconstructed. I reached the stifling boredom of equality, taking care to intern myself less than halfway. No womanly becoming was possible through, with, in, or by means of the knowledge transmitted via these apprenticeships within the family, the schools, and the academy.

Nothing, it seemed, would allow me to escape from this accursed circle; neither my mother's determined illiteracy nor a first passion for a young girl, vital and destructive, the naive homosexuality whose lesbian impasse I may have been anticipating too early, nor marriage for love. Everything always seems to come back to sameness, even the poets who would have me be a mother.

The law, whether I was its victim or its accomplice, was blind and deaf to my most elemental need: to exist. I had a choice between slavery and absolute mastery, hystero-feminine or homo-psychotic, hetero-feminist or homo-lesbian. I believed that I was midway through the journey of life. I felt lost.

Twenty-seven years ago (I was about to turn twenty-seven; today I am fifty-four), pregnancy struck. Necessity more than coincidence, chance more than bad luck, an ordeal, in any case, that obligated me.

Ten years earlier I had fallen ill. The etiologic diagnosis was vague: prenatal origins, some prehistoric illness that was to affect my motor skills definitively and increasingly, contracted at the time my mother dreamed I had no feet. At the time this illness (a form of multiple sclerosis) constituted both a medical contraindication against pregnancy and a legitimate therapeutic argument for abortion. Today one would call on a surrogate mother, a substitute childbearer. I tried my luck: since I'd taken the first step, I carried on regardless. I wanted to make a child. I was also afraid. Anxiety and hope always go hand in hand: this was the subject of my DES thesis.[1] In the face of both, *jouissance* is hard to identify, but I sensed it at this turning point.[2]

On March 3, 1964, I brought into the world a girl in perfect health (she will soon be twenty-seven); her father and I agreed to give her my mother's first name, just as I had received from my father my maternal grandmother's name. Antoinette, he said. Vincente, we responded. (A. V.: initials that mirror each other vertically and form the letter X, the central X of my father's first name, or a lozenge shape, a female symbol.) The mute word *flesh* that haunted my entire pregnancy (fruit of thy womb, flesh of my flesh), accompanying the fear of transmitting my illness, inscribed in these initials, triggered reveries about latent thoughts of a female genealogy, a genealogy of thought.

I was to pay very dearly for the risk I took, even though at first, paradoxically and contrary to all medical forecasts, my health improved. The responsibility for giving birth to a child would make walking more difficult for me. But what I was to lose in walking, I gained in the approach to what has preoccupied me as far back as I can trace my own questioning.

The unconscious work of gestation was for me, in its dynamics, a regression that worked toward reintegration and narcissistic restoration, a factor in the awareness and transformation of my own identity: I was born a girl and reborn a woman after giving birth to a girl. Thus despite the oppression of all the symbolic institutions (reinforced by the *diktat* of a certain feminism), I assumed the psychophysiological destiny of my sex.

I am not providing these autobiographical elements here to talk about myself—who would that be, myself in 1964 or myself today?—but rather so that I can come as close as possible to what I would come to know intimately of the identifications and the disidentification of a being presumed to be a woman.

Pregnancy as an experience confirmed for me, in a more exalting way than I could ever have imagined, that there truly are two sexes. Though a man and I had conceived, really, phantasmatically, symbolically, and legitimately together, I had to create, alone, for nine months. In the wake of the sexual play and the "pleasure of love" came an intense and unceasing bodily work that my physical condition did not allow me to forget even for a second and an activity of thought that was flowing, elementary, *flesh*, in a word, most often unconscious, clairvoyant, blind, very often also preconscious, foresighted, too rarely conscious, clear, like the attention I am predisposed to, my first name being its anagram: an activity of thought that never let go of me, during the whole time of gestation, both expectancy (*attente*) and management (*gestion*), during which I promised the three of us that I would hold on until the birth.

Conscious that a first cycle had come to a close with that event, I set out, once again on man's land, in search of instruments to forge that would allow me to approach what was thinking in me without me.

THE OBSTACLES

AT THE SYMBOLIC LEVEL

It was at a moment when I had every reason to be convinced that there are two sexes and that no measure of equality could absorb the differences—it was at this moment that I learned, very officially, that there is only one libido and that it is phallic.

That was what the only existing discourse on sexuality stated: Freud, reinforced by Lacan, reinforced by Françoise Dolto, who was more phallicist than the absolute Phallus.

An equivocal silence on the part of the others who from time to time, according to the movement, the place, or the opportunity, denounced but never really took up the task of elaborating. Elisabeth Roudinesco rightly pointed to a few initiatives, but these had never really won a following.

In other words, in psychoanalysis, you are not born a woman (as Simone de Beauvoir also said, from a different but nonetheless convergent viewpoint). You are born a little boy or, more precisely, a castrated little boy. From this perspective, the female identity can only be a derived and negative identity, since (according to Freud and Lacan) it is determined by the absence or the inadequacy of a penis equivalent.

Within the space of phallic monism, one is trapped in the alternative: phallic for the boy, castrated for the girl. The order (the law) of castration ordains the phallic economy to which all jouissance and consequently all desire is suspended (Lacan). From the moment women recognize themselves as castrated (in the real), or as castratable (symbolically), they are legitimized, albeit negatively, in the phallic order. Many women prefer to designate themselves in this place rather than to conceive of a symbolic order that would complement the phallic order.

The genital stage, the stage of psychophysiological maturation of sexuality, on the basis of which I am capable of engendering living beings, is assimilated with the phallic stage, that is to say, reduced to the infantile genital stage of the boy, characterized by his interest in his penis. As a result, it becomes impossible to symbolize and elaborate on the uterine dimension and the uterine activity without which access to the genital stage is properly unthinkable for a woman.

The uterus is considered not as an active/productive organ, symbolizable as such, but as a pure "space" (lieu; we speak idiomatically of a uterine "milieu")—moreover, as the etymology of the word tell us, as a space that is "behind" (husteros), prehistorical, prenatal, and that calls, and calls only, for regression. Female genitality is thus dismissed as pure biology, as belonging to the natural-material realm of the preverbal (even pre-preverbal) and pre-psychic. This space, for the person who can imagine nothing beyond the phallus, is fantasized as the absolute beneath (en deçà), as the black hole of the black continent, and even worse, as a generator of psychosis, of "white noise." Now this uterine space remains definitively "behind" only for the one who has come out of it without looking back and who has lived the contact with it in an essentially passive mode: the son. Nevertheless, in the space of phallic programming everything takes place as if man and woman could think the mother—the maternal flesh or body—only as a (mi)lieu, an environment or object for the child, the sole subject.

And yet the parturient is not an object, no more than the child is an object for her: the woman who procreates and gives birth does not remain "behind," she labors, she accompanies, she stays alongside and goes ahead to meet the subject-to-be. In so doing she does not return to the maternal body, she integrates this first body inside herself, at the very moment that she projects herself forward and outside, by procreating.

If women see only the phallic milestone, if they do not understand the necessity (psychic, not biological) of undertaking a process of identitary regression-reintegration, the only one that enables an escape from the logic of phallic identity, they cannot really progress. Either they will become "girl-sons" (filses),[3] not-quite-sons, or they will remain hysterics (literally, women who suffer in and owing to the uterus), suffering from both amnesia and reminiscence, as if by a badly executed amputation of the matricial, since it is from the cutting off of/from the uterus, from the foreclosure of the uterus, that every subject is supposed to organize itself, and not from the integration of the uterus within the whole maturation process that would be completed in a heteronomous adult genitality.

This process of regression-reintegration is in some ways mirrored recursively when a woman engenders a girl. But only a woman who engenders a son really has the right to the title of mother in the cultural imaginary. In other words, it is not procreation that makes a woman a mother, it is her designation and her place within the patriarchal structure and patronymic transmission. Similarly, one thinks of the young girl's passage from girlhood to womanhood only in her relation to a man (who deflowers/marries/legitimizes her) and not for her procreative capacity: this is decidedly the syncopated moment, the black hole of a thought that shirks thinking (itself).

We could almost say that "woman" (that is, not the concept but the reality of every woman, at once unique and shared) does not come about, has not yet taken place in history, for even what we call feminine is, most often, only a metaphor, man's phantasmatic representation (re-creation or fabrication) of a woman or even a gender (*genre*) that man bestows on himself, that is to say, a kind of transvestism. A certain femininity—which displays and markets itself as such—is not the expression of a woman's inner speech, of her body or her jouissance: it is the gender that a woman picks up in return, thus imitating, through a kind of reduplication, the one who conceals her by imitating her. Hence, here again, the psychopolitical logic of a certain lesbianism (as distinct from authentic female homosexuality) that I describe as a kind of countertransvestism (on the model of a counterinvestment), because it consists not in seeking the place(s) of a woman in oneself but simply in reduplicating the process of imaginary inversion, exchanging one fetish for another.

This is why I prefer the adjective *femelle*, "female" (as it has been retained and used in English in "female writing"), to the adjective *féminine*, "feminine"; for me the word *femelle* does not refer woman back to a prepsychic, antecultural, biological register;[4] it enables me to convey, within the space of the thinkable and the cultural (a space that defines the human itself), the work of the body and of the flesh that belongs specifically to women.

It is not a question of embracing the antiphallic or the antioedipal, which would be tantamount to advocating the abolition of the phallus. The phallic stage of a girl child (even of a woman) that corresponds on the sexual level to clitoral activity is at least as structuring for girls as it is for boys. But unlike what happens with boys, in the case of girls this stage is not terminal. And even for men, is there any reason for their desire for infinite erection other than a fantasy of pure prestige and power over the so-called weaker sex and over nature? We can thus challenge the notion that the phallic stage is the end point of speculation, and even the idea that it would be the ultimate stage for man, by questioning the reduction, for him too, of the genital to the phallic.

The phallus, representation of the penis, detached from the body and in a perpetual, imaginary erection, is a narcissistic fantasy. It is erected and maintained as such to express resistance to castration and especially denial of the difference between the sexes and of the body at work—a denial that shores up this erection. It is a fiction that contradicts the reality of the penis and the procreative and cocreative capacity of female flesh and a simulacrum of a fourth stage that obscures the reality of this "fourth dimension," which, for the woman, is the uterine dimension (the stage and the thing). It is the sign of a denial not only of the reality principle but of the real itself. In this sense one can say that phallic organization is in reality pregenital. The idea of the phallus is inherently metaphysical and signifies its primacy over thinking/procreative matter. This is an illusion of psychoanalysis.

The adult man can only acknowledge the posterective flaccidity of his real penis. The economy of the "genital penis" will integrate this reality in place of the barbaric fantasy of castration (as an anal-sadistic punishment for phallic priapism). The adult man will have to renounce, at one and the same time, his resistance to castration (the narcissistic defense of the little boy) and bodily and psychic mastery over gestation during the time it takes place.

But God, according to the fantasy of those who have imagined him, does not want to renounce his power over gestation. The Bible is filled with examples of his delusions of mastery: after pulling Eve from Adam's rib (a reverse genesis that still doesn't strike many people as astonishing), and after bestowing on woman only a "derived identity" and not one of her own, he opens and closes at will the uteruses of the matriarchs (Sarah is sterile for one hundred years; Abraham thus needs Hagar to engender his first son, Ishmael, who is illegitimate in God's eyes; then Sarah becomes fertile and engenders Isaac—this is the root of the current conflict between Israel and Palestine, Judaism and Islam); then God condemns adulterous women (an adulteress might introduce into the family a child that does not come from the father); finally God concedes that his son-made-man may have a flesh-and-blood mother, provided that she remains a virgin, like Athena for the Ephesians' Diana, but deprived of divinity. All that is too well known to warrant further emphasis here.

We know that the churches have never ceased claiming their mastery over the bodies of women, but we easily forget that states too share this obsession with mastering gestation: some outlaw abortion, others impose sterility. Is there a single state anywhere that does not legislate on and over the bodies of women?

So how can we think and put into practice the symbolic independence of women? By refusing egalitarian symmetrization, we posit ourselves as potential partners in a heterosexed symbolization rather than as castrated twins in an immovable order decreed immutable.

But to attempt to think the role specific to each sex in the production of living-speaking beings (that is, of the human), to demand both the acknowledgment of differences and the economic, cultural, political, and symbolic equality of women and men is to come up against—at every level, not just at the symbolic level—the theoretico-political machinery that neutralizes, that is, conceals, women's sexed reality and experience in the name of the dogma of phallic monism.

AT THE LEVEL OF THE ARTISTIC
AND SCIENTIFIC IMAGINARY

Genital production (that is, production of the living-speaking, or *anthropoculture*,[5] a task and responsibility that today and throughout the world fall almost entirely to women) appears, oddly, to have been relegated to a secondary level, on the scale of symbolic and cultural values, where the pregenital organization of little boys—in which sadism and anal eroticism play the leading role—reigns in absolute sovereignty.

The imaginary of artistic creation (literary in particular), imitating the theological fable of Genesis, repeats the foreclosure of uterine production by fantasizing it as an idealization or at best as a sublimation/transposition of anal activity: earth, mud, shit, and gold are exchanged for pleasure, infinitely equivalent, substituting for each other to satisfy the fantasy of the all-powerful Narcissus, whether his face be that of God, a poet, a philosopher, a psychoanalyst, or any old despot-son.

"I kneaded mud and turned it into gold," each says in his own way, both the poet (this is how Baudelaire sums up his poetic enterprise of capitalizing transmutation in The *Flowers of Evil*) and the theoretician of the capitalist economy. It is better to produce gold (verbal or sociomaterial) than thinking flesh, unless the production of living beings, fragmented, fetishized, merchandised, enslaved, denied in its female origin, is transformed into a flourishing industry through the magic of technology. We have lost count of sperm banks, blood banks, organ banks, and it is now quite common to speak of human capital, of red gold or gray gold.

It's a question of screening off, of eclipsing the unquenchable *uterus envy* of the Creator,[6] of creators, unless one makes oneself, as every true poet does, an "imaginary transsexual," an inventor of a poetics of the real. This transsexual temptation is also, today, that of the physiologist, of the scientist—René Frydman, for example, from "test tube babies" to the title of his latest book, *Ma grossesse, mon enfant* (My pregnancy, my child);[7] in the order of our metaphysical, pregenital, and prethinking civilization, all creation would tend to impose itself as expropriation, exploitation, and replacement of the procreation that haunts it.

AT THE ECONOMIC AND SOCIAL LEVEL

It thus seems quite natural that the same censorship should order the economic and social sphere, where our hyperproductivist organization penalizes women both professionally and symbolically. The only women considered active are those with a professional activity, even if it is raising children other than their own. Women who make children and do domestic work are counted among the inactive population! There is no country in which the production of living beings, the work of renewing the generations, of renewing human wealth—work accomplished by women—figures in the calculation of the gross national product. The production of women's bodies, their labor power, is only valued or quantified in a technological or industrial context that forgets woman and origin, woman as the origin of living-thinking beings. And yet demography, a discipline within the social sciences and economics, is primarily based on the concept of "fertility rate per woman." Such are the contradictions, the inconsistencies, the aberrations of the social sciences that continue to erect themselves on infantile fantasies.

Moreover, women are less than ever in control of the creative process that is the distinctive property of their own bodies. Even as they deny this form of creation, traditional societies continue to make it a production of slaves, while industrialized societies exploit it in a technocratic, industrialist, and capitalist manner.

It is obviously not a question of demanding salaries for mothers, but rather of refusing the distinction between women declared "active" or "inactive," refusing the shameless exploitation of those who make children, and of establishing the concept of the triple production of women, the majority of women being workers three times over in our society; pregnancy must be considered not only in its economic and social aspects but also in its ethical and universalizing dimensions.

AT THE POLITICAL LEVEL

The functioning of our democracies is far less well-known than that of religions, and yet the founding myths of the Athenian democracy continue to evangelize or imperialize the world, through culture and theater in particular, by its fundamental principles, which are all the more powerful today to the extent that they are hidden to us, unconscious, repressed.

What do the Eumenides tell us in the last play of the *Oresteia*?

1. Orestes, who killed his mother, Clytemnestra, who had killed her husband Agamemnon, in part because he had sacrificed their daughter Iphigenia, will be found innocent by the virgin goddess Athena. His case will ultimately be dismissed with a *non-lieu*,[8] and he will be allowed to regain his kingdom and become the privileged ally of Athens.
2. The Erinyes, goddesses avenging matricide, in becoming Eumenides, will lose all power. Exit matricide as a crime.
3. Following the example of Athena, born solely to her father, Zeus, who swallowed his spouse as she was about to give birth so as to give birth in her place, indigenous Athenians will be born to the mother-earth, without women. And Athenian democracy, as we know, will deny women, slaves, and half-castes the right of citizenship.

Nowhere but in *The Eumenides* do we find expressed with so much clarity, precision, rigor, and arrogance the mythical, historical, political defeat of women; the masculine dictatorship that founds the democratic model is haunted from the outset by the exclusion of the other, by *uterus envy*, by the hatred of the mother-woman and the expropriation and foreclosure of her body as the place of creation of the human being, of the living-thinking.

Women's bodies are foreclosed to the advantage of the mother-earth and Gaia is excluded from symbolization. Freemasonry, which is one of the primary ideological agents of democratization and secularization, particularly in Sub-Saharan Africa, excludes women from its principal rites, asserts itself as resolutely monotheist and, in the initiation rites of mixed or women's lodges, leaves earth outside the temple of light.

"Liberty, equality, fraternity": two centuries ago, with the great revolution, we entered the era of simultaneous affirmation of the individual ("liberty") and the universal ("equality"). Desire for identity and desire for sameness were displayed in a single movement. God and King were dead (or at least recognized as mortal) and the blow to theocratic and state monotheism favored the flowering of individualistic liberation movements and, simultaneously, of egalitarian surges of solidarity (or rather of mutual acknowledgment).

A little later socialism and feminism made their entry onto the politicocultural scene and more recently the May '68 movement put the finishing touches on this evolution by encouraging the formation of narcissistic brotherhoods, that is, by insisting both on fraternity (among men) and on the right to the unlimited expression—the power—of a sovereign ego marked and constituted on the side of the phallus: the 1968 graffiti slogan "power comes from the barrel of the phallus" is reiterated today by the rap-graffiti group NTM (Nique ta mère [Fuck your mother]), superstars at the zenith of Canal-Plus,[9] subsidized by the French Ministry of Culture.

All this leads me to think that we, women and men, have gone at best from patriarchy to a filiarchal or fratriarchal regime. Feminism is the demand for undifferentiated, stereotypical equality, modeled on images lent by the power in charge, to satisfy that demand, sometimes with and sometimes without knowledge of the fratriarchal hegemony. Yet if the affirmation of difference without equality produces only reactionary hierarchy and archaism, it has always seemed to me that an equality incapable of acknowledging differences only creates hom(m)ogenization and assimilation,[10] literally sterilizing for those who have simply chosen/yearned to act like their so-called fellow human beings, their brothers.

To produce life, actually and symbolically, is it not necessary that the One enter into relationship with the Other? The apostles of the great Neutral, who dominate the Western media at present, deliberately lump together the demand for recognition of the difference between the sexes and the demonstrations of separatist nationalisms and other fundamentalisms that proliferate all over the world. Yet ancient and contemporary history alike show that nationalism is not the opposite but rather the corollary, the specular inverse, of universalist individualism. The aspiration to undivided sovereignty, source of today's conflicts and wars, proceeds from the same narcissistic logic, immune to all division, as the republican pretention to reduce every other to the one, in a community that is one and indivisible.

Finally, the affirmation, made in ignorance of reality and the unconscious, that the category of sex does not exist (or has ceased to exist) and that there are only individuals, all similar but each working for itself, throws every woman and man back to the narrowest and most selfish form of individualism and deprives women of the capacity to recognize misogyny and to struggle together, that is to say, politically, against it.

To complete this brief tableau of our politicocultural evolution, I shall add that, in the West, all this seems to be accompanied and reinforced, at the economic level, by the shifting of the industrial economy strictly speaking (which falls within the anal imaginary of production that I briefly described earlier) into a total market economy that implies absolute control of exchange value; in other words, an economy that is still on the order of representation, the fetish-effect or gold-effect—an economy that some have described as the emergence of a spectacular society or a society of the spectacle.[11]

AT THE JURIDICAL LEVEL

If, in the phallic order, the identity of women is conceived as a derived identity, in the juridical order, which commands social organization and political discourse, this identity is not even mentioned. Women in France, not to speak of those in other countries, have not yet been recognized as such by the law: they still do not have full access to citizenship and, beyond that, to a symbolic existence, since our Constitution does not even mention the word *sex* among the distinctions between human beings that have the right to respect and to existence in the polity.

Here is the preamble, dated October 27, 1946:

In the morrow of the victory achieved by the free peoples over the regimes that had sought to enslave and degrade humanity, the people of France proclaim anew that each human being, without distinction of race, religion or creed, possesses sacred and inalienable rights. They solemnly reaffirm the rights and freedoms of man and the citizen enshrined in the Declaration of Rights of 1789 and the fundamental principles acknowledged in the laws of the Republic.

They further proclaim, as being especially necessary to our times, the political, economic and social principles enumerated below: The law guarantees women equal rights to those of men in all spheres.[12]

Yet there can be no real equality, as demonstrated *a contrario* by this preamble, unless a distinction is made first, at the outset, symbolically, by naming the very ones, men and women, who would be promised equality, juridical-political nondiscrimination: in other words, there can be no true, full, concrete equality, indeed no parity, unless differences are taken into account. Indifference goes on producing new forms of discrimination. The perverse effects of symmetrization and egalitarian neutralization are no longer even noticeable because institutional misogyny remains so steadily unthought.

Law continuously inhibits the political. We must therefore go back to the principles that founded it in order to analyze its contradictions, its inconsistencies, its denials and negations, and unveil its immaturity, so true is it that democratic principles founded on a neutral, abstract universalism in contradiction with its own ideals lead, where symbolic power is concerned, to a real sexual apartheid. Universality, on the contrary, would stem from the fact that subjects under law are biologically, therefore ontologically—since we are talking about human beings—sexed. Juridical monism recognizes on a social level that there are women, without recognizing this symbolically, just as Catholicism recognizes the Virgin Mary as a saint but not as a divine being.

By refusing to sexualize the status of citizenship in the Republic, law, in an unconscious reference to monotheistic dogma, neurotically denies reality, shrouding it under a veil of ignorance rather than facing it through analytic work on its philosophical presuppositions—in other words, through an effort to democratize. Law thus authorizes a denial that there have been any attacks on personal rights in the sphere of the difference between the sexes, since it has not inscribed that sphere on its own pediment.[13] Like every object foreclosed from the symbolic, this difference has not ceased to haunt the reality of a psychotic political-symbolic power, incapable of responding fairly and with justice to the questions that the historical existence of women, henceforth indelible, raises for democracy.

And is it not owing to this "constitutional misogyny" that everyday misogyny, in contrast to racism, is still not recognized as a crime? Every day, all over the world, the misogynist plague rears its ugly head.[14] Here and now, little girls, young girls, and women are being humiliated, degraded, sold, beaten, deported, tortured, raped, subjected to incest, and killed because they were born women—not because of who they are but because of what they have the capacity to make: children. And this is such a scandal that it seems scandalous to say it, to evoke the reality of the scandal. The mildness of penalties (often going so far as dismissal of the case, a verdict of non-lieu) sanctioning murders linked to matricide or sororicide reproduces every day, at the juridical level, the political and symbolic coup constituted by the passage from the Erinyes to the Eumenides.

In the general mutism and immobility pierced every once in a while by a television personality's burst of laughter, it is difficult not to remember Robert Antelme, who writes in The Human Race: "You can burn children without that disturbing the night. The night is unmovable around us, who are enclosed in the church. Above us, the stars too are calm. But this calm, this immobility are neither the essence nor the symbol of a preferable truth; they are the scandal of nature's ultimate indifference."[15]

Faced with the increasing gravity of crimes committed against women, which will finally have to be considered as crimes against humanity, Amnesty International has introduced the category of sex, next to those of race, belief, and religion, in its international statutes.

It is urgent to modify the preamble of our Constitution so that women will truly conquer the right to law. For the meaning and the role of law are also to name, to designate, to recognize, to tear away from silence, oblivion, and denial. The right to a nonderived law would make women subjects of a specific legal regime that would recognize and legitimize (as has been done with regard to identity) their specific function as producers of living beings, guarantors (until further notice) not only of the survival but also of the life of the human species, a species that will advance or decline according to whether this law is respected or violated.

This full recognition of woman's "supplementary" capability, of her integral personality, would be a basis for making procreation, symbolically founded in this way, a universal personal right, in turn, instead of a demographic duty, a right that would necessarily include the right to abortion.

On the frontispiece of all the constitutions of the world we should find the following inscription: "Each human being, without distinction of sex, race, religion, or creed, possesses sacred and inalienable rights."

AT THE LINGUISTIC LEVEL

As we know, in language (at least in the Indo-European languages), it is the term *man* that expresses the human, while the word *woman* can never speak for the human. In French there are two genders, masculine and feminine, but these genders do not refer to the sexes (to sexed reality) even if they function, if they are made to function, in their stead. And in French grammar the masculine gender prevails over the feminine, even annuls it, as soon as the masculine—and there need only be one element—takes its place alongside the feminine.[16]

There is thus only one language, and two bodies, differently sexed, that are both prey to the same language. The syntax and lexicon of French demonstrate—as if a demonstration were needed—that not even language is neutral, or rather that its neutrality, here again, is marked in the masculine.

If the neutrality of language is not neutral, the logic of discourse is even less so, as Jacques Derrida has shown; his term for its mechanism is *phallogocentrism*. And now, after leaving behind the adjective *femelle*, language tends increasingly to forget the mark of the feminine. This is a constant on television, but all too frequent elsewhere as well.

The question of the subject of writing—who speaks, who writes when "I" write?—is infinitely complex, and I do not pretend to do it justice here. It is certain that at every moment our writings, our representations, and, of course, our words, are in agreement or disagreement with the constraints the body imposes on language and on its phantasmatic effects. Born a girl or a boy, one becomes a woman or a man, but also masculine or feminine, son or daughter of the mother or of the father. This is the whole problem of the distance between gender and sex, of the complex identifications with which each subject structures and composes himself or herself: in sum, we must take into account here the dimension of psychic bisexuality. This said, and quite rightly, the act of writing will never be neutral.

I would like to formulate, here and now, a hypothesis that you may well find shocking, and yet . . . I wonder whether, as Jean-Jacques Annaud implied in *La guerre du feu* (*Quest for Fire*), women were not the ones who invented language. Many anthropologists have shown that women were the first to practice agriculture and fishing while men were off hunting and at war. I think that women are the *anthropocultivators* who, by talking to the fetus during pregnancy and then to the child, invented and transmitted articulated language. In fact, if we consider the philosophical question of address involved in "speaking to," we are led to think about the patience involved in listening and speaking to another. For a pregnant woman necessarily both listens and speaks to the fetus. This is, for me, the inaugural scene of language.

TOWARD A NEW HUMAN CONTRACT

My thinking is organized around submission to a reality principle that could be formulated as follows: There are two sexes and they are irreducible to one another. This irreducibility arises from the dissymmetry between man and woman in the work of procreation, from the experience of gestation as the specific time and space for welcoming the other, for hospitality and responsibility toward the unfamiliar, as the common origin in which, for the human species, the genealogy of thought can be understood, the advent of ethics is announced and pronounced: gestation as the paradigm of "thinking of the other."

This reality is denied at all levels by our civilization, which functions by means of a totalitarian assertion that there is only a (male) one, there is a (male) one without a (female) one, there is only a one without an other. Recognizing this reality—that there are two sexes—would enable us to move from a homosexed, repressive, inegalitarian, and exclusionary history to a heterosexed, fertile, just history; it would enable us to move from the old order erected by the sons, in the name of the father and then of the brother, to a new civilization. For this, we must work toward the formation of a new analytics and a new ethics of procreation.

THE ANALYTICS OF PROCREATION

This must come about, as I have already suggested, through the elaboration of a theory of genitality for each sex, one that accounts for the formation of "female" genitality—and even of male genitality—beyond the boundary of the phallic and that would consequently admit into its field of investigation and reflection what I call the *uterine stage*, corresponding to a *uterine or female libido*. For a long time I have called this libido 2; nevertheless, the woman precedes; she came first and she is moving ahead.

Imagine a tertiary process, a sort of principle of strangeness or of integration, which would displace the fixation on the two onto an oscillation between the two and the three: a new distribution that, by recalling the forgotten woman, would integrate her capacity to welcome instead of foreclosing it, would dissolve the drive to envy and to hate, would reduce the defensive splitting of the ego. We can predict the economic effects (on underdevelopment), the political effects (on xenophobia), and the symbolic effects (on gynophobia). From the vital knot untied to the vital link retied, that is, to the *human contract*; from a bodily constraint to a contract of free association.

Neither an everyday oral-anal transit nor procrastination, but progression (no doubt this is what leads the engendering woman to reintegrate drives), genital time is a historical and political time, in the strictest terms: nine months, no more; scansion, maturation, term, and decision. It is the historic time of conception, rather than a historic conception of time. It is women's time, the time of a promise that can be kept. Time to understand, to free oneself in fertility's openness, to take with oneself the woman, mother, sister, or daughter.

Such an epistemological turning point should logically lead to a reformulation of relations between sex, body, and psyche as they are articulated, separately and together, with the cultural order. On the one hand, because the uterus (the function and the organ), while it is genital, is no less sexual (it provides uterine jouissance); the matrix of living beings, it is at once the sex that plays and that experiences jouissance, the body at work and the thinking flesh. A fleshly materialism from which each monism is subverted one by one and from which what is called thinking can presumably be initiated. On the other hand, because such an analytics of the production of living beings/the living, which would separate the biological neither from the psychic (both as the unconscious and as language, because a woman in gestation, it must be recalled, is a speaking being) nor, at another level, from the symbolic, would give its full cultural dimension to an activity vital to the future of our species, its genealogy, its memory, its transmission, and its history. In other words, such an analytics would put an end to the reign of culture as a metaphysics that opposes creation to procreation, valorizes the former at the expense of the latter, and conceptualizes the existence and functions of the two sexes along that dividing line.

It is on the condition that creation and procreation, genius and genitality, conceptions of/about the flesh and flesh that conceives, cease to be antagonistic or divided, that men and women will together be able to elaborate an ethics of procreation and an aesthetics of creation without mistaking one for the other.

THE ETHICS OF PROCREATION

In order to arrive at the formulation of a new *human contract* that would take into account the physical, juridical-social, and symbolic dimensions of the existence of living-speaking beings, we must first think through, at the level of collective organization, what has remained unthought in our societies: the production of living beings the living. We must sketch out the economy of this production practically and theoretically—in short, we must invent a *gyneconomy* (or a *feminology* with a larger epistemological field) as a human science dealing with women's share in production in all its forms.

The children of the earth, after a very inadequate social contract, are concerned today with forging a new alliance with nature: the ecology of the elements, plants, animals, and human beings is focused on a vital "natural contract." In the beginning were the waters, and the waters are now polluted. In the beginning was the air, and the ozone layer is shrinking. In the beginning were the forests, and the forests are disappearing . . .

In the beginning, for each of us, there was a woman's body. But in millions of pregnant women numerous pollutions (radiation, AIDS, and so on) are attacking the amniotic fluid and the placenta, the first protective and nutritive membrane of the human being. Alongside physiological pollution, mental and psychic pollution are transforming mothers' "capacity to dream," their function as sublimators, their activity as *anthropocultivators*, into sterile neuroses, into desertifying excitements.

The maternal body is the first environment, the first natural and cultural, physiological and mental, fleshly and verbal milieu. It is the first welcoming (or rejecting) world, where the human being is formed, is created, and grows. It is the first earth, the first house a human being lives in. The living, speaking, intelligent flesh of women is the first thinking matter; at the same time it is the first factory, the most formidable production machine of all. What a fantastic computer it is, with the uterus connected to the brain, to the hormonal system, to all the organs, but also to the psychic apparatus, to the soul, to love! Creative flesh is like a fifth element, the quintessence that contains the four natural elements—water, fire, air, and earth—and sublimates them. Gestation is the unique place and time of the common and universal origin of our species.

Like the body twenty years ago, *flesh* is still overlooked. Flesh wants the jouissance of sex, wants the caress of hands and body, wants the work of the flesh: the full presence in the hollow of the body, not incorporation but a double reciprocal incarnation, desire fulfilled, a project lived, sexuality beyond sex, the yes and the no. Flesh is both clairvoyant and invisible; it is a coupling and an uncoupling; it is memory, a thinking element, in unceasing maturation of self and nonself, premeditation and foresight, a sensitive element, an anticipated reminiscence, a lexicon of affects, pre- and reapprenticeship, source, organization, management of passions, regeneration of drives; the crucible of senses and sensations, transference-countertransference of moods, of affects and of intermingled, chiasmatic thoughts; it ties and unties, summons and sorts, retains and delivers; at once archive and prehistory, it wants the whole but shapes the singular; its unconscious is structured like thinking; the flesh is hospitable: not only does it welcome the guest but, being thrifty, tolerant, strategic, tactical, managerial, dreamy, and enthusiastic, it informs, forms, nourishes, equips, and arms it, withholds it inside only to better accompany it and render it up to the outside, to itself, as unique. For the genital, any contretemps would be harmful.

Thus, just as ecology attempts to establish a contract of rights and duties between human beings and nature, the *human contract* I have proposed should permit the establishment of new rights and new duties between men and women, and also between both men and women and the transitory subjects we know as children. For production of a living being is tripartite: the two must not exclude the third, and human adults are at once the fruit of their double heterosexed origins, of their double lineage, and of the child each once was. The new *human contract* would reestablish the vital link with the matricial space and time, would make men and women partners in a multiple alliance: between women, between men, between men and women, and with their own nature.

Ethics does not appear to be possible without working on (and I say working on, not returning to) origins.

Thus, at least a recasting of the symbolic, if not an exit from the symbolic (insofar as the symbolic implies the two, such an exit does not seem necessary), would be possible, opening and articulating itself around the semantic field of gestation, on and with reality: there are two sexes.

Gestation as *generation*, *gesture*, management, and inner experience, experience of the intimate, but also *generosity*, *genius* of the species, acceptance of a foreign body, hospitality, openness, desire for a regenerative graft; an integrating, aconflictual, postambivalent gestation of differences, an anthropocultural model, a matrix for the universality of humankind, the principle and origin of ethics; gestation, a fleshly and spiritual conception of the other, always already subject, rather than Genesis, that autistic fable that men and the religions of the Book have substituted for it; gestation, a transformation in the present toward a real, nonutopian future; gestation, living attention and heteronomous experience, which knows how to make a place within the self for the nonself; gestation, the promise of the being to be; gestation, finally, the paradigm of "thinking the near/future other," a paradigm of ethics and democracy.

What can we women do in these times of despair and sterility? It is hardly possible for us to act, and we can't do much to make our voices heard, but we can always practice thinking. Perhaps we should try to go through and past the place where hysteria has always put us in an impasse; perhaps we should try to succeed where the hysteric has always failed. By starting with the following proposition.

It is the symbolization of what the all-one excludes, the symbolization of our foreclosed knowledge concerning primordial thought, of our foreclosed knowledge concerning the experience of gestation as a trial, that can not only go beyond monistic totalitarianisms but can also promote a mode of ethical thought beyond animist, religious, or scientific ways of thinking.

Allow me, then, to express a few wishes: rather than the biblical and Greek mythologies, which falsify origins by substituting fabled, motherless geneses for female gestation, rather than unisex, matricidal democracies, we want a process of democratization that recognizes the irreducible difference between the sexes, the dissymmetry and privilege of women in procreation, a process that makes procreation a universal right, that reestablishes reality, the fleshly and sexual truth of human origins, that expresses its gratitude to women for their unique contribution to humanity in its genealogy, its memory, its ongoing transmission, its capacity to think.

We want a democratization that recognizes the *genius of women* as regards their genitality and their own identity, a process that considers gestation as the paradigm of an ethics of generosity where the foreign body, the other, is welcomed by means of a spiritual as well as a fleshly graft, the model of all grafts, where the other is loved and created as the near and future being.

We want a democratization that recognizes that reproduction is in fact production, production of the other through oneself and of oneself through the other, that considers that this gesture of gestation must take place apart from all technological and commercial speculation, away from all devastating pollution, that it must be protected by a new alliance of humans with women, through a *human contract* that guarantees the durability of our vital link to the uterus (in Arabic and in Hebrew the same word designates the uterus and mercy).

Gratitude, as a replacement for envy, is the atheological virtue I prefer. Gratitude is the very "poethical" sentiment, in other words, a *re-co-naissance* in its infinite polysemy: being born anew, coming to birth, the birth to come (the pro-birth of procreation) and also of birthing together, investigation, discovery, knowledge, etc.[17]

As I thank you for having listened to me, I would like to read you a letter from Martin Buber to Emmanuel Levinas, quoted by the latter in *Proper Names*, where he develops a line of thought already expressed by Paul Celan in 1958,[18] in his "Discourse in Bremen":

Once again the hour for uncommon gratitude has come for me. I have much to give thanks for. For me, this was a time to meditate once more upon the word thank [*remercier*]. Its ordinary meaning is generally understood, but it does not lend itself to a description that would define it unequivocally.

One sees immediately that it belongs to that category of words whose original meaning is multiple. Thus it awakens a variety of associations in various languages.

In German and English, the verb for "*remercier*," which is *danken and thank*, is related to *denken and think*, in the sense of *having in one's thoughts*, remembering someone. The person who says "I thank you," "*Ich danke dir*," assures the other person that he or she will be kept in the memory, and more specifically in the good memory, that of friendship and joy. It is significant that the eventuality of a different sort of memory doesn't arise.

It is otherwise in Hebrew. The verb for *hodot* means first *to come in support of someone*, and only later, *to thank*. He who thanks someone rallies in support of the one thanked. He will now—and from now on—be his ally. This includes, to be sure, the idea of memory, but implies more. The fact occurs not only within the soul: it proceeds from there toward the world, to become act and event. Now, to come in support of someone in this way is to confirm him in his existence.

I propose to vow a thankful memory and to come in support of all who have sent me their good wishes for my eighty-fifth birthday.

Jerusalem, February, 1963[19]

The twenty-first century will be *geni(t)al* or else it will remain narcissistic and murderous and it will not be.

4. Does Psychoanalysis Have
an Answer for Women?

April 2, 1991

PASSAGES: To begin at the beginning, so to speak, what is your personal contribution to psychoanalysis?

ANTOINETTE FOUQUE: My contribution may lie in my insistence on asking analytic theory a few questions; naturally enough, these questions contain the outline of some answers. Why, for example, does the only scientific discourse on sexuality, psychoanalytic discourse, assert, from Freud to Lacan, that there is only one libido, and that it is "essentially male" or "phallic," when there are obviously, in reality, two sexes? Might not this phallic monism, which is more contaminated by the *vir* than analysts themselves might like to admit—as the phallus is very often confused, even in analytic theory, with the penis—obey the pleasure principle rather than the reality principle? So what is conventionally termed the symbolic order would appear to be based upon a denial of reality, in the claim that there is a single, male, libido for both men and women. This monophallicism cannot fail to evoke the various monotheisms. Might psychoanalytic theory thus derive from a religious rather than a scientific way of thinking?

This theory has all sorts of implications, not to say perverse effects. It is, for example, impossible to describe women's sexuality except in terms of castration—negative phallicity—or to designate it "feminine"; yet "feminine" characterizes a gender that can also be applied to a man. For a long time I have been saying that femininity is a form of transvestism. In any case, because Freud often gives it connotations of passivity, it refers back to the anal register of sexuality; it is therefore pregenital.

Because it is encapsulated in pregenitality in this way (for men too; I shall come back to this point), psychoanalytic theory is caught up in a regressive attraction from the phallic toward the anal, in a perverse phallic fixation that powerfully inhibits it from elaborating a theory of genitality, since genitality is, of necessity, heterosexed.

This has a further perverse implication: hysterical neurosis is seen as the obverse of the phallic perversion. But if the discourse of the master is illuminated by that of the hysteric—hysteria being the lease that is taken out on the uterus by the phallus—why shouldn't it be illuminated, in a progressive sense, by the discourse of women? Its subordination to the reality principle would then allow psychoanalytic theory to make progress by allowing it to elaborate a theory of genitality, which can only be heterosexed, as we know. Strangely enough, women analysts who work with, or through, their female analysands on their common sexuality continue to assert this "only" in theoretical terms ("there is only one libido"; "jouissance can only come from the phallus"). Do they do this so as to avoid the risk of losing the father's love, or a place in one or another of his institutional mansions?

Women's right to the symbolic, and therefore the right of both men and women to a "dialogic order," might allow a better understanding of how things stand, or do not stand, with sexual relationships. But women's right to the symbolic requires us to take the view that, given that there are two sexes, there are two libidos: every woman bears within her a libido of her own. Twenty years ago I called this libido 2, but since, after all, we are talking about a uterine libido, about a matricial economy, it could also be called "libido 1," as it is primary, principial, and primal for both sexes.

PASSAGES: Are you saying that psychoanalysis is a male science?

AF: The theory, or rather psychoanalytic discourse, was elaborated de facto by Freud the man—who was both vir and homo sapiens—and based on the words of young women he described as hysterics; however, Freud the writer partially repressed the women subjects of these words because, starting with the *Studies in Hysteria* and later with *Dora*, where he conjugated dream and hysteria, he finally described "the interpretation of dreams" as the royal road to the unconscious, usually with himself as his object of study; his own male obsessional neurosis was the basis for psychoanalytic knowledge.

The repression of hysteria, which is itself a trace of the foreclosure of the uterus, can be read in more than one place in Freud's works. Freud himself admits that he did not know how to take Dora's homosexuality into account and that his interpretation of the countertransference was mistaken; elsewhere, during his analysis of the poet Hilda Doolittle, he refuses to assume the maternal position in the countertransference. We now know that he did little work on his relationship with his mother during his self-analysis and that, when he wrote up the final version of his notes on his sessions with the Rat Man, he repressed almost all references to the maternal. We also know, finally, that, while it appears in one of the key dreams in the *Interpretation*—the so-called dream of "dissecting my own pelvis," it does not give rise to any discussion of his own uterine drive, his female being, except through the use of an encrypted metaphor. Now, while repression is one of the fundamental concepts of psychoanalysis, its cornerstone, perhaps, the *foreclosure of the body of the mother*, like the foreclosure of the name of the father conceptualized by Lacan, can generate psychoses: what is foreclosed from the symbolic returns in the real.

Being at once on the far side and the near side of the anal-phallic problematic, which takes up virtually the entire field of analytic theory, women's sexuality might be elaborated around an oral-genital articulation. The writer who preyed on the talking cure discovered by Anna O. died of a cancer of the mouth that reduced him to silence toward the end of his life; he had planned to theorize orality, but that project was aborted because work on the prenatal, on pregnancy, on the sexed body, on the thinking flesh of women as the space of the *production of living-speaking beings*, was foreclosed from the science of the unconscious. If I dared, I would say that, even before it could be written, the epistemophilic drive degenerated into an epistemophallic drive, to the detriment of an analytic and conceptual advance that could have geni(t)ally freed the son from a mother who is seen, in fantasy, as omnipotent. For sons pay a high price for wanting to be loved with a nonambivalent love, for wanting to see themselves as God and wanting to remain tethered to Her, to the mother, both as fathers and sons, rather than admitting that they were born of mere women and that, like those women, they are human beings, nothing more and nothing less, even though they are sometimes geniuses.

Mono-phallo-theism may have led to spiritual progress, but it cost us a misogyny which increasingly seems to be a factor in humanity's sclerosis, its perverse fixation, and its impoverishment. Because it has been foreclosed from the symbolic, the vital link with the matricial returns in the real in the form of dependency on the archaic mother, while the misogyny, fear, and hatred men feel towards women make the human contract obsolete.

PASSAGES: So what work has to be done within psychoanalysis, in your view, to get out of this impasse?

AF: Secularizing and democratizing psychoanalytic theory is a matter of urgency; that is, we must not only make room for the mother in the father's house, but we must also free ourselves from pregenitality and infantile dependency. Far from wishing to destroy the body of Freud's construction, whose foundations and roof are admirable, from cellar to loft, we have to repair parts of it and extend it by adding a few more indispensable rooms. When it comes to genealogies, birth certificates, proper names, and family ties, it is time to reconsider the matricial function, maternal responsibilities, and the woman subject's place in the house; in a word, we have to think through postpatriarchy in order to invent ourselves as men and women, but we must do so together.

The work that has to be done therefore means recalling this unknown relationship, elaborating this vital link with the matricial. Going beyond envy and recognizing, as Wilfred Bion did, the mother's ability to daydream or, to be more accurate, the drive to know, woman's capacity to welcome the other: this would be a way of arriving at a form of gratitude that would in itself bring us closer to what we might call thinking. Perhaps it might be a way of getting away from a religious mode of thought, which is all too often obscurantist, and of coming closer to a scientific and ethical mode of thought.

The symbolizable experience, virtual or real, of pregnancy is, for every woman, an intimate way of working on the self and the nonself. It is the model for all successful grafts, for "thinking of the other," a heterogeneous "between-us," a tolerance of the other's jouissance, a hospitality shown to a foreign body, a gift that creates no debts, a fleshly hope that is disavowed by all absolute narcissism, all totalitarian undividualism, and all racism. These specific capacities can be transmitted, can be shared in the man-woman cocreation that is human procreation.

It is time to do away with misogyny; it is time for knowledge, gratitude, and thought to triumph over the relation with the unknown, over the envy of women and over obscurantism towards women. It is time to do away with the fantasy of the "dark continent." A women's ethics would converge with the woman-inspired ethics of the poet-philosophers Rimbaud and Rilke and others . . . In his Bremen speech Paul Celan recalls that, in German, *denken* and *danken*, to think and to thank, have the same root.[1] This is an echo of Heidegger, for whom the word *thinking* directs us to the essential sphere of memory, devotion, and thanks.[2]

5. The Plague of Misogyny

June 7, 1991

Thank you for inviting me to this conference to speak about a very specific racism—the one with which I am most familiar because I have always been its object and its witness. This is a racism so old, so familiar in human history and in the history of every human being that its victims had scarcely begun to shake off its yoke, to break the silence surrounding it, twenty years ago, at a time when I was already over thirty and had reached the canonical age at which, according to Balzac, a woman no longer exists.

I feel very lonely, coming here to speak to you about this racism, if that is what it is; but if racism is a hatred of the other's jouissance, then misogyny is the worst of all racisms.

Misogyny is the most widespread form of racism because it victimizes half of humanity, as though that half were a species within the species, a separate "race" that the entire human species can mock. A half of humanity that is at once its own victim and its own executioner, a victim subject to ridicule, so triumphant is the executioner—think of The Taming of the Shrew: a victim who inspires fear, so irrational is the hatred.

THE PLAGUE OF MISOGYNY 61

The hatred of this racism—it is not really racism and yet it is—has a woman, women, as its object. But the subject who feels that hatred can just as easily be a woman as a man.

In ancient Greece a man or a woman who hated women was described as a *misogynist*. The cognate term *misogyne* is attested in France as early as the sixteenth century; it was firmly established by the eighteenth century and was the object of a short entry in the Littré dictionary. However, unlike *racism*, and even though *racism* is a very recent formation, *misogyny* does not figure in contemporary dictionaries of philosophy.

In order to remove all ambiguity as to its object, women, I speak of *misogyny* rather than *sexism*. The latter term is a neologism modeled on *racism*. As a result of the way it was used by the feminists of the 1960s, it entered the lexicon in France in 1975, defined as follows by the *Dictionnaire Quillet de la langue française*: "Sexism: Masculine noun, neologism. The fact of ascribing major importance in social relations to sexuality, and especially the male libido. Term forged on the model of racism, describing the behavior of those who consider the male sex to be superior to the female (or vice versa) and take the view that it must be dominant."[1]

The word *sexism* is reversible in terms of its object and therefore in terms of its subject. The same reversibility is not present in the word *misogyny*. Five years later we could read in the Quillet-Flammarion *Dictionnaire usuel illustré*: "Sexism: Masculine noun. The dominant attitude of individuals of one sex towards the other, especially of men towards women."[2]

Misogyny, then, describes the hatred of which women are the object or what Freud, in several texts, and especially *Inhibitions, Symptoms and Anxiety*, describes as disavowal, by both sexes, of femininity or castration; *misogyny* describes the discriminations that result, and they range from the disparagement of women (which goes hand in hand with their idealization) to the murder of women.

While the difference between the sexes informs every principle and system of difference and provides the model for all binary opposition systems and all dualist domination, the roots of the hatred of the other—which we mistakenly term "racism" even though the notion of "race" is very slippery—may, and this is the hypothesis I am advancing, lie in the masochistic hatred that humanity feels for half of humanity. Now, while it is true that there is no such thing as "race," there really are two sexes. This is a reality, and it will remain irreducible and unavoidable for a long time to come. The intercrossing that some are so keen to see, and which would supposedly reduce the dissymmetry and erase its borders, would lead to the sterilization and then the extinction of the species. The human species is a sexed species, and its survival or perpetuation therefore depends on this reality and this principle: there are two sexes, and that is what fertility means.

Misogynist journalists turned the "Manifeste des 343" into the *manifeste des 343 salopes* (the 343 sluts),[3] and everyone laughed. If we replaced the word *women* with *Arabs, blacks,* or *Jews,* followed by "assholes, the lot of them," everyone would rightly be up in arms and screaming "'racism" . . . The basis for misogyny, and this may be the reason why all fundamentalisms use it as their ultimate weapon, is not the fact that women *exist,* but what women *do.* It is an ability to do, or to make, that the men of the human species lack: using a male seed and a female ovum, a genitor and a genitrix, and thanks to the labor of their own flesh, body, and soul, women produce children, girls and boys who can speak and think, in a differentiated process of individuation.

Misogyny's roots lie in envy rather than hatred and fear, in the male's envy of women's procreative capacity. Freud hammers home the message that we women are the slaves of our penis envy. Surely this is just a bogeyman, masking the *uterus envy* that so obsesses men, the envy that demands its foreclosure, and which is rooted in and erected into the surrogate phallus tree that symbolizes all power ("power comes from the barrel of the phallus," "power comes from the barrel of a gun," and—why not—"power comes from the barrel of a pen").

This thought has always haunted me, and I experienced it vitally when my daughter was born; years later I found that it had been expressed in magisterial terms in the work of Melanie Klein.[4] I drew the relevant political conclusions by founding the MLF in October 1968 as a movement in which we could fight the most obscene form of that envy: misogyny. A combination of male envy and an excessive and exclusionary valuation of one sex at the expense of the other leads to the disparagement of women, on the one hand, and to their immaterial and disembodied idealization, their nonexistence, on the other. Here we find the roots of primal violence against women, their enslavement and what men call Law or the symbolic order.

How could this symbolic law recognize and condemn misogyny as a crime without putting itself outside the law, without outlawing itself and declaring itself criminal? A democratic law must account for the crime of a symbolic law that puts half of humanity outside the law. It has a duty to think it through and transcend it.

THE PLAGUE OF MISOGYNY 63

If primal repression means that woman, as mother, must be left behind and foreclosed and that everything that was once familiar must be stamped with the mark of the un---unheimlich, uncanny, unconscious, unknown, unknowable, unthinkable—we are indeed dealing with a misogyny that has become almost natural. And because what psychoanalysis calls "primal repression" is the precondition for the formation of the ego, in other words for the maturation of the psyche, this formative process definitively holds women back, husteros, as genitrix (mother or hysteric), forever foreclosed from the symbolic, an unnameable thing and object of hatred and horror for men: monster, medusa, sphinx when she appears at a man's side or before him. What is most familiar, the heimlich, the space of conception and gestation, becomes strange, uncanny, alien, unheimlich; what we know best becomes the unknown itself, and the prefix un- will henceforth bar access to it: uncanny, unknown, unthinkable, unconscious, and so on.

The space where sexual, genetic, and identitarian differentiation is engendered will be the object of an absolute discrimination, of a real symbolic apartheid, or the object of repression, an egalitarian nondifferentiation.

It is because we are dealing with two types of misogyny that it is so difficult to think about the problem today. On the one hand, the advocates of motherhood go on exploiting the sexual division of labor when it comes to procreation by speculating on it and penalizing women in all their activities, in an enslaved procreation, a production of living-speaking beings that is never recognized for what it is. The irreducible dissymmetry between the sexes when it comes to procreation induces endless discrimination and endless inequalities. Everyone is familiar with that misogyny. On the other hand, by denying, to the point of paranoia, the most elementary reality principle—there are two sexes—the supporters of egalitarian universalism reduce humanity to a neutral pseudo-integration, which is therefore in fact masculine, monosexed and therefore homosexed, narcissistic, divided, sterile, and literally egoistic. An ego with no other is all that exists. There is only one God, and He is either the Father or the Son. There is only one libido, and it is phallic.

This misogyny, which is modern and progressive, is much more difficult to spot: it throws the baby out with the bathwater, and difference out with discrimination. According to its logic, any woman who wins glory, visibility, or rights hitherto reserved for men immediately becomes a man (Florence Arthaud, Edith Cresson).[5] This is the modern republic of transsexual, symbolic sons and girl-sons (filses): madame le Premier ministre.[6]

It is about this hatred, then, that I am speaking, the hatred directed toward women by the sons and girl-sons of the human species who, in order to advance, flee headlong—often backward—sacrificing part of themselves as other in the name of the most perverse One.

Everywhere, always, in all places and at all times. Here, today, they are humiliating, mocking, scorning, killing, beating, raping, subjecting to incest, torturing, and killing little girls, girls, and women because they are female. They, those impersonal *they*, as Elie Wiesel said yesterday, are the fanatics; we have to say that *they* are also the misogynists.

This is such a scandal that it is scandalous to evoke it. It is so total that our democracies do not want to know about the totalitarianism that exists at the very heart of their ideals. It is global, worldwide. This is barbarism on a planetary scale. This is permanent, organized self-destruction.

In recent years feminist movements have constantly recalled that massacres and sometimes mass murders of women have been common throughout history. Witness the European witch hunts of the past, the female infanticide in China; witness the women who were buried alive in accordance with the tradition of ancient Arab tribes or the Indian women who were burned alive on the funeral pyres of their husbands and who were described as faithful wives. These are by no means phenomena from another age: female infanticide has made a comeback in China, and in certain Third World countries girls are systematically undernourished. Women are still burned alive in India when their dowries are deemed to be inadequate or are not paid on time. We also know that millions of women still suffer genital mutilation (excision, infibulation), especially in Africa, and that the same practices are widespread in Paris. The very existence of shelters for battered women and the number, finally, of rape complaints make it clear that the women of the industrialized Western countries are not spared either.

Amnesty International has published a damning report on the condition of women around the world. In both peacetime and wartime the world is a place in which women are always in mortal danger. Our century, which is so keen on denouncing all the evils that threaten humanity, and the destruction of the earth, the seas, animals, and peoples, still takes no notice of the destruction of women.

The Observatoire de la Misogynie has shown that, in France, in 1990, freedoms and equality for women were flouted at every level: economic, political, ideological, and symbolic.[7] In France, 1 woman is killed every day because she is a woman; 362 women were killed in 1990. But even before these crimes have been denounced or named, mitigating circumstances are found: the killers are said to be insane and therefore not responsible for their actions (article 64 of the penal code) or they are said to have committed crimes of passion, in which case their crimes are understandable (reduced penalties). Over four thousand women are raped every year in France (two of every three rapes are gang rapes).

Today's Republic of Sons is, in general terms, a democratic improvement over the patriarchal Republic, but it is women who are paying the price for this sonocracy, in which the Oedipuses so often drift into a matricidal, monstricidal, priapic, and narcissistic anti-Oedipus. "Power comes from the barrel of the phallus" becomes the taggers' "Motherfuckers." Macho games and rituals—soccer, bullfights, wars—either exclude women or assimilate them. The "Zulu" street gangs have adopted the gang rape of blue-eyed blondes as a rite of passage and integration. And there is a real danger that a certain antiracism will give rise to a new misogyny: replace the mère (mother) in Nique Ta Mère ("Fuck Your Mother," a rap group) with black, Jew, or pal and you'll get the point.

Turning to the uprisings in the banlieues,[8] where unemployment and racism reign, what do we know about the multilayered suffering of immigrant women, about the exclusion and confinement of women, who are doubly invisible? We find the same silence that was forced upon the deportees who were not allowed to speak about the internment camps when they came back. The daughters of Algerian or Tunisian fathers are the social group most affected by the scourge of suicide: between the ages of fifteen and twenty-five twice as many of them commit suicide as French girls of the same age; they are five times more likely to kill themselves than their brothers.

At the economic level, a real threshold of tolerance applies to women when it comes to the right to work, despite laws on equality in the workplace. French unemployment figures attest to the discrimination: 12 percent of the active population is unemployed: 8 percent of the male population and 14 percent of the female population. Over 60 percent of the long-term unemployed are women of working age.

Women are still objects to be bought and sold, and the porn industry is expanding rapidly: underage girls are still sold into prostitution in countries where there are no laws to repress prostitution or to protect women.

Women are penalized in both economic and social terms because their triple productivity is still not recognized: the human riches that they alone produce remain invisible and unrecognized. As a result, women are still penalized even when they do the same work as men.

Women continue to suffer discrimination in terms of access to knowledge, worth, and power.

In legal terms, and despite the UN Convention on the Elimination of All Forms of Discrimination Against Women, which has been ratified by all the democracies and many developing countries, the UN secretary general could state in 1990 that, for women, a world of democracy or of developed countries does not exist anywhere. And although France ratified the convention in 1990, the country has introduced only timid, not to say timorous, reforms. At a time of identity crisis, the lack of any antimisogynist laws modeled on antiracist laws condemns women to the reality of death. Its existence still denied, misogyny is not recognized as a crime, as though, where women are concerned, we are afraid to punish men. The proposed reform of the criminal code speaks in general terms of the "strong" and the "weak" and of "crimes against humanity," even though in three out of four cases the criminals are men and the victims are women. The crime remains unnamed, and therefore does not exist, just as used to be the case with rape. So long as the word is not there, the specificity of the crime can be denied. The role of the law is not simply to punish: the law names, designates, and recognizes. It wrests crimes out of silence and denial and makes it possible to speak of them: a democratic, democratizing law thus makes it possible to think.

Making a distinction between the sexes and giving women access to a law of their own is not only a way of fighting discrimination; it is a way of promoting democratization.

In ideological and cultural terms, in the era of visibility, of names and fame and "golden boys" in the media, women are absent, anonymous, invisible, silent, or dead to the world, everywhere from Bari and Mantes to Algiers. Either that, or the old images of the whore and the Madonna resurface, together with classic femininity.

At the symbolic level, the preamble to the Constitution still makes no mention of sex, a category that Amnesty International enshrined in its statutes this year alongside race, religion, and creed. The constitutional framework, remaining reticent, paralyzes the law and inhibits the urgent need for democratization, inhibits political action.

In political terms, the Constitutional Council's rejection of quotas for women in 1992,[9] which was justified on the grounds of a hypocritical equality, is one of the reasons for the political underrepresentation of women and for the breaks in women's careers.

The scourge of humanity known as misogyny, defined as the hatred of the other, can now be analyzed on four levels:

—The endemic, day-to-day, or banal level: 99 percent of men are unconsciously misogynist.
—Misogyny is the typical attitude of self-proclaimed good-natured male chauvinists who make smutty jokes; however, such incidental pronouncements have far-reaching political and symbolic implications and are related, sometimes by just one man, to collective beliefs: the pope has compared abortion to Nazism.
—Misogyny is contagious; it is passed on from individuals to groups and incites hatred.
—Misogyny can at any moment manifest itself at the state level if women's right to have their own rights is challenged, if women are denied "inalienable and sacred" citizenship in their own right, or if they are not inscribed in the Constitution.

The women and men who denounce this scandal appear scandalous themselves; those who attack this irrational hatred are described as madmen and madwomen; those who fight for the elementary rights known as the rights of women are shamed and described as extremists.

It is time for us to begin to stop destroying one another. It is our duty as democrats to fight misogyny.

6. And If We Were to Speak of Women's Powerlessness?

1991

To speak of the power of women in France, where their presence in positions of political power is so negligible, would almost be a joke. The statistics are quite damning; France very clearly brings up the rear in this particular area. Moreover, just as a single swallow does not make a summer, the presence of a woman as French prime minister, despite the indisputable symbolic effect of this presidential initiative, does not represent a rapid transformation of reality. In fact, there are no more women in Edith Cresson's government now than there were in that of her predecessor, Michel Rocard. More important, the current French government has made no real attempt to strengthen its policy toward women, except for reintroducing a ministry solely dedicated to women, as we had in 1981.

Today almost a quarter of a century after the democratic revolution of 1968 and the organization of the Women's Movement, women's access to the ranks of political, economic, and symbolic power remains difficult, not to say impossible. This is the case, despite women's partially acquired access to knowledge, at least in the West, which does not represent a concomitant access to "worth."[1]

Don't women like power? Or is it power that doesn't like them? Women are segregated, more often than not, with their special problems, and when it comes to considering major options for the future the powers that be act as though women have no opinions on such matters. No one remembers to ask. The newspaper *Vu de gauche* (Seen from the left), edited by Jean Poperen, is noteworthy in this respect, but an infinite number of examples could be found in the media. Do women actually like power? It's like asking whether poor people like money. . . . No, because they don't have any; yes, because they don't have any.

In this rather dreary political summer, two news events or issues that concern women have stirred up a few waves in the murky backwaters of the media, the trade unions, and French politics. A third, the most serious, is not an issue but a tragedy: I refer to the rape of seventy-one young women and the murder of nineteen of these women by their own male classmates in a high school in Kenya, an event that seems to have received virtually no press coverage. Here in France the only media attention given to everyday rapes and violence against women has taken the customary form of shining a spotlight on their murderers.[2]

The first current event, then, was the publication of *Horizon 2000*, a study conducted by INSEE (National Institute of Economic and Statistical Information) in 1991; this study predicts a shortage of manpower in 2005. According to INSEE, if the fertility rate remains at its current level, the segment of population known as "active" will diminish. To remedy this situation, the authors propose four solutions: increasing the productivity of the working population, extending the retirement age, increasing employment opportunities for women, or once again encouraging immigration. Virtually everyone seized upon the fourth solution: the political left predicted increased immigration in 2000, while the right and the far right expressed support for what was the aim of the study—to promote a pronatalist policy. The right's solution came down to two competing and convergent exclusions: the exclusion of immigrants, so threatening today and tomorrow that we must rush to lock down the borders again, and the exclusion of women, who, while destined to reproduce the French workforce, are considered "inactive." In the future, these women will not even hold the lead they have today in the category of the active but long-term unemployed population. Women constitute 57 percent of the long-term unemployed, and young women 76 percent of the young long-term unemployed; they are thereby marginalized economically, politically, and socially.

The mobilization of society's resources for a policy that would recognize women as triply productive members of society should be a priority for the political left. In reality the left has neglected women and made them the most excluded category in this competitive and production-oriented society. And this has occurred despite the fact that women are indeed triply productive in human society—as reproducers who have the exclusive task of perpetuating the species; as productive housewives responsible for the family, the private sphere; and finally, and in large numbers, as working professionals whose activities are now indispensable for the maintenance of a barely decent standard of living. But as a result of their multiple duties, women find themselves the majority among the large numbers of the long-term unemployed; in other words, they find themselves the most excluded of the excluded in this competitive society.

Moreover, the "inactive" and "active" categories that demographers apply to us not only make the female population a divided one, arbitrarily separated by social affiliations and diverse cultures, but also make of each one of us, each individual woman, a person torn between her need for private achievements and her legitimate social ambitions.

The fertility rate is the blind spot around which this type of demography is organized, this pseudo-human science, so surreal in its attempt to saw off the very branch on which it sits that it forecloses women—the very life source of its legitimacy—from its analyses. In fact, if demography does not consider women of reproductive age part of the active population, how can an active workforce be produced by such an inactive source? And how will future generations renew themselves except through the reproductive capacity of the female population, which, while counted as "inactive," makes up the very core of the active population, generation after generation. In other words, humanity, as Lacan once put it, would be a woman who makes a woman who makes a woman, one after the other, inactive according to the demographers but always present as a factory for the production of the active population. When we speak of electricity or atomic energy, we include power plants in figuring the cost of production. Human procreation, however, is left out of the calculation of human productivity and the resources that this productivity creates. Human procreation remains the ultimate—but formidable—site of slavery.

The capacity to procreate, the specific power of women, instead of engendering power (some speak of demographic power), has shackled us to a very real powerlessness, precisely because reproduction is so negatively inscribed in democratic thinking—which, while rightly concerned with principles of equality, is oblivious to the reality that there are two sexes and the dissymmetry between them where this primary difference is concerned. And, as we know from psychoanalysis, what is foreclosed from the symbolic returns in the real; what democratic thinking refuses to think consciously will resurface as a symptom at every step along the path toward democratization. In virtually all their activities women are penalized for their reproductive power, for an activity that is qualified as inactive.

Even to speak of procreation, of maternity, often appears to reflect a regressive and reactionary stance in and of itself—mainly because, up to now, only the political right wing has discussed it, and when representatives of the right discuss it in the context of their program for a pronatalist policy, they exacerbate this penalization. In fact, the Women's Movement has always stood on the political left, has always put nurture before nature (the reverse of the environmental movement), and has always viewed reproduction as a choice, a culturally rather than naturally determined fact of life, which a woman's control over fertility would humanize even further. Not the least of the advances made by the Women's Movement lies in its proposal that there be greater articulation between the private and the public spheres, between the subject and history. In addition to the Women's Movement's rethinking of the body as capable of both suffering and joy, as more than a mere bearer of a work force, it has also brought to the fore a topic forgotten by Marx: the political nature of the subject, whether embryonic or already born. Once qualified as a social movement, the Women's Movement has always defined itself as a cultural and civilizing movement with a universal mission.

As producers or creators of living-speaking beings, women are the source of the principal human resource: humanity itself. The demographers should not refer to them only as members of the "active population" but also as endowed with ingenious brains and creative intelligences. Reproduction remains foreclosed, as I have said before, from the productivity-oriented thought that it feeds and that defines it as powerlessness.

The second current event confirms this analysis. The European Court of Justice recently lifted the ban on night work for women in the name of equality between the sexes. From the workers, those archaic dreamers, we heard charges of regression: we must eliminate night work for both sexes. From the managers we heard claims of progress: women are achieving and being promoted as fast as their male counterparts, except in the "special case of maternity" (these were the terms used in the declaration by the CGC).[3] Affirmative action for women is inscribed in French labor law and is a protection against sexual abuse and the financial burden of raising a family. But, as far as I know, rapes and violent acts against women have not diminished in our country. Moreover, if one is to believe INSEE, the fertility rate per woman is 1.8 (or 2.1 according to INED [National Institute of Demographic Studies]), which means that every nonpubescent and nonmenopausal woman in this country is potentially responsible for producing two children, and this is true for 53 percent of the population. Is maternity then a "special case" or a more general one, the case of the majority of women?

We cannot simultaneously credit each woman with a fertility rate—thus holding her responsible for the renewal or the aging of the species and blaming her for any demographic imbalances—and continue to consider pregnancy or maternity a "special case." The concepts of fertility rate and demographic equilibrium turn an innate capacity into a universal socioeconomic competence; thus imposing a requirement of solidarity among women—whether childbearing, adoptive mothers, or child free—so that this "production," "service," "competence," "gift," or "creation," as one prefers, will be integrated into the very core of democratic ideals.

No doubt it will be argued that we now have very sophisticated machines that work nonstop, day and night. But at least three eight-hour shifts have been organized around these new automatons. In contrast, a qualified woman technician (there are many such, these days, and there will be even more tomorrow) who has a three-year-old child and is pregnant with another could not under any circumstances manage to cope with three eight-hour shifts during pregnancy, which mobilizes huge amounts of her energy around the clock. Still, in the name of equality, we will make her work a supplementary night shift and in the name of protective discrimination, or affirmative action, we will then proceed to penalize her when she seeks a promotion. This is a scandal: the egalitarian and production-obsessed ideology that excludes the urgent issue of reproduction from its dynamic excludes women from the very outset. In other words, obtuse and nondifferentiating egalitarianism generates a blatant injustice.

In Honduras three thousand young girls between the ages of fifteen and twenty were forcibly sterilized to satisfy employers who wanted to abolish maternity leave, claiming it disrupted the organization of their work.[4] All over the world women are slaves and martyrs to reproduction, whether it is forbidden or obligatory. Totalitarian and egalitarian societies alike are opportunistic and sadistic in their obsession with productivity; women are invisible slaves to a kind of production that has never even been considered by any economic theory as such. Women have been martyrs since the earliest days of human history, and even today they die in childbirth by the millions; they were martyrs owing to their exclusive knowledge of the flesh, deemed diabolical, when they were subject to *gynocide* by an Inquisition that burned them by the hundreds of thousands.

Today, misogyny takes the form of a fanatical antifeminism, which means that even a women's elementary right to knowledge carries the risk of death. Do we need to recall the Quebec tragedy, replayed in an even more horrific version in the Kenya tragedy? In Canada, in December 1989, a young man assassinated fourteen students at the Montreal Polytechnic in an attack against women who were seeking higher education. In Nairobi, on July 13, 1991, a horde of three hundred boys, aged fourteen to nineteen, students in a mixed-sex Catholic school, engaged in a collective massacre of their female counterparts. Drunk and drugged out, armed with iron bars, these boys stormed the girls' dormitory, wounded seventy-five of the girl students, raped seventy-one of them and killed nineteen. These girls had preferred to continue studying during an examination period rather than join a strike against the leadership of the school, which they felt did not concern them. "Murderous insanity," read the headlines in the newspapers, which only gave a few lines of coverage to the tragedy. Insanity should under no circumstances ever be considered an attenuating factor to justify misogynist and antifeminist crimes and violence, any more than it should ever be used to justify racial violence or crimes of a racist nature. However, while racism is now considered an offense, misogyny remains an opinion, and sexist murders are written off as the work of madmen whose madness renders them irresponsible and thus utterly unaccountable.

The task of democratic men and women can be defined on three levels. First, the struggle to eradicate a deep-seated misogyny that either maintains women in a state of powerlessness or plots *gynocide*. The decline of Marxism threatens to bring about a renaissance of a metaphysical philosophy that would make women its primary victims. Considered reflection on the issue of reproduction is probably the first condition for elaborating a system of thought that is not metaphysical. By taking human reproduction into consideration, this way of thinking, far from being regressive, would eliminate more than one type of deranged logic; it would also finally recognize the social dimension of reproduction, one of the most vital activities of our species—for its genealogy, for its memory, for its transmission and its history.

Second, we must struggle through our involvement in counterpower structures, taking the side of those who have been excluded from and disinherited by the competitive international production-obsessed system.

Third, and finally, we must struggle to pave the way for women's access to all existing power structures according to democratic principles: equality with respect for difference and not the inverse. From now on, the process of democratization must inscribe the existence of the two sexes and their dissymmetry in an egalitarian framework, and it must put women in control of their fertility not only on the biological level but on the civic and symbolic levels as well.

7. "It Is Not Power That Corrupts But Fear"

Aung San Suu Kyi

1991

On October 24, 1991, for the sixth time in its history, the Nobel Prize was awarded to a woman. And for the first time in its history—thanks to this same woman—it was awarded to a Burmese. A few months prior to the announcement of the award, on July 19, 1991, Aung San Suu Kyi had received the Sakharov Prize from the European Parliament. Unfortunately, she wasn't there to receive it. Aung San Suu Kyi is under house arrest, but even this expression delicately conceals the fact that she is being kept in absolute solitary confinement somewhere in Burma, not far from the capital city of Rangoon.

It is with the utmost simplicity and with deep emotion that Aung San Suu Kyi's husband, Michael Aris, introduces us, in the preface to an anthology of texts of which he is the editor, to a woman whose life takes the form of an odyssey from Rangoon back to Rangoon via India, England, Bhutan . . . Her life reads like an epic, a legend, an exemplary destiny not only for the Burmese people but for human history.[1]

Aung San Suu Kyi was born in 1945 in Rangoon, the Burmese capital, in a country that was both governed by the British and occupied by the Japanese at the time. Her father, Aung San, the charismatic leader of the Burmese resistance, was assassinated in 1947, shortly before his country gained its independence on January 4, 1948. In 1960, when she was fifteen, Suu Kyi moved to New Delhi, India to live with her mother, the Burmese ambassador (and the first woman to hold that post). Between 1964 and 1967 Suu Kyi studied political science at Saint Hugh's College, Oxford, where she ultimately earned her degree. In 1972, after working for several years for the United Nations Advisory Committee on Administrative and Budgetary Questions in New York, Suu Kyi married Michael Aris, a British Tibetologist from Oxford University and a specialist on Buddhist religion. Suu Kyi and Aris have two sons.

From 1972 to 1988 Suu Kyi continued her graduate studies and traveled with her family from Bhutan to Japan via India, though always keeping London and Oxford as her moorings.

By 1984 Suu Kyi had finished and published a biography of her father.[2] In compiling the portrait of a man she never really knew, Suu Kyi sensed the inevitable, that she was to be his successor, "an icon of popular hope and longing" for the Burmese people. Or, in the words of her husband, Michael Aris: "In the daughter as in the father there seems an extraordinary coincidence of legend and reality, of word and deed."[3]

In 1988, Suu Kyi was admitted to the School of Oriental and African Studies at the University of London to pursue a doctorate in Burmese literature. At the time she also dreamed of creating, and had begun to plan, an international study fellowship for Burmese students as well as a network of public libraries in Burma. But that same year, after receiving news that her mother, Dan Khin Kyi, aged seventy, was seriously ill, Suu Kyi returned home after twenty-eight years in exile. Suu Kyi cared for her mother, the widow of a national hero, until the latter's death in December 1988. On January 2, 1989, her mother's funeral attracted huge crowds; this was to be the only time that the Burmese government would cooperate with Suu Kyi.

Upon her return to Burma, Aung San Suu Kyi found not only an ailing mother but an ailing country. Once the rice bowl of Asia, now a socialist republic in the throes of popular insurrection, Burma is a country that in economic terms has been bled dry, ruined, and starved by the incompetence and corruption of a "revolutionary" military junta and torn apart by the ideological battles of its ethnic minorities and their struggle for recognition.

The French barely know Burma: this country of 40 million inhabitants, with a land area 25 percent larger than France, is bordered to the east by India and Bangladesh and to the west by China and Thailand, with the Himalayas to the north and the Andaman Sea to the south. Enslaved by both the Communist arms trade and the capitalist drug trade, Burma, which is one of the world's poorest countries, is also ruled by one of the world's most oppressive regimes. Burma has been closed off to journalists and humanitarian organizations for more than thirty years; it is a country run by means of torture, political intimidation, deprivation, and fear. The France-Burma Association recently warned that prostitution is spreading rapidly—and, in the absence of condoms, so are all the associated risks. The devastation of Burma's tropical forests is paralleled by intensive cultivation of opium fields (the source of 90 percent of the heroin consumption in the United States). Prostitution and opium sales help the Burmese regime finance its purchases of China's most sophisticated weaponry. On August 8, 1998, the Burmese government, an extreme nationalist socialist regime, a drug-trafficking dictatorship, put down a popular insurrection with a blood bath.

This was the state of affairs, the backdrop to Aung San Suu Kyi's intuition, an intuition that would lead her to request a promise or a "favor" from her husband Michael Aris before their marriage: "I only ask one thing, that should my people need me, you would help me to do my duty by them" (xvii).

This woman, who has remained so faithful to her primary identity, to the values and language of her country, that she refused to relinquish her Burmese citizenship and passport and, despite her marriage to an Englishman, only aspired to be worthy of her father's painful legacy: "I could not as my father's daughter remain indifferent to all that was going on. This national crisis could in fact be called the second struggle for national independence" (199).

For months, Burmese dissidents flocked to the house where Suu Kyi was then caring for her dying mother. Finally, on August 26, 1988, at the Shwedagon Pagoda, a site of great symbolic importance in Burmese Buddhism, Suu Kyi spoke for the first time in public in front of a crowd of hundreds of thousands of people. In the months that followed, Suu Kyi crisscrossed Burma—a country that was then and is still under martial law—insisting that the nonviolent struggle for human rights and democracy be the first principle of the National League for Democracy, the party she cofounded and now leads. As her husband describes it, "she spoke to the common people of her country as they had not been spoken to for so long—as individuals worthy of love and respect" (xxi).

On July 20, 1989, along with the majority of her fellow league members, Suu Kyi was placed under house arrest. However, despite a xenophobic government campaign against Suu Kyi (on the grounds that she was married to a British citizen and could thus never be a true national leader), her party won a landslide victory, earning more than 80 percent of the votes. Again, her husband Michael Aris describes the emotion and the irony of that moment: "The vote was a personal one for her: often the voters knew nothing about their candidate except that he represented Suu . . . There is a great irony in this, for she had become the focus of a personality cult which she would have been the first to decry. Loyalty to the principles, she had often said, was more important than loyalty to individuals" (xxiv).

The military junta has never acknowledged that Aung San Suu Kyi won 80 percent of the votes.

Everything in Suu Kyi's life, the life of this serene woman, this woman who at a time of "frenetic activity" still made her house "a haven of love and care," this woman who for so many years had taken responsibility for her family so that her husband could conduct his research, helping and encouraging him in his work—everything predisposed Aung Sang Suu Kyi to sacrifice her peaceful family life, in the midst of great suffering, to be faithful to her mythic heritage, to become this "indomitable" heroine, this sage, this Mother Courage to a tyrannized people. This was the legacy of her parents, and it was both a paternal and a maternal legacy, masculine but feminine too, a legacy that drew on a deeply rooted Asian tradition of female leadership, from Indira Gandhi to Benazir Bhutto, on both Buddhist religious and cultural values and on Western democratic cultures grounded in the spirit of freedom articulated by the United Nations and the principles of human rights and—finally and perhaps most deeply—on the ideas of Mahatma Gandhi.

In her speech, "Freedom from Fear," Aung San Suu Kyi's analysis of the origins of fear exposes unequivocally the universal nature of fear, in Burma and elsewhere—even here, in France. "It is not power that corrupts but fear. Fear of losing power corrupts those who wield it and fear of the scourge of power corrupts those who are subject to it" (180).

Vaclav Havel, who nominated Aung San Suu Kyi for the Nobel Prize, has also analyzed the phenomenon of fear under a Communist regime: "The fear I am speaking of is not, of course, to be taken in the ordinary psychological sense as a definite, precise emotion. . . . We are concerned with fear in a deeper sense, an ethical sense, if you will . . . "[4] The more brutal forms of oppression—fear of trials, fear of torture, loss of property and even deportation—have been replaced by more refined forms. The principal weight of this pressure has now been displaced to the sphere of existence where it becomes, in a certain sense, more universal: "Everyone has something to lose and so everyone has reason to be afraid."[5]

The greatest fear for the year 2000, as it was for the year 1000, as it is today, is the fear of thought and science, of the foreigner, of the Other, the green fear,[6] the brown fear, the fear of women, the misogynist fear, the fear that undermines the fundamental liberties and the sacred, inalienable rights of every human being, regardless of ethnic origin, religion, nationality, beliefs, or sex. Here in the West, from Austria to Louisiana, through Wallonia and Scandinavia, this fear has given rise to young chieftains who take Mussolini as their model.

If fear, from East to West, can today be considered as universal simply because it is human, then the faithfulness to herself, the respect for her fellow human beings, the unrelenting effort, the resistance, the humble daily gestures, the acute sense of responsibility, dignity, and wisdom manifested by the "indomitable" woman Aung San Suu Kyi may also become, through her exemplary struggle, universal virtues, simply because they too are human.

The daily asceticism, the daily ordeals, the courage and wisdom that triumph over this fear and this destructive madness: these are the nonviolent gifts Aung San Suu Kyi has given us and the world; we must learn to accept them in order to wrest her from the shadows and the silence of her prison so that we can give her back to those who love her and need her. If we are like children afraid of the dark, then in these shadowy times, the words of Suu Kyi light the way for us.

A political prisoner since June 1989, Aung San Suu Kyi has not been allowed to see her husband since December of that year, and the last letter her family received from her was dated July 17, 1990. Today international concern for her plight is immense. Last October three members of the Médecins du Monde (Doctors of the World) told the press that "in reality, no one knows where she is being held."[7]

8. My Freud, My Father

1992

If I try to conjure up his image, I see double. So I focus my vision and two photos appear, superimposed in a single image. He is a small man, refined, even elegant in appearance. Outdoors he always wears a hat. He is a man of another generation. His gaze is piercing, painful; it is at once the gaze of a man and that of a dog. I create this tension by superimposing two portraits by the same painter: the man-fruit and the man-book by Arcimboldo. One is the handsome Alexis, Virgil's faithful shepherd. The other, my father, is the knight of the Alliance, the adventurer. Abraham and Montaigne, rather than Moses and Pascal. These two men would have nothing in common if not for me, through whom their two names crossed in time, for the space of a story, in a book.[1] The worker and the thinker are both men of exile, experience, independence, men of honor, men of ethics more than morals. At the heart of my memory and my unconscious, these two men will continue to play, work, think, and travel within me.

I remember now. I am three years old, it's a suffocating day in August; my father takes me by the hand; I trust him; he takes me to a bullfight. It's a real massacre; I pee in my pants. From then on I understand that all games are sexual and bloody, that joy for one can mean suffering for another. Michel Leiris, *L'âge d'homme* (The age of man), preceded by *De la littérature considérée comme une tauromachie* (Literature viewed as bullfighting): a study of murder viewed as one of the fine arts.[2]

I am seventeen years old; he is teaching me to drive, in his car, the one with front-wheel drive.

I am thirty years old and, no matter how familiar this man is, the one who will lead me into the psychoanalytic arena, I side with the wild beast, our prehistory, wisdom through tears. Never will I be able to identify with the brightly clad son who kills, with the spectator who applauds and who, generation after generation, has still never reached "the age of man." He will try in vain to offer me all his objects, his toys, his concepts, he will give them to me or he will lend them and then take them back; they will never be mine. He would like us to be contemporaries, would like fathers and daughters to become brothers and sisters—the eternal seduction.

"My little one, you have to see everything, do everything in life." I was three years old; I was thirty years old. He renews the invitation: "The important thing is to say everything." I shall learn the lesson, without really making it my own—and yet I do not lack words or audacity. I have also learned that truth lies in half-saying and that I am not all His, not all Him, God, the Father, the Phallus. I am not even his *filse*,[3] his girl-son, his Antigone, half victim, half accomplice—even if, after yielding to the "object transfer" by getting married, I have kept her initials, A. F., Anna Freud, his own daughter.[4] If he has landscaped a huge portion of the wild terrain of my unconscious, he only knows me as he has made me, still such a small part. My father, Freud, Lacan, all my androphile fathers, you don't understand me through and through. They have not managed to decode my "Linear A," my intimate writing.

Without him, I wouldn't be alive; without them, I might not be in the world. I feel respect, gratitude. They have often wounded me; I have sometimes been ashamed; when the one wanted my sister to be his son's slave; when the other demands that the mother's love for the son be exclusive and without ambivalence; when, always and *Encore*, he claims that the hysteric says what she knows "without knowing what she is saying," he, the father-son longing for a Name, who pretends not to know that the "Father doesn't exist."[5]

Even if here where I live you are still present and always will be, we shall never be contemporaries. Time to call a halt to matricidal writing, the matricidal Écrits,[6] the confusion of genders, the life drive and the death drive on equal footing. The era that is beginning is the age of women. As for me, I belong to the generation of women.

9. From Liberation to Democratization

July 1, 1992

Appearing before you today to defend a *doctorat d'État* based upon a body of work produced during a career of almost twenty-five years spent outside the university, in a place where the university may often have come in for criticism, may look to some like an act of defiance or even provocation.

They forget the multiple administrative, symbolic, historical, political, friendly, and emotional ties that have bound me to the university for much longer than that.

It was at the University of Aix-Marseille that I received my initial (literary) education. It was in that institutional context that I became a student teacher in 1956; it was there that I met the man I married; and it was at the Sorbonne that I took my *diplôme d'études supérieures*.

The MLF chose the Université de Vincennes as the site for its first public demonstration, or its first outing, in the spring of 1970. It was at the University of Paris VIII–Vincennes, the mother campus of Saint-Denis, that I was asked to teach courses on philosophy and psychoanalysis, and I taught some of them together with the Psychanalyse et Politique group between 1970 and

1973. And it was also there that I met several of the women who have shared in my political struggle ever since.

The decision to present and deposit some of the propositions I developed as part of my work at Saint-Denis, the mother university's daughter university, is therefore inscribed within the history of an encounter between a movement of cultural action and militant research and a university born of the desire to innovate in knowledge, if not to bring about a revolution in knowledge. Once again, there is nothing fortuitous or circumstantial about the overlapping of those territories; on the contrary, it is a mark of fidelity, affinities, overdeterminations, maturations, and renewals. Saint-Denis is indeed Paris VIII, but it is no longer Vincennes. Here we find signs of the site's renewal, thanks to my political friendship with the woman who was once its president and who offered to be my supervisor. Which means that this is no longer Vincennes and that I am no longer the woman I was in the 1970s.

Less insistent upon maintaining an untamed externality in the attempt to "speak the truth," but more grounded than ever in these dark times (which seem intent upon spreading to every place, both natural and cultural, in the world), in an awareness that, "to be in truth," the object of my desire and of my research (the foreclosed knowledge of women) can and must engage in self-questioning and install itself in a place where an adequate ritualization of speech can facilitate its elaboration in a discipline such as *feminology*. While I am not afraid of losing my heretical status as a result of this excursion, I shall be so bold as to risk the reciprocal integration of a twofold exclusion; I shall risk trying to liberate myself, symbolically perhaps, from my excluded internee status; I shall risk trying to forge a chiastic or open alliance between more than one inside and more than one outside, between mine and yours; I shall risk trying to confront the rigor of academic knowledge with not-yet-legible traces of the foreclosed (in other words, unconscious and excluded) knowledge of women, with a knowledge that I often compare to the Minoan-Mycenaean Linear A script, which has yet to be deciphered.

Being here today does not strike me as a return but rather as a displacement. And my gesture finds in displacement its whole political sense—both its direction and its meaning—of promise. The "homodidact" that I have become—for I was never completely absorbed in any of my institutional formations—is perhaps trying to test (and in my case it really was a test, in the sense of trial or ordeal, attested by several months of psychosomatic symptoms, nightmares, and insomnia) how little autodidacticism there was in my analytic training when I realize that the affirmative component—the epistemological articulation and recomposition of a field and genealogical desire—has always competed with the critical element, the reading of exclusion and the need for deconstruction.

In the life-as-experience that has been my life, in my permanent apprenticeship to the "trade of living," the university has always been there, on the margins of my work, or my work on its margins, in a permanent counterpoint with which I always had to reckon, without caring too much whether I was going backward or forward, toward an end or a beginning.

The heterogeneous and heteronymous nature of my work is testimony to my displacement; and, as I have said, the feeling of being displaced, here or elsewhere, of appearing where I am not expected, is a trial, one that may, for me, mean wandering between the negative knowledge of women manifested by various institutional discourses and women's own nonknowledge or unknowledge about themselves.

Fortunately, you members of the jury are here to recognize—with both rigor and benevolence, I hope—as an interpretive act this sign of stubbornness on the part of the subject that I am, adrift, but desiring and waiting.

That the object of my research is also the object of my desire inevitably brings me—me and my research—into contact with psychoanalytic thought and with its masters and its instruments. Lacan (whom I first encountered through his Écrits) was the first to conceptualize (to name and substantiate) "the real" as such. Then, and only then, came Freud and his contemporaries, and especially Sándor Ferenczi, whose texts I encountered thanks to my second analysis with Belá Grunberger, a training analyst at the Institute, a Hungarian Jew by origin who was the first analyst to introduce Ferenczi in France. And after him came, quite naturally and in the course of that same second analysis, Melanie Klein, Donald Winnicott, and then, in recent years, Wilfred Bion.

Basically, a classic use of the instrument in both training and practice, loyal to the first of Freud's principles: "Where id was, there ego shall be."[1] It seems to me strictly orthodox to want to lift the censorship on the body, just as Freud began by lifting the conscious mind's censorship on the unconscious; that, as we know, was his major coup, and a political act. At that time the body, which has since become a theoretical object, struck fear into the psychoanalysts who had dedicated themselves to the dead Father. Lacan said much the same thing about it as he said elsewhere about women: "It does not exist, it is pure surface." The body, the site of dream work, the phantasmatic place par excellence, and therefore the site of the son, who was very much alive, compared with the Father who had already died in the analytic institution.

The transition from psychoanalysis of the subject to psychoanalysis of the body, or "natural psychoanalysis," resulted in a democratization of symbolic power, even if it did not necessarily give any legitimacy to the *flesh*, which is the site of the real (and of living thought). Haunted by gestation, which is the paradigm of the other scene, for transference, for what is analytically possible and for "thinking of the other," psychoanalytic thinking refuses to trace the genealogy of its thought or to think its genealogy. Only Ferenczi made any real attempt to elaborate a theory of genitality, but it remains one of psychoanalytic theory's fictions, one of the son's phantasms.

In the 1970s Bion, for his part, fled Germany for that very reason and took refuge in California; he began to theorize thinking (the "alpha function" or "the mother's ability to daydream") and revealed women's ability to contain the other, their responsibility to experience the foreign body as a subject and not an object, without that subject necessarily constituting women as an object, as an object to be forgotten. Where women and their specific libido are concerned, the question of genitality, which either precedes the oral stage or goes beyond the phallic, remains foreclosed, just as the writing of gestation, or the privileged time and space where genealogy comes into play, the time and space of creation as program and project, as proposition and as promise, is usually absent from psychoanalytic discourse.

The fact that the object of my desire is the (living) real—and not the thing—inevitably ties me to the treasures of literature, the science of texts and the practice of writing. One of our counterslogans, in an MLF that thought it was reasonable to desire the impossible, was to want to make the real possible.

The text as the site for deposing stereotypes and universality (a term that can be heard and read as "university"), writing as the moment of the depowering and the deconstruction of what Jacques Derrida calls phallogocentrism, could not but echo women's powerlessness or their desire to take power only in order to dispossess themselves of it (Monique Wittig expresses this wonderfully in Les Guérillères).[2]

For me, "poetry as experience"—as an experience of liberation, as an escape from language, which is sometimes analogous with mysticism—naturally entered into an alliance, a relationship, with gestation and found an echo there, for gestation is an experience that takes place outside language,

a leap from language into the intimacy of the flesh. The utopian and antito-
talitarian character of both these worlds, the old back country that preoc-
cupies poetry and the obscure destiny that lies ahead of us, created, in my
view, an indissoluble link between the poetic and the political. This was
what led me to establish the publishing house in 1973.[3] It has been an honor
to publish—to limit the discussion to French fiction—Chantal Chawaf's
first novel, texts by Emma Santos, Denise Le Dantec, Jeanne Hyvrard, Michèle Ramond, and, above all, from 1975 on, Hélène Cixous, of whom I have
had the pleasure of saying, wherever I went, that I regard her, and that I have
long regarded her, as our greatest contemporary writer. And I say that in a
universal sense, without any distinction as to sex.

Our legal work was the "natural" outcome of the earlier actions that had
been the Women's Movement's high points; at a moment when there was a
lull in the Movement's activities this work resulted from a series of political
acts that had taken us from a call to abstain from voting in 1973—by no
means a banal action at the time—to the call to support François Mitterrand
in the first round of the 1981 elections; we campaigned with a view to making a transition, perhaps, from a Father's voice that was becoming stifling
(de Gaulle speaking through Giscard) to what I later called a "republic of sons."
The latter, even though women have not greatly profited from it, has at least
opened the way to a certain democratization, and it has had the effect of
bringing about a change of government and bringing the left to state power.

But our legal work was also the outcome of certain avatars of the struggles
that were tearing the movement apart. Oedipal triangulation, the appeal to
the law, and the legal charges brought during the court cases of 1976–77 provided a way out of the savage sororicidal struggles that were often orches-
trated by male intellectuals or politicians who wanted to see a gladiatorial
battle between women.

The Oedipal law in politics takes us from totalitarian violence, from rep-
etition (volte-face, revolt, revolution), and from the omnipotence of the narcissistic subject to the task of democratizing the body of the law.

The law, then, functions as the arbitrator in massacres, as an instrument
for partial symbolization, even though foreclosure, in the analytic sense,
has not really been analyzed (the concept of foreclosure is also a legal concept). When phallic monism and a pseudo-egalitarianism of unisex symmetry, on which I dwell at length in the documents I have submitted, still
hold sway, foreclosure still rules because matricide remains foreclosed (not

enshrined in law and dismissed for lack of evidence). We are familiar with what happens when matricide is dealt with in this way, from the Eumenides to Althusser.[4]

By foreclosing women's bodies as the space of production of living beings, the law maintains and perpetuates the erasure and nonexistence of the matricial, overlooking its anteriority. The law justifies murder and, by exalting the delirium and perversion of the phallic whole, condemns a humanity that has been cut off from its past to the absence of any future or to a deadly future. (There is now talk of lethal overpopulation, and the UN has just established a commission to look into ways of limiting overpopulation, which is experienced as a cancer, at the very time when George Bush is setting up a fetal tissue bank. While the law takes no account of the matricial, capitalism goes on storing living matter in banks, in a multifaceted industry. That living matter is, I remind you, the speaking-thinking flesh of matricial production).

And, finally, I ask myself, here and now, what "natural law," as opposed to "the law of the subject," really is.[5]

In conclusion, I might say that, in everything I have done, I have been asking, in various ways, just one question: how are we to give a voice to a chapter of history, to a signifier, that has no voice? How can we give existence to foreclosed knowledge? How can we help the women (myself among them?) who are the world to bring women into the world?

In reply, you might ask me: why women, in these distressed times? And I would reply: in order to reinvent ethics.

10. Our Editorial Policy Is a Poethics

September 1992

There is no difference between the translation policy of the publishing house Des femmes and an editorial project that was itself originally part of the strategy of the Women's Liberation Movement (MLF), organized around Psychanalyse et Politique, and is now part of the strategy of the Women's Alliance for Democracy.[1] Or, rather, the only difference is that the field covered by our translation policy is more specific, while that of the movement is broader.

One of my first preoccupations as a political activist was to organize an international colloquium (at La Tranche-sur-Mer in June 1972). It seemed to me that, in the years to come, Europe would find its true place among women. At the time, I was interested in establishing an original movement, as opposed to America's "women's lib," which was too outwardly oriented, too concerned with winning equality at work and with struggling against discriminatory laws and actions. We needed a European movement that could draw upon the wealth of contemporary ideas, a cultural, civilizational, and intellectual movement that was in touch with the emotions, interiority, and identity of the subject and that was concerned with the personal and private realm. We needed not just to raise consciousness but to discover the unconscious; we needed a *revolution of the symbolic*, to use the expression I employed at the time—I would now speak of a *reinvention of ethics*. The time was at hand, it seemed to me, for Rimbaud's prophecy to be fulfilled: freed from their age-old servitudes, women would become the translators of the real, messengers of the impossible, and poets.

Founding a publishing house in 1973 was a way of formulating these multiple demands, of making part of the dream of abolishing linguistic frontiers come true, and of reaching a new stage in our liberation. No literature and no writing will ever be alien to Des femmes. Two of the first three books we published were translations. Even now, only half the titles in our catalogue were written directly in French. Let me use an anecdote to illustrate this geo-politico-poetico-editorial policy. During a "feminist" trip to England, Françoise Ducrocq introduced me to her friend Juliet Mitchell, whose thought and activity were close to those of the antipsychiatrists associated with *New Left Review*. We had a long discussion about the importance I attached to psychoanalysis for theorizing and advancing the women's movement. Juliet Mitchell does not speak French, and my English is poor. Even though we could not really understand each other, we managed to get a few questions across. Our political moorings are perceptibly different. Shortly afterward, Juliet Mitchell paid me a long visit in Paris, and I spoke to her at length again about Lacan, Barthes, Derrida . . . A few months later, she began her analytic training and wrote *Psychoanalysis and Feminism*. We published it, in a translation by Françoise Ducrocq and others. Echoing our psychoanalytic and political work, the essay traces an original path for the entire women's movement; it met with international success. A further stage, our collection La Psychanalyste (the female psychoanalyst) led to an encounter with women who had explored the unconscious; they came from the four corners of Europe and beyond. Margarete Mitscherlich, Hanna Segal, Joan Riviere, Margaret Little, Lou Andreas-Salomé, Karen Horney, Janine Chasseguet-Smirgel, and many others attest to this multifaceted movement and to the complex exchanges and textual interplay that took place between women and psychoanalysis.

A translation policy can, in my opinion, be based only upon analytic thought and poetic creation. The real is the object of both; the motive behind them is wish fulfillment; their work is that of translation, and their common source is the "trance." In my view, the prefix *trans-* presides over the loving trade known as publishing. Like a dream, a text is translation, transliteration, transaction, transport, transfer, transference, literally a metaphor: translation of unconscious thoughts, transfiguration of the unfigurable, translation of the relation of unknown, transliteration of the lost letter, transaction between translator and author, between author and translator, transference from one state to another, and transport from a body to a text. A publishing house is thus the transitional space where these transformations take place, the matrix for such transpositions. Gestaïon, or the capacity to think, welcome, and be with the other, strikes me as the paradigm of the linguistic and *fleshly hospitality* known as poetry, thought, translation, and publishing.

I forgot, though, that texts, dreams, and translations inevitably involve transgression. Because they resist the language of Creon, which Barthes audaciously describes as "quite simply fascist,"[2] dreamers, poets, and translators, who are all perverse polyglots, free us from its stereotypes. A dangerous and vital transgression takes place between the flesh and the word, between the idiom and the law. Elementary captives of the mother tongue and lexical virtuosos alike will need more than one language, familiar or unfamiliar, heterogeneous or original, phallic or maternal, if they are to be born into the world of their own texts. Writing, translating, or being a woman always implies at least two genitrix languages. Most poets are translators, and many translators are poets, but the majority of translators are women. Thinking writers recall the maternal idiom; women of letters (I love that expression) know that they are consubstantial with the father. Sibilla Aleramo, Lou-Andreas Salomé, Natalia Baranskaïa, Chantal Chawaf, Hélène Cixous, Assia Djebar, Hilda Doolittle, Jeanne Hyvrard, Denise Le Dantec, Clarice Lispector, Nata Minor, Irmtraud Morgner, Anaïs Nin, Nelida Piñon, Sylvia Plath, Amrita Pritam, Michèle Ramond, Nawal El Saadawi, Emma Santos, Duong Thu Huong, Yuko Tsushima, Virginia Woolf, Maria Zambrano, Friderike and Stefan Zweig and many others are witnesses to a living present.

While any writer worthy of the name is part of the (r)evolutionary promise, many revolutionaries have had an international destiny thanks to their books. The dissidents imprisoned by Franco (Eva Forest, Lidia Falcón . . .), the feminists hunted down by Communism (Tatyana Mamonova, Julia Voznesenskaya), and the democrats persecuted by the Burmese junta (Aung San Suu Kyi) are also in the resistance; translating them opens up the world of books to solidarity and symbolically frees these rebel women from Creon, especially when literary creation and political analysis are closely entwined, as in the case of the Vietnamese writer Duong Thu Huong.

Not so long ago—it was in 1978—Laure Bataillon was astonished when I suggested that I should interview her: "I might say that it's very unexpected, almost unlikely, for a translator to be asked to express her views; translators are usually asked to keep quiet at all costs, and to make absolutely sure that they do keep quiet, their approach and function are usually ignored."[3] While I travel the world in search of writers and women engaged in struggles, our women translators, working at home and crossing borders at the same time, propose to "liberate"—sorry, "publish"—a secret text that had been forbidden to enter the country and that has long been repressed by publishers. This happened with Viviane Forrester and Virginia Woolf's *Three Guineas*, with Sylvie Durastanti and Clarice Lispector's *La paixão Segundo G.H.*, and with Nicole Casanova and Lou Andreas-Salomé's *Fenitschka* and *Rodinka*.

Des femmes is a small publishing house that has sought to remain apart from both the national and artisanal regression and the lying poker games of the industrial publishers who create "best sellers." Our ambition is at once modest and modern: to create an ensemble or set, in the musical, mathematical, and convivial senses of the words, where the individual can flourish within a group, where a singular destiny can echo a shared destiny, and where the polyphonic translators known as dissidents, dreamers, poets, and women can recognize one another, understand one another, and forge an alliance.

THE LIBRARY OF VOICES[4]

Reading sets the voice of the text free and allows us to hear it. This is not the voice of the author. This is a matricial voice that is inside the author, in the same way that the genie is inside the bottle in fairy tales. This is a genius-voice, a genital voice that generates text. I am not sure that Nathalie Sarraute's *Childhood* doesn't come from Madeleine Renaud's reading of *Tropisms*, which succeeds in recapturing a child's voice.[5]

Read Proust, listen to Proust. The primal scene is not the one with the madeleine. It is the one before: "I had not then read any real novels" said the narrator when his mother read him *François le Champi*.[6] His mother's voice, which he associates with his grandmother's, returns, moreover, at the end of *La recherche du temps perdu*, at the point where he decides to write the novel—which is in fact almost finished. This becomes all the more interesting when we notice that *François le Champi* is a novel about a search for the body, for the voice of the other, and that the name of its heroine, François's adoptive but still "incestuous" mother, is Madeleine. George Sand, a woman of letters with a masculine name, plays subtly on genres and genders: masculine and feminine, oral and written, body and name, flesh and pen. When read by these two women, *François le Champi* is the latent, manifest, matricial novel of *La recherche* that has been lost and found again, perpetually *in statu nascendi*. This is the origin, the alpha and omega, of Proust's writing. Proust the writer saw himself as a pregnant and parturient female who was giving birth to a text that was permanently in gestation. *Female writing* rather than "feminine" writing. The love between women that fascinated him was not so much lesbian homosexuality—even though he analyzes perversion better than anyone—as his own homosexuation to the mother, a *native, naive homosexuality*. He was born as a writer to the female couple constituted by his mother and his grandmother, rather than as a son born to his parents, to a father and a mother. The voice of these women was the one that told him, dictated to him, that he had a vocation to become a writer; this is the Orient of his text, its birth, its fleshly trace.

The voice orients the written word, from the oral to the genital, from the genital to the oral, toward the old back country, toward primal thought. The voice is fecundity, conception, gestation, and promise. It makes a gift of the text to the world to come.

11. Dialogue with Isabelle Huppert

December 15, 1993

Buried speech
Shapeless speech
Silent speech
With Antoinette Fouque
Speech acquires a body
Ideas become clear
This is the generosity of listening
The pleasure of understanding
—Isabelle Huppert, *Cahiers du cinéma*

ISABELLE HUPPERT: I've been wanting to meet you, just as I wanted to meet Nathalie Sarraute. I've wanted the issue of *Cahiers du cinéma* that I've taken on to be open, not just about film.

ANTOINETTE FOUQUE: First of all, let me thank you. I found your offer very touching. Give or take a few years, you could be my daughter. Feminists of my generation have often been criticized for not having passed anything on. Your wish to meet suggests to me that it has been possible to pass something on, that something has been transmitted. I'm grateful to you for that.

I would also like to say how honored I am to find myself in the company of Nathalie Sarraute; in terms of writing, she is my heart of hearts—I'd like to see her get the Nobel Prize—and I had a youthful passion for her. When I was an adolescent I would have done anything to meet her.

IH: Nathalie Sarraute has probably told you that she doesn't like to be defined as a woman writer. You must have talked to her about that.

AF: She's right. It seems to me that the source of her writing, or the stratum she mines, if we take a geological section of the terrain where a writer finds her raw material, is a presexualized stratum of absolute pre-figurative and prerepresentable narcissism, a sort of nebula of drives. I've always thought that Nathalie Sarraute was the writer who took writing from the figurative to the nonfigurative. It's the same revolution as in painting. I don't know if this revolution will ever come about in cinema. Perhaps *Malina* gets away from figurative cinema and attempts some kind of cinematographic abstraction. It's very difficult. Nathalie Sarraute's writing is a writing of the drives, of what Freud would have called the elementary passions; we might say that it is presexed and, at the same time, constitutionally female and/or embryonic. It is on the side of gestation, of the embryo or the gestatrix. It is concrete writing, a writing of the flesh, of something living. Nathalie Sarraute snatches this reality away from the impossible, the unsayable, the improbable; she brings it into the realm of meaning and offers it to the world to read. As Rilke did; as Hofmannsthal did. But she doesn't handle it in a poetic way; she handles it in a narrative way, as a woman novelist.

IH: Do you think she is the only woman who does this?

AF: I think she's following in the footsteps of Virginia Woolf, but that she goes much further than Woolf. The extraordinary thing is that she is not mad, if we can say such a thing.

IH: Yes, she works on the edge, on the border of madness. The bridges between her work and her personality are, unlike those of Virginia Woolf—who drew on her own life, on incidents in her life—completely invisible. In Sarraute's work there seems to be nothing that has to do with her life. What she makes visible in her work is what is invisible in her personality. For me, that's a completely mysterious zone. That's her secret.

AF: She is a woman who explores the real. She has confronted what I call the archi-unconscious, which lies below the unconscious, below its figurability. This is a shapeless, amorphous zone. In *Childhood* she reveals her defense system, shows how she organizes the framework, the scene of writing; how its stage is furnished and what its protocols are and how she resolved, or did not resolve, her relationship with her mother.[1] This is no écriture féminine, but it so happens that, in literature, it is a woman who has accomplished this beautiful tour de force.

No one seems to have wanted to base a film on *Martereau* or *The Planetarium*. Do you think there are some literary forms that can't be transposed into film?

IH: On the contrary. From my point of view as an actress, I think that the states she transmits through her figures of speech could easily be turned into films.

I would even go so far as to say that they could be turned into films much more easily than the so-called figures that are restricted by the way they usually sketch out characters. She tracks life to such a point that it strikes me as representable. As you were saying, what she writes has to do with flesh.

AF: I saw both *Malina* and *Après l'amour* again, and I said to myself that you were a writer in both films, but of two very different sorts. We need to find cinematic equivalents for the categories Barthes gave us, though they may have become a little hackneyed: the *écrivant* and the *écrivain*.

IH: Yes, like *actante* and *actrice*. For me, being an *actante* would mean playing an active part in transmitting a role. I have often wondered whether I was a subject or an object in my films. I have always felt myself to be more of a subject than an object, even though I am well aware that there might be a hiatus between being a subject and being an object and that the gap might be unbridgeable. Isn't it often said, isn't it a cliché to say that an actress is supposed to be just an object? I like being both subject and object in my films, in other words, being able to create a space in which I can stand back. As it happens, that is both a freedom and a constraint, to the extent that I cannot help but have that double gaze. Why do I say double? In theory, it should be the director who stands back and looks on. When I adopt this analytic approach, I adopt the position of the writer rather than that of the actress.

AF: That displacement toward the author's creative space is quite perceptible in your work. With you, the actress is more important than the character. The transference takes place inside the actress's body rather than the actress getting into the character's skin, clothes, or costume. The character is forced to come and live with you, to submit to the ordeal of a transference onto you.

The first time I saw you in *The Lacemaker* and *Les Indiens sont encore loin* you immediately reminded me of Ingrid Bergman. My unconscious compared you with her. When I was a girl I saw *Spellbound*, in which Bergman plays the role of a psychoanalyst who saves Gregory Peck from his guilt. My first contact with psychoanalysis took place in that film and my first transference was onto Ingrid Bergman. Her role, which is decentered with respect to the codes of woman-as-object—and this is Hitchcock's genius—allowed me to discover the transferential function. Throughout the film she is trying, from a completely active position, to undo the knot of a neurosis. The actress has turned out to be the site of a real psychic transformation, of unconscious work on the viewer's part.

An actress is in fact always available for a transference, unless she is a pure Narcissus and therefore an object. What you did from the outset in *The Lacemaker* and *Les Indiens sont encore loin* was to introduce a gap between the woman who is caught up in the perverse space of the world as it exists, the woman who is being hunted, and yourself. That gap produces a cathartic effect. The viewer, male or female, can analyze what is going on even though, in most of the films of yours that I've recently watched again, the heroine is hurtling toward destruction; she goes to prison, dies, or goes mad.

If directors always put women into the same structure, the actress can make this explicit; by remaining in the gap she creates and introduces as a supplement she can spell out in what respect the world is out of joint or perverse. This gap is very perceptible in all your creations. This is the creative part that you take on; this is your writing. It's very modern. You are definitely the most resolutely, absolutely modern actress, because you maintain the gap within a divided subject in your films. Were you aware of this when you made *The Lacemaker*?

IH: No, not at all, but I was aware, or rather I knew intuitively, that for me being an actress did not mean being completely an actress in the classic sense of being seductive. Being an actress was a live experiment, not an imitation. It was a total commitment on my part. And that inevitably meant anticipating the mystery of the truth.

AF: Do you have a relationship with psychoanalysis?

IH: I went into analysis when I was twenty, at about the same time I started to act. I very quickly sensed that there were certain images, certain clichés that were associated with the actress function and that that was not the way I was going to experiment with the fact of being an actress. I thought, to begin with, that being an actress meant expressing something to do with pain. Perhaps what I called pain was the gaze.

AF: Whose gaze? The other's, or your own?

IH: Mine. Seeing the truth. Perhaps that's what I called pain.

AF: Violette Nozière is both "looked up and down" by her father, as she puts it, and a *voyeuse*. So is the heroine of *La truite*. You have surveyed all these aspects of exhibitionism, and they are almost compulsory for an actress.

IH: I think that, right from the start, for me it was a question of working on the truth. Actors often say that they love surrendering to their characters, lying, dressing up, or thinking that they have other lives. That discourse has always been completely alien to me. I have never believed that being an actress meant going to live in someone else's life. On the contrary, for me it's always been a tireless exploration of myself. It means moving to somewhere deep inside me and not being swept away into the outside world; it's a verticality. Which brings me back to what I was saying to you a moment ago, ultimately, I don't go toward the characters; it's the characters who come to me. And it's in that sense that I tend to compare the job of an actress with that of a writer. I should say autobiographer, because a writer can also write fiction, novels. Right from the start, being an actress was never a way of ceasing to be myself in order to become someone else; on the contrary, it was a way of finding out who I was. And never finding out who I am was, of course, the whole idea.

But since then, I have also discovered that the truth is not always the painful truth or the truth behind the tragedy. It can also be the truth of lightness or well-being or, quite simply, the truth about the wish to be.

AF: You've just outlined what might be called "the actress's paradox": seeking the truth means getting rid of what analysts call the "false self," the "as if" personality, and it may seem paradoxical that one way of getting closer to your true self and getting rid of the false self is to embody characters and use your body to get them across.

IH: Yes, it's paradoxical, but dressing up is the best way of revealing yourself.

AF: That calls for almost a twofold effort. Freud, borrowing an expression from Michelangelo, says that there are two possible ways of creating art: "un per via di posare, un per via di levare." The painter adds matter and the sculptor takes it away. You tend to adopt the sculptor's approach: taking away matter in order to give shape to the ego, the true ego. Which may seem something of a paradox, but it seems right to me. Seeing through falsity, flashy rags, imported or pasted-on identities is an extremely contemporary attitude. The artist wants what is true or what is real. Your approach is that of an artist or a creator rather than an actress.

IH: I'm not sure whether it's an artistic approach.

AF: Someone who's trying to transform reality. You don't like the word artist?

IH: Let's say that I don't recognize myself in it. For me it's very much tied up with the idea of the artiste maudit. And artists are no longer maudits. Too many people would like to be credited with that curse, which would legitimize them.

AF: I'm using the word in a categorical sense. After years of work, practice, and theorization, I am trying to see how women can not so much escape the structure in which they are trapped as transform it, how they can emerge or speak as women. They can use several types of discourse: a discourse that cannot be spoken, the discourse of mutism or that of the primary female homosexual who sinks at one point or another into blankness, complete depression, nonexistence, foreclosure, and drops out of the symbolic, out of speech, or that of the actress, the hysteric who is inhabited by the discourse of the master and who is in drag; and then there is the discourse of the woman I call the artist, the writer. This is the discourse of Virginia Woolf, aching, in pain, in danger of dying. This is the discourse of Clarice Lispector, Ingeborg Bachmann, Marina Tsvetaeva, of all the women who try to express themselves by writing and who often commit suicide or descend into madness. They do not want to be just actresses or to be vehicles for the text of the other, as though they were its spokeswomen.

IH: I think it's a matter of occupying the field in a different way. It's a rather tangential power, not the usual power of comedians or actors, which is more frontal with respect to director.

AF: In order to create your own field, your own territory; it's almost animal or perhaps it is actually very human.

IH: You were talking about the alternative for women: being silent, always being in drag, or . . .

AF: Yes, I still think the world is topsy-turvy. There are two sexes, and all the laws that govern us take only one of them into account. It begins with monotheism: there is only one God. Woman does not have divine status. The Virgin is nothing more than a saint; she is holy, but not divine. There is no possibility of women identifying with something maternal, something matricial, with a female divinity, and, conversely, all the values that women contribute are subordinated to this structure of the one. There is only one God, there is only the father, and this world overlooks the fact that there are two sexes; it denies reality and it is perverse. Men can come to terms with this generalized perversion. The husband in La truite is homosexual. If he isn't homosexual, he commits adultery or incest. According to Freud, a man who has daughters has to be adulterous to avoid being incestuous; his wife is not enough for him. Women are therefore caught up in this perverse structure. And they have what I call a derivative perversion. Violette Nozière and Madame Bovary are roles for echo-women, for women with a derivative perversion, one that echoes Narcissus's perversion, because Echo reproduces Narcissus's law.

But I'd like to ask you: who are you? How do you write what comes next? There is nothing realistic about your acting. There's an "un-acting" (déjeu), a decentering that makes it difficult to pin down.

IH: That's true. In *Orlando* I explored something very special. Bob Wilson is the very opposite of a realistic, concrete director. With him one is in an abstract world, and yet I have never felt more in touch with myself. It's a bit like what you were saying about Nathalie Sarraute. Not so much abstraction, perhaps, but it is nonfigurative, it produces life, flesh, because the absence of identifiable figures was totally liberating. All I did in *Orlando* was just be completely myself. Then there was the discovery of androgyny, my own androgyny. And yet I had a tendency to say that roles did not teach me anything about myself because they just confirmed what I already knew. I was just thinking a moment ago that the first two stories to fuel my imagination were two of Anderson's fairy tales: *The Little Mermaid* and *The Little Match Girl*. One dies of love and the other dies of cold, but the idea of androgyny is also present in *The Little Mermaid*. That fishtail is the absence of a sex. I think that what I discovered in *Orlando* was androgyny, not defined just as a sexual disorder or the possibility that an actress might appear in drag, but in the deeper sense of the difficulty of choosing between activity and passivity. Virginia Woolf captures that difficulty. Nathalie Sarraute reminded me that Virginia Woolf said that the writer is androgynous, as though there were a sort of subversion, an in-between, between man and woman, where she is neither on the side of power nor on the side of passivity.

AF: She's on the side of play. Don't you think that this is very much bound up with childhood?

IH: Absolutely. Everything in *Orlando* takes place under the sign of play, all those explorations, all those ramblings and substitutions are very closely bound up with childhood. So expressing an androgynous femininity means both taking refuge in childhood and rebelling.

AF: It is true that, in *Orlando*, childhood rediscovered, or "childhood clearly formulated," as Baudelaire says of genius, is very present. And because you and Bob Wilson are so demanding, you give it a formal perfection that allows all the drawers to be opened. That kind of androgyny is as rich as childhood. That's more or less what Nathalie Sarraute has done. It is no accident that one of her latest texts is called *Childhood*. We get back to where it came from. It is one way of creating, of producing. How do you relate this androgyny to your life as a woman, to the fact of having children?

IH: I don't know. I don't relate the two. My life is one thing, and these projections of myself are another. They probably do meet, but I don't know where. Everything seems to be in separate compartments.

AF: Playing with androgyny is surely very important for an actress because otherwise she's heading for disaster. It's like Greta Garbo or Martine Carol. Perhaps Garbo did what you were saying; she used splitting mechanisms to save her own life. Why does no one say that her extreme beauty and her captivating charm had to do with her homosexuality? She used splitting mechanisms, and so she did not commit suicide. I believe that there is a certain symbolic homosexuality and that it plays a very structural role for women. This really is not the lesbianism that is experienced or illustrated by transvestites, but something completely internal; the relationship with the first love-body, and that is the mother, for both girls and boys. A trace of that intimacy remains.

IH: Perhaps that allows me to understand more about why I venture into androgyny. Why do you say it's a form of survival for an actress?

AF: It's the same as it is for a writer, because bringing the masculine into play allows her to play with gender difference rather than being completely trapped by a sex that is hers but that isn't entitled to exist.

IH: Perhaps androgyny is a form of protection against a certain image of femininity that is perceived by the woman who embodies it as a threat.

AF: I was also thinking of Bergman and *Persona* and of Cassavetes and *A Woman Under the Influence* or *Opening Night*. Cassavetes went a long way toward giving an almost entomological description of the trap in which women are caught. "A woman under the influence" is ultimately the theme of all those films about women who are trapped by a sort of derivative perversion, a secondary perversion that echoes the perversion of men. I find it very hard to see how the scene of women's madness can be transformed in films. I always wonder where the great directors are going and what women directors could offer that would be different.

IH: Garbo was the emblematic embodiment of that paradoxical moment, of the opaque zone that lies between withdrawal and the moment of appearing. I think that, for an actress, that's what it's all about. How to be visible and invisible at the same time. You were asking me how I write what comes next. I don't know, but I think I'll always try to be at the heart of things, at the heart of the projects.

AF: Keeping ahead of people and things, being active. Have you ever thought of directing?

IH: No, not for the moment. I've thought about doing it much later. The much later will come closer one day. For now, I feel like an actress through and through, even if I do feel I'm both a subject and an object, and I would find it very hard to give up my object status, this state of seduction. I feel I'm an actress from head to toe.

AF: How does your career as an actress interfere with your career in life, your career as a woman?

IH: The opposite is also true; the career of living interferes with the actress's career. But being an actress is also a way of relating to the world, of being there and not being there. We embody states, drives.

AF: It has to do with passion. In Latin, a passive verb with an active meaning was used to express that state. A *deponent*. You might say that a state is a passive act or an active passion, which does not stop at one moment or another, which comes back in dreams that haunt you. How does this sort of permanent transference between you and your characters come about? Between you and the body's guests, the guests of the unconscious, the guests of thought? What do they mean to you, your body's guests, those of your unconscious or those of your thoughts?

IH: I think all three were there in *Orlando*: the unconscious, thought, and the body. In the theater it's more the body's guest because the body is much more involved, especially in the way it was in Bob Wilson's play, with a whole memory coming back in the gestures, the attitudes of childhood, dancing the way little girls dance. I watch my daughter dance for a moment, and I find myself using the same gestures. All I did in *Orlando* was play, play make-believe. What I did not know about myself was, perhaps, that capacity to rebel, that will to set myself free, to be freer, and *Orlando* allowed me to discover it. Even if you believe you are free, you always want more freedom, don't you? You'll tell me that a film actress has achieved a certain degree of freedom, but actually there is always the fantasy of having greater freedom. As the various parts I've played have always allowed me to glimpse different possibilities, different states, I always feel that my life is somewhat in danger, that I'm always standing on the edge of a cliff.

AF: When you find yourself standing on the edge of a cliff, as you put it, don't you have the feeling that, having come as far as you've come, you have a body of work behind you? That something has been built, perhaps despite yourself, that there is something you can lean back on?

IH: No, not really. Actresses also feel that they are both everything and nothing. That's their form of hysteria!

AF: Do you feel you've opened all the drawers, got your ego in a complete state, so to speak? What are the female egos or emotions that might not have been expressed?

IH: Probably the egos of freedom . . .

AF: There are of course little boys in a little girl's world too. Like Tom Thumb, who saves his family: his majesty the child. Those roles aren't on offer where we're concerned.

IH: I'd like to move toward states like that in the future. I wanted to give Emma Bovary a certain arrogance, a certain understanding of what she was doing. I think that arrogance made her more modern. Like Flaubert, I gave the viewer the opportunity to understand the mechanisms that are at work in history, and outside history. As I was making the film, I kept thinking that Emma was the first great feminist heroine in literature, that she was, to the best of her abilities (and God knows they were limited!), fighting a battle that prefigured the great battles women would have to fight in the future.

AF: Ingeborg Bachmann says, in Malina and in all her books, that women learn to play chess and always lose. Whereas a certain feminism would have us believe that there is a liberty, or a liberation, to be found in feminism.

IH: You don't think there is?

AF: At the outset I wanted to find an ethics, that is, a form of thought that went beyond feminism. I wanted to work on the experience of thought and its limits, and that is what I did. I was accused of being an antifeminist. When we started this movement, in 1968, we had the means to go beyond feminism. In France especially we had intellectual tools with thinkers like Lacan and Derrida, with ourselves, with our own experience, that allowed us to get beyond feminism, which is basically a form of hysteria. My project was to succeed where feminism and hysteria had failed.

The risks were enormous. I asked myself a lot of questions. Reestablishing the specific link between daughter and mother means trying to blow up the fortress of the One, of monotheism, of "there is only one God" and monodemocracy. In Athens only the men were citizens; ultimately, it is the same here. I was trying to reveal the perversion of a world that forces on us patriarchy, gold, language, and a logic of the one, when in fact there are two: there are two sexes, and the two are not only different but dissymmetrical in the work of procreation. A woman can do anything, or almost anything, a man can do, but she is also capable of gestation. This may be where I distance myself from the problematic of Virginia Woolf and what we might call pregenital androgyny. Pregenital androgyny is perfect for an actress. For a writer, it didn't keep Woolf from committing suicide. Mrs. Dalloway is saved by her daughter. Virginia Woolf could never have a daughter because her husband and her doctors forbade her to, decreeing that she had to choose between creation and procreation. Perhaps if she had had a child or children she would not have committed suicide.

I think that this feminine genealogy of the transmission of women's practices—of what women have learned and are capable of doing—from mother to daughter and from daughter to mother, which is by no means a return to maternity, is perhaps the bearer of something other than the old model, the bearer of what philosophers such as Levinas call an ethics or as the welcome given to the other. Women have a capacity to welcome the other, a capacity for active containment that is bound up with gestation. And, given that we are human beings with the gift of speech, this is not merely a biological capacity; it is imaginary and symbolic. That is what happens with a fertile actress. She does not slip into her characters; she hugs them to her breast, welcomes them into her heart, into her body, and—why not?—into her uterus. A woman's pregnancy, gestation, is the only natural phenomenon of bodily—and therefore psychic—acceptance of a foreign body. It is the model for all grafts.

Some men do have this capacity to welcome, of course. As I was watching *Orlando*, I said to myself that Bob Wilson had acted as your matricial container. You say unconscious to unconscious, but it is almost flesh to flesh. It is as though he had brought you into the world. All at once there was a new birth, an event. At the same time, it is not impossible that, having given *Orlando* a body, you engendered in him something his fecundity needed. This is an interrelationship, because he certainly has female capacities within him. Androgyny is transmitted in a presexual mode, but it might also be transmitted in the mythological or mythical mode of a twofold fecundity.

For your part, you have the experience of a woman who has had children and the experience of being an actress. That is why I am interested in the question of being a container for characters rather than being contained within them. It is the same in analysis. A real analyst is generous, acts as a container and brings you into the world. I think that the whole of Freud's theory is haunted by his desire to have a uterus. *Uterus envy* in men is as important as penis envy in women, and perhaps more important. While his wife was making a baby, Freud was, by his own admission, giving birth to *The Interpretation of Dreams*. In 1973 I made a film about his "Psychogenesis of a Case of Female Homosexuality." In all the cases of female homosexuality that he analyzed he thought he was the site of the transference to the extent that he was a father; he failed to see that the girl's transference was to the mother, to a woman. In the particular case on which the film was based, the homosexual woman was in love with a film actress. So what exchange is taking place here between psychoanalysis, the young homosexual woman, and the film actress? How did the actress act as a screen for the dream and a screen for the transference? How did she embody both the difference between the genders and the difference between the sexes?

Someone like Lou Andreas-Salomé stopped short of procreation. She theorized elements of the symbolization of feminine qualities or values, but she remained a mystic. A mystic embodies, makes herself flesh and then burns, bursts into flames, or, as in The Little Mermaid, becomes a cloud. She spiritualizes herself and does not pursue her experience to the end, which would mean transmitting what you call the invisible. Ultimately, the invisible is the flesh, the inside. It is matter itself, the thinking matter that is at work in dreams or the drives. Perhaps it was not the Word that was in the beginning, but the flesh, the substratum of the unconscious, the prenatal unconscious.

Biological exchanges and psychic exchanges between the fetus and the genitrix do take place. We still don't know everything about them. We don't know, for example, to what extent the pregnant woman and the fetus share their dreams. But at all events many exchanges do take place between the two, and those exchanges are the model, the paradigm, of transference. And, besides, a pregnant woman does more than dream; she listens to the fetus and talks to it. For me, this is the scene that inaugurates language. I think women were the ones who invented articulate language by trying to communicate with the fetus and then with the child. Women are anthropocultivators.

Men cannot go back to the experience of gestation. Women can, and they actively relive what they once lived in a passive way. They were once contained, and they can be containers. This is quite exceptional. I think that is why we are persecuted. I think that God and the monotheisms are substitutes for gestation. Genesis is an imaginary, illusory form of gestation, and God is a son who dreams of taking the container's place. He, noncreated, creating man and then taking woman out of man. This is an inversion, and, so long as women do not put the world the right way around, everything will be upside down. There is an investigation to be carried out into how women live this inner experience, this experience of moving from inside to outside. Psychoanalysis has yet to look into this. Psychoanalysts talk about the mother, about the child who is born, but never about the prenatal period. But why do women who know about gestation allow themselves to fall into the trap of feminism?

IH: Of feminism? That takes the cake!

AF: I think that feminism has sought to dissociate creation from procreation and to force women to choose between making films, for example, and making children. It has condemned women to sacrifice part of themselves. And when women did both those things, they did so by maintaining a gap. I think that in the twenty-first century we'll find a way to build a bridge between creation and procreation.

IH: I have experienced, very deeply and personally, what you have just theorized. At a very young age I was obsessed with the idea of having children. I was very much aware of the fact that being an actress and having children was the same thing, that it was a comparable transformation, the same waiting—and we do in fact "give birth to a role"—or at least I understood that the two things were not antagonistic.

AF: I was very naive when I was pregnant; I knew in any case that it was what I wanted and I was haunted by certain landscapes, as when you go back to someplace in a dream. We speak of "being" pregnant, it's a state, like a dreaming state. At the same time, you are working twenty-four hours a day.

IH: I don't know if you've seen Jack Clayton's film *The Pumpkin Eater*. It's a very good film in which Ann Bancroft is perpetually pregnant. In the film, being a container is portrayed in more negative terms than those you describe; there is also the idea that a container is by definition empty if it is not filled.

AF: No, because it is a container that transforms. It's not a vase.

IH: You said something about the woman writer that evoked a void for me, and that is something I have experienced very powerfully. I often think that an actress is empty, that her function is just to be filled, that she is waiting, and that this emptiness can often be painful.

AF: Your work as an actress often makes me think of a writing that allows blanks to appear in the sentence, or silence. It has to do with a certain gaze, a coloration or a transparency of the skin, a mask that can appear on the face of the actress, but that has nothing to do with make-up or lighting; it gives the event a new opacity or transparency or something in between the two, something opaline. Perhaps a little amorphous, even, as in a certain nonfigurative art. It is very concrete, as though the flesh or the drive, something from inside, was breaking through the surface. It seems to me that this is an unconscious that is more fleshly than Freud's unconscious, an elementary unconscious. I have always thought that the flesh was the fifth element. You have water and air with the Little Mermaid, fire with Joan of Arc or Malina, and you have earth—you've often been compared to a peasant woman. In reality, in human beings, these four elements are one and the same: flesh, which is their quintessence. And flesh thinks. It is primary thought, primal or archi-archaic thought.

IH: You are in fact expressing in very clear terms what I feel, sometimes in a confused way. I'm in a somewhat awkward position because, while I do feel I have the ability to think abstractly, I don't necessarily have the ability to formulate that abstraction. That's why I'm an actress. I would find it hard to write, for example, to work with the concreteness of words. I think I exist in the zone of nonformulation, which you need to be an actress. Or rather, being an actress is the only possible way to express that nonformulation. You were asking me if I'd ever thought of being a director; it seems to me that being a director means formulating things. Perhaps I exist in what you call the preunconscious, but I am also involved in the analysis of this nonformulation. I exist both within thought and within nonformulation.

AF: But you formulate it very well. Thought is preverbal too. Real thought, not philosophy, not theory. Psychoanalysis is brilliant in that it allows us to think with the drives, within the preverbal, and yet it becomes organized, becomes ordered, becomes clear. All at once we can perform an act that is not an acting out; an act that has been thought through somewhere else, something intimate that can be "excarnated," expressed outside the flesh. Something is elaborated as though in a dream. It's extraordinary to follow Colette through all her transitions: adolescent, androgynous homosexual, then actress, artist, writer, and then her relationship with her mother and her daughter as she transmits a particular experience, her relationship with the real, with the materiality of things, with nature and with animals. Children love her. I used to read *Dialogues de bêtes* to my daughter. Colette relates to the living-speaking. And yet the fact that she never took any historical stand bothers me. She does have a blind spot, after all.

IH: I'd like you to repeat what you were saying about feminism.

AF: During the feminist years, when everyone was a feminist and when everyone thought I was a feminist, Simone de Beauvoir loathed psychoanalysis—even though one of her heroines (Anne in *The Mandarins*) was a psychoanalyst, albeit a very oedipal one, very father-oriented—and had a horror of what she called motherhood. De Beauvoir could not see the ethical dimension of gestation, the narcissistic experience of the fact of being pregnant and producing something with her body. In those feminist years, when everyone thought everyone was a feminist, there was one model: one man in two is a woman, and two men in two are men. The only possibility for women was to become men who were like other men.

IH: I have the impression that women are now having children in order to experience the truth behind what you're describing.

AF: Yes, we've now gotten away from the madness of sterility. Fortunately . . .

IH: I think that I like having children as much as I enjoy playing a role.

AF: Is that because you feel empty or, on the contrary, because you feel you are going to make something?

IH: Because I feel I'm going to make something.

AF: You are going to make a little miracle, a surprise, happen. What event could be more important than a birth? There are also metaphorical births, of course: a part, a play, a film.

IH: I'd have found it difficult to put up with a life in which there was nothing but metaphors. For a metaphor to exist, there had to be some reality behind it. *Malina* was made in a state of great euphoria, and it was very pleasurable because my children were there. It was summer, and we did everything together. In concrete terms this meant I could play ball in the corridor with my son and then be on the set immediately afterward, even for difficult scenes. And most of the time it's like that. I'd say it's a way of constantly displacing the center. You might think that the roles are central, but in fact it's often the children. Roles and creative life are peripheral. But that periphery exists only in relation to a center. Part of this desire for children is obviously a desire to go back to one's own childhood, to bring it back to life.

AF: You are very calm in many films, and one has the feeling that it isn't you who lacks something. You are tranquil in *Loulou*. When a woman is not in a state of lack, when she is in her body, that's all it takes for hysteria to manifest itself on the masculine side. One of Freud's strokes of genius was showing that hysteria is not the prerogative of just one sex. That is obvious in all your roles. I am sure that you're filled with the thought of something you know, but not necessarily in a theoretical way. It's a kind of quiet strength, and there's something right about it. If we worked on all your films we would see the emergence of something that you've created, the contemporary contribution you've made to the cinema as a woman. Someone could write you a great scenario with a heroine of our time, a woman who accomplishes things.

IH: Yes, I feel as though I'm excavating my own film inside all the films I move through. All these women's destinies are metaphors for the condition of women, but also for my own life.

AF: The actress has an ethical function. It's central to her desires. When we're adolescents, we're looking for new identifications and we change, not our point of view, but our point of desire. One of the most important things of all is giving girls beautiful thoughts.

IH: And that means running the risk of giving them thoughts that might look like bad thoughts.

AF: Beautiful thoughts, not good thoughts! Form is important too.

IH: What counts for me is rhythm. There is a rhythm to *Malina* and even things that are funny at times; it's not a slow film.

AF: That's what is missing in French films. Dynamics and cadence. They lack rhythm.

IH: In France, we identify tragedy with slowness and comedy with speed. Speed has nothing to do with it. Labiche is one of the funniest of all comic authors, and his plays are never funnier than when they go slowly.

In your view, is cinema primarily about actors?

AF: Actresses have a lot to say about their unconscious, their childhood, their permanent gestation, about the state of being an actress. *State* is the word you use most often.

IH: Yes. It takes my whole personality into account. What's more, I prefer being to saying.

AF: Perhaps you are more of a poet than a narrator. A *state* is the state of being in love, the state of passion, the poetic state. I'd also like to talk to you about the voice in *Orlando*, which is a magnificent piece of work. In a very fine text that we are going to publish with Des femmes, Ingeborg Bachmann says that the voice, the human voice, has all the privileges of the living (*le vivant*)—warmth and coldness, gentleness and harshness—and that it supports a quest for perfection, for the truth. Like your voice in *Orlando*.

Sound systems have completely transformed the theater by giving it a real modernity.

IH: It's only by working on the voice that you can express the movement of the language as, not the expression of thought, but the expression of, well, a state.

AF: The language sprang from different parts of your body, from different strata, and it took on volume. It became three-dimensional.

IH: The signification, the meaning of the text might have come to the fore. However, that was not the point, precisely because the beauty of this language lies in its not being reduced to its meaning, but rather in its being extended to something much more expansive, virtually limitless. That was an abstract approach to the word. The point was to use vocal and sonic forms to show feelings and sensations. With Bob Wilson the issue of what the words meant never came up. That's how we were able to communicate with each other. That reminds me of something very beautiful that Grotowski once said: acting is not something that happens between you and the audience, not something that happens between you and yourself, it is something that happens between you and something very mysterious that is above you. Something like the unconscious, moreover. In *Orlando* I had the impression that I was expressing the virtuality of dance. It expressed itself through me, and I am no dancer. Wilson succeeded perfectly in getting it across by going through what I was. I prefer to go through what might be called the lie of a metaphor or the secret of a metaphor. Metaphors can be deciphered, but deciphering one is more difficult than deciphering actual words. And metaphor implies form.

AF: You must know that text by Kleist, the essay on puppet theater where he expresses the view that the most rigorous form can give access to the greatest abstraction, to what is most amorphous. It can succeed in creating a grace that is more than human. It's both aesthetics and ethics. This is not mysticism. It's art. The greater the formal rigor, the more we can express the inexpressible, what you call the invisible.

IH: Yes, *Orlando* was like that. A very abstract form that made it possible to say everything. But if I try to talk about the inexpressible, I don't stand a chance. If we concentrate too much on naming things, there is always the slightly anxious feeling that the outcome might be an irreparable loss. I don't know what of. I was just talking about having the impression that a building is collapsing. I often have a feeling of being in great danger; hence my paranoia about interviews. It's not capricious; it's a real anxiety about the spoken word, about giving away secrets, unveiling mysteries, as though it might lead to an irreparable loss. I don't know what of.

AF: That's one of the reasons I have such difficulty in publishing. It's not just the irreparable effect of unveiling things; it is the issue of who I am addressing. Who can you address yourself to when it's something intimate, something intimately real that you are bringing out into the open, as though you were extracting a precious stone or precious flesh. What will become of it, who is going to do what with it? The world is cruel to the things that women do. It is only within the analytic space that it is possible to believe one will be received and protected. And even that's not true because analytic theory gives women a rough time too.

IH: When you're an actress it's hard to resist both the temptation and the need to be popular, because we also depend on that for our survival. I resist it as much as I can, but with great difficulty. Nathalie Sarraute was saying the other day that she has always walked a lonely road and that it didn't matter to her. I too feel that I am walking a lonely road, but it doesn't really bother me!

AF: You feel lonely?

IH: Yes. I get lots of work, but trying to walk a very specific road, come what may, is not always easy. It's like pursuing an obsession. But, let's be honest, what matters in this life is choosing, after all, and not just putting up with things.

AF: Why did you want to see me? I can understand wanting to see Nathalie Sarraute . . .

IH: Precisely because of what we have just been saying about androgyny, about creation, about procreation. I've often wanted to talk about the relationship between the state of being an actress and motherhood. Godard has thought about the intimate circulation between life and the cinema. Those are things that lie at the heart of an actress's intimacy, and I thought I would be able to talk about them with you. I was right.

I was very interested in what you said about the actress as container. I talked about this with Nathalie Sarraute too, but it took a different form. I talked with her about the absence of characters. I've been saying for a long time now that I no longer interpret characters (*personnages*), but that I interpret persons (*personnes*), and that the more abstract and apparently impossible to embody the substance I embody becomes, the easier it seems, paradoxically, to embody it. When a character is sketched out, dressed, I find it very difficult to get into the role. The more abstract, the more boundless the proposition, the more it can be embodied. Because when there are no limits I can throw myself into it, myself and my different states. When you talk about woman as container, about the way you can welcome a role into yourself, like a child, you're talking about the same thing. I don't define myself as an actress who interprets a character, who espouses a role, but as a person who welcomes another person. Talking to Nathalie Sarraute, I defined that approach in terms of form, style, and mind; talking to you, I define this approach in terms of the body. So I finally find myself all together! There is a mental approach to what I do, but that mental, cerebral element also involves the body.

AF: The brain is also part of the body. There are such things as brain hormones. And during pregnancy everything circulates. The child is swimming in brain hormones. We know that, but we also know very little about it; women know a lot of things, but their knowledge is closed off from scientific knowledge, and all my work is an attempt to bring out what we know without knowing it, yet at the same time knowing it. This is not abstract knowledge but subjective knowledge in which subjectivity, flesh, flesh and mind are not dissociated, but in a relation of exchange.

IH: Yes, that's true. I have the impression of knowing without knowing, but knowing all the same.

AF: What is coming to the surface might be called the unconscious, the knowledge that you call "knowing all the same." I think that Freud discovered the unconscious and that women have since discovered their bodies and the body in the unconscious. But these discoveries are not heard; hence the difficulty. What is madness? Not being listened to. You send out a message in a language they tell you is inaudible, foreign, hieroglyphic. It is a writing that still cannot be read.

IH: That's why I became an actress: to decipher hieroglyphs.

AF: The key phrase in Freud's work is "Where id was, there ego shall be . . . " I think that where id was, there women's "I" shall be. It will be on the side of what I call the creation of life. Our future lies ahead of us, not behind; it will grow out of something that has lagged behind and not been thought through, something to which we, unlike men, do not need to return via incest. For women, there is no obsession with the eternal return. The prefix that characterizes women is pro-, that is, forward: procreation, proposition, programming. Pro is women's preposition par excellence. The promise that, despite anything Claudel may have had to say,[2] women are now capable of keeping.

12. Recognitions

March 9, 1994

The cultural education I received in secondary school, and my early apprenticeships—which, to be more specific, echoed two texts I studied in ninth grade (*classe de troisième*)—inspired in me, as an aftereffect of a precocious childhood curiosity, a sort of vocation for research, for seeking to learn in order to know and seeking to understand in order to live. The first text was *Il vecchio scolaro* ("The Perpetual Student"), by a late-nineteenth-century author (was it Pascoli or Fogazzaro?), and the second was Montaigne's *Essays*, and especially the text that I would retitle "On Fainting as Experience."[1]

After completing my university education, I committed myself to two projects: first, research on the sociology of literature, on the French and Italian avant-gardes, and on the thought of the 1960s, with Roland Barthes at the École Pratique des Hautes Études; then, after some years of adult life, in the course of which I became "a puzzle to myself,"[2] research on psychoanalysis, which, as everyone knows, is an experiment in knowing (*connaissance*) that requires a personal analysis and not just access to the established body of knowledge transmitted by theoretical seminars, clinical seminars, and study groups linked to particular schools. In my case this meant undertaking a personal analysis with Jacques Lacan, attending his theoretical seminars at the École Normale Supérieure and his clinical seminars at Sainte-Anne,[3] and, finally, participating in study groups with the psychoanalysts of the École Freudienne, with Serge Leclaire in particular, but also with many others, including Michèle Montrelay.

My MLF,[4] if I may be so bold as to call it that, was permeated with this same orientation toward research. Some years ago, I established the Institute for Teaching and Research on the Sciences of Women or Feminology; its work has recently been made more public. At a session held at the Institute on March 5 of this year, a paper on the movement's infancy by Françoise Ducrocq (an English professor at Paris VII) reminded me that the MLF was initially, for the most part, at once activist—we acted, were involved in struggles—and, in ideological terms, rather dogmatic—we followed master thinkers such as Marx and Althusser, although not uncritically: this was our legacy from the revolutionary left. But the MLF very quickly made allowances for what we then called "lived experience," and in the highly original "consciousness-raising groups," which were almost unique among the many small groups formed at the time, women's speech began to make itself heard in the margins of, or in opposition to, all forms of institutionalized knowledge. In the light of two major experiences—that of procreation, which I described at length in the body of my thesis, and that of psychoanalysis, as I have just noted—it seemed to me that it was essential to rework both what was being said and the way it was being listened to.

Action and revolution required established knowledge and master thinkers; women's reason and madness required them to distance themselves from the system and to detect, beneath it, the masculinist ideology of Freud, Lacan, but also Althusser, Marx, and others; wisdom, finally, demanded that we not let ourselves be trapped in the impasses of acting out, through activist actions that were repetitive or even suicidal, or trapped in preanalytic motivations that claimed, whatever the cost, to know nothing of the existence of the unconscious.

The creation of the research group called Psychanalyse et Politique in late 1968 allowed us to explore a "dark continent,"[5] to discover a new world; it was an effort to embark on the adventure of articulating the unconscious with history, and the subject with culture. Attempting to work with and against psychoanalysis and politics at the same time meant attacking what Michel Foucault described, in his fine inaugural lecture at the Collège de France, as the two major poles of power; it meant trying to deconstruct ideologies, to reinvent and even to reconstruct the political. It meant concluding that an experience specific to women, their universal contribution—what Engels, in The Origins of the Family, Private Property and the State, describes as human production, as opposed to the production of commodities (although this description did not lead to any conceptual work or elaboration)—was still foreclosed, as such, from the theory of political economics and from psychoanalytic theory.

As far as methodology is concerned, I would like to insist here on the value and function of experience and of the foreclosure imposed on the *production of living beings*. On the concept of "experience" I refer you to Roger Munier:

> First there is etymology. *Experience* comes from the Latin *experiri*, to test, try, prove. The radical is *periri*, which one also finds in *periculum*, peril, danger. The Indo-European root is *per*, to which are attached the ideas of *crossing* and, secondarily, of *trial, test*. In Greek, numerous derivations evoke a crossing or passage: *peirô*, to cross; *pera*, beyond; *peraô*, to pass through; *perainô*, to go to the end; *peras*, end, limit. For Germanic language, Old High German *faran* has given us *fahren*, to transport, and *führen*, to drive. Should we attribute *Erfahrung* to this origin as well, or should it be linked to the second meaning of *per*, trial, in Old High German *fara*, danger, which became *Gefahr*, danger, and *gefährden*, to endanger? The boundaries between one meaning and the other are imprecise. The same is true for the Latin *periri*, to try, and *periculum*, which originally means trial, test, then risk, danger. The idea of experience as a crossing is etymologically and semantically difficult to separate from that of risk. From the beginning and no doubt in a fundamental sense, *experience* means to endanger.[6]

Speaking of experience rather than of what we had "lived" was a way of freeing ourselves from ready-made doctrines and isms—in my case from feminism in particular—and a way of trying to make room for the subject, the unconscious, the body: I mean, of course, the sexed body. It was therefore a way of remodeling reason and modern consciousness as represented at the time by the humanities and the social sciences. Wanting to be both subject and object of research, seeking to make ordinary what had once seemed impossible to learned men, we found that many difficulties stood between us and our aims.

The first experience of every living being, incontrovertibly, is the prebirth and birth experience. We are familiar with the importance Hannah Arendt attaches to birth in *The Human Condition*;[7] she almost turns it into a concept. However, she does not develop the point that being born a girl or being born a boy makes a difference and that this difference between the sexes conditions different destinies in that it is not simply an anatomical difference, because it is welcomed into what we call the symbolic order. The birth of a human being is not a natural phenomenon but a cultural phenomenon.

Since the dawn of time, being born (merely) a girl (*n'être fille*, as I put it) has been experienced as a catastrophe; it still is, in many countries.[8] Being born (merely) a girl means being subjected to the radical oppression of a sex that is dedicated to the reproduction of the species. But being born a woman (*naître femme*) conjugates the destiny of being born (*naître*) with that of giving birth (*faire naître*). The same is not true of being born a man. Being born a man means to a large extent feeling that one is excluded from giving birth. Hence a series of contradictory affects: wonder, curiosity, a feeling of mystery, of secrecy, but also rejection, phobia, envy, and then substitution, exploitation, and imitation of the phenomenon of gestation. The specific experience of giving birth seems to be the basis for the very condition of modern woman, given the present state of knowledge. That is at least a hypothesis. Following Hannah Arendt, I would say that the anastrophic[9] nature of women's being born and giving birth brings about a return of the foreclosed in the genital, creative mode rather than in the psychotic mode that entails being forever walled up in silence.

Gestation, which is the initial and ultimate experience of the narcissistic development and accomplishment of women, constitutes the original experience, the first thought, the very heart of knowledge, and the *paradigm of ethics* for thinking of the other as a subject. It is a capacity to welcome the other and a recognition of the other: love of one's neighbor and democracy. For women it is the royal road to thought; for men, on the other hand, it is the impossible experience, the real that is forbidden and therefore foreclosed.

The concept of foreclosure is not easy to define. It is a concept that was forged by Lacan in psychoanalysis, but it is not alien to juridical discourse. Let me cite the historical dictionary of the French language:

> Of all the verbal prefixes of "*clore*" [to close] only "*foreclore*" [to foreclose] was formed in French from the old preposition "*fors*," "*hors de*," "*dehors*" [outside] and "*clore*." The word was replaced by "*exclure*" (from a similar Latin formation: "*ex + claudere*" [to exclude]) but survives as a specialized legal term: "to take away the ability to perform an act or to take legal action

after the expiry of a time-limit." The active noun "*foreclusion*," formed from "*exclusion*," is a legal term reintroduced into psychoanalysis by Jacques Lacan to translate the word *Verwerfung*, "rejection," which is used by Freud with reference to psychosis; the word concerns the primordial rejection of a fundamental signifier from the symbolic world of the subject. This mechanism, as distinct from repression, is said to lie at the origin of psychosis.[10]

There are other, broadly similar definitions, for example in the *Manuel de psychiatrie*,[11] and a new and specifically Lacanian definition in *The Language of Psychoanalysis*.[12] The latter also alludes to the term's linguistic meaning, which enriches it considerably.

This production, this giving birth that is impossible for men, will therefore, as a result of all the contradictory affects I have just mentioned, be the object of a radical, primal repression in Freud (the origin of repression and the repression of origins). I remind you that repression is one of the basic concepts of analytic theory. In *Leonardo da Vinci and a Memory of his Childhood*, we can see how Freud, the discoverer of the unconscious, the specialist in lifting censorship, the stubborn investigator of dream work, the eternally curious child who wants to know "where babies come from," a scientist rather than an artist dedicated to understanding secrets—this Freud underestimates the artist da Vinci's *libido sciendi*, or epistemophilic drive, in order to impose his own childhood theory of genitality and privilege the work of art over the work of psychoanalysis.

In his seminar on psychoses, Lacan concludes his remarks on matricial and paternal functions with this sentence, which really is cavalier: "There is nevertheless one thing that evades the symbolic tapestry; it's procreation in its essential root—that one being is born from another. . . . There is, in effect, something radically unassimilable to the signifier. It's quite simply the subject's singular existence. Why is he here? What is he doing here? Why is he going to disappear? The signifier is incapable of providing him with the answer."[13]

For his part, Claude Lévi-Strauss admits to André Green, in a discussion of the elementary system of kinship, that he took little interest in the maternal function when he elaborated his theory:

CL-S: The question of the nonqualification of relations between mother and child is much more interesting. And I hardly need say that it is a problem that has given me more than a little trouble. But the reason I did not introduce it is that I did not need that hypothesis; in most cases the soci-eties we study normalize the relationship between husband and wife, normalize the relationship between brother and sister, and normalize the relationship between father and son, but do not normalize—or at least not to the same degree—the relationship between mother and children. For you psychoanalysts, on the other hand, this is an essential relation-ship. But I would say that the two things are related, that that relationship must, for us, precisely not be normalized, in order to allow you to inter-vene and find your place (*laughter*). For if the anthropologist made it his business to specify, for every society, the relationship between a mother and her children, he would tell the psychoanalysts: "We have explained everything; there is nothing more for you to say." Now, there are things we cannot say. What do we do? We try to determine, for each society, a sort of collective paradigm of attitudes. And you start out from the obser-vation that this paradigm is not respected in the same way by all the family configurations within the group, that there is some free play, that there is some variation; the gap we leave you with is the site of that free play and its variations, and your essential mission is to study it . . .

AG: The question that concerns me is that you say you can do without that (mother-child) relationship, that you do not need it because there is no social regulation involved.

CL-S: I do not need it in order to explain collective behaviors.

AG: For our part, we say that it is essential, for two reasons: the mother-child relationship is considered not only in its structuring or normative nature in relation to the social group; it is quite essential for the problem of identity, for seeing how this mother will "see" her child.[14]

There is no question of seeing how she will make the child, produce it with her body and her flesh over a period of nine months.

In a study of Proust and George Sand, André Green, for his part, speaking about the difficulty and creative genius of Proust, refers to a "reserve of the uncreatable" and thus avoids having to address the homosexual Proust's genital problem with the "unprocreatable" rather than the uncreatable.[15]

The impossible experience has two repercussions. The major theoretical constructs and systems of thought overlook gestation, procreation, and even the mother; women, who live and think in accordance with the prefix *pro-* (projects, promises, programs, progress), are relegated to and marked by the *un-*. The experience that is impossible for men becomes the poetic experience, an ethical, unspeakable, unliveable, untransmissible experience, and women are condemned along with it.

The genitrix, defined as the producer of living-speaking beings, is foreclosed from the law of universal man and his monist orders. That is what I tried at length to demonstrate in the work collected in my thesis.

And the reality of gestation, which has been expelled from the symbolic field, naturally keeps on coming back in political, economic, social, and juridical reality and in certain mad sciences such as demography. Denied in its necessary values and in its indispensable function, human production returns as an alienating prescription, a sacrificial duty, and an enslaving obligation whenever, in the course of a history in crisis, a conservative state decrees that women must be locked away, adopting a program intended to strengthen the family or a policy designed to increase the birthrate.

Freud lifted the censorship on dreamwork, Marx lifted the censorship on the proletariat's labor force, and they gave us the tools and the means to lift the censorship not only on women's labor, work, and action—what Hannah Arendt calls the *vita activa*—but also on their specific form of thought, their original way of thinking, and the censorship on procreation, on flesh-thought—or on what Arendt calls the *vita contemplativa*; they even gave us the means to advance the hypothesis that gestation in itself conjugates *vita activa* with *vita contemplativa*, removes and transcends the opposition to which these two components of human activity have always been deliberately confined.[16]

This abolition of censorship should allow women to emerge from a psychogenic underground, from the excluded-interned status (to use a concept elaborated by Jacques Derrida), from the status of outlaws, radical foreigners, immigrants with regard to citizenship, a status to which they are condemned, paradoxically, by the prescription and foreclosure of the matricial.

Elsewhere in my work I have attempted to demonstrate how the access of foreclosed knowledge to a scientific mode of knowing could give birth to a materialist rather than an idealist mode of thought, to a political rather than a metaphysical mode, and how it could give rise to an anastrophic, ethical being-for-life and being born/giving birth rather than the being-for-death of the Apocalypse and a catastrophic demography.

In these times of serious crisis, especially for women, now that state power is trying to restrict their right to knowledge and right to work, the urgency and contemporary relevance of this research will not escape vigilant minds and specialists in philosophy, literary creation, and the law such as you. If we are unable to think about women's right to procreation, "freedom and equality" will remain principles that mislead and delude us, and "frater-nity" will never give birth to solidarity between men and women in a hetero-sexed world. Only the translation into law of a rigorous theorization of this issue can result in political actions that can benefit women. When politi-cians do not think, the law bogs down in quibbles over technicalities and legal excesses while citizens regress into dependency and depression.

The doctorate, which represents a maturational stage, can thus be said to have born fruit. In 1992–93 Professor Francine Demichel suggested that we run a joint DEA seminar on "The Law, Economics, and Sociology of Medical Decision Making" directed by Professor André Demichel.[17]

Three DEAs were awarded under this joint supervision, and the work that was done made our methodology explicit: we wanted to establish links be-tween experience, reflection, and action. We undertook a collective three-part study of the question: "Is rape a crime against humanity?": a synthesis of knowledge (historical, social, juridical, and political) about rape, con-crete actions in solidarity with women victims (and especially with women who had been raped and tortured in the war in the former Yugoslavia), and legal action (actions, for example, to have rape recognized as a crime against humanity by bringing pressure to bear on international agencies).[18] It was, therefore, at once a set of situational actions, a summary of existing knowl-edge about the subject, and analyses that attempted to promote new theo-retical, political, and legal thinking about rape.

The seminar continued in 1993–94, and it led to the creation of a research group that has taken up and expanded the body of knowledge by women and about women: their store of skills (savoir-faire) and of empirical and prag-matic knowledge (savoirs). The group has collected documents, elaborated concepts, and set up the Observatoire de la misogynie, an "observatory" to document misogyny. These efforts ought to energize the university, and the university should confer legitimacy upon this body of knowledge once it has met a certain number of requirements to become an academic corpus that can be transmitted.

The strategy of this research group is modeled on the strategy behind my thesis: the mutual subversion of academic knowledge and foreclosed knowl-edge and the transformation and integration of each by the other. The re-sulting knowledge is doubly chiasmatic, thanks to the doubling of research structures: the extra-institutional research carried out by the Institut d'enseignement et de recherches en sciences des femmes ou féminologie stands alongside the intra-institutional research undertaken in the academic context (Paris VIII, the DEA). The two structures, both inherited from the Psychanalyse et Politique experiment, make it possible to critique and correct the flaws in the MLF's methodology and to expand upon some of its strengths.

From the methodological standpoint, being both the subject and object of our research created many more problems in the 1970s than it had done for Montaigne, all the more so in that, being largely inherited from psychoanalysis, for which saying is doing and doing is transforming, our method was based upon an oral practice and in that we ourselves, rather than books, were most often the raw material for what we were producing, for our work and for our actions.

As for the *production of living beings*, which has been forgotten and left behind (*husteros*), it is still difficult, even today, to represent it (even to ourselves) as something that lies beyond the phallic agency, as something that theorizes genitality and the cornerstone of the *human contract* into which (this is my hypothesis) a higher form of humanism will transform the social contract.

However, international events—the UN conferences I mentioned a moment ago—have intervened, and they impel us to refine our existing research practice with a view to taking broader political action. And I note that, in recent months, the right to procreation, which I have tried for years to bring to the attention of feminist or socialist thought, has appeared, and is identified as such, in the latest UN texts.

The men and women involved in our research group (some eighty of them) come from very different backgrounds. They have all been politically active in the past; they have specialized professional skills as lawyers, doctors, academics, mathematicians, literature professors, engineers, and so on; they have some experience with psychoanalysis and they share a "feminist consciousness." All these men and women have come there to despecialize themselves, as it were, and to try to learn and develop "the sciences of women" together.

The authorization to supervise research that I am requesting here would come less as a way of recognizing twenty-five years of work or as an encouragement to persevere than as a tool, a passport for exploring the new pathways and difficulties that will punctuate the creation of an epistemological field whose complexity and richness it has not been possible to describe in detail here. It would facilitate progress at the psychoanalytic, political, and legal levels, or so I hope. And we have known from the start that this would be the longest march in women's history.

13. Wartime Rapes

March 14, 1994

They tell us that Sarajevo has been liberated, but they also tell us that mortars are still pounding several regions in the former Yugoslavia, and we, the European women of France, less than fifteen hundred kilometers away from that country, know that hundreds, thousands, of our sisters there are still being held in camps where they are being raped and impregnated by force.

On March 8, 1994, International Women's Day, the Tresnjevka feminist group in Zagreb, acting on the initiative of Nina Kadic, called upon the International Criminal Tribunal (created on May 25, 1993, by the United Nations) to judge the crimes against human rights that are being committed in the former Yugoslavia and to judge the rapists as criminals.[1] The women in the group alerted international opinion to the existence of forty-five camps in which women are being systematically tortured, raped, and deliberately impregnated and to the fact that rapes occur constantly in certain parts of that country. The group sought to make April 15, 1994, an international day of protest against rape, a "crime against humanity."

It was also Tresnjevka that undertook field studies, submitted a report to the United Nations on the mass rape of women, most of them Muslim, and then alerted the press in the summer of 1992. At that point in the war, several missions had already been dispatched to the former Yugoslavia and had observed widespread violations of human rights but said absolutely nothing about the rapes.

In France the media resistance was spectacular. Although news about these systematic and particularly cruel rapes had appeared in the German and American press as early as September, it was only in November that it reached us (in *Libération*); and it was not until January 1993, following the Warburton Report (the European Community Report on the treatment of Muslim women in the former Yugoslavia) that a real press campaign to inform the public began. It lasted scarcely two months and, as usual, completely ignored the mobilization of women in France (news, appeals, petitions, debates, subscriptions, fact-finding missions, letters to the United Nations, a demonstration mobilizing nearly ten thousand people on March 6, 1993, and so on). More than nine months later, a politicocultural demonstration, which did receive media attention, together with an evening program on Arte,[2] failed to attract more people and, not without misogyny, forgot about women; the warlike emblem brandished over the proceedings was a chimera, an enormous, monstrous creature with a woman's breasts!

Moreover, it seems that rapes had to be systematic and on a massive scale before the media would talk about them, and even then the emphasis was put on the racist rather than the sexist nature of the crimes, because the victims were mostly Muslim women (a Serb statement declared that rape would be used as a weapon of war in the strategy of "ethnic cleansing"). These misogynist crimes were scarcely recognized as a political phenomenon.

And yet, while it is true that a few men and boys were raped, women were the ones being raped in massive numbers (we do not have precise figures, but does that really matter when it is certain that we are talking about several thousand women—twenty thousand, fifty thousand?) They were raped in the most atrocious fashion, often in front of their families, and almost always repeatedly by gangs of men: women, but also girls, even very young girls, and old women. Many of them died as a result.

We have been reminded that traditionally war, which tortures and kills, also rapes and that raping a woman is a way of raping the wives, mothers, sisters, and daughters of the enemy in order to destroy, "through them," as we are told, the power and honor of a man or a people. For bands of brothers, either fraternal or fratricidal, women do not exist. They do not count; similarly, ethnologists do not need women—and they acknowledge this[3]—to establish the "elementary structures of kinship." The assaults on the integrity, dignity, and honor of the women of the former Yugoslavia were scarcely acknowledged in the French press, even though rape has been recognized as a crime in our country since 1980. But, in the absence of any antisexist law, misogyny, unlike racism, is still not a crime; it is merely an opinion.

Such is the ignorance of the history of women that even those who reported on the fact-finding missions, and, in their wake, the media, believed that this was an episode without precedent. Yet recent history teaches us that this was not the first time such cruel rapes have taken place on such a vast scale. There were, for, example the rapes in Nanking in 1936 (over twenty thousand women were raped by Japanese soldiers in the space of one month) and the rapes in Bangladesh in 1971 (between two and four hundred thousand women were raped by Pakistani soldiers during a nine months' reign of terror).

What is absolutely scandalous about the current war, however, is that, for the first time, women have been deported and held in camps for the purpose of "getting them pregnant." The goal has not been simply to massacre these women's children in front of them, to gang-rape them in public places in front of their families and their neighbors, and then to go on and on raping them in the camps; it has been to use them as machines to produce new generations of Serbs. The madness specific to this war, which outdoes even fascism, is a macho-national frenzy. Every rape is accompanied, explicitly or implicitly, by the words "you will give birth to a Chetnik," in other words, to a boy, a Serb, a warrior, a son without father or mother. The phantasm of ethno-spermatic omnipotence would engender men with no genitrix (no trace of the genetic heritage or of the woman's work of pregnancy) and with multiple and anonymous genitors (almost all the rapes were gang rapes).[4]

And this is happening in Europe in the 1990s. In Europe, where for the first time in the history of the human species women and couples are able to control their fertility and enjoy freedoms and rights that make women citizens of the human community.

Little has been said about the devastating effects of these rapes and forced pregnancies, but we know about them thanks to the women activists and/or specialists looking after the women who have managed to survive and find help and thanks to a few eye-witness accounts: mutism, anorexia, insomnia, apathy, loss of interest in life, depression and even suicide; above and beyond the clinical symptoms, there are the moral reproaches—guilt, shame—that lead to humiliation and loss of self-esteem, despite the fact that imams have intervened on behalf of the women who were raped and left pregnant. In 1971 the imams of Bangladesh tried to convince the population that the Muslim women who had been raped were heroines; they tried to convince men that these women could still remain their wives or that, if they were single, they deserved to be married. The imams failed. Rejected by their families, the women who survived either turned to prostitution to eke out a marginal existence or they committed suicide.

Only the condemnation of such *gynocide* by the International Court in The Hague (which must find the rapists and the organizers of the rapes guilty as "criminals against humanity") can restore the dignity of the women victims of these crimes and reaffirm their right to life and—this is our most ardent hope—put an end to these crimes now in the former Yugoslavia, in Rwanda, in Djibouti, in Somalia . . . and, in the future, all over the world.

14. Religion, Women, Democracy

March 19, 1994

More than a century ago, the visionary Jules Ferry predicted a free and modern culture for girls. In a vibrant speech on the need to educate girls at a time when they were limited to church schools, where they received a rudimentary and discriminatory education, he said: "The bishops know very well that whoever controls women controls everything. Women must either belong to Science or belong to the Church."[1]

A few decades later, Freud undertook a rigorous deconstruction of what he called the religious illusion—an infantile fiction based upon the pleasure principle and man's narcissistic omnipotence—in *The Future of an Illusion* and contrasted it with science and the reality principle. But, while he repeated his critique of the religious mode of thought in *Moses and Monotheism*, the last text he wrote, he forcefully reinstated monism in the name of patriarchal power and the absolute paternal function, not only by alluding to the biblical hero—the German title refers to "der Mann Moses," and the French translation to "l'homme Moïse"[2]—but also by appealing to Aeschylus's *Oresteia* and Greek democracy. As you know, Athenian democracy was founded by Athena, the motherless daughter who absolved Orestes of his matricide, drove the Erinyes, avenging goddesses, into the underworld, and silenced them by transforming them into the Eumenides. Freud hails all this as marking an essential spiritual advance for humanity. I remember that, a few years ago and before Khomeini left Neauphle-le-Château,[3] Michel Foucault, writing in *Le Nouvel Observateur*, hailed him as the incarnation of the renewal of Islamic spirituality.

Like Greek democracy, monotheism can do without women. In Catholicism—to restrict the discussion to the religion in which I was brought up and with which I am quite familiar—the spiritual trinity is made up of the Father, the Son and the Holy Spirit. While the Virgin Mary was later elevated to the status of a saint, she does not have the status of a divinity; man alone is God, One God, father and son.

Just as it was for Freud ninety years ago, so it is for Levinas today: Europe means "the Bible and Greece."[4]

So let us take a look at Europe and its immediate southern periphery, at the very cradle of the three monotheisms—the Mediterranean is especially dear to me because I was born in Marseille and spent more than twenty years of my life there. We see Bosnia, in turmoil and torn apart by wars; we are told that these are not wars of religion, but the clashes between bands of brothers are more fratricidal than fraternal. The role reserved for women is that of absolute victim, as is the case further afield in Rwanda, and in Africa in general. The treatment inflicted upon women entails repression, imprisonment, torture, rape, and death. In Bosnia we see the triumph of the illusion of male omnipotence thanks to the oldest of all patriarchy's theological and philosophical phantasms: the phantasm of generating children with no trace of a mother. The foreclosure of women's bodies in the monist symbolic system has never been more powerful than it is among the Serbs, who say to every woman they rape and claim to "get pregnant": "You will give birth to a Chetnik!"[5] The theme of purity, common to all religions, is now being distorted into the theme of ethnic cleansing.

Every day we can read in the newspapers about the deadly effects the rise of fundamentalism in Algeria, our closest neighbor, has had on girls. They must hide away either behind their veils or in their homes, abandon all hope of taking the baccalaureate exams, or risk having acid thrown in their faces or even being killed. Whereas the UN designated March 8 as International Women's Day and, in a similar spirit, adopted a Convention on the Elimination of All Forms of Discrimination Against Women, on March 8 of this year, in a sort of inverted symbolism, fundamentalists stabbed a fifteen-year-old girl so as to terrorize all girls still further. Hidden away in their clothes and shut up inside their homes, women are executed if they do not execute themselves. It will be argued that fundamentalisms are not the same thing as religion, but, where women are concerned, all religions are fundamentalist.[6] It is gross hypocrisy to try to make a distinction between fundamentalism and orthodoxy on this point. Under both Islamic law and the patriarchal regime, fundamentalisms, like neuroses and psychoses, reveal the foundations of the norms of religious orthodoxy.

We have seen the effects on schoolgirls of the inequality, the apartheid to which women are structurally subjected by the monotheisms, the very effects Jules Ferry warned us about. We can also see these effects in the way mosques are laid out; as in synagogues, women—wives and daughters—are confined to a small area, while the chosen sex enjoys a monumental space. The theme of purity reappears: women are relegated to insignificance because they are impure, especially when they have their periods. They talk to us about respect for women in religion—they talked to me about it throughout my childhood. I was born into the Catholic religion, married in church, and some of my academic work was on a very Christian author, namely, Bernanos.[7] In short, I understand this religion and I do not mock it, but one would have to be blind or have no self-respect—it would be necessary not to be a woman, in a word—not to see and resent the permanent humiliation this exclusion represents, above all its devastating effect not only on relations between mothers and sons but on all family ties. That the monotheisms are misogynist, anti-egalitarian, and discriminatory now goes without saying.[8] When the Anglican Church seemed to be seeking, democratically, to reestablish a degree of justice by accepting women into the priesthood, most Catholics and some Anglicans declared in thunderous tones that this was transvestism: Christ had the body of a man—and we are not talking about a symbolic body here; he had a real body, and it was male—so priests must have the same male body; women cannot become part of the priesthood because that would be obscene. We can, like those who cry transvestism, also say to ourselves that, when the Anglican Church took into consideration the reality of the existence of two sexes, it nevertheless remained subject to the monist and narcissistic arbitrariness of the "Only One," according to which there is only one God—a male God—and not simply a universal "Man."

The wars and uprisings that are now taking place in Europe are based upon identitarian or narcissistic, nationalist, and religious demands, and women are their first victims. Women experience these demands as so many fundamentalisms. To the extent that, whatever is said about them, the wars that are now being waged in Europe are wars of religion: they are primarily wars against women, and, as I have said elsewhere, misogyny is the basis of fundamentalism.

In France, the media—and the Observatoire de la misogynie that I created five years ago can provide numerous examples[9]—have noted that the condition of women, especially girls of North African origin, is moving in two contradictory directions. The first direction shows women and girls being both physically and verbally abused, frustrated and repressed in their freedoms, and insulted in the name of a tradition to which they themselves say they must submit, rather than attributing their subordination to the brothers who force the tradition on them, though the young men often fail to respect it themselves. Girls are usually absent from the picture, though, whereas the young men of the *banlieues* are depicted either as angry hooligans or as nice kids who are looked after by sports and cultural associations. Tagging, rap, and street art are activities from which girls are essentially excluded, because, as everyone knows, girls are not supposed to "hang out" on street corners. A couple of weeks ago, I went to see a street art exhibit at La Villette,[10] and it was obvious that the girls had been invited to watch and not to create something. The emblematic and best-known group of this integrational street art goes, as I have often mentioned, by the name of Nique ta mère, "Fuck your mother." I am ashamed to pronounce the name because, in my city on the shores of the Mediterranean, this is an insult that no decent boy, and certainly no girl, would ever dare to use.

When Salman Rushdie is the object of a fatwa, progressive intellectuals, Muslims as well as Westerners, rise up and mobilize; when Taslima Nasrin, a thirty-one-year-old Bengali doctor and feminist writer, writes against the oppression to which she and her sisters are subjected, she too becomes the victim of a fatwa, but only a few voices are raised to prevent her from being killed in the house in which she has had to shut herself away, with her mother.[11]

Both here and in Bangladesh women are being brought back into line by the repercussions of what is happening in Algeria and elsewhere. Last month one of my students had to abandon her plans to marry a European Frenchman and continue her graduate studies. Women are brave, but they are also lucid and they are afraid. Yesterday evening, we went to a "Nana beurs" meeting,[12] and the women told us they no longer felt completely safe here, in our country, in their country. They too are well aware that the difference between fundamentalism and orthodoxy is quantitative and not qualitative and that they are in danger.

The second direction revealed by the media emerges from Baudelot and Establet's book *Allez les filles!*(Come on, girls!).[13] Now that they have been given equal opportunities and equality of access to knowledge, girls are performing very well in all areas and are much better integrated than their brothers, both in school and in civic life. The authors say "Come on, girls!"; however, it is not really the girls but secularism that has to make an extra effort, because, while girls are now doing very well and while more of them are passing the baccalaureate exams and going on to university-level studies, a sort of *numerus clausus* is being introduced in higher education, especially at the postgraduate level, for example, in law or biology: girls are being refused the right to pursue advanced degrees on the grounds that there are supposedly too many of them.

The aim of this roundtable discussion would seem to be to ensure that secularism will adopt and adapt (and adapt to) certain religious specificities in its relationship with Islam. Yet in today's France secularism, which is seriously afflicted by its oldest enemy—Christianity—has been seriously undermined and may even be in great danger. Some would like to go back to the era of the *loi Falloux*[14] and abolish the separation of church and state, the very Church that the state had to fight for a hundred years in order to guarantee girls a full right to learning on equal terms with boys. Catholicism is returning in force in Europe, thanks to a papist morality which, having opposed painless childbirth until 1956, is now violently opposed to abortion and anti-AIDS contraception.

Christian democracy has not laid down its arms,[15] and it can now rely on the support of what Alain Finkielkraut calls the "Holy Alliance of Clergies."[16] Precisely because girls are excelling at what Jules Ferry offered them, they are victims of new forms of discrimination. The patriarchal alliance converges with the alliance of monotheisms to block the pursuit of their emancipation. Certain devout democrats are now prepared, following the example of the Constitutional Council, to accept discriminatory practices on the grounds that they are based on differences at a time when public life, more homosexed and more undifferentiated than ever, is putting itself on display and exhibiting itself without women.

To the extent that it states that girls cannot be granted French nationality until they are eighteen, the latest legislation on nationality puts them at risk by leaving them—as is the norm under French law—under the jurisdiction of the national laws of their parents' country of origin, and this considerably undermines the role these girls can play in public life. When the same government outlines "an ambitious family policy" and suggests that the role of fathers should be strengthened while women should go back to the home, as the draft framework law on which we will be voting in a few days proposes, one might say that it is contravening the principle of parental equality, which is one of the latest secular and social rights women have won in recent years. While there has been a lot of talk in recent days about the CIP,[17] which most young people see as a sort of SMIC for youth,[18] very little has been said about the suggestion that a parental allowance should replace the maternal wage equivalent to half the SMIC paid to women when they have a second child. The suggestion is not designed to allow women to get an education but to allow them to give up their jobs without any welfare protection either now or in the future. Not only should women give up their jobs, become dependent on their husbands or the state, and look forward to a future living on the RMI;[19] they should also be making children and taking responsibility for their education because fertility rates are supposedly falling.[20]

On March 8 a committee on the French language was created by the minister for culture; it is made up of forty men and not a single woman. At the same time everyone now knows that, as well as being excluded from social life, women are being excluded from political life and from symbolic life; they are even being excluded from knowledge, because it is well known that women will put off having their first child until they have completed their education. Now, if women are supposed to have children at a very young age, some would like to encourage them to interrupt their education to hasten the arrival of the first child.

Unlike Freud, I will not contrast science with religion or the reality principle with the pleasure principle. On the contrary, I am willing to bet that they can coexist if they both acknowledge the primacy of reality. There are indeed two sexes, and in a republic such as ours the two sexes are born free and with equal rights. This reality should encourage the monist narcissism to which our religions are still clinging to mature a little more quickly.

I shall opt not for the future of a monist, religious, social, or political illusion, but for the future of a reality that is secular in both educational and civic terms, a reality that is mixed in terms of sex and based on parity. If democracy is to be able to defend itself, it must do so by reinforcing the philosophical bases of secularism by and for women. They need one another; they must be able to support one another, to maintain the right of women to education, work, freedom, and equality. I shall opt for nonsectarian and multicultural social and public spaces; I shall opt to encourage girls who define themselves as of immigrant origin to become guardians of integration and guarantors of democratization.

It is because they exclude women and want to remain homosexed and narcissistic that fraternal bands of brothers turn to fratricide: with the cult of the Supreme Being, the Terror following the French Revolution is the most terrible example. The real democratic alterity that must be considered, integrated, counted, thanks to which we shall be enriched, is first of all women.

To overcome the discontents in civilization, democracy must take into account and count on women. There are two sexes. That is the reality, and if that reality appears to contravene the pleasure principle of "there is only one" we need to make yet another effort of maturation before the two can coexist and come together in a democracy.

Yet another effort, secularists, if you wish to be republican!

15. Our Bodies Belong to Us

Dialogue with Taslima Nasrin

June 1994

ANTOINETTE FOUQUE: The fatwa that threatens your life was pronounced by the fundamentalists because you dared to criticize the apartheid that Islam inflicts on women.

TASLIMA NASRIN: I became aware of discrimination between men and
women as a child. My brothers could go out, but I couldn't. This discrimination leaves its mark on all women. They are constantly kept under guard;
they are guarded by their fathers until they reach adolescence, then by
their husbands, and finally by their sons. Many women have, like me,
been to university and have jobs, but they are kept shut up in the workplace
or at home. They spend their lives in captivity because they are the slaves
of men. So long as women—even educated women—do not have access
to equal rights, neither their bodies nor their minds will be free.

The Koran oppresses women: it says that the first woman was born of a
man's rib, that women are the slaves and sexual objects of men, who are
their masters, and that men can have four wives and divorce them as they
see fit. I have denounced the harmful effects of Islam and social taboos in
my articles.[1] I even dared to write against the prophet Mohammed, against

the texts in which he threatens women with hell if they do not submit to their husbands' sexual desires and promises them heaven if they drink their husbands' blood and pus. That's why the fundamentalists issued a fatwa against me. I've been living in captivity ever since.

AF: Confinement, like the headscarf, is a sign that the churches have always, as we know, asserted their control over women's bodies and their fertility. As Freud demonstrated in The Future of an Illusion, monotheism is the illusory triumph of the pleasure principle of narcissistic male omnipotence, the pleasure principle of a sex that wants to be chosen, absolutely unique and sovereign, over the reality principle, which teaches us that there are two sexes. It is the sons' envious appropriation of women's creative capacity and it reflects the oldest of all theological and philosophical phantasms: engendering children without any trace of the maternal. It is uterus envy, which is misogyny itself. Women disappear; they are enslaved, imprisoned, made invisible, and foreclosed. On this point the difference between fundamentalism and orthodoxy is quantitative, not qualitative. For women, all monotheisms are fundamentalisms.

In Europe Catholicism is returning in force, thanks to a papal morality that, having opposed painless childbirth until 1956, is now violently opposed to anti-AIDS contraception. By allying itself with Iran, the Vatican is trying to force the UN to omit any mention of the right to abortion in the papers to be presented at the Population Conference,[2] advocating that women should go back to the home.

TN: In Bangladesh, which is a people's republic, 80 percent Muslim and 20 percent Hindu, Islam became the state religion when the army seized power in 1988. Before, it was a secular state. Our constitution, which was inspired by British law, established the legal equality of men and women. But the Islamic Family Code allows men to take four wives, to inherit two-thirds of all family property, to have custody of children over the age of seven in the event of divorce, and so on. There are no equal rights. There is no democracy in the family, in society, or in the state.

Politicians, the government, and society have turned Islam into a weapon. Any civilized country has to opt for secularism. When I speak of secularism I do not mean equal rights for all religions. I mean a society in which religion remains in the private sphere. And a civilized country also means a country in which women have equal rights in every domain, in which they are treated as human beings, in which there is no discrimination

between blacks and whites, and in which property and wealth are distributed on an equal basis.

AF: If it is to make any progress, democracy must indeed reinforce the philosophical basis of secularism with and for women. We can see this in
Algeria, where women are behind the democratic mobilization that is trying to get the country out of the impasse of fundamentalism: on the one
hand, fundamentalist terror and, on the other, a state in which Islam has
been the official religion since 1963 and that imposed a family code on
women in 1984,[3] despite the long struggle women waged against that proposal. Secularism must rely on women, and women must rely on secularism in order to preserve their right to education, work, freedom, and
equality.

However, the democratic model has always been haunted by the exclusion of the other. This is what a reading of the Greek texts teaches us. In
order to found Athenian democracy, Athena, who was the motherless
daughter of Zeus, absolved Orestes of matricide and drove the avenging
Erinyes into the underworld. The alliance of males combines with that of
religions to block women's pursuit of emancipation. Ever more homosexed
and ever more undifferentiated, public life here in France is unfolding without women, and we have been fighting for parity for several years now.

TN: In Bangladesh a law introduced a parliamentary quota that gives an extra thirty seats (out of three hundred thirty) to the women of the majority
party, because no more than two or three women have ever been elected to
parliament. The women who take those seats have not been elected; they
are named by the ruling party. People make fun of them because, in their
view, politics is men's business. And in fact there are no openings that
would allow women to become involved in politics. Those who do so usually inherit the role of a husband or father who has been killed, like Benazir Bhutto.

Our prime minister and the leader of the opposition party (both
women) are elected members of parliament, but they are implementing
the policies of their husbands or father and doing nothing for women.
As for the parties, the women involved act on the advice of men and do
not want to change the system. When, in accordance with Islamic law,
the fundamentalists issue a fatwa forbidding women to work outside the
home or condemning a woman who has denounced the system, no woman
politician protests, because she and her party would be accused of being

anti-Islamic. And, given that the majority of the population is Islamic, she keeps quiet.

AF: Like the other monotheisms, Islam is the primary obstacle to women's entrance into public life, and into political life in particular. But in secular states women face other very constraining obstacles. The principle of equality, for instance, is essential and has to be defended, but it is dangerous for us because it has not been thought through. It helps to conceal misogyny. The hatred of women, of "Woman," on the part of both men and women, is the root of all rejections of the other. It is the root of all racisms. Perhaps at bottom it is not so much hatred as a primordial, archaic *envy* of women's procreative capabilities. And that envy is all the more influential in that it persists in denying the existence of what it envies.

The principle of equality is perverse, and it denies reality: there are women, and there are men. Because the dissymmetry with respect to procreation has not been thought through, it reappears in the form of obstacles to equality and the penalization of women for their contribution to humanity. Equality and difference cannot exist the one without the other, nor can either be sacrificed to the other. If we sacrifice equality on the altar of difference, we go back to the reactionary positions of traditional societies, and if we sacrifice the difference between the sexes on the altar of equality, we sterilize women, deprive them of their identity, and sterilize humanity.

TN: A new generation of women is being born in Bangladesh. On March 8, last year, they celebrated Women's Day by marching through Dacca chanting "It's my body; it's my decision." I had adopted this slogan in my own texts, and I felt less isolated. All over the world women are assigned to reproduction. In the Third World, governments decide whether or not they must be sterilized and whether they may have one child or two. Women are used in Western countries too. They are used in all social systems, by all government and all states. This dictatorship over women must be abolished. It is up to them to decide whether or not they have abortions, how many children they have, and with whom they have them.

AF: "Our bodies belong to us" was one of the first assertions to be made by the Women's Movement in France in the 1970s, and it is a precondition for our liberation. Later, on October 6, 1979, we marched to demand the renewal of the Veil law and the reimbursement of the costs of abortion,[4] with a banner on which I insisted on writing "The uterus belongs to women, the factories belong to the workers, the production of living beings belongs to us." The slogan led to a lot of polemics, and yet it is up to women to produce, or create, living beings.

The ancestral duty to procreate that churches and states have forced upon us for thousands of years now has to be transformed into the right to procreate. There will be no justice and no freedom for women until procreation is enshrined in law. The universal right, not a duty or a prescription but the affirmative right—and the right to abortion is obviously part of it—of all women in the world to procreation and full control over their own bodies.

16. Homage to Serge Leclaire

October 23, 1994

Serge Leclaire, my friend.

Someone said to me recently that there are no friends in politics. Are there any friends in psychoanalysis? In my case, there was one friend: you. From the very beginning, you honored me with your friendship, and I was as proud of it as I was intimidated by it. Thanks to your good offices I very quickly accepted the risks and the pleasures involved, without ever becoming accustomed to them. And today, I thank Geneviève Leclaire, who has done me the honor of inviting me to talk about you here.

I met you as you were going from one bank to the other, going against writing (*à contre-écriture*), swimming with the tide of history from the right bank to the left. For me it was a few days before I left for China, for Peking, for the first time, a few days before my daughter's eleventh birthday and at the end of a seven-year analysis with Lacan. I felt as though I were a woman in parentheses, between West and East, between mother and daughter.

I came to you with a demand for work that was imprecise, undecided, and perhaps undecidable. You almost immediately skewed the deference, displaced the respect, subverted the place of the master, and abolished the analytic generations in order to establish a reciprocity between us, to make me your partner, to make yourself my contemporary. Neither analyst nor father, neither brother nor son. The scene between us was neither analytic nor incestuous. Instead, informed by your analytic history and oriented by my political history, the relationship between the man that you were and the woman that I am, between you and me, similar but nonidentical, was one of equality within the differential dissymmetry that concerned us. It was, as we desired it to be, a relationship of parity.

There was little resemblance between us. You were born in the North, and you were a solid bourgeois. Your voice was poised, chocolaty, unctuous, even. Your discourse was slow and composed. We had little in common, except perhaps our small stature. We remained small.

I recognized in you the primal friend, the one I had known before we first met: the little boy I had known when I was three reappeared in my life a grown man, just as I was a grown woman; we met in our maturity. From the very start you joined me in the parenthesis between father and son in order to free yourself from some secret that was weighing on your man's heart.

We turned the primal ground between us—childhood—into a time that existed before the written word or, rather, into a writing that existed before writing, into an undeciphered writing like Linear A. Through what we shared we practiced friendship, friendship as experience.

Our common objective was to take over, fulfill a promise, and work toward the future. The object of our (unconscious) work was our ongoing invention or what I would now call the democratic personality.

Nothing was agreed between us, nothing was familiar, nothing was fixed, nothing was natural. We never shook hands, never called one another. We were just there, simply, quietly there together, facing each other, in the joy and the smile of one another's presence. We used to meet in gardens, in paradise. I loved your house in the mountains, and you loved my houses in other places.

But while you liked to welcome and receive, perhaps you liked coming and going even better. You liked coming to my home, for example, and presumably to the homes of others as well. You liked me to invite you, and when I forgot to do so for too long you would remind me: "I'd love to pop over for a few days." You would turn up, cheerful, in good form, with almost no luggage, no phobias, ready for anything. Everything was to your liking: the water, the air, indoors, outdoors, the gardens, the kitchen. You would make yourself at home, frisk about and purr, half-dog and half-cat. And we talked a lot. A lot.

Childhood smiled at us in our respective homes, which we often exchanged, like a promise that could finally be kept. We were attentive to each other, accepting and understanding. It's simple: we got on well. There was a bond between us, a space that was incurably fresh and innocent. Before and beyond envy and hate, before and beyond sexuality and transference.

Love between a man and a woman, between two men or between two women is difficult but possible. Friendship between two men is normal; friendship between two women has been decreed impossible. But friendship between a man and a woman is suspect, as though it were always a matter of frustrated love, as though the beast were always prowling in the jungle. It is a truism to say that friendship (amitié), which should be written as âmitié with a circumflex accent, true âmitié comes from the soul (âme), and many still hold the view that women have no soul. But you were one of the few men, the precious few, who have known from birth, naively and natively, that women do have souls. What we had was, precisely, that state of the soul, a friendship that was gracious and fervent, light and dense, joyous and thoughtful, idle and curious, episodic and constant, dispassionate and sexed, blossoming and reserved, primal and definitive, elective and nonexcluding, voluble and studious, open and faithful, nonexclusive, sharing, and loyal, frank and straightforward. In a word, and to use our respective and allotted signifiers, our friendship was living and thinking.

When we were together, we let each other be. We had, each of us in our own right, a taste for escapades, a sense of escape, an ability to break ranks, to set off in the opposite direction from where the killers of hope were lying in wait for us. It was hard to shut us up in the fortress of dogma, in the prison of ideologies, or to force us to wander endlessly in the labyrinth of libertinage. We had both survived, come though the persecutions and the bombardments of war and Nazism. Perhaps conjugating endurance and humility was all we had to do in order to escape.

We confided in each other, told each other our secrets, but never those of others; we were never complicit, never waged war on anyone. We would meet for, never against.

You would discreetly evoke the youthful love you felt for Geneviève; after more than twenty years you were still astonished at her youthfulness.

I never saw you out of your mind. Which means that you were not afraid. I never saw you act in a cowardly fashion. You had decided once and for all to trust a woman who was your friend, to trust her judgment, to trust her choices, to trust her. That took courage, and I was proud of you. You committed yourself and, at my side, you crossed so many fields of tittle-tattle as though they were so many minefields, never stepping into a calumny, a prejudice, or a what-will-people-say. A cautious adventurer, and one who was too aware of the foundational value of the forbidden to accept any prohibition or intimidation, you rejoiced at the fact that I could make my dreams come true and approved of my moments of madness because you thought them wise, right down to the most recent one, in May, and I loved your moments of madness, loved your enthusiasms, and, always, your new projects.

We did not prevent each another from doing anything, forbade each other nothing. On each other's behalf we took the risk of adopting an open-minded attitude toward the adventure of being a free man and a free woman. We loved our projects, even when they were not joint projects, because we knew that they would—would have to—come together in a place and a time to come, a place and a time of greater maturity. We respected the legitimate, creative transgression that honors what conservatives of all parties would like to keep foreclosed. We called for this liberation, this extension of democracy, with all our work, with all our might, with all our heart.

You left us on August 8 of this year, just as my mother did six years ago.

We had plans: America, New York, Los Angeles . . . You were going to come to my island between the sea and the sky in August. In September you were to come to Strasbourg, your city, with its Babel-Parliament, to plunge head first into the swimming pool of a Europe in movement(s), to mix with all those serious and committed members of the European Parliament who were intent on trying to prevent wars and to promote justice.

This week, scarcely two days ago in Vienna, we celebrated both Austria's accession to the union and the birth of a little girl in Sweden, the Sweden where Taslima Nasrin, a woman who rebels against fundamentalisms, has found some freedom once again. That little girl, the first to be born in the history of the world—this is an event, an advent—is called Real Democracy, or parity-based democracy. For the first time in any state institution, there are as many women as there are men to pass laws and to work for the future of the human species. It sounds unlikely, but it is true. And you had something to do with it.

What your Tbilisi text announced in premonitory fashion was already visible in Cairo: women are the beating heart of the movement of history.[1] They are central to it and the source of its courage.

You had something to do with it. The history of life goes on, and I know that tomorrow I will invite you, as I invited you yesterday, to share, in my heart and in my consciousness, some of the adventures in which I shall be involved.

Yesterday when, with you, I was thinking about today, I received the latest book by our philosopher friend, *Politics of Friendship*. I have not had time to read more than the epigraph, which is taken from Cicero (*De amicitia*). Allow me to address it to you:

"Henceforth, even the absent are present and—more difficult to say—the dead are alive . . . "[2]

17. How to Democratize Psychoanalysis?

October 24, 1994

PASSAGES: What gave you the idea of setting up the research group known as Psychanalyse et Politique as soon as the Women's Liberation Movement was born?

ANTOINETTE FOUQUE: You probably don't know this, because it has been forgotten, but when the Women's Movement first began, most of the women involved, and especially those who called themselves feminists, would have nothing to do with psychoanalysis. In their view Freud was just a horrible male chauvinist.

As I have often said, the ideology of masculinity that was holding back the psychoanalytic revolution was not enough to make me reject such an instrument of knowledge, still less to use a feminist counterideology to fight it. Psychanalyse et Politique was my attempt to understand the unconscious element in political commitment and the political element in psychoanalysis, in institutions, but also in theory.[1]

I asserted, right from the beginning of our Movement, that there is not only the phallus, that this "only" (ne ... que/noeud ... queue) was imperialistic and dangerous for women,[2] that this fixation on the phallic phase, this feminism, kept them in a state of pregenital immaturity, deprived them of their genitality. Feminism was (is) clinging to ante-oedipal positions, often with a lot of hatred for the father on the pretext of the struggle against patriarchy; it clings to the father as an authority who has to be challenged and not as a symbolic function that has to be introjected. It is a regressive, anti-establishment, illusory, and infantile position; as I used to say at the time, feminism is, to parody the famous slogan, the infantile disorder of the MLF.[3] Rejecting the illusion that we will one day have the phallus is not a loss but a differentiation. The phallic stage is not the final stage for women. It is possible to surpass it, and its surpassing really is inscribed in the body of every woman: this is what I call the *uterine stage.* Lacan derives this symbol—the phallus—from Freud's theory, but he fetishizes it: he turns the One into the Only One and he puts Freud's proposition "there is only one libido, and it is phallic" in an absolutist position.

PASSAGES: How did your work with Psychanalyse et Politique begin?

AF: In the 1970s we set off to find a *libido 2,* the "2" being simply a plural, the first figure that comes after "1." I now tend to refer to this libido as the *female libido* or *uterine libido.* There is the one, a phallic function, a "Name of the Father." There is also the two, a postphallic genital stage for women. I later spoke, in this connection, of a *revolution of the symbolic.*

Why has this phallic function found itself in an imperialist position, an absolutist position? For a little boy, it is the penis, or even the phallus, that allows him to distance himself, to differentiate himself, from the body in which he was a parasite, from the body that fed him and to which he remains in a state of extreme subjugation and dependency. The boy's first relationship, with his mother, is heterosexual, and his homosexual relationship with his father is already caught up in a secondary process that represses the body. In contrast, a girl's first relationship is homosexual; her first love-body is that of a woman; her homosexuality is *native, primary.*

Given that we women are "natively" homosexed, a failure to take into account this first relationship, which is the land of our birth, condemns us to an oral conflict, with all the hysterical or even schizophrenic sequences that implies. This native land is usually simply foreclosed as a space for withdrawal, a dark room, a shadowy room that makes women frightened of themselves, frightened of the other who is their likeness, and frightened at the same time of difference.

Bringing to light the girl's relationship with the other woman, that is, the daughter's relationship with her mother, with the woman part of her mother, with the part of her that is not subservient to the patriarchal system, that is not assigned to the mother-function, means abolishing the *foreclosure of the body of the mother* (equivalent to Lacan's formula the "foreclosure of the Name of the Father"). "Body of the mother" is a symbolic function: we are not talking about the real body or about the uterus as biological organ; we are talking about a relationship with a body, a land, a place of birth, an inscribed trace, the relationship between a daughter, or even a son, and the mother's body.

In order to make himself independent of the phantasm of maternal omnipotence, which has caused him to suffer, the boy uses the phallus to bar it. The girl does not have that bar to cling to so as to assert a difference; caught in her mother's grip, she is, or so they say, sucked into psychosis, or into what they call a defective or inadequate relationship with the mother. I don't want to describe this relationship either as inadequate (Grunberger) or as devastating (Lacan).[4] But it is a fact that oral conflict is devastating, that it is itself already a result of the primacy of the phallus and of the refusal to articulate the same-sex relationship of a woman who gives birth to a daughter.

The rediscovery of a prehistory of women's bodies should result in the elaboration of a history and a society that has at last been genitalized in a postphallic history and society. What was once a prehistory will become a posthistory with respect to the phallic stranglehold that restricts women's psychosexual maturation in both the "beneath" and the "beyond."

Women's *native homosexuality* is the first "room of our own," a place where we can develop a language, a thought, a body, and a life of our own; yes, it is narcissistic, but it is also topographic, dynamic, a- and postphallic; it is a structuring homosexuality that is vital to any becoming-woman; it is a homosexuality that has nothing, or very little, to do with lesbianism, which refers to a secondary homosexuality constructed on the basis of an identification with the father. On the contrary, I am talking about a *primary homosexuality* that takes priority in the elaboration of self-knowledge. It has priority and it is permanent; it is the only place from which we can assume the surpassing of the relationship between the *filse*, the girl-son (a daughter legitimized by the father) and the Father.[5] This is Antigone's only way out of the oedipal stage, the only escape from being no more than a stick for her father's blind old age, the last pillar of the patriarchy that is established more than anything else by the Father/Girl-Son couple under the double headings of hysteria and feminism.

PASSAGES: So how can we take the psychoanalytic statement "there is only one libido and it is phallic" and think it differently?

AF: There are two sexes. There are men and there are women. There is a phallic libido and there is also, necessarily, a libido specific to women. You have only to listen to women talking to feel the way they suffer because they have not been listened to by theory and therefore cannot be received into the symbolic order as women. What women say is regarded as inarticulate, inarticulable, null and void; they are condemned to silence or mutism.

I have been working on what, for want of a better term, I am provisionally calling *uterine libido* for twenty-five years.[6] I think the uterus is a space that is not at all outside the psyche. Women are speaking, thinking beings; gestation is a cultural and human act that is related to the unconscious, to speech, and to thought.

Perhaps the reason analytic theory cannot advance is that it is, like all institutions, in the hands of men who are shut up inside the monarchic, narcissistic bastion. The limits of this oedipal and all-phallic hell are a double foreclosure; "before," at the stage at which we ourselves are created or, in other words, intrauterine life, the fetuses we once were, and "beyond," in the procreative capacity to generate and to have descendents; a double foreclosure, of the uterine within the procreated beings that we are, and of the uterine beyond the oedipal and the phallic as the capacity to procreate. I think that we have not advanced very far in this direction, probably because men do not have, in their bodies, this capacity for procreation, the capacity to relive the experience of bringing into the world in the active mode. That creates a frustration for them, a *uterus envy* that cannot, it seems to me, be overcome; they do not want to, they cannot regard gestation as a psychic moment because they have no experience of it. If they could recognize their uterus envy, it could be sublimated into gratitude. The vital link with the matricial, with the maternal, could be restored, and the anamnesis of what has been foreclosed could be abolished. We could then begin to think about genealogy.

The main envy that haunts psychoanalysis is not penis envy (where women are concerned), which I do contest, but uterus envy, an underlying and more powerful force. There really is a universal obsession with controlling motherhood, procreation, and lineage, and it is tied up with an inability, on men's part, to come to terms with that production and the idea that it escapes their control.

PASSAGES: How do you see psychoanalysis evolving today?

AF: I still wonder how women psychoanalysts in particular can function with the idea that there is only one libido and that it is phallic. And I regret the fact that the Lacanians (or Lacanists) are fixated on this dogma in a fetishistic way, because the work I did with Lacan did give rise to something to do with women, with certain formulations such as "Woman is not all," she is not caught up entirely in the phallic, and "supplementary jouissance," which introduces something like a "beyond the phallus." Lacan himself was always on the lookout for anything that could help him advance. As for women psychoanalysts, I think that, in both their practice and their clinical work, they know much more than they say in their theoretical texts; much more about women's *native homosexuality* and the *uterine libido*. But we are just beginning to come across a few articles here and there that are based on these concepts. We are slowly making progress.

Psychoanalysis must be democratized and must move from the one and the mono to the two. Democracy means acceptance of the other. It must elaborate a theory of genitality for each of the sexes, and that theory must take into account the constitution of "female" genitality—and of male genitality.

There are two sexes, but when the modality of the two is dual, dualist, and warlike, it is regressive, sending us back toward the anal and the pregenital; if we turn to genitality, the modality of the two is *coupling,* which provides the paradigm of procreation and ethics.

Serge Leclaire and I worked together on what I now call the *democratic personality,* which recognizes and welcomes the existence of the other. The seminar that we planned to hold at the École Freudienne in 1977, and which we were barred from holding there, was to have dealt with the two; the outcome was an ironic response in the form of a little text entitled "Pas de deux"![7] In 1979, in "Un soulèvement de questions" (A raising of questions), a report from Tbilisi, Serge Leclaire explained clearly how the dogma of the phallic-whole could be subverted.[8] He showed what the driving force behind the psychoanalytic movement might be and, commenting on our work with Psychanalyse et Politique, declared that "[these women] have at last given the other a place that escapes all reductionism: *women* and, by the same token, men."[9]

Unfortunately, all monisms bear within them the seeds of their fundamentalisms, and phallic monism is no different from any other monism. Perhaps Freud only analyzed religion in order to reinstate male monism all the more firmly. That is the only real danger with psychoanalysis. The pope can now cite Malraux: "The twenty-first century will be religious, or it will not be." I prefer to think that the twenty-first century will be democratic.

18. Democracy and Its Discontents

January 21, 1995

Almost seventy years ago, it occurred to Freud that religion is "like the obsessional neurosis of children" and that its roots lie in a nostalgic and powerful need for "the protection . . . provided by the father." He contrasts religious fiction with a "sense of reality" and with trust in rationality and a science that is imperfect but in movement and making progress.[1]

After fourteen years of Socialist government, which I have described elsewhere as the republic of sons, the reemergence—via the conservative candidate (Jacques Chirac) who seems best placed to win the presidential election—of "the revenge of God" and the image of the Father is indicative of a psychological regression and reactionary political turn on the part of our compatriots.[2] And this regression-reaction has a direct effect on the preconditions for the permanent democratization that is needed in our country and in any modern state in its national, European, and global identity.

Democracy is ailing, here and elsewhere, because it has become trapped in monocratic dogmas and oligarchic behaviors. Democracy is ailing because the republic of sons has been unable to evolve into an adult democracy of men and women; it has been trapped in a narcissistic posture where it can only be overtaken, as it slides into an essential depression, by the politics of the Father. Whoever fails to advance retreats. The characteristic feature of narcissistic logic is its self-contemplation, its indifference to anything other, its adolescent perversity, its sterility, and its exclusivity (socialism, like feminism, is one of democracy's adolescent stages).

The left has not only forgotten the struggles and the movements of the living forces that brought it to power; in the name of an equality that is as abstract as it is hollow it has also forgotten to think through the differences between classes, races, and sexes; these did not figure in its self-speculative mirror for self-admiration. The left has been incapable of foreseeing that, before the three great forces that have been excluded from its reign return in the form of protest demonstrations, the old demon and its horror of the other will seize its turf. Socialism will have been no more than a second conservatism, in the same way that Christianity is no more than a second monotheism. And the protest movement, together with the reforms that have come in its wake over the last twenty-five years, will end in a Vatican-inspired counter-reformation that is in fact a truly conservative reformation. Does not the removal of the bishop of Evreux, which has been announced by the anti-abortion commandos,[3] recall the revocation of the Edict of Nantes (just as the rise of Islamic fundamentalism in Algeria was announced by the introduction of the Family Code in 1984)?[4]

When religion takes over politics, and when moral values take over religion, these moves encourage discrimination, exclusion, and the most scandalous of the old orders. The pronatalist nationalist's fear of the other reproduces the identitarian obsessions that see beings who are different in terms of their class, culture, or sex, as dangerous forces that will undermine the virile, national, and aristocratic ego. Athenian democracy excluded women, metics (resident aliens), and slaves. Thanks to its reference to a universal man, modern democracy has brought about the repression of the workers and the colonized, and the introduction of apartheid for women.

A power that was already gynophobic and heterophobic (is it necessary to recall that fewer than 6 percent of the deputies in the National Assembly are women and that the political class is almost exclusively cast in the same mold?) has become so "demophobic" that it describes as "populists" those who are not afraid of the people and accuses them of putting our democracy at risk, only to adopt their proposals a few months later.[5] Is it really populism that threatens our democracy, or is it this "demophobia" and its rejection of the other? Is it populism that poses the real threat, or is it a fundamentalism that used to crawl on its knees but is now riding high? De Villiers, Pasqua,[6] and the Vatican are all fighting for the values of the day before yesterday, while the Socialist shepherd,[7] Narcissus and Endymion, is in a state of self-hypnosis.

Democracy is ailing because it has not made sufficient progress, because it has not familiarized itself with analytic thought, because it has been unable to develop a "democratic personality," that is, a personality capable of otherness. Like the proletariat, which is etymologically "that which procreates," women can and must contribute the specificity of their talents and their own genius to politics. The process of democratization, which has to be modeled on coupling, insists that we cannot have the (male) one without the (female) one.

Before we administer murderous miracle cures, we have to make an etiological diagnosis of democracy's discontents. To rid ourselves of the symbolic handicap of excluding young people, immigrants, and women, we require new, forceful analyses and propositions that will allow us to wage a real fight against unemployment and exclusion, that will enable us to establish real parity between men and women and between civil society and political parties.

It is our present and pressing duty to bring about the advent of democracy. Democrats of all countries, let us wake up and unite!

19. Tomorrow, Parity

March 8, 1995

International Women's Day takes on its full historical meaning today if we recall that it was proposed and instituted by Clara Zetkin in this very place in 1910.

From the beginning of the century, this celebration has punctuated critical and often tragic moments of our history: in 1914 and 1915 in France, in Germany, in Oslo women demonstrated against the war; in 1917, in Petrograd, against czarism; starting in 1937, in Spain, in Italy, and in Ravensbrück in 1945 against fascism; in 1974, in Saigon, against the American occupation. During the 1970s, taking advantage of the women's liberation movements in the West, International Women's Day established a tradition of affirming our rights, and it became, de facto, as much a day of protest against the inequalities that remain as a day of ever stronger determination to advance our cause. Exactly twenty years ago, I celebrated this day in Beijing with some ten comrades from the MLF and my daughter,[1] who had just turned eleven. We knew nothing of the barbarity of the so-called cultural revolution that was devastating the country, all the less so given that, for an entire day, we had been able to engage in dialogue with Chinese women who had already turned, with all their needs and all their intelligence, toward democracy.

I could evoke every March 8, year after year. They were not all equally flamboyant. But each one has marked a stage of consciousness, of strategies and struggles for thousands of women, showing solidarity with millions of others in the world. Our primordial rights to freedom over our bodies, equality in the familial, socioeconomic, and political spheres—rights that are questioned, even endangered, every day—have often been put forward in the streets on March 8, proclaimed in assemblies, so they could be won and then written into law.

On March 8, 1979, we were in Tehran, demonstrating with fifty thousand women against the wearing of the headscarf imposed by Khomeini. The documentary film we made there, *The Liberation Movement of Iranian Women, Year Zero*, attests that, even if our Iranian sisters have since failed to gain their freedom, the forces of regression may still be unable to eradicate this embryo of liberation and permanently block women's birth to the sexual, economic, social, political, and symbolic independence for which they clamored with us in 1979. On March 8, 1980, we expressed our solidarity with the Irish women imprisoned at Armagh and we issued the Leningrad appeal in support of Tatiana Mamonova and the Russian women persecuted by the KGB.[2] On March 8, 1981, in a double gesture of protest and commitment, a twofold gesture that always conveys the urgency to denounce, to deconstruct, as well as the will to go forward and to create—on March 8, 1981, then, we issued "Cahiers de doléances contre la misogynie" (Registers of grievances against misogyny), as was done during the French Revolution, and we launched an appeal to vote for François Mitterrand, candidate for the French presidency, on the first ballot, even though we were not members of his party. In support of making March 8 a national holiday, starting in 1982, I had written a letter to the French president on December 3, 1981, saying in part:

> The acknowledgment by nation-states of March 8 as a symbol of women's struggles has so far been too narrowly restricted to popular democracies, although the day is celebrated throughout the world. It would be right and proper for the French government to make March 8 a legal paid holiday, thus becoming the first in Europe to connect the initiative and action of a majority of citizens—women, viewed as a minority because they are female citizens—with a decision on the part of the state.

In this way the Socialist government would honor the women who have made a major contribution this year to the victory of the left, just as, in 1947, a left-wing government honored the workers' struggle by acknowledging May 1 as a day for demonstrations and a holiday for workers.

Three days later, François Mitterrand's answer, "nice, but difficult," had the effect of granting the easiest part of my proposal: March 8 was declared a "national day," although not a "paid holiday." And while I declined the overly selective invitation to attend an event at the Élysée Palace along with three hundred other women, all very officially chosen, we expressed ourselves in full force: on March 6, in the main amphitheater of the Sorbonne, we held the first Estates General of Women from All Nations Against Misogyny, with Nawal El Saadawi from Egypt, Eva Forest from Spain, Maria de Lourdes Pintasilgo, a former prime minister of Portugal, Domitilia Banios de Chungara from Bolivia, Fetouma Ouzegane from Algeria, Kate Millett from the United States, Kumari Gawardena from Sri Lanka, Alla Sariban from Russia, Cheryl Bernard and Edith Schlafer, representing Amnesty for Women, from Austria, and many others. On March 7, at the Cirque d'Hiver in Paris, first-rate women athletes and singers gathered for a splendid party. And on Monday, March 8, there were twelve thousand of us from all parts of France in the streets in Paris, twelve thousand of us who had gone on strike in order to demonstrate. Our weekly newspaper, *Des femmes en mouvements hebdo*, bears witness to this event, opposing the obdurate censorship and systematic misinformation by the media, which preferred to cover March 8 in countries other than our own and to focus on oppressive situations for women elsewhere rather than mention the strength of determined women who came from everywhere to gather here in a land of freedom.

On March 8, 1989, in the spirit of the bicentennial of the French Revolution, we organized other Estates General of Women after reissuing the *Cahiers de doléances des femmes en 1789*. For several years I served as international president of the San Diego Women's International Center, which granted a Living Legacy Award every year. Consequently, I wanted to make March 8, 1990, a day to express collective gratitude by celebrating women who had been exceptional, each in her own field. Coming from virtually all over the globe, they embodied the now indelible existence of women who are at the forefront of progress in the democratic, legal, and humanistic as well as the humanitarian, artistic, and athletic domains. Pioneers in the advances of humankind in their countries—that is, in the world—included Doïna Cornea from Romania, Ela Bhatt from India, Charlotte Perriand from France, Elena Bonner from what was then the U.S.S.R., Yvonne Choquet-Bruhat from France, Khunying Kanitha Wichiencharoen from Thailand, Jeannie Longo from France, Albertina Sisulu from South Africa, and so many others stood as so many beacons casting light on a planet still very dark in the eyes of young girls and women.

This survey, too long yet incomplete, is a way of indicating that each March 8 we faithfully observe this historical occasion, one in which we shall certainly never stop participating; furthermore, we are now convinced that its future depends to a great extent on our determination to transform it so that it can finally take on a human face, a just and worthy direction and meaning.

Today, March 8, 1995, it is particularly meaningful to me to be in Copenhagen as a French woman, a European democrat, and a world citizen, as well as a militant in our movement and a deputy in the European parliament, serving as vice chair of the Committee on Women's Rights.

In 1992, the last time France held the presidency of the European Union during his term of office, François Mitterrand proposed that a world summit on social development be held to "renew our reflection" and "emphasize the human dimension of reality," thus expressing his attachment to a European model of development as theorized by President Delors in his white paper.[3] Mitterrand was no doubt aware that the clause spelling out the right of all employees and workers to social welfare and respect for their status could exert a democratizing influence on the many countries in transition.

But once this summit set out its three primary goals, fighting poverty, building solidarity, and creating jobs, something that was clearly expressed in the fifth of the ten commitments of the draft common statement against poverty that will be submitted to the heads of states and governments in three days quickly became self-evident: what was at stake was "respect for human dignity and improvement of the status of women in society."

Indeed, as soon as we mobilize ourselves to fight poverty at the global level, we again discover, as we did at the Rio World Conference on the Environment in 1992, at the Vienna Conference on Human Rights in 1993, at the Cairo Conference on Population and Development in 1994, that, regretfully, women are the bruised heart of the human species, but that also, through an amazing reversal of the present disorder, they are on their way to becoming the pulsing heart of a just and sustainable development everywhere in the world.

THE PRINCIPLES

If we look at the major international texts, we can say that the condition of women in the world has changed considerably in the course of the last few decades.

The Charter of the United Nations, drawn up in 1945 just after World War II in order to promote and defend human rights, "the dignity and worth of the human person," is the first international text to proclaim equality between men and women. The UN Universal Declaration of Human Rights, adopted December 10, 1948, came next to declare that "all human beings are born free and equal in dignity and in rights," and this "without distinction of any kind, such as race, colour, sex, language, religion, political or other opinion, national or social origin, property, birth or other status."[4] International agreements concerning civil and political rights, as well as economic, social and cultural rights, strengthen these principles of nondiscrimination and equality for all in the eyes of the law. The Geneva Conventions and their additional protocols provide for the protection of the civilian population in war time and stipulate that "women shall be especially protected against any attack on their honour, in particular against rape, enforced prostitution, or any form of indecent assault."[5]

In 1975, under pressure from international women's liberation movements, the UN General Assembly decided to focus attention on obstacles to equality. It declared the International Women's Year, highlighted in June by the 1975 World Conference held in Mexico City, the first conference on women ever organized on a worldwide scale. A plan of action was adopted proposing that the "United Nations Decade for Women: Equality, Development and Peace" be proclaimed in all countries; this was followed in 1980 by a conference in Copenhagen, and five years later by a conference in Nairobi that set forth "Forward-Looking Strategies" for action between 1985 and 2000. The resolution on future prospects and equality of opportunity emphasized not only the need for legal measures to ensure equality of treatment between men and women but also the importance of dealing with existing inequalities. The Development Fund for Women (UNIFEM), designed to finance new types of activities in the interest of women, and the International Research and Training Institute for the Advancement of Women (UN-INSTRAW) were created in 1976.

Another important step took place in 1979 when the UN adopted the "Convention on the Elimination of All Forms of Discrimination Against

Women," signed in March 1980 and effective as of September 1981. This major text reminds us that "discrimination against women violates the principles of equality of rights and respect for human dignity, is an obstacle to the participation of women, on equal terms with men, in the political, social, economic and cultural life of their countries," and that it "makes more difficult the full development of the potentialities of women in the service of their countries and of humanity." Recognizing "the social significance of maternity," the convention states that "the role of women in procreation should not be a basis for discrimination."[6]

Active throughout the world, nongovernmental organizations continue to spur the reflection of the United Nations, urging the organization to take action in favor of women. At each conference NGOs show their fighting spirit and appear as the creative forces driving these international summits. Thus, in June 1992, during the Conference on Environment and Development held in Rio,[7] more than four hundred NGOs led a *Planeta femea* (a women's tent in the alternative Global Forum); they made it clear that the dominant model of development constituted a threat not only to the planet but also to the human species, for which women feel responsible, through procreation and child rearing. This gave me the opportunity to develop a theme to which I am deeply attached, the idea that the first environment of the human species is the maternal body, and we all know to what extent physical or psychic aggression toward the child bearer can be harmful to the child-to-be.

In 1993 the rights of human beings were more than ever under threat. In February, to address the systematic rapes, tortures, and practices of "ethnic purification" carried out in the former Yugoslavia, the UN Security Council voted to create a special court to rule on war crimes and crimes against humanity. This was the first time the council was led to create a jurisdiction similar to the Nuremberg and Tokyo courts set up to judge World War II criminals. In June the World Conference on Human Rights supported measures taken "to ensure the effective protection and promotion of human rights of the girl child" and urged the states "to remove customs and practices which discriminate against and cause harm to the girl child" (II, 49). In an earlier declaration the conference asserted that "the human rights of women and girls are an inalienable, integral and indivisible part of universal human rights" (I, 18).[8]

In December 1993 the General Assembly adopted a Declaration on the Elimination of Violence Against Women, asking for "the universal application to women of the rights and principles with regard to equality, security, liberty, integrity and dignity of all human beings."[9] On the occasion of the Day of Human Rights, Mr. Ibrahima Fall,[10] then UN under-secretary general for human rights, appealed for a five-point plan of action that would support the various conventions that had been ratified, in particular the Convention on the Elimination of All Forms of Discrimination Against Women, and that would integrate women's rights "in all activities related to human rights." The plan was adopted in March 1994. The Commission on Human Rights then decided to appoint Mrs. Radhika Coomaraswamy from Sri Lanka for a three-year period as a "special spokesperson to report on the question of violence against women, including its causes and consequences."

In May 1994 the World Health Organization (WHO), which has condemned the practice of female genital mutilation since 1982, "urge[d] all member states to establish national policies and programmes level that will effectively, and with legal instruments, abolish female genital mutilation."[11] The High Committee for Refugees considers that women who risk persecution for opposing the practice of such mutilations upon themselves or their daughters are entitled to the provisions of the 1951 convention regarding the status of refugees if they are not protected by their governments.

In September 1994 the International Conference on Population and Development held in Cairo made it possible not only to speak openly about the condition of women in the world but also to assert that their liberation has taken on a universal dimension. The twenty-year Programme of Action aims at "advancing gender equality and equity[12] and the empowerment of women, and the elimination of all kinds of violence against women, and ensuring women's ability to control their own fertility."[13] The determining role of women in development was unanimously and clearly emphasized for the first time. Summing up the overall consensus, Nafis Sadik of Pakistan, general secretary of the conference and executive director of the United Nations Population Fund (UNFPA), suggested that the twenty-year program might well change the world.

EUROPE, A SOCIAL MODEL

Today, March 8, 1995, we are here both to prepare the World Conference on Women in Beijing and to celebrate Europe, since Denmark is now part of the European Union. This is why I would like also to speak to you about the European model of equality between men and women, which is still poorly implemented, no doubt, but can help us to progress.

From the moment of its creation in 1949, the Council of Europe has expressed its interest in "safeguarding and realizing the ideals and principles which are [the] common heritage" of the member states, in order to lay down the basis for a "genuine democracy."[14] The Convention for the Protection of Human Rights and Fundamental Freedoms, drafted in 1950, expressly guarantees to women, equal to men, the use of rights and liberties "without discrimination on any ground such as sex, race, colour, language, religion, political or other opinion" (article 14).[15] Since then numerous recommendations, declarations, and conferences have aimed at or resulted in removing obstacles to equality between the sexes and finding solutions for cases of inequality. This commitment on the part of the Council of Europe has been reinforced by the United Nations Decade for Women. Thus, in 1981, equality became a guiding principle for intergovernmental action. In a symbolic and entirely political way, the Steering Committee for Equality Between Women and Men (CDEG) has become part of the section of the council devoted to democracy, freedom, and fundamental human rights.

The European Union proposes a social model benefiting women globally. The few pages on this topic in Jacques Delors's white paper offer a synthesis of the policy in favor of equal salaries for men and women, a policy initiated as early as 1957 by the Treaty of Rome, twenty-two years before the UN Convention. This model is the common foundation for the various nation-states that make up the Union. Since then the construction of Europe has kept pushing this principle of equality forward by means of directives on equal pay for men and women (1975), equal treatment of men and women in employment (1976), and equal treatment of men and women in statutory schemes of social security (1979). In 1992 we adopted a code of practice on measures to combat sexual harassment (followed in France, for instance, by a law against sexual harassment at work). In 1992 the social protocol of the Maastricht Treaty made it possible to implement "measures providing for specific advantages in order to make it easier for women to pursue a vocational activity or to prevent or compensate for disadvantages in their professional careers."[16]

Contraception is legal everywhere, although information remains insufficient, but the right to abortion is not granted in all European countries. It is still prohibited in Ireland and in Germany, and it remains precarious everywhere. Rape is called a crime in almost all European Union countries, except in Germany and Great Britain. Divorce through mutual consent is authorized everywhere, except in Greece and Ireland. In all European countries women are granted maternity leaves (but in Great Britain, in Belgium, and in

Spain,they do not receive their full salaries). In New York, during the last preparatory conference for this summit, Europe led the way in matters in defending social gains and equality of treatment. And, above all, Europe is the birthplace of parity, which I shall define provisionally as the political will to ensure equality at all decision-making levels. I shall say more about this shortly.

FRANCE, A LAND OF PARADOXES

Ever since the 1789 Revolution, France has declared itself the country of human rights, yet it is paradoxically the country that has shown the greatest resistance to the progress of women's rights. At this historical moment, when the issue of inequality between men and women is being raised, in our country too, in terms of parity, it may be helpful to recall briefly how—but also how slowly—our victories were won.

The right to knowledge had for a long time been denied girls. It was finally granted to them under the Third Republic, with Jules Ferry's legislation on elementary schools. And in 1924 girls were allowed to take the baccalaureate examination and thus have access to university-level studies.[17] Entrance to the *grandes écoles* was even more difficult to obtain.[18] The École Centrale was the first one to open its doors to women, in 1930,[19] and the École de l'Air the last one in 1978. Probably under the influence of the International Woman's Year in 1975, the law on education instituted compulsory coeducation in all state schools and, in 1989, the law on governing higher education asserted its mission of equality.

Work outside the home was virtually forbidden to women, for it had long been linked with prostitution. However, with the demand for labor produced by the industrial revolution in the nineteenth century, nearly half of all French women took on professional activities. Only since 1965 has a married woman been able to work without her husband's consent, and the requirement of equal pay for equal work did not appear in French law before 1970. In 1983 a law on professional equality attempted to improve a de facto situation of glaring inequality.

In politics the paths to equality for women have been particularly obstructed, even more in France than elsewhere. The Revolution of 1789 did not give women access to citizenship. Despite the enlightened proclamations of Condorcet and the courageous and genuinely revolutionary stance of Olympe de Gouges, the 1793 Constitution confirmed the exclusion of women, just as it maintained slavery. The Revolution of 1848 abolished the poll tax as a basis for suffrage, but did not grant any more political rights to women than it did to the insane; however, this new suffrage was—and sometimes still is—called universal. The Constitution of the Third Republic confirmed this exclusion of women from "universal" rights. Nevertheless, in every generation since the 1789 revolution women have come together and organized to claim the right to vote. Exemplary women, Olympe Rodrigues, Hubertine Auclert, Marthe Bray, Louise Weiss, and many others: six generations, 150 years of struggle. They showed tenacity, those women called suffragettes. In 1936, with the Popular Front, the French Parliament unanimously endorsed giving women the right to vote. We had to wait almost ten years more for the decree signed by General de Gaulle on April 21, 1944, just after World War II, which finally declared the right of women to vote and to be elected on the same terms as men.

Kept until 1938 in a state of "civil incapacity" by the Napoleonic Code, women obtained the right to freedom very late: their incipient legal emancipation has progressed more rapidly since 1970. Beginning that year, women shared parental authority; starting in 1973 a mother could transmit her nationality to her child. In 1975 divorce by mutual consent was granted, and in 1985 husband and wife became equals in matters of property management and child care.

Laws have progressed as a result of women's struggle for the right to control their own bodies. As early as 1968–69, in the Women's Movement, at the earliest meetings of the group Psychanalyse et Politique that I was leading,[20] the focus was on sexuality, and the question of rape as a specific form of violence appeared simultaneously with the question of the procreative independence of women and their control of their own fertility.[21] The work of the movement, as a whole and in its diversity, led to a wide mobilization, to numerous publications, to the first major women's demonstration when we demanded freedom to procreate ("No laws over our bodies," "Free and available abortion and contraception"), in 1971, and to the first day devoted to denouncing crimes against women, with a demonstration at the Mutualité in Paris in 1972.[22] The decriminalization of abortion, won in principle in 1975, was not passed definitively until 1979, after another powerful protest movement, and reimbursement of the cost of abortion by Social Security was granted only in 1982. In 1980, two years after the start of feminist struggles in the legal field,[23] the penal code registered women's demands and made rape a crime: on the same basis as homicide, it became a crime against the individual. The new 1992 code increased the penalty for rapists.

In 1989, echoing organizations that had been combating family violence for more than ten years, the secrétariat d'État chargé des droits des femmes (secretary of state in charge of women's rights) introduced a television campaign to this end. The following year, organizations were authorized to bring civil suits. The same year, following the adoption of European legislation on the subject, a law was passed punishing sexual harassment at work.

REALITY

Measured against international principles, egalitarian proclamations, and laws, the reality is quite different and quite bleak: women are the excluded among the excluded, the poor among the poor of the planet. Everywhere, no matter how poverty is assessed, the figures provided by experts reveal a tragic reality. 1,300,000,000 human beings are in a state of absolute poverty[24] (that means 1 human being out of 5); they lack resources to get adequate food or to meet basic needs in housing, health, and education. And of this 1,300,000,000 poor people, 70 percent, or nearly a billion, are women.[25] Two-thirds of the 990 million of those who are deprived of the right to education, and who will never have access to it, are women: a total of 660 million.[26] The latest report on human development has shown that, in developing countries, discrimination is found not only in education but in nutritional support and health care; according to the same report, statistics in forty-three countries reveal that the mortality rate of female children, from a few months old to age four, is clearly higher than the mortality rate of male children in the same age group.[27]

However, poverty and exclusion are still signs of women's survival, compared to the ongoing *gynocide* perpetrated against them. According to studies by Amartya Sen, a brilliant Harvard economist, women are being denied the very right to exist and to live. Sen's research led him to estimate that at least 100 million women are missing from the census of world populations.[28] One hundred million women have disappeared because they were women: 38 million in China, 30 million in India, and the other millions in the rest of Asia and Africa. These disappearances, referred to as a "demographic deficit," are mostly attributable to abortions, infanticides, malnutrition, selective health care, sexual mutilations, and pregnancies or deliveries performed under poor conditions.

The number of abortions of female embryos has increased quite markedly in China, in India, and in South Korea over the last fifteen years. In India today, there are only 927 women for every 1,000 men, in contrast to the developed countries, where there are more women than men.[29] Malnutrition and lack of proper care are the primary causes of death for young girls in India. UNICEF estimates at more than a million the number of very young girls who die every year, worldwide, because they are born female.

Every year 2 million young girls, that is five thousand a day, three every minute, are subjected to the torture of excision and infibulation. The operation takes about twenty minutes, which means that at this very moment, sixty young girls are being mutilated somewhere in Africa, in Asia, in the Middle East, and probably in Europe as well. In Sudan one out of three girls dies from infibulation. As for those who survive, 110 million of them suffer all their lives from severe injuries caused by these mutilations.

During the Cairo Conference on Population and Development in September 1994, the minister of family life in Egypt committed himself to prohibiting sexual mutilations, which concerns 80 to 90 percent of Egyptian women.[30] But I have just learned that in October, one month later, the Egyptian minister of health had a decree passed, not to prohibit these mutilations, as he had announced, but to have them performed in hospitals; he even listed the qualifying hospitals. This medical treatment may save human lives, but it will not stop the mutilation of women.

UN reports indicate that in India the dowry system is the cause of death for five thousand to nine thousand women a year; that one married woman out of three in developing countries reports that she has been beaten; and that one woman out of every two thousand, worldwide, has filed a complaint for rape.[31] Human trafficking, whether it concerns women, young girls, or young boys, takes place with impunity: slavery is rationalized as a form of international and domestic sex trade. Amnesty International reported that there were fifteen thousand cases of sale of a woman or a child in China in 1993,[32] but China is obviously not the only country at issue. It is no wonder that, in such a barbaric situation, surviving women are in an extreme state of destitution, while also in charge of procreation, of transmitting life through generations, even at the cost of their own lives.

In the armed conflicts that are devastating the world, specific acts of violence against women compound the horrors of war. The denunciation by feminist militants[33] and by many international missions of massive rapes and forced pregnancies in the former Yugoslavia did not prevent the programmatic use of such torture against women in Rwanda the following year.[34]

In Algeria, as in Iran and in Bangladesh, fundamentalist religions make women a privileged target. A particularly barbaric form of religious fundamentalism is devastating Algeria.[35] Subjected to intimidation, kidnapping, sequestration, rape, torture, exorcism, and murder, Algerian women are caught in a veritable misogynist delirium, a deadly madness. Bound to the Family Code,[36] which imposes upon them the status of minors and abandons them to forced marriages and brutal repudiations, they have been exposed since 1989 to assaults from armed groups. In January 1994 the Algerian Union of Democratic Women (RAFD), which brings together several organizations of women democrats, published a manifesto denouncing the situation:

> We speak of women who are subjected to persecution in daily life, powerless victims of barbaric attacks ranging from acid to fire, as well as whipping or sexual abuse, when it is not simply murder. . . . We speak, too, of the terrorized women living in villages or suburbs close to Algiers, who have been forced into seclusion by recent openly circulated propaganda leaflets to hide themselves away; they have no choice but to hide themselves away or wear the hijab, for fear of having their throats slit.

A more and more widespread Shiite practice known as a "marriage of pleasure" entails a "marriage" that lasts a few hours or a few months, according to the needs of the "madmen of God." In November 1994 Algerian television showed two young girls murdered and beheaded by alleged members of Islamist armed groups for refusing to submit to this violence. In February 1995 Laila Aslaoui, who came to the European Parliament to denounce the fate suffered by Algerian women, reported that 267 women had been murdered in this way. The association of Armed Islamist Groups (AIG) is multiplying threats against women whom its members deem "impious." In the name of sexual purification, religious barbarians are exorcizing imaginary devils, to the point of death. In The Female Devil, Hafsa Zinai Koudil,[37] an Algerian woman filmmaker, denounces an event that took place in the north of France one day in July: a nineteen-year-old woman died, victim of an exorcism session led by her brother along with the imam and the president of the Roubaix mosque.[38]

Nevertheless, women are also in the forefront of the battle. This very day, March 8, a "Tribunal Against Fundamentalism" is being held in Algiers, organized by the RAFD, which women from several countries are expected to attend. I take this opportunity to assure them once again of our complete solidarity and to warmly salute their courage and their determination.

When minute after minute, day after day, universally, the right to be born, the right to live, the right of very young girls, of girls and of women to exist in dignity is being violated, how can we still speak of freedom? When 500,000,000 women under Islamic law lack the right to inherit, how can we make equality a universal model? No wonder that under these conditions the perverse notion of equity tends to replace the principle of equality: it allows the nation-states that make up the group of 134 developing countries to try to avoid any reference to equality between the sexes—as the Muslim states do—along with all references to human rights, thus to the rights of women— as is the case for China and the other Asian countries that maintain traditional moral standards. The notion of equity constitutes a serious regression with respect to the principle of equality. Notwithstanding the decisions made at the Vienna Conference, the pressures exercised by these countries and the need for consensus have produced a dangerous coexistence between the notion of equity and the principle of equality in the preparatory texts for Copenhagen.[39] Under these conditions, it is almost impossible to insert even watered-down social provisions in commercial agreements.

The political representation of women in the world decreased from 15 percent in 1988 to 10 percent in June 1994. Many countries in Africa and Western Asia (for example, Djibouti, Mauritania, Kuwait) have no women in their parliaments. The Seychelles Islands and Europe have the highest percentages, for example Denmark (33 percent), Finland, Norway (39 percent), and—since September 1994—Sweden (41 percent), the first country to have a parity-based government, with an equal number of male and female ministers. France and Greece, where less than 6 percent of the members of parliament are women, bring up the rear among European countries on the road to political equality. The Parliament of South Africa that emerged from the first multiracial elections includes 25 percent women in the National Assembly, while women's representation in the United States comes to 11 percent. Very few of the 178 parliaments throughout the world are headed by women: only eighteen, or slightly over 10 percent.

In the economic realm, the same situation prevails everywhere. Where there is not apartheid, there is always powerful discrimination. In other words, where freedom and equality, as well as solidarity, are concerned, the condition of women in the world is closer to that of slaves or subhumans than it is to that of citizens. To demand that this change is a priority, not to say an urgency.

IN EUROPE

Europe, which tends to associate women to the model it proposes, as we have seen, nevertheless hardly protects against poverty. A recent report from the European Parliament[40] demonstrates the feminization of poverty in Europe. Women comprise the immense majority of the 55 million Europeans who are poor. They constitute 55 percent of chronically unemployed workers, 90 percent of single parents, and 80 percent of the elderly living on welfare. In the European Union they receive salaries that are inferior to men's by 30 percent and they are subjected to persisting discrimination in the areas of training, specialization, and promotion. They constitute 80 percent of the part-time work force.

The EU is torn apart by the imbalance between North and South and between East and West. The situation is getting worse in the South. Handicaps accumulate—being from the South, being young, being a woman—and multiply. In Spain, for example, the unemployment rate for both sexes is the highest in the Union; the rate for women under twenty-five comes to 42 percent, the European record: a sign of future poverty and exclusion. In the East as in the West, the same logic of profits requires that women from the former DDR obtain a certificate of sterilization to get a job,[41] while in France a pronatalist policy is promoted so that women will have more children and give up their jobs. And much more could be said about European countries still not part of the Union, where women who are traditionally vulnerable are literally devastated by the cataclysmic effects of the end of Communism.

Still, according to all observers, despite the widespread unemployment that is their fate and despite their crushing poverty, women are organizing so that democracy may come into being.

IN FRANCE

I ought to list here the countless facts recorded by the Observatory of Misogyny concerning the mistreatment inflicted upon women by the media, pornography, television, advertising: in short, by daily life. Let us not forget that France's ratification, in 1983, of the UN Convention on the Elimination of All Forms of Discrimination Against Women has not been followed by the adoption of any antisexist laws, on the model of the antiracist law voted after the ratification of the UN Convention Against Racism.[42] And misogyny, still not considered an offense, remains an opinion like any other in the name of freedom of expression.

In France, then, a few figures are sufficient proof that the war against women is not a pure fiction. Every day a woman is murdered because she is a woman; every day one woman out of seven is a victim of violence at the hands of her spouse.[43] Each year four million women are beaten; each year, thirty thousand are raped—this means one every fifteen minutes—because they are women and girls, even very young girls. Only fifty-five hundred women have pressed charges, which have led to condemnations in only 17 percent of the cases. So we can say that rape is the least punished crime in France.

As for incest, it is impossible to make a plausible estimate, for crime is most often kept secret within families where it functions as the basis, the bond, and the major symptom of familial madness. It seems that after two decades of denunciation by women—whether they are victims, militants, mothers, or health care providers—this training of young girls for a totalitarian patriarchy remains the most resistant pillar of our culture. It has often occurred to me that the mystery of the Virgin Mary and the cult around her might be a foundational idealization of incest at the heart of the Catholic Church. Just before coming to Copenhagen, I heard a militant ecologist who claims to be a feminist declare in a television broadcast, when her opinion on the subject was not even requested, that incest in France was of secondary importance.[44] A candidate for the presidential elections, she probably had in mind her potential supporters, who are mostly farmers. In fact, we know that incest is most common and least denounced in rural areas. Psychologists and psychiatrists have shown us that when a young girl is the victim of incest she tends to fall into silence, anorexia, and/or depression. It impedes her studies, if it does not interrupt them for good. The devastating effects of incest are incalculable: the vast majority of women prostitutes have been victims of incest.

Abortion rights, obtained by women after a hard struggle, are being called into question once again. Illegal actions against centers where abortion is practiced are multiplying in spite of the 1993 law punishing such actions. The commandos that carry out these actions are endorsed by the highest Church authorities. A truly conservative reform movement is trying to question the rights women have gained in the last twenty years.

If we examine the advances made in education, employment, and citizenship, we have to admit that equality between men and women is not always respected. What about higher education, for instance, since it has been women's first step to autonomy? Where are we, seventy years after granting girls access to the baccalaureate degree, that is, access to university-level study? Too often, they must choose between so-called feminine career paths, which means they remain victims of discrimination, or so-called masculine fields, where their specificity is denied. However, girls have not only caught up with boys at the level of the baccalaureate, but they have pulled ahead. In 1988, 33 percent more girls than boys earned this diploma.[45] During the first two years at university they tend to get better results; however, by the end of this period, their number has diminished. Their long-delayed entrance to the *grandes écoles* still remains impeded.

The goal of equality in education had just been set forth by the 1989 law on governing higher education when it was put to the test with the appearance of the Islamic headscarf in schools. The council of state, supreme judge of schools, chose to reassert freedom of conscience and to disregard the enslavement of women, though it is clearly manifested by the veil; and secularism (*laïcité*),[46] refusing to consider the political message, totally ignores discrimination against women. To my regret, I can only touch on this question superficially. It would require not only careful review but a theoretical elaboration that has yet to be undertaken, for want of precise *feminological* instruments. This question has most often been dealt with in a partisan, ideological way or by nonpertinent social sciences, such as political science, sociology, or anthropology, which always reduce the priority of sex to a secondary consideration. But, in any case, we know that immigrant Muslim young women often do much better in school than their brothers. Might not the issue of the headscarf have arisen to slow down the successful integration of these young women? If our institutions do not support their efforts, what will happen to their desire to learn and thereby to free themselves from the constraints religion imposes on them?

France is still among the leading European countries in terms of women's professional activity. In 1991 71 percent of adult females are employed.[47] But working conditions are difficult, for the majority of working women continue to be responsible for a *triple production*—childbearing (for those who choose to have children), domestic work, and professional work—that still remains largely unacknowledged as such. Practical help to women who bear and rear children is still not offered by the state; it remains difficult, costly, and unorganized. As a result, women continue to be penalized in their professional lives by virtue of the gift of life they make to the world.

Besides, their right to work is being challenged yet again. Right-wing technocrats are proposing the return of women to the home as one of the solutions to unemployment, and our conservative government has reinstated a parental allowance for education, with the hidden aims of removing women from the workforce and increasing the birthrate. This ridiculous subsidy, proposed for the third, then the second, and soon the first child, is called a parental allowance, but 95 percent of those who receive it are women. Thus, in 1993, fifty-five thousand women gave up their professional lives, but, in spite of guarantees of reemployment, six out of ten failed to find work again the following year.[48] In short our government chose to stem unemployment by using the oldest and most reactionary methods of all—undermining the rights of the least privileged women, sending them back to dependency on family and procreation, secretly reinstating an old family code.[49] When the members of our government boast that they reduced the number of unemployed workers by sixteen thousand in January 1995, and when they plan a yearly reduction of two hundred thousand unemployed workers, they seem to be unaware that they are also planning the exclusion of several hundred thousand women, who will become dependent on the community in the years to come. Stay-at-home mothers already rank among the poorest in the country.[50]

As with many European countries, unemployment figures attest to discrimination against women, who constitute the majority of unemployed workers, everywhere and in all categories.[51] In 1994 the number of unemployed men aged twenty-five to forty increased by 2 percent; the number of unemployed women in the same age group grew by 7 percent. Considering these figures, the minister of labor had to acknowledge that the growth of unemployment concerned women exclusively, while the situation remained stable for men.[52] Women represent 58 percent of long-term unemployed workers and 80 percent of part-time employed workers. The 1983 law on professional equality, for want of the political will to control its application, failed to reduce wage inequalities between men and women. The gaps between men's and women's salaries are 12 percent for unskilled workers and 20 percent to 35 percent for executives; the latter gap can be as high as 40 percent in Île-de-France.[53] Women are also subjected to persistent discrimination in regard to education, specialization, and promotion.

In consequence, we can say that in France there is still a threshold of tolerance for women where their right to fair remuneration and to promotion is concerned. Obviously, equal career opportunities for women and men will remain a pious hope as long as women do not have access to decision-making positions. Perhaps only real politicosymbolic equality will make the laws and measures taken at the socioeconomic level truly effective.

France, which was late in granting women the right to vote, remains in the rear guard when it comes to electability. In 1945, one year after women received the right to vote, 6.05 percent of the deputies in the National Assembly were women; in 1995 the proportion is only 5.6 percent.[54] In the last fifty years we have advanced by moving backwards in history! France comes last in Europe, notwithstanding the multiple, steady, and repeated proofs we women have given of our will to attain freedom, of our competence as equals, and of the fight we have carried on together for the democratization of our country.

LIBERTY, PARITY, SOLIDARITY

Everywhere in the world, gaps like these between great principles and reality indicate not only that democracy has not been achieved but that we need to devise new means to make it happen.

A country like Denmark, where the memory of March 8 has its roots and where this summit conference is taking place, can be taken as exemplary and paradigmatic: it has a ratio of 33 percent women in Parliament and can be proud of having a professional activity rate of 76 percent (as opposed to 51 percent in the European Union as a whole).

THE PATHS TO PARITY IN FRANCE

Mao Tse-Tung's famous line, "women hold up the other half of the sky,"[55] is unquestionably one of the sources, the most poetical one, of the Women's Liberation Movement in France. As early as 1968, a few of us became aware that we represented more than half of humankind. Becoming political partners and then full-fledged citizens: this was the dynamic impulse that motivated us.

In order to bring balance to a universal history, allegedly neutral, but in reality hommosexed and entirely built on a system of apartheid for women,[56] and in order to assert our existence in the face of religious, cultural, political, and symbolic monism, we had no choice but to come together in a women's movement. This partitioning impelled us to highlight the fact that there are indeed two sexes and to find a notion that would work better than the principle of equality to ensure a fair distribution of responsibilities and power between men and women. Beyond equality and the dead ends to which it can lead, the term parity—still too vaguely defined to claim the status of concept—confirms the failure of the feminist ideology of sexual nondifference.

Paradoxically, it is because of the slow and circuitous development of our political identity and the complex and even contradictory strategies implemented that, in the 1970s—when we were also victims of the prevailing anti-parliamentarianism—we chose not to use our right to vote.[57] The candidates were not sufficiently aware of our demands and of our project. On March 8, 1981, I called on women to vote for François Mitterrand in the first round of the presidential elections and then to support the candidates of the left in the legislative elections that followed.[58]

In 1989, the year of the Bicentennial of the Revolution, I founded the Alliance des Femmes pour la Démocratie (Women's Alliance for Democracy) to help women obtain the full exercise of a citizenship based on their specific identity. That year we launched into the battle for equality in politics. We decided to present electoral lists mostly composed of women, first in the 1989 municipal elections in Paris, in the sixth district, and in Marseille, in the fourth district, then in the 1992 regional elections in the Bouches-du-Rhône.[59] Actions such as these gradually implemented the initial project of the movement, and their concrete results made way for the notion of parity. Finally, in May 1992, I created the Club Parité 2000, setting a historical deadline for this desire for parity.

Meanwhile, an amendment to the electoral law instituting the first quota was adopted by the Parliament almost unanimously,[60] then invalidated by the Constitutional Council, based primarily on a reference to the 1789 Declaration of the Rights of Man and the Citizen, which is the fundamental text of our Constitution. Let us not forget that, when this declaration was conceived, it totally excluded women from citizenship. And since then nobody has felt the need, while keeping it as an ultimate reference in the successive preambles to our Cconstitutions, to specify that, from now on, it would apply to both men and women.

Contrary to international texts, such as the United Nations Charter or the 1948 Declaration of Rights, the preamble to the 1946 Constitution, to which our current Constitution refers, fails to mention the category of sex when it declares that every human being has "sacred and inalienable rights," "without distinction of race, religion or creed."[61] I have been asking since 1989 that this preamble be modified so that the human person, regardless of her or his sex, may obtain these sacred and inalienable rights and fundamental liberties. The preamble to our Constitution is at the core of the legal inscription of the symbolic exclusion of women, with all the consequences, political and otherwise, with which we are familiar. In the founding texts, we are still not citizens equal to men. In this respect, we can speak of constitutional misogyny. Without a strong symbolic inscription of women at the legal level, equality between men and women remains fragmentary, subsidiary, and scattered throughout the legislative field. This is why, for a long time, I have been pointing out the importance of modifying this preamble, and on the occasion of the revision of the Constitution, at the beginning of 1993, I wrote to the president of the republic to propose a new version.

PARITY IN EUROPE

The question of parity appeared at the European level in 1989. That year, at the Council of Europe, the philosophical foundations of democracy were questioned, the difference between the sexes was rehabilitated, and "parity-based democracy" was discussed,[62] coming into harmony with my own long-standing critique of universalism, of the notion "one as all and all as one."

In November 1992 the European Council organized a European summit in Athens titled "Women in Power," followed by a charter demanding equal participation of women and men in public and political decision making. The Athens declaration, signed by top-level women politicians, was widely distributed and helped the idea of parity to have a noticeable impact on mentalities in France.

In November 1993 the "Manifesto of the 577 for a Parity-Based Democracy,"[63] published in Le Monde, was the turning point that made sure the lists established by the principal or secondary parties on the left would include parity in their electoral strategy for the June 1994 European elections. The Socialist Party observed quantitative parity,[64] with the appropriate masculine bonus: a man at top of the list, which led to the election of eight men and seven women; a parity observed by the Communist Party and by ecologists, already familiar with this practice. The Énergie radicale list proposed that I appear at a threshold rank, the thirteenth, perceiving me as symbolically conveying a project for women; it ultimately and quite unexpectedly got five women elected out of thirteen candidates.

The distinction that I had made between quantitative parity and *qualitative parity* seemed to be confirmed at the time of the European elections, and even more so later on. Quantitative parity means an alternation between men and women—women running for office without a specific project for women. Ecologists have observed this form of parity since their first electoral list, but we have not seen any positive results for women, except for those who have been elected. As for the seven women elected to the European Parliament on the Socialist Party list, none of them chose to sit on the Committee on Women's Rights or to intervene in the interest of women on any other committee. Each of these women has remained simply a Socialist among others. I shall come back to this distinction between qualitative and quantitative parity.

In late 1994, in Vienna, during the preparation for the Women's Conference in Beijing, European women appeared as promoters of the idea of parity, even if this idea could also be found in the United States. The initiatives of the Council of Europe and the extension of the Union to the Nordic countries, where the number of women present in parliaments exceeds 30 percent everywhere, support the strategy of women's empowerment.

AN ETIOLOGICAL DIAGNOSIS

As history demonstrates, the right to equality was built up in a slow, difficult, and fragmentary manner. In the name of an abstract and neutral equality, affirmative action based on sex has been forbidden, making true equality difficult to achieve. But, above all, legal logic has not registered the fact that there are two sexes and that neither one can be reduced to the other.

The many explanations for the impasses of equality are relevant, but they remain caught in the trap they denounce, for they do not take into account the infrastructure and the superstructure that border, upstream and downstream, the egalitarian imaginary—a philosophical phantasm of the social contract. In *media res* logic goes around in circles in the social and sociological fields, where the democratic government of the Republic is still being thought through, at levels that are not only subsidiary but secondary and relative, compared with the political level, which is both real and symbolic.

The scandalous political underrepresentation of women, in the country that boasts of having invented universal human rights, seems mysterious, as long as one doesn't try to understand the situation as the product of a French-style misogyny, somehow inscribed as much in the tables of the republican law as in a perversion based on a denial of reality: I know there really are two sexes, but let's pretend that we need only one.

This denial of the fact that there are both men and women has unquestionably led to abuses of a logic of equality that has almost become a dogma by now, with very obvious inegalitarian effects. For nearly twenty-five years, I have kept on presenting the perverse results of this logic of sameness as evidence that leads from women's invisibility, their powerlessness, their inexistence, to their total disappearance. This logic is still advocated today by many feminists, however, whereas the concept of parity, provided it is conceived rigorously, may well provide a way out of the impasse.

The passion for the sovereign One—God, almighty Father, only Son, Emperor or Phallus—that has inspired the absolute monarchy has been turned into a universal republic, one and indivisible, by the philosophers of the Enlightenment: so many metamorphoses of the One with a complete disregard of the at-least-two, or more, that should be the source of the modern democratic spirit. In its inspiration, both monarchic and republican, our Constitution remains in keeping with this passion for the One, when it fails to specify that a human being is not neuter, and when it construes the fact that there are two sexes as a secondary difference and at the same time considers differences that are indeed secondary—since they are reducible in the course of life or in the course of history—as fundamental. This is the symptom showing that what is really major must remain foreclosed, that is, definitively abandoned, exhausted, unthought: the irreducible real, the fact that there must be two sexes in the destiny of the human species, considered as "a citizen species." Once more, the mechanism of foreclosure is set up to penalize women for their specific contribution to the real by ignoring them in the politicosymbolic era.

By omitting to express unequivocally that a human being is born male or female, that he or she is male or female for all his or her life, the preamble to the Constitution repeats the denial, reiterates the foreclosure, and refuses to acknowledge the nonidentity between the two sexes, whereas it is precisely this nonidentity that enables the species within which they are similar to be fertile not only on the biological level—as is the case for all living sexed species, animal or vegetable—but also, because it is the human species, on the anthropological, cultural, historical, and political levels.

The well-known universalism to which Western man has remained bound like Ulysses to his mast, for fear of the regression the sirens of his elementary drives might bring about, is just the premature stage of an adolescent consciousness. The existence of a two can be considered only according to the logic of the One, with no other, or with another reduced to the same, so as not to alter the narcissistic power of the Whole. The economy of the One-Whole seeks to exclude difference or, under constraint, tolerates its corollary: the carefully planned, quantified, controlled, homeopathic or vaccine-like inclusion, the foreclosed internment of difference. With such a logical basis, abstract, neutralizing, undifferentiated equality can only lead—as long as there is a two—to the opposite extreme of the direction it has claimed for itself: to ever more inequality, ever more discrimination.

No wonder the road to equality has required a long forced march, a paradoxical agonizing struggle, both in contradiction and in agreement with the reappearance of the Declaration of Human Rights in our Constitution. The preamble to the Constitution purports to serve two masters at once: on the one hand, the republic and the monarchy, that is, the One, and, on the other hand, the democratic concessions of contemporary governments (womens' right to vote for one, professional equality for another; and so on), all against a background of monophallic tyranny.

QUALITATIVE PARITY

Since "the people" actually comprises two sexes, each of the two should logically represent the whole on an equal basis. The fact that only men have had access to linguistic representation of humanity—the expression "rights of man" is still being used—and to political representation, always and everywhere, is the major symptom indicating that *homo universalis* is indeed a male and not a female individual. Humanity may be heterosexed, but the church and the state require either a male representation or a representation of men and women subjected to a unique referent, still and always male. In this perspective, if, today, one citizen out of two is a woman citizen, tomorrow, in the one, indivisible, and universal republic, two citizens out of two will be men citizens. For if France, the eldest daughter of the Church, recoils—as the Catholic Church does—at being represented in any way other than by sons in the image of the Father, in the near future it will be able to tolerate a more democratic representation—as the Protestant Church does—by its "girl-sons" (*filses*),[65] without giving an inch with regard to the all-powerful symbolic referent. Filiarchal parity will certainly include daughters or girl-sons (as if they were sons) in a philosophical "as if" that, according to Freud, has nothing to do with the real, yet it can fulfill the religious or ideological illusion of an obsessional type enslaved to a phobic ego.

What an odd citizen species, which, having recorded the existence of two sexes, would have committed itself to parity and would ultimately find itself reproduced in an identical clonelike way, entirely "hommosexed"; a citizen species in which the self would forever be protected from an inner division, from the existence of an unconscious, from contamination by those who at last would have been eliminated; a citizen species without women—in a word, a citizen species purified.

If this notion of parity is only a sort of compromise between a heterogenous real and an abstract principle, we can expect that its use will produce more discrimination than it reduces. If ideological neuroses are opposed to a rigorous theorization of the notion and its development as a concept, the word *parity* itself will soon begin to function as a sterile fetish, and any strategy for its implementation will necessarily lead to the same dead ends as those the principle of equality has reached and will continue to reach.

However, the logic of parity has the means to organize its own way out of the egalitarian logic. It can instrumentalize it, in order to plan, prepare, and proclaim the way out of an infernal circle where our species alienates itself in endless self-destruction. The real logic of parity not only appears irrepressible but inherently dialogical: it can impose itself on the consciousness of both sexes as the invention of an enlightened diversality. Instead of a now totally static universalism, the diversality engendered by the coupling of the two sexes representing it might lead to a heterogeneous republic, exceeding rather than falling short of the One. Here, freed from the quantitative model of a radical quota (50/50) in the terrorist politically correct version offered by an unchanged ideology, a concept of parity could unfold.

What has actually been happening since this notion imposed itself in the Women's Movement and is now being imposed, at least as a question, in political parties? Parity has different lines of logic and goals according to the libidinal investments and psychic types of its actresses and actors much more than according to their political affiliations. Thus we can say that this notion goes beyond right-left divisions.

In fact, there exists a conservative parity, conservative inasmuch as it preserves the absolute primacy of the One and sets reformed neutralism as its ultimate goal: it is the quantitative parity of ecologists or that of the Socialist Party in the European elections. In a very similar category we have to include the quantitative parity of many feminist projects, which tend to keep the One, *gendered* neuter (masculine-feminine) on the Protestant rather than the Catholic model.[66] This parity has to be distinguished from truly *qualitative parity*, determined from a field worked mainly by the difference between the sexes. In this respect, some consider that parity means giving up equality. For my part, I prefer to consider the notion from a perspective of (r)evolutionary maturation: to find a way out of the logic of equality, we have to have gone through it and gone beyond it for fear of finding ourselves within it, just as in libidinal evolution we can find ourselves beneath the One, divided up, discriminated against.

Beyond, and only beyond, a well-integrated equality, however, parity will go on gaining strength with phallic proclamations and provocations before it brings the ethical values borne by women to fruition. Indeed, to go from quantitative to *qualitative parity*, it is not enough for women representatives of the people to have—in addition—a project for women; this project must consider them as women, not as men-to-be, which means that their political project must take into account the reality of their experience as women who are sexed human beings—with regard to the work of procreation, the adventure of gestation as the specific time and place for welcoming the other—and as women who are persons in charge of the world.

The issue that is really at stake in parity today, then, is whether the passion for the One is going to pervert it into a One-Whole or whether the generous, genital wisdom of the two will lead it into a risky, genial adventure; whether parity is going to be a warlike strategy of hegemonic domination in the guise of sharing or the promise of a multiplication of chances for the species; whether it is going to be used as an inclusion of sisters, next to their brothers, in a republic of sons, without any structural change or whether, beyond all isms—socialism, feminism, universalism, and other outdated notions, all based on denial and on the resulting suicidal perversions—it will allow the expression of the foreclosed knowledge belonging to the only living species capable of creation. Beyond equality and to achieve equality as a matter of justice, yes, parity: but a parity that is heterosexed in its historical destiny as in the premises on which it is based, even including those men and women who deny it and distort it at the very moment when they are forced to acknowledge it. Parity is equality plus fertile heterogeneity.

I could also describe our coming together today at this roundtable as parity based, we female representatives of NGOs and members of the Parliament, each one perhaps, like myself, both a militant and a representative. By parity-based, where I myself am concerned, I mean that I feel as much a militant as a member of Parliament, just as I was convinced, when I was simply a militant, that I was playing an active role in politics.

There is no doubt about the impact of NGO representation in official UN conferences on women. Such representation demonstrates that, at this level, a well-conceived parity between governments and civil populations could balance and at the same time accelerate development and peace in the world. Needless to say, society, made up mostly of women, and governing powers, made up mostly of men, illustrate a kind of sexing which has everything to gain by conjugating the two terms. Parity tomorrow would mark the end of the refeudalization of civil society, and it would mean multiplying, rather than sharing, democratic power in the polity. Through a fair distribution, each citizen, eligible to run for office as well as to vote, would have a share of power at his or her own level and would hold hegemony in check. This is the democratic revolution that can be brought about by the arrival of women in public life.

We have often been told that our women's movements were made up of intellectuals cut off from the reality of the world. But what do we see today? The model of liberty, equality, parity, and solidarity, adapted to each culture, is bringing us heroines of democracy from the far corners of the earth. I shall mention only three of them as examples: Taslima Nasrin, exiled today in Sweden, is fighting for equality between men and women in Bangladesh. Aung San Suu Kyi from Burma founded the National League for Democracy, which won a resounding victory in the May 1990 elections. She received the Nobel Peace Prize for her political work in 1991. Under house arrest for almost six years, she is still engaged in democratic progress. Leyla Zana, a Turkish member of parliament, the first Kurd woman to be elected, imprisoned after a rigged trial, proclaimed: "Our only crime is our firm and determined commitment to our democratic and pacific demands."[67] A few heroines who are the tip an iceberg made up of millions of women, messengers of hope, who everywhere in the world are awakening, listening to one another, coming together, organizing, starting movements: this is the pioneer front of democracy.

20. Women and Europe

1997

The Treaty of Rome is forty years old. For forty years its very famous article 119 has served as the basis for the European construction of the principle of equality between men and women. Seven directives, five recommendations, three decisions, twelve resolutions, the implementation of action programs, the adoption of codes of conduct, and the large number of precedents established by the Court of Justice have allowed us to make the transition from the principle of equal pay to the principles of equal treatment and equality of opportunity in the labor market and have had a direct and determining influence on all the progress that has been made toward those goals in each member state. There is, however, a big difference between the recognition of a right and its implementation, and the legal advances that have been made are themselves under threat.

Poverty is being feminized in all the member states. 70 percent of the 36 million Europeans living below the poverty line are women; 55 percent of the chronically unemployed are women, as are 90 percent of single parents, who are particularly affected by extreme poverty, and 80 percent of those in part-time work, most of them in precarious jobs that are not covered by the social welfare system. Discrimination in the workplace is exacerbated by structural economic changes, and the new jobs are being created by cutting-edge technologies. Traditional values and prejudices based upon the archaic principle of a negative and preegalitarian difference between the sexes are projecting new discriminations for the future, in addition to those values and prejudices that have never changed. Another alarming sign: the budget for the fourth medium-term community action program on equal opportunities for women and men has been cut by half by the council, and the third antipoverty program has been tabled.

For a few years now, a certain interpretation of the principle of equality between men and women on the part of the Court of Justice of the European Communities has been working against the interests of women. In the name of an abstract concept of equality, the court has challenged national measures aimed at compensating for or limiting the inequalities suffered by women as a result of their activities as mothers and their responsibilities for children and other vulnerable individuals. The recent and very controversial Kalanke ruling,[1] as many will recall, has placed drastic restrictions on affirmative action. The proposed amendment of the 1976 directive on equal treatment of men and women, which was put before the European Commission as a result of that ruling in an attempt to clarify its implications, tends in fact to ratify it. The Committee on Women's Rights has persuaded the European Parliament to postpone discussion of this proposal until the findings of the Intergovernmental Conference have been made public.

The treaty is the Union's primary and foundational law, the basis of its values and its identity. Now, as things stand, everyone agrees that the legal basis for equality is quite inadequate. Women do not appear in the treaty as subjects of law, and the principle of equality is restricted to a mere social right. Hence the extreme fragility of the gains that have been made and hence the worsening position of women throughout the Union. The European Parliament's Committee on Women's Rights sought to see the principle of equality between men and women enshrined as a fundamental right at the heart of the European project, which would make it a decisive contribution to the democratization of the Union and of the countries that are about to join it.

We have therefore defined the inclusion in the treaty of a broad and coherent legal basis for equality between men and women as the highest priority; this would allow its implementation in concrete situations. For my own part, I would add that equality must be discussed in the light of the irreducible difference that exists between men and women, for the latter are still responsible for gestation and, to a large extent, for mothering. This positive difference, which is necessary, fecund, and vital, must not lead to discriminations, but it must not be denied, either. As matters stand, instead of adding up the various forms of wealth produced by women—procreation, domestic labor, professional activities—the economy deducts them all from women's paid work and their future in the workplace.

Recognizing that equality is a basic right and obliging the Union to adopt positive measures in all domains, ensuring in particular that women are part of the decision-making process on equal terms with men, would be no more than minimal reparation for the prevailing injustice and a very small step toward recognizing the debt that is owed to women.

At the close of the Amsterdam summit, equality between men and women became one of the community's missions, as introduced by articles 2 and 3 of the treaty. This is a first step beyond the restrictive framework of article 119, extending its field of application to all community actions and policies, but it does not go so far as to make equality a basic right in explicit terms.

We had further recommended that the treaty should recognize the principle of "parity-based democracy" elaborated by the Council of Europe. The increased participation of women in the decision-making process is a basic element of the necessary democratization of European institutions. The European Parliament stressed the need for such democratization during the preparatory session of the intergovernmental conference.[2] The recommendation that was unanimously adopted by the council on December 2, 1996, further stressed the need for democratization. Only parity can bring about the balanced participation of men and women in the government of the world; it is both an assertion of equality and a promise of something more than equality. *Qualitative parity* implies a project for women and guarantees the representation of their specific interests. It is highly regrettable that neither the Irish presidency, the Dutch presidency, nor the member states have recognized it.

Proposals for affirmative action have also been extremely inadequate. In order to move from de jure equality to de facto equality, positive measures are required. They must be able to be adapted without restriction, and the resulting equality must take precedence over strictly equal treatment in every individual case.

Now, despite the apparent consensus as to the need to recognize the inadequacy of formal equality, and despite the support of the European Parliament,[3] no new provision to this effect has been included in the revised treaty, and this constitutes a major regression. The terms used in the Agreement on Social Policy were simply integrated into article 119; these provide for the nonprohibition of specific advantages intended to promote employment among the underrepresented sex and not the formula "to improve the position of women in the workplace." This may pave the way for discrimination against women in sectors where they are in the majority.

As for article 119, it now includes the notion of equal pay for work of equal value, but our demand for new and additional provisions covering all domains of social, economic, and family life, as specific goals with respect to access to education and training, working conditions, and the right to social security, was not accepted.

I also regret the fact that the demand put forward by the Committee on Women's Rights and Parliament that sexism should be condemned on the same grounds as racism has not been satisfied to date. I will mention one victory that makes me particularly happy, however, given my commitments in this area; the struggle against human trafficking has been recognized as a priority for the Union on the same basis as drug trafficking. I greatly regret the refusal to extend the right of asylum to women who are persecuted because of their sex, as the United States and Canada have been doing for several years now.

Although significant progress has been made, it has to be said that the draft treaty falls far short of satisfying our demands, especially where the implementation of real equality is concerned. Many of the priorities we defined—basic rights, parity, positive measures, obligation of result—have at best, and despite the support of the European Parliament, been adopted only partially, not in terms that would allow the spiral of regression to be overturned and become a spiral of progress. There is therefore still a great deal to be done.

21. If This Is a Woman

September 24, 1999

This text never stops being written. Ended, it remains endless. It comes off the telex machines, interminably, every day crueler than the last. It is the text of the human tragedy of the condition of women. I have written it a hundred times, and others have written it at the same time. This is not writing; at the very most it is a transcript of the daily hell in which women have lived for all eternity, all over the world.

Why so many murders, why so much hatred, why so much suffering? In these questions, which lie at the root of all racisms, we find the dark continent of human stupidity, the whole species' refusal to take stock of the greatest genocide in the entire history of speaking beings.

"If This Is a Woman" struck me as a fitting title for this article, in an allusion to Primo Levi's *If This Is a Man*. In Levi's introductory poem I found the few lines he devotes to the condition of women in Auschwitz:

> Consider if this is a woman,
> Without hair and without name
> With no more strength to remember

Her eyes empty and her womb cold
Like a frog in winter . . . [1]

In *Aujourd'hui*, the national edition of *Le Parisien*, on August 25, 1999, we learn of the existence of "breaking-in camps" in Italy where women and "girls" are turned into prostitutes. "Imported in groups of fifteen or twenty under false identities by pimps from the Yugoslavian, Russian, or Czech mafia, they are forced to turn more than a hundred tricks a day! They come away broken and submissive. Some become hooked on heroin or cocaine so they can stand it. Most of them drink . . . " I am certainly not confusing either this camp in Italy or the brothels that have been organized in Bosnia with the Nazi camps. And yet in all these camps the torturers' desire to dehumanize their prisoners is the same.

This news was not picked up by any other paper. I read the so-called popular dailies assiduously because they are slightly less misogynist than the so-called quality press. They do not ignore the murders and the rapes to which women fall victim every day, even though they confine them to the "news in brief" column rather than putting the stories on the political or social pages, which are reserved for racist murders.

So women and "girls" are brutalized just as they were in the old brothels—and from time to time the question of reopening these "closed houses" in France is raised, under international pressure. At the end of this millennium, what was at the beginning of the century a craft industry—whose "charms" are now celebrated by libertine intellectuals, men and women alike—has been turned into an industry that is listed on the Stock Exchange, and the "oldest profession in the world" has been turned into a so-called career in its own right, one that can be exploited to the full. Some countries in the European Union have become pimps of an ultraliberalism that is as untrammeled as it is barbarous by getting involved in the regulation of so-called forced prostitution—what a tautology!—and profiting from the houses of torture and indignity known as eros-centers.[2] Prostitution reveals the truth about relations between West and East, North and South, rich and poor, and men and women. There are at least two million prostitutes in Europe. You'll tell me that prostitution poses no threat to the majority of women; my answer is that this most complete form of sexual slavery, this commodification of thousands of millions of people because of their sex, is a threat to any women who is driven into poverty, into destitution.

As early as 1991, Amartya Sen, whom I often cite, noted that more than one hundred million women were absent from the roll call when the world population census was taken, if we apply the sex ratio of the developed countries at the international level.[3] The French press sang his praises when he won the Nobel Prize for economics in 1998 for his work on the Human Development Index (HDI),[4] but not a word was said about what I call the ongoing *gynocide*. More than one hundred million women have disappeared because they were women. No one seems to be alarmed by this demographic deficit, which is due to feticide of female embryos, undernourishment of girl children, selective medical care, sexual mutilation, and childbirth in precarious conditions. As early as 1991, Sen took the view that this was "one of the more momentous, and neglected, problems facing the world today."[5] And yet nothing has changed. On the contrary, the problem meets with the same indifference. The number of female embryos that are aborted has risen steeply in India, South Korea, and China, where thousands of girl children are abandoned at birth and left to die. Every year over one million girl children are left to die somewhere in the world because they were born girls.[6] Two million are subjected to the torture of excision and infibulation. At this very moment over sixty girl children are being mutilated somewhere in Africa, Asia, the Middle East, and probably in Europe.[7] As for incest, its devastating effects are incalculable: mutism, anorexia, depression, prostitution, suicide.[8] And yet, in France, libertine intellectuals with high media profiles sing the praises of both incest and prostitution. In the poorest countries over six hundred women die each year, uncared for and in silence, as a result of pregnancy or childbirth.[9]

"If," for reasons that could be analyzed, "hundreds of thousands of men were suffering and dying every year, alone and in fear and in agony, or if millions upon millions of men were being injured and disabled and humiliated . . . then we would all have heard about this issue long ago, and something would have been done."[10]

In the armed conflicts that are devastating the world, women suffer mass rape and forced pregnancies in addition to the horrors of war. Denunciation of the rapes that occurred during the war in Bosnia did not stop the same tortures from occurring again in Rwanda, in Turkey, in Sierra Leone, or, this year, in Kosovo. Not to mention the shame and silence to which rape victims are usually condemned by their communities.[11] In Afghanistan, Algeria, Iran, Bangladesh, and Sudan, religious fundamentalists have wreaked havoc, and women are the favorite targets of their misogynist delirium. But peace does not always put an end to violence, and rape has always been a weapon of war all over the world. In our so-called advanced democracies a woman is raped every six minutes. In France one woman dies every day because she is a woman,[12] and one woman in seven is beaten. In Russia almost fifteen thousand women die every year as a result of conjugal violence; this is equivalent to the army's losses over the ten years of war in Afghanistan.[13] Being the wife of a singer (NTM) or being a famous singer in one's own right (like Lio) provides no escape from the violence of lovers.[14] And yet there is still no antisexist law in France to protect the lives and dignity of women. Unlike racism, misogyny is still regarded as an opinion and not a crime.

Nowhere in the world does the Gender-Related Development Index (GDI) show equality between the sexes.[15] Poverty affects women first and foremost: 70 percent of the 1 billion, 700 million human beings living below the poverty line are women, and more than two thirds of the 840 million adults who are illiterate are women.[16] Women, who carry out two-thirds of all the human labor performed in the world, receive only 10 percent of available income and only 1 percent of the world's wealth. They are responsible for almost all the (nonmarket) *production of living beings*, along with most domestic labor, and most of the informal sector. None of this productive activity is included in national gross domestic product figures, and it is still part of an underground economy that is neither recognized nor remunerated.

Even in Europe, the continent where women's rights are at their most advanced and where the principle of equality has been proclaimed, poverty is being feminized, as is shown by European Parliament reports from 1994 to 1999. And when they are economically active, women earn only three-quarters of a man's wage for doing the same jobs. Despite the existence of an active and vigilant Committee on Women's Rights, a clear decline was recorded during the 1994–1999 legislative session in which I served as a member of the European Parliament. The latest European directives fall into what, in 1998, I called the liberal trap: the agencies and instruments of the policy favoring equality have been devalued, credits for the fourth equal opportunities program have been cut by half, affirmative action to reduce the gap between the principle of equality and its implementation has been delegitimized by the Court of Justice, and there has been talk of abolishing the Committee on Women's Rights.[17]

In France, one of the European countries in which women are most active in the workplace, their working conditions remain difficult and are becoming more and more so. When women are employed on a part-time basis, the reduction in the hours they spend at work does not give them more freedom; it burdens them with even more work in the home. Their jobs are now being taken away from them and given to men. Most of the women who opted to take the parental allowance for education have still not returned to work after their three years' leave. There is no real child-care provision for very young children, and nothing has been done to make things easier for young mothers.[18] On the contrary, and for the first time after thirty years of continuous progress, there has been a dangerous decline in women's economic activity.[19] All over the world women are being penalized because they bear children, because of their unique contribution to humanity.

As for the power to take decisions, whether economic or political, we can only speak of the powerlessness of women. Only 10 percent of the world's parliamentarians are women.[20] Thanks to the voluntaristic policy of its government, which was encouraged by women's parity movements, France has now achieved that international average, but ranks next to last in the European Union. There are now nine women in the government, but the policy on women that social justice demands has yet to be drawn up. In our country the aberrant dogma claiming that "women are men, just like other men" makes it impossible to envisage "affirmative action" where there is an absolute and urgent need for it if we are to reduce the gap between the principle of equality and real equality between men and women.[21] And there is still no women's commission in Parliament and no meaningful budget.

When they are not condemned to invisibility or slandered, women appear in the media only when they are being flattered as the bearers of the flame of femininity or reduced, as a second sex, next to—or to the left of or below—an athlete or a president. And even when they are leading figures in their own right, first in their own field, like Jeannie Longo,[22] or like Nicole Fontaine, who has just been elected president of the European Parliament, they always take second place in the press.

Why so much misogyny everywhere? And what makes it so durable? Why is our century, so eager to denounce the evils that threaten humanity, the destruction of the earth and the seas, of animals and peoples, and every other injustice, still not concerned about the destruction of women and discrimination against women?

For the last thirty years I have not been satisfied simply to catalogue the permanent *gynocide* that is being perpetuated all over the planet. I have tried to analyze its causes. I think that this hatred for women, which is devastating the human race, is based upon a primordial, archaic, and universal but radically denied *envy* of women's procreative capacity, of the specific role that, together with gestation, devolves upon them in the production of the human species. This envy, which is misogyny itself, is the basis for all the systems that exclude the other. It lies at the root of all racism and all exploitation.

The same envy is also the basis for a whole series of constructs and theorizations that substitute the phallus for the uterus, the better to deny, exploit, and appropriate the *genesic function* of women. These constructs turn the phallus, as an erect penis, into the tree of life, the source of all desire and all value, while relegating the procreative capacity of women, and even women themselves, to secondary or even negative status. At every level we find the reversal that turns women into a castrated, derivative, and relative "second sex" that excludes and/or interns them, but that always deprives them of their libido. The entire system of universalist thought has been constructed on the basis of envy and denial of the genesic function and on what that implies: the imperialism of the phallus and its passion for the One. The passion for the one sovereign god, father, son, emperor, or phallus, lies at the basis of the universalism to which Western man is more attached than to anything else. The existence of a two is conceivable only if it does not damage the narcissistic omnipotence of the One. The other sex, which is in reality the first sex, since every human being has been born of a woman, is therefore excluded or at best tolerated as a second sex and included as a foil for the male sex.

We can see the effects of this monosexed universalism at every level—economic, sexual, political, and symbolic—and above all in the triumphant, untrammeled economic ultraliberalism that is, as we now recognize, responsible for the exclusion and the poverty of the majority, and especially of women, who are the proletariat of the human species. Men are demanding an ever greater tribute from women's bodies and women's production.[23] Worldwide economic growth derives mainly from levies on women and from their unrestricted exploitation. Owing to globalization, women are being used against women to promote the victory and power of ultraliberalism. That is the characteristic feature of slaves: their labor feeds into slavery. They have no choice but to be the agents of their own poverty. And we go on ignoring the genital mode of production of the living, which only women can experience, in order to force them into the industrial mode of production whether they like it or not. For ultraliberalism is not just an economy; it is also a philosophy of the freedom of the individual, the narcissistic and egocentric individual who takes the view that his freedom begins where the freedom of others ends.

Many people criticize ultraliberalism at the economic level, but no one talks about its libertine ethics. That ethics is the pinnacle, roof, or foundation of the ultraliberal economy. Ultraliberalism as an excess of capitalism in the economy and libertinage as sexual free trade come together in a pincer movement to block any process of liberation and to introduce, moreover, the additional bodily slavery known as the trade in women. That is why the sex industry, which is bound up with organized crime, is booming. At the same time, Sade and other libertines are returning in strength with their disemboweled mothers and their daughters subjected to incest, while transsexuals are being turned into models for a third sex: a woman without a uterus but with a penis is the old dream of men who fear women. Ultraliberalism means, finally, the rule of secondary differences, of differences between languages, cultures, and genders that not only do not challenge the phallic order but actually reinforce it. The difference between the sexes, which is the principal, primal difference, goes on being denied all the more.

Quite apart from the traditional misogyny of the advocates of maternity, with which we are all familiar, what makes it so difficult to think through the question of women is the fact that we are faced with a modern and supposedly progressive misogyny that is much more difficult to identify, because it throws the baby out with the bathwater and abolishes the difference between the sexes along with discrimination. I have endlessly tried to demonstrate the perverse effects of this logic by showing that they lead to the invisibility, nonexistence, and powerlessness of women and, quite simply, to their disappearance; they lead to a *symbolic gynocide* that reproduces the *real gynocide.*

And yet this logic of sameness is still promoted by the many *nondifferentialist* feminists who would like women to be men and who reduce procreation to nature, when it is in fact the human experience par excellence. I have been—and still am—met with violent opposition in France for trying to advance beyond the fence of uni(sex)versalism and to develop a "beyond feminism" in both thought and action. To assert that there are two sexes, while never forgetting that nothing that is human is natural, is not "differentialism"; it is a way of abolishing the foreclosure of women's genitality.

A just society can neither overlook biological determinations nor exploit them because what it refuses to think through becomes a symptom. The denial of human production in its indispensable function and its necessary values is an alienating prescription, an absolute prohibition or a penalization of women. So long as the dissymmetry between the sexes with regard to procreation is not recognized and reconsidered at every level of society— economic, social, juridical, political, and symbolic—it will be an obstacle in the path of concrete equality.

And yet women are the primary producers of wealth and can now be seen as the beating heart behind a triple hope, a triple dynamics: demography, sustainable development, and democratization. For over ten years all United Nations conferences have demonstrated that the women who were once the beneficiaries of new rights are now the main agents of progress. All over the world they are restoring the demographic balance by using contraception, wherever it is no longer banned. Once they can read and write they pass on education. As the UN says, "Educate a man and you educate an individual; educate a woman and you educate a family."

All over the world, women are finding solutions that allow them to survive, to live, and to create life; they are restoring the social bond and the solidarities that allow the integration of the most fragile populations; they are working to preserve the environment. Wherever they can, they are implementing a genital mode of production, of which they know the secret. It is a secret that they are always ready to share: a different relation to time, space, giving, and life. There are countless examples of their courageous collective initiatives. From South Africa to the outskirts of Paris, in India, Kenya, and Burkina Faso, women are inventing and acting together. All over the world they are forming movements and promoting democracy. The heroines we know so well, like Aung San Suu Kyi, Taslima Nasrin, and Leyla Zana, are no more than the tip of the iceberg. The submerged part consists of the hundreds of thousands of women who are fighting for their rights, their own dignity and that of their children, and thus for future generations.

"So long as one woman remains a slave, I too remain a slave; my freedom begins with the freedom of the other"; that is what we said at the time of the Women's Liberation Movement. We did so in order to rebalance a universal history that was supposedly neutral, but that was in reality hommosexed and entirely based upon women's enslavement and a system of apartheid;[24] in order to assert our existence, we had no option but to come together. The freedom and responsibility of women lies in the brave assertion of women's solidarity with other women and their special competence and not in a denial of the fact that they are women. Equality and difference must go hand in hand; one cannot be sacrificed for the sake of the other. If we sacrifice equality on the altar of difference, we revert to the reactionary stance of traditional societies, and if we sacrifice the difference between the sexes, with the wealth of life it brings, on the altar of equality, we sterilize women and impoverish the whole of humanity.

As the procreators of living-speaking-thinking beings and as the *anthropocultivators* of the species, women are the source of human wealth, even though, all over the world, the vital task of reproducing the generations and renewing the labor force continues to be excluded from registration in any social, economic, professional, political, or cultural domain. We must ensure that the *genesic function* is recognized as vitally necessary to the human species and acquires political responsibilities. This is the right and duty of every female citizen, and it symbolizes the *female libido* proper to all women. *Uterus envy* might be sublimated into gratitude, the vital bond might be sublimated into the matricial, the maternal, and renewed, and the repression of what is foreclosed might be removed.

Once thought through, the experience of gestation will allow us to leave behind the passion for the One and advance toward knowledge of the two. A place of memory and a moment of becoming, a model for loving our neighbor and thinking of the other, this experience endows women with the *genius of the living* (*génie du vivant*) at the level of the real, with a democratic and xenophilic personality at the level of the imaginary and an ethical dimension at the level of the symbolic.

Thirty years ago, my MLF, and the theoretical practice of Psychanalyse et Politique in particular,[25] proclaimed themselves, not without a certain provocative intent, to be a civilizational movement that went beyond economic and social issues and proposed to bring about a novel and radical revolution: a *revolution of the symbolic*. That revolution is on the march. Without ever ceasing to be procreators, memories of the future handed down from mother to daughter and from one generation to the next, many women have also become creators in every domain—economic, social, environmental, scientific, political, and artistic. To mark the World Conference on Women held in Beijing in 1995, women from all five continents asserted their radiant, diverse, colorful existence and their conception of a world for the third millennium, a world in which egocentrism and envy will be replaced by *generosity* and *gratitude*, a world that will reconcile the human species—men and women—with life. Thinking-living in the plural: that is our future.

22. They're Burning a Woman

October 9, 2002

You will, of course, be aware of the "incident" that occurred in Vitry-sur-Seine on October 4, 2002: the murder of Sohane, the seventeen-year-old girl who was burned alive in the trash bin area of an apartment complex on the outskirts of Paris. She was taken there by force and put into a bin by a lover she had rejected. He had the support of several boys from the neighborhood.

On the same day a young man of North African origin was shot dead by a drunken maniac in Dunkirk. That act was immediately, and quite rightly, described as a racist murder and condemned by the highest authorities of the state. Racism is "a cancer that must be rooted out from our society," said the minister of the interior. Despite its obviously sexist nature, the barbaric murder of the girl, on the other hand, was not interpreted as such and did not give rise to any official protests.

Both the media and public opinion used double standards, as became abundantly clear in the aftermath: demonstrations of anger and therefore violence in the case of the young man and abyssal silence in the case of the young woman.

Now Sohane's murder is, in structural terms, no different from the general degradation suffered by women in these housing projects. This time death has revealed the end result of the insecurity and violence of which women are the victims.

For many years I have tirelessly pleaded—addressing the president of the republic, in 1992 and on other occasions; the United Nations' World Conference on Human Rights in 1993 and its conference on women in 1999; and also, as a member of the European Parliament, speaking out from within the Parliament's Committees on Women's Rights, on Civil Liberties, and on Foreign Affairs from 1994 to 1999—for the rights of women to be made an integral part of human rights and for an antisexist law modeled on the existing antiracist laws. These measures would advance the fight against sexism:

- In France I have proposed that our Constitution should be modified in such a way that the enjoyment of the "sacred and inalienable rights" enshrined in the Preamble of 1946 be extended to "all human beings, *whatever their sex*, and without distinction as to their ethnic background, religion, opinion, or sexual orientation."[1]
- At the international level I made a direct approach to Ibrahima Fall, the secretary general of the 1993 World Conference on Human Rights, proposing that the basic rights of women should be enshrined as an "inalienable, integral, and indissociable component of the universal rights of human persons."
- In Europe I have proposed that we broaden the fight against racist, xenophobic, and anti-Semitic discrimination to include sexist (misogynist and/or homophobic) discrimination and that we amend all texts, reports, and resolutions accordingly.

As you know, proposals to enshrine and implement these demands have, for over thirty years, met with—and still meet with—very stubborn resistance. And yet women are still being immolated in France, in Europe, in India, in Bangladesh, indeed all over the world.

President of the Republic Jacques Chirac put it forcibly in Johannesburg: "Our house is on fire, and we are looking away. The earth and humanity are in danger, and we are all responsible. . . . We cannot say that we did not know. We must be careful to ensure that future generations do not see the twenty-first century as the century of crimes against life."[2]

This time it was the body of a woman, the first home, the bodily home of all human beings, that was burned. How can we say nothing and do nothing?

I count on you to help us in our efforts to raise awareness, educate the public, and amend the laws.

23. What Is a Woman?

2008

The real, the living (*le vivant*): this is what was at stake at the beginning of the MLF.[1] This is why it is so hard to document its history. One would have to be a poet more than an academic, a *feminologist* more than a feminist, to depict the fecundity of its birth and its early years, the outpouring and liberation of life. One would have to prefer "intimacy with the world of living women," one would have to produce an opera, the opera of women at work, to write the story of these years of creation. Rather than taking shelter in the shadow of libraries, which hold only texts from which women are excluded, one would have to agree to hear the witnesses, the oral history, history in the present, each witness an actor in history becoming a historian. One would have to have the courage to deconstruct the history of men in order to be able to write the history of women.

In offering testimony here, the idea is not to tell my life story but to inscribe the Movement of which I was one of the founders, while making the pathways of my own action and thought visible. Thus I shall deliver this brief account from memory, out of love for truth, having been more concerned with making history all these years than with writing it; I shall recount the event whose genealogy can be established here. I ought to call it an "essay in ego-altruism," because, by proclaiming that, "as long as one woman is a slave, we shall all be slaves," the MLF expresses absolute solidarity. Never dissociated from the other, the ego-narrative becomes an altruistic narrative.

Nineteen thirty-six, 1964, 1968, three dates that marked my path, three births: mine, that of my daughter Vincente, and that of the MLF, the last reinscribing the first two.

I was born on October 1, 1936, from my father's desire to have a third child who would symbolize his proletarian freedom, a daughter; my mother didn't want a third child. The Popular Front was concurrent with my own gestation. Then, in 1964, the fleshly, psychic, and symbolic experience of pregnancy, the royal road to the unconscious, diverting me from my intellectual pathway but remaining in continuity with my personal one, constituted an anthropological and epistemological rupture for me. May 1968 was the external, cultural, and civilizational event that permitted me to braid the three strands of the personal, the political, and the historical together, both an event and a late political birth; I had finally found my space of engagement, that is, the space where I could be politically and psychically present, a way out of the prohibition on thinking. The encounter with Monique Wittig, the deeper analysis of the homosexuation to the mother and to the daughter that I had experienced since the birth of my child four years earlier, constituted a political shift. The mutation spread out over nine months, a sign of genital time. We needed this time to give birth, together, to the MLF.

For women there was a before '68 and an after. The emergence of the Women's Liberation Movement was the *genesic event* of the late twentieth century, hence the stress I place on genesis.

In 1968 I was a literature teacher in Paris and enrolled in graduate study at the Sorbonne. A PhD student with Roland Barthes, I worked on the so-called avant-garde movement, principally Italian. I attended Lacan's seminars at Sainte-Anne;[2] in analysis with him, I maintained a critical stance. I considered the avant-garde a form of aesthetic, political, or ethical thought, or all three at once. I anticipated that it would be liberating. My young husband and I were passionate about culture; we had a powerful desire to learn, to understand modernity. We translated Italian poets. We moved from the south of France to Paris in 1960. In 1965 we wrote a piece called "*Novissimi*, an Essay on Recovering the Real Through Language" for *Les Cahiers du Sud*. At Éditions du Seuil, where I had been hired as a reader, I encountered texts embodying the movement of thought in the 1960s, a modernity without precedent in French culture. A revolution in all areas of knowledge, with Lacan in psychoanalysis, Derrida in philosophy, Althusser in Marxism-Leninism, Leroi-Gourhan and Lévi-Strauss in anthropology . . . They brought French intellectual life to new heights with their incisive thinking, their research, their discoveries. This state of incessant creation could be described as a decade of Enlightenment, a genuine Renaissance that already heralded the events of 1968.

Two opposing concepts stood out in those years: the modernity of engagement according to Jean-Paul Sartre and *Les Temps Modernes* and the intransitive modernity represented by Claude Simon and the New Novel. Shortly before 1968, these two modernities confronted each other. In fact, it was a battle between the Ancients and the Moderns. I sided more with the Moderns, because the Ancients wanted nothing to do with structuralism, linguistics, psychoanalysis, or Derridean theorization. But while I had chosen my side, I felt ill at ease there because liberation by way of this avantgarde seemed to me actually to reflect a regression, a subversion of the sexual order by perversion, from Genet to Guyotat, with, for some, a fixation on "the anti-Oedipus" or on the adoration of Sade, who, in a reversal of Diderot's bright Enlightenment, portrayed the hell of a dark Enlightenment. The birth of my daughter in 1964 put me in an awkward position vis-à-vis all these ideas; in contrast, it drew me closer to my own genealogy, to my own competence, if I dare say so; at the same time I continued to grapple with this culture in order to situate myself, to situate the fruits of this experience.

Until my pregnancy I had lived on the myth of sexual difference, undoubtedly, but without difference between the sexes. My republican schooling had led me to believe that I was a man's equal, since I was taking the same courses and exams. At the university we were so-called equals and almost the same, free and transgressive, in a sort of circulation of genders. But republican equality ceased to exist when I became pregnant. Pregnant, I felt that that equality was only an illusion; if I existed as an intellectual, I didn't exist as a woman. I noticed that there was something irreducible in the difference between the sexes. I suddenly became aware of the obvious fact of a responsibility, a competence that I had sensed unexpectedly when I entered maturity, enlightened by the obscure work that, although an atheist, I had done for my DES thesis,[3] "Anguish and Hope in Bernanos's *Diary of a Country Priest*." Anguish, "at the border between the visible and invisible world," jouissance,[4] neither masochistic nor ecstatic, in a matricial erotics, and hope in the future, in what was to come, in the neighbor, in the other. The anguish of living and giving life, of thinking and acting. I entered another world, a world of before and beyond the Fall, hell and paradise, it can be understood either way, in any event something that I shared only with the child to be born and that impelled me to think the unthinkable in a universe that I hadn't suspected and that I made my place, the place of nonplace. The hope that I sensed with the formulation of the title of my thesis was there, in this back country that was a turnaround, a reversal that put yesterday ahead.

During the two years after I wrote my thesis, I had had the choice between incorporating myself into the phallocentric, republican culture, without women, or instead persevering in my own being and asserting my identity. Despite my fragile health, by choosing this inaugural pregnancy in which anguish and hope were embodied and conjoined in the work of gestation, I understood that the capacity to think not only belonged to women too, but that pregnancy was the answer to "what does one call thinking?" Before, I had only learned, understood, studied, and this was not useless, but it was not the same as producing, creating a thinking, living being; I was looking for a pioneering experience, a path that led not only to the unconscious but to what was specific to human beings, to thought. Pregnancy was the sudden emergence, in linear time, of a different time. With the time of gestation, see-ing another memory burst forth and be reactivated, the sexual, uterine mem-ory, and realizing right then that this other culture had to be inscribed in his-tory in order to complete it or invalidate it or go beyond it, or all three at once.

"What is a woman?" For Lacan, the fact that one being is born from an-other "evades the symbolic tapestry."[5] But procreation doesn't evade the symbolic; it is the symbolic that is based on matricide. The foreclosure of procreation that Lacan carried out allowed him to seize the child at birth and to insert it, even as an *infans*, in the symbolic, homosymbolic order. If procreation has a legitimate place in the human sciences, the symbolic will no longer be able to produce myths in lieu of developments in the human species. Hence my persistent determination to date the birth of the MLF.

Pregnancy allowed me to deconstruct myself as identical and to recon-struct myself as a woman with competencies and capacities, to give me ac-cess to something real that had had no place. It drew me out of the mirage of the hysterical conversion to the phallic world. That experience obviated all the introjected culture I had acquired in elementary school, in high school, in my university studies, and in the intellectual circles that I frequented. I believe I can say that I stopped being a feminist the day I became pregnant and doubly so when I had given birth to a daughter: I felt that I was outside the patriarchal enclosure, perhaps extraterritorialized with respect to one filiation and at the same time belonging to another lineage. Freed from all spirituality, I devoted myself to the materialist experience of thinking flesh, to the human experience. A kind of liberation in statu nascendi: the moment of birth as liberation. The freedom I found once again when my daughter was born was the love of women, which meant that fertility, or the matricial, was linked for me to the Movement that we would create later on. What remained in fact was to create an external place for the intimate place from which a woman procreates.

Vincente's birth was a psychic birth for me. Maternity, considered as a kind of slavery, pushed me to take my distance from the Master. It allowed me to fight against intellectual slavery and move toward symbolic independence, renewing my childhood dream of one day becoming the Spartacus of women and liberating Marseille, my birthplace, from prostitution and Nazism. At thirty-two, the age at which for the entire nineteenth century, for Balzac and even for Freud, a woman was dead, I had fulfilled the stereotype of a traditional life: an education, a profession, a husband, a child, an apartment in Paris. At that moment things could have turned hellish by renewing the alienating model of our mothers and grandmothers. Women who turn away realize that daily existence has wrecked their dream of the ideal family; they prefer to flee toward an earlier paradise, the adolescent paradise, rather than face the reality of a petit bourgeois existence, the reality of male chauvinism. They prefer to head off in the opposite direction to recover something of the adolescence that had remained fallow. Having suspected very early on that childhood lay at the end of life, I still had to live thirty-two years to get there, to return via the MLF to women only, women among themselves. A progressive regression, the world not rediscovered but never lost, since I was a woman; the world of women found anew every day. Not revolution but evolution. The world to be invented, to be created, the world that creates itself and to which each woman gives birth. And that men poets rediscover. A departure in the opposite direction, but not an inversion: a women does not go back to where she came from, does not incestuously return to the source. She stops being thwarted in her development. The real was already a word that haunted me even before I was in analysis, when I was working on the Novissimi, but this time I wanted to treat language through the real of experience.

It was time, and I knew it, to be born as a woman in history, to give birth to the political. At the age of thirty-two we either had to die or draw up a critical balance sheet and be born from everything that had come before.

And then the revolution arrived. Exit the avant-garde: what remained was the revolution among women, between avant-garde and revolution. I gave up institutional research to search in a different way . . .

In January 1968 Josiane Chanel, a friend from my seminar with Barthes, introduced me to Monique Wittig. It was the "before-spring," as Ponge would have put it. Nine months later we founded the MLF. Monique was already a recognized writer—she had received the Prix Médicis in 1964 for L'Opoponax, published by Minuit—but she was never included in photos of the New Novelists, no more than was Marguerite Duras; only Nathalie Sarraute escaped this ostracism occasionally. We both observed the ill treatment of women in the Republic of Letters, the intellectual milieu, the publishing houses, and even the university, everywhere, and I, who had given birth to a child, noted it doubly. We felt that we were discriminated against within this revolution of thought that was nevertheless very modern.

On May 13, at the Sorbonne, we created a Revolutionary Cultural Action Committee with a substantive two-page tract. André Téchiné, Bulle Ogier, Danièle Delorme, Marc'O, Dominique Isserman, Umberto Eco, Marguerite Duras, Nathalie Sarraute, and Maurice Blanchot joined this group or passed through it. There were students from the March 22 movement, workers, artists . . . It was very active, a kind of permanent manifesto of contemporary thought. We did street theater, we held meetings, we improvised. It was the alliance of the student movement with the worker movement, women and artists, the troika that, as Auguste Comte had said a century earlier, brought together the three driving forces of the revolutions to come.

It was the idea of the people's university, which Rancière so eloquently discusses in La nuit des prolétaires,[6] the idea of abolishing the division between the active life and the contemplative life, between gestures and words, in which there are no longer two classes set against each other in a single human being, with reference to manual or intellectual occupations, but valorization of the one by the other, of the manual by the intellectual, and consequently the worker's desire can be affirmed, rather than his anger, with respect to those who think and write. This was my obsession: not only to bring in bourgeois culture but also a certain avant-garde culture, a certain dissidence with respect to culture, the arts, and creative practices, while keeping in mind Marcelin Pleynet's critical observation that the avant-garde is "ahead of the reaction that it protects." There is no proletarian culture; in contrast, there is a very powerful creativity that is crushed in the classes kept at a distance from culture; and what is crushed is in fact materialism. Up to that point I had seen only Charles Péguy extol the creativity, honor, and ethics of the man who makes a chair rung. I came from a proletarian background in the noble sense of the word, I was familiar with the decolonization movements, but until then I had never gotten involved in a political movement. I wanted Psychanalyse et Politique to be a kind of people's university that would bring the highest culture, the most contemporary thought, to the greatest number of people, while looking at them from a critical perspective.[7] May '68 crystallized all these aspirations. And for me, all that had to be kept as far as possible from being sensationalized by the media.

May '68 was a liberation of thought, an event that happens perhaps just once in a lifetime, the end of confinement, the end of the taboo on thinking, a breath of radical transformation, a breath of life—it was my birth into history. But Monique and I observed that this was a male-dominated revolution, one in which women could not express themselves and one whose chief actor was the phallus, as the posters proclaimed: "Power from the barrel of a gun," "Power from the barrel of the phallus." Young men threw paving stones, they launched actions and organizations, while women in this warlike, narcissistic-phallic movement were restricted to the mimeograph machine, or even to the bedroom, and could not speak out in meetings. They were not there as sexed persons but as derivative revolutionary subjects, the second sex. We saw clearly that sexual liberation applied above all to men and that young women, thinking that they were liberated, often found themselves pregnant, having trouble getting abortions, suffering.

At the Sorbonne we already understood that we had to create a women's movement, had to free ourselves from '68; while we could draw on it for support, we had to continue doing critical work on the thinking of the 1960s, which had maintained the same old discriminations against women. We had to systematize critical freedom so as not to get engulfed in the dead end of isms,—leftism, feminism, socialism—and so as to escape the fossilized ideologies through a movement of thought, of continuous surpassing, and a revolution of the symbolic.

During the summer break Monique joined me in the south, at La Redonne (a family vacation home) with her then boyfriend, who had just come back from Vietnam, where he had shot a film on the liberation movement with Joris Ivens and Marceline Loridan. He explained to us that Vietnamese women participated in the fighting. Every day Monique read to me what she had written, which would become Les Guérillères.[8] And we decided to create a women's group in the wake of, and against, May '68. I am speaking here of an act of birth and not of a mediatized baptism.

Between May at the Sorbonne and the MLF in October, we went from culture to a fleshly materialism. During the first meeting, on October 1, 1968, in an apartment on the rue de Vaugirard that Marguerite Duras had lent us, with a few young women who mainly came from the film world, we talked about our bodies, about virginity. One might say that these were already "The Vagina Monologues." We absolutely rejected the idea of virginity as alienating for women. The first accounts dealt with intimate questions, sexuality and violence in the family. One woman recounted that she had been raped by her uncle, a famous photographer. Another said that her father, a lawyer, beat her mother . . . Monique and I discovered horrors; as the women talked, it was as if a stone had been lifted, everything came pouring out. We worked on this wounded sexuality. We saw each other almost every evening, every night, our numbers increasing, in Jo's apartment on the rue des Canettes. There was protest, revolt, and anger and there was joy, excitement, enthusiasm. But also a great deal of difficulty in naming and describing suffering.

The extreme leftists wanted to launch a revolution for the masses, for "the people's" classes. But we were the people. We ourselves were "the substance of our struggles." We worked on our own oppression. It was an activism of proximity. And we had tools that Freud lacked. We read a lot: Engels, Marx, Marcuse, Reich, Flora Tristan . . . I read Freud; Monique didn't like him.

I very quickly found these "consciousness-raising" groups insufficient: we needed a vessel to receive these words that came tumbling out so they could be treated on more than just the conscious level. We had to channel this energy more toward creativity than toward dangerous psychic suffering. I was convinced that we had to succeed in articulating two different scenes without conflating them: the extremely private scene of a wound and the scene of political engagement. While the one did not go without the other, they could not be confused; each had its specific place of treatment. Our MLF meetings had to attempt this articulation without doing collective or amateur psychoanalysis and also without programming actions that would turn us inside out. I was concerned with our work on ourselves, an in-depth work, a slow maturation.

Thus, within this nascent MLF, I immediately created a research group, a laboratory for reflection that I called Psychanalyse et Politique. Psychoanalysis because, at the time, its discourse on sexuality was the only discourse available and because it could allow us to go deeper into the political instead of making it merely a place for revolt. Politics, to highlight the fact that in psychoanalysis there is a form of power that must also be questioned. The originality of the MLF in France was that it introduced this type of thinking, and on a very large scale. Beginning to think for ourselves, rejecting all the intellectual masters: this was the great liberation.

We had decided that the first meeting would be for women only, as a first act aimed at liberating a way of speaking that women used only with one another, without the weight of domination and male discourse. Being for women only was what constituted a complete break for the MLF.

The initial homosexuation, which was only a moment in the history of women, was perhaps a necessary moment in the history of each woman so that she could succeed in existing. One cannot progress without going back to take hold of what one has had to give up, something that is still alive and lively. It is like a continuous archaeology of the living. Yet homosexuation to the mother is structural, and I think that it structures the daughter's desire for procreation, which I call the libido creandi. Unfortunately, most women don't know that, in common with their mothers, they have this genital function that needs to be symbolized. They know it on the level of the real, but, as this knowledge is foreclosed by a patriarchal civilization, they often remain mired in division and hatred toward the mother, as almost all psychoanalytical texts attest. I wanted the work of psychoanalytical theory to go back to this first, primary link and restore it, make it a competence for encountering a man or a woman and for sharing a procreative life with a man or a creative life with a woman—although creation between a man and a woman and procreation between two women can also occur. We weren't a movement against men, but a movement for women. However, we were against the misogyny that exists in men and also in women. The women-only structure was indispensable to the process of developing a female identity that could be conjugated with the male identity. A female Other with a view to the encounter with a male Other, so as to move toward a heterosexed society. Both men and women are necessary for a society to be fertile.

For nearly two years, starting in October 1968, we built the Movement through trips around Europe, through meetings in Paris and the working-class suburbs, through relentless efforts to understand and transform the condition of women. The question of sexuality brought with it that of day care centers and the right to control one's own body, one's own fertility. The pill had just been made legal. But we still had to take hold of this technical advance and make it into a tool for consciousness-raising. The first assertion had been: "Our bodies belong to us." Then the second: "A child when I want one, if I want one." I had never had an abortion, but I was one of the initiators and signers of the Manifesto of the 343.[9] It was extremely important to create an alliance and then demand not only decriminalization of abortion but also freedom of the body. For the first time women rose up as one to demand justice. It is hard today to imagine the freedom represented by this gesture. If 1945 marked the Liberation of Europe, 1968 marked the beginning of the women's liberation process.

The slogan "our bodies belong to us" indicated, right from the start, two contrasting trends in our shared determination to liberate pleasure and maternity from enslavement:

- the orientation favoring abortion to the detriment of what certain women even today call "unbearable maternity," with desexuation and gender as corollaries; this radical feminism, or "how not to become a woman," has led to the queer movement;
- the assertion of an unconstrained right to procreation as the principal demand in which the battle for abortion would be a negative moment. This was my choice. I looked for the desire for a child in the heart of abortion or in the failures of sterility. Right from the beginning, I sought to connect procreation and sexuality in order to stop cutting women in two. The idea was not to liberate women from procreation but to liberate procreation for women and for men. A woman has the right to the full development of her psychosexual components; procreation and gestation are integral aspects of her sexuality. The matricial has to be understood as an absolutely vital contribution to a regenerated and fertile humanism.

When I call to mind the images of those first years in particular, I rediscover all the gaiety and joy that we experienced in creating this Movement. I think it was starting with the MLF that political demonstrations became lively, joyful, colorful affairs that included children. Those first years were characterized by women's laughter, women among themselves, away from the male gaze, looking toward the liberation of life. It was an extremely dynamic and sensitive movement, a high-performance movement, a perpetual creation. We absolutely distrusted power; we wanted the power to do, to make, to create. A "room of one's own," a libido of one's own, we wanted to make a revolution of our own, a "silk revolution" of the self.[10]

This period culminated at Vincennes, the university representing every form of modernity, the university of contemporary knowledge. Our first public appearance came about in this place that had been the kingdom of May '68, its chosen land. It was in spring 1970. There were probably about thirty of us. Monique and half the group decided to wear T-shirts, American-style, bearing the slogan "We are all hysterics." The others—and I was among them refused: we were not willing to go on embracing this insult. A debate began; people stamped their feet; Monique, who found it hard to speak in public, begged me to intervene. My prior experience enabled me to take the floor in this large auditorium holding more than five hundred people to say the most surprising thing imaginable: "We women are going to succeed where the hysteric has failed." Marie-Claude was there, and we have been together ever since.

I started from the hypothesis that if hysteria is an illness of the uterus (something that one is still not allowed to say among analysts) it is because the uterus has been colonized by an economy of reproduction, the phallo-centric, patriarchal economy. It has to be decolonized, restored to free, not enslaved, production. I pondered what psychoanalysis had to say about "feminine sexuality" and about that absolutely unshakable dogma of ana-lytical theory, reinforced and perpetuated by Lacan and still acting as a law today: "There is only one libido, and it is phallic." This dogma is imperialis-tic, a violent blow aimed at women, who are excluded from the symbolic and therefore consigned to psychosis. With the MLF I proposed to get out of this double impasse that seeks to condemn the hysteric to forget that she has a uterus and at the same time to remember, without words, that it has to function. The hysteric is a woman thwarted in a certain way by the change of object, in her homosexual passion for her mother—hence the relationship between the matricial and what I call native homosexuality. And I wanted women not to be driven to suicide because they have been de-prived of giving life, as Virginia Woolf was. Giving life, writing books, and perhaps loving women: having this broad spectrum of love without losing the love of men and without the love of men making women lose the love of women.

Based on the experience of my pregnancy and what it led me to conceptu-alize, I told myself that penis envy, which structured women's sexuality, ac-cording to Freud, was actually a screen for men's uterus envy. Since I formu-lated this concept, anthropology has taken it up in part, but nothing has ever been said or thought about its devastating effects.

One day, perhaps, the influence that the MLF may have had on Lacan, with whom I was in analysis, will become apparent. Starting in the 1970s, while he remained misogynous and paternalistic, he began to modify his theorization of hysteria—this can be seen at the beginning of *Encore*. All his work bore on the symbolization of psychosis, maintaining the primacy of the phallus but asserting the existence, in women, of a supplement that escapes the phallic.

In May Monique, with her sister and two American women, published an article in *L'Idiot international*: "Fight for women's liberation." It was the first time the oral was repressed by the written: bringing together all our work, she raised to the rank of text a living object made up of all the voices, all the activities, all the work that had given birth to it. The author took authority over the child and erased the mother. In August 1970, the placing of a bouquet on the Tomb of the Unknown Wife of the Unknown Soldier took the form of a mediatized baptism within a religion other than that of knowledge, a pure speculation, a simple effect of representation. In an era when the media, intangible and above criticism, had become a religion, many people considered the Movement to have been born that day, as, in the past, people thought that a child was born the day of his or her baptism. However symbolic or religious it may be, such an event can never be a real birth. In October an issue of *Partisans* bore the title "Women's Liberation, Year Zero," displaying the same determination to send back to prehistory the two preceding years, forgetting, censoring, repressing the real origin. The "prehistory," here, is what precedes each woman's arrival; if she does not take into account what has been done before, it is matricide. History must be a history of the symbolic that confronts the reality principle that takes into account genesis, genealogy, and even gestation. There is no spontaneous generation, there are no miracles, there is no obligatory baptism. Instead of a mythological, biblical genesis, the profound movement of engendering should be brought to light. All these recuperative gestures, by systematically blurring the origin, modify the structure of what the Movement really was: how can a movement that deconstructs patriarchy develop if it keeps placing itself back under the patriarchal yoke? From the very beginning of the MLF, the foreclosure of the one who produces was reenacted—matricide was enacted.

From Vincennes on, the movement broadened. Before 1968 and until 1970, in France, there was no feminist tradition or no longer such a tradition. Many women presumably thought that, since they had acquired the right to vote after the war, the struggles were pointless and we had won the match.

In 1970, after two years during which the MLF had known an intense existence, feminists showed up and asserted themselves through their determination to create a "revolutionary feminist" movement rather than a "women's liberation movement." I persisted in not adhering to this ism, which for me evoked all the radical ideologies. And the important questions that we wanted to answer—questions of sexual identity, procreation, education, work, the desire for thought and creation, that is, acting-thinking-creating—seemed to me to outstrip egalitarianism and feminist identity, which were expressed in slogans like "one man out of two is a woman" or "one is not born a woman, one becomes a woman."

Our movement was created more along the lines of the right to take inventory, in a break with traditional feminism, in a sort of resistance in order to try to think differently. Even if the earlier descriptive work was necessary, it was far from sufficient; it was inscribed directly, like the work of a derived subject, within the dominant history. Getting away from this discourse means moving toward a different memory that is still inscribed in an anteriority, a back country, in a writing that was in advance: it is Virginia Woolf, it is Colette, it is Melanie Klein, and it is not the discourse of assimilation, of conversion and integration, anchored in the abhorrence of the matricial even more than of the maternal. Feminism has not taken the turn that I call ethics. "Woman" has remained an accursed word, maladetta, naming the one above all whom you must not become, since it was a word of alienation as if produced by misogyny. The MLF then grew larger and became fragmented, became a string of discrete parts, with Psychanalyse et Politique refusing to adopt the term feminism.

I think that the glorious years were the MLF's year of birth and its first two years. Around 1973 I became aware that the movement was suffocating. Repression succeeds oppression, an inevitable phase after a liberation movement. And women were dispersed in men's homes, having left the father's house for the husband's. One could say that the patriarchy organized the diaspora of women; they were in their Masters' homes, noncitizens. Next came a subculture of femininity. When women go from the condition of pariah to that of woman, when they achieve an active and structured solidarity, they reach a political position. The shift from the feminine condition to the historical condition of women constitutes liberation.

A certain number of gestures needed to be made with this in view. Houses evoke both the real and the metaphoric and that is why we created a house open to the other woman: the first, the *maison des femmes*, the women's house of Les Gobelins; the house open to other writing, the publishing house Des femmes, the first in Europe; the house open to the other unconscious, a film, *Une jeune fille* (A young girl), a critical reading of Freud's "On the Psychogenesis of a Case of Female Homosexuality"; magazines, *Le Torchon brûle*, *Le Quotidien des femmes*, the monthly and weekly *Des femmes en mouvements*; the much larger house, the one open to solidarity, all the political venues, the demonstrations, the encounters, the colloquiums, the universities, the international appeals.

I founded Des femmes at the end of the year so that we could go from words to writing and so that something of the movement of civilization could be continued. It seemed to me that political action alone was a dead end, that there would not be a revolution, that certain women would be tempted by terrorism and others would go toward neoliberalism. We needed a place for research, to build on the six years during which women had begun to speak out. The question was how to write in a nonmatricidal way, how to produce texts that would not repress the oral, but would be situated beyond phallocentrism, a sort of alliance between the oral and the genital. Later, I would create *La Bibliothèque des voix* (The library of voices). What resonates in a text, what carries it, is the voice, the genital voice. It is the first contact with the exterior, one that comes from outside but that resonates within. The voice is the Orient of the text. The first text that Proust said he had read was one he had actually heard read aloud.

And I told myself that we needed bookstores not only for our books but also to gather together all the books written by women and published elsewhere. The Des femmes bookstores are places that also welcome men (this is not the case in other places, in Germany, for example), activist intellectuals or other honest men who are fascinated by the historical condition of women. They are spaces where women and men mix on a truly equal basis rather than spaces where women are neutralized by masculinity.

In founding the MLF, we wanted to understand the why of women's inferiorization. In a period when the battles for liberation were taking place through decolonization, my first hypothesis was that women were in a situation analogous to that of colonized peoples, colonized because they possessed wealth; reading Zola's *Fruitfulness* (*Fécondité*) confirmed this for me. The appropriation of women's fecundity very quickly struck me as the first cause of their servitude, their exploitation, their enslavement. This colonized dark continent contained a tremendous spiritual, psychic, ethical, and sexual resource, which I called the libido creandi or dark energy, something that cannot be found in the workings of phallocentrism.

I have always thought that the Women's Movement represented the historical emergence of the body. Until that point we were in abstract, spiritualized history, as Freud or the French Republic posited it, with a single sex; then all of a sudden women said our bodies are here, slaves of maternity, vassals of the species. This lifting of the censorship on women's bodies was the most serious narcissistic wound after the ones inflicted by Galileo, Darwin, and Freud. I called this wound the genesic blow: it was not God who created man and woman, it was women, who, pregnancy after pregnancy, generation after generation, regenerated humanity. The idea was to turn Genesis the right way around again in the name of genesics. As God did not create the world, neither did he create Eve from Adam's rib. This creationist fantasy, spread by speculation, technologies, neoliberalism, and libertinage, aimed to make the alternative disappear: to eliminate everything that was not identical to it—fertility, the class struggle, the Jews, any otherness—or else to set up an alternative globalization, an alternative humanity, an alternative memory.

Genesic history was about to bring to light the limits of the metaphysical history contained in Genesis and myths. Writing succeeds in foreclosing the thought of what concerning woman eludes it, not only over the short and medium term but over a very long time, the time of the evolution of humanity, which will need to adapt, like prehistory, archeology, or paleography, and will need to use genetic decoding to obtain the information and datings without which history could not be made. If Jean-Pierre Vernant is to be believed, my memory is on the side of this past that is not a past. If Freud is to be believed, if the unconscious is alive, in contrast to archaeology, which can only gather ashes and shards, this past of the species is not only alive in every gestation but is the program for the future.

Based on the genesic experience that made me, in my turn, a natal body, I read in all these Judeo-Greek narratives (which constitute Europe, according to Levinas), in all the fables with which we were raised, the same male autoerotic phantasm establishing the omnipotence of men's narcissism. In them I see the self-evidence of men's appropriation of procreation as the supreme creation, with the annihilation of women and their competencies, whether we are looking at the Bible with Eve or Greece with Athena, who was born fully armed from Zeus's head.

During Pope Benedict XVI's recent visit to Paris, the entire mass was centered on the maternity of the Virgin Mary, "source of life," "Mother of us all."

With the highlighting of this iconic figure of the servant of the Lord, an incredible character in monotheisms, who uses all the language of the goddess and to whom everything is given except what is essential, the Catholic Church created a true Counter-Reformation. The very same day, the front page of *Libération*, announcing an article on pregnancies in women aged forty, included a photo of a pregnant woman's abdomen and a finger pointing at her belly button.[11] It was not the *Creation of Adam* in the Sistine Chapel but the first judgment. She was pregnant from the finger of God. It was almost the Annunciation. The pope may be planning to remodel the rooftops of St. Peter's for solar energy, but he is above all trying to capture the dark energy of the dark continent, the South and Latin America. From East to West, men are confronting one another in order to appropriate this wealth.

To explain the "French exception" that "has both the highest birth rates in Europe and that of mothers of young children with a professional activity,"[12] this same daily newspaper, which could hardly be suspected of complacency toward me, credited what it called "my original feminism," which took into account the importance of maternity in a woman's life. A feminism of assimilation—thus not very original at all, and very misdirected, since, in women's desire, it was fertility that prevailed—continued nevertheless to reject any "differentialism." The stress I placed on procreation was taken up again, but distorted in a process of dematerialization that culminated in the phantasm of technophile scholars who denied the origin, repressed and censored women's competence. Women's bodies entered the neoliberal economy as production machines, and genesic, matricial gold became the object of speculation. Poles apart from fleshly and psychic materialism, there is the artificial uterus; poles apart from what is freely given, from the gift, there is commodification, surrogacy, and the rented uterus. The label *biological mother* dehumanizes the pregnant woman and is a sign of Western domination over the uterus, the first colony and the last historically known. And these sex workers, these uterus workers, the two oldest professions that aren't professions, are the women of the third world, slaves among slaves, over which the hypercapitalist, rich, and sterile West continues to exert its domination.

Ethics no longer intervenes except in a transcendent, amaterialist manner. Ever since Diderot posited in *Les éléments de physiologie* that everything the child knows at the moment of birth he has learned in his mother's womb, philosophers preoccupied with ethics have left aside the fruitfulness of this questioning. Metaphysics does not seem to be able to think of the gift except from the viewpoint of the receiver without considering gratitude vis-à-vis the source of life. We find this perversion again in law, which legislates on abortion year in, year out, and we find it in the bias of the media that focus on the child's viewpoint, the status of the fetus, deviations in childbirth, such as pregnancies at advanced ages . . . Yet the first environment of every human being is the mother's body; it is human ecology. To forget the thinking flesh is to pervert all thinking. One does not restore to women what is already theirs: childbirth is attributed to the couple even before the ego-altruistic consequences of the pregnancy have been identified, and in a caring approach what would properly stem from genesics is ascribed to simple moral qualities. The refusal to work on this primary question produces dilapidation and exploitation. As much on the symbolic level as on the economic or imaginary level, it is forbidden to talk about *uterus envy*, and everything is reduced to a paraphilosophical social issue, whereas, on the philosophical level, unisex dominates, with the rejection of a specific libido and of materialist symbolization. This ongoing distortion feeds the dominant structure. It is always, in fact, the question of the genesis of the event, birth, and gestation.[13]

This book gives an account of each woman's genesic genesis,[14] which means that at a given moment a woman gives birth to herself, becomes the *woman giving birth to a woman* (*l'enfante femme*); then, for me, the time comes for giving birth to theory: a philosophy of birth and gestation, which can only be an ethics. But when I talk about pregnancy I am talking about symbolic fertility. Starting from the real, because, in the human species, it is women who make children ("woman: female of the species," the dictionary says), it is a matter of building an imaginary for all women that is symbolized for every woman, a matter of establishing an identity that makes it possible to better define and then decenter phallic identity.

For forty years the MLF has asserted a sexed identity. The woman of assertion is an invention of women's liberation. Today not a single woman is exempt—and this is a good thing—from a liberation movement that has revolutionized the historical condition of women and therefore of men and of the human race. It is likely that the most disruptive of the disruptions that has affected democracies as well as nondemocracies is the massive entrance of women into history. This advance is the work of the women's movement even when it denies the difference between the sexes.

When I stressed procreation, it was an innovative opening of a path between the *tota mulier in utero* of right-wing conservatism and the *tota mulier sine utero* of the elitist avant-garde. Control of fertility, provided that it is a *gyneconomy*, liberates, opens onto the most creative fertility. This is what revolution means. We have moved from one human era to another. The uni-dimensional man, to use Marcuse's vocabulary, died out in 1968. Humanity begins with two: there are two sexes. Women's access to freedom of thought seems to me to include the freedom to create and to procreate. There is in gestation—and not only in the fact of giving birth to children—a form of liberation, of creativity in which I see true poetry, true thought. My challenge in founding the MLF was to place genesics at the heart of the libidinal and political economy, at the heart of thought.

It is the MLF that has produced political and legal advances that go from the decriminalization of abortion and the institution of voluntary termination of pregnancy to the law on parity, and these laws, endorsed by deputies on the right as well as on the left, concern the majority of women, that is, the least privileged and the most vulnerable. It is perhaps because the MLF was strong, because with psychoanalytical work on phantasms it was able to emerge from extreme leftism, that there has been no terrorism in France. Women have for the most part chosen the democratic process, without compromise but in dialogue. And this movement has preceded and accompanied many other current movements, the homosexual movement, for example, which gave rise to the PACS.[15] The return of religions, with the fundamentalism, terrorism, and violence they attract, is, I believe, a defense against women's entrance into history, a "virile" protest in the face of a phallocentric West that has, even if only partially, let go of its fundamental male chauvinism, of men's omnipotence over women, and in so doing has shaken the world. During his visit to France the pope stated that religion will meet humanity's need for hope. It is secularism withstanding the test of women's historical condition, women's secularism, and future generations that will fulfill human hope and, beyond that, motivate and reinvent it.

For the first time in history, the Women's Liberation Movement is absolutely irrepressible. It is an irreversible movement contained in a territory much larger than itself, larger than France or Europe—as large as the entire world. I did not meet a single woman during those years who hadn't been an activist, a warrior, a fighter for liberation. While I may not have chosen to be (born, *n'être*) a girl,[16] I was determined to be a woman in movement, in a liberation movement. Each woman in her own singularity and all of us together, as George Sand put it so powerfully: "All existences are linked to one another, and human beings who would present their own, separately, without connecting it to those of their fellow creatures, would only be offering us an enigma to decipher . . . That individual self, by itself, has neither meaning nor importance of any kind. It takes on meaning only by becoming part of all creation, by blending with the individual selves of each of my fellow creatures, and through this blending it becomes history."[17] I think that together we women of the MLF have tried to evolve toward history. Women—a very large number of women—with the MLF have succeeded.

Forty years ago I tried to get people to acknowledge that the MLF was a symbolic movement and not just a social movement. If it concerned women, it also concerned all of humanity, the environment: women are contributing what they have been deprived of; they are rebuilding history in a new alliance in order to reconcile what has been separated by war, by the war between "nature" and "nurture," and, more broadly, by the conflict of oppositional pairs. Today, in Europe and in France in particular, the women's movement has massively chosen parity rather than war between the sexes; the movement is advancing alongside ecology and transforming women's relation to the world. Thus it is clearly a movement of civilization and, as such, an advance in liberation.

Through our battles we conquered the right to assert the dual desire of not separating procreation from sexuality, that is, the desire to save love and the desire to take part in production without cutting it off from procreation. From now on women can affirm bodies that produce the living, a creative imaginary, a body of thought on their condition in history. From the most real to the most symbolic, what remains to be done is to organize a society in which women represent half the population of this country or of the human species. Whereas the time that takes us from childhood to death is a time without generation, women ensure regeneration and the linking of generations in the life drive. A change in civilization is underway and is inscribed in a different time, the time of fertility.

Forty years already constitutes history—a long time that goes on indefinitely—and it is made up above all of the living. The revolution has not come to an end; it is unending. It has to integrate the event of '68 and the advent of women in history as uterus bearers. Because it is not fraternity without women that will resolve the conflict between liberty and equality, but ethics. There are two sexes, and that fact is what will make possible the shift from metaphysics, the love of wisdom, to ethics, the wisdom of love.

What is a woman? Genius, geni(t)ality, the genius of permanent gestation and childbirth, that can enable her to evolve from "not being" (n'être) to coming into the world through giving birth to a woman (l'enfante femme). The little girl to be born will be the birth-giving woman of tomorrow, not caught in the eternal return but in the permanent movement of generative thought . . . Ceasing to be "acosmic," assuming, in the full light of day, her share in humanity, evolution and transmission, not only in terms of the mitochondrial DNA passed from mother to daughter, from generation to generation but in terms of a symbolic and *anthropocultivating* transmission, assuming that share in what I call *ego-altruism*, in the ego-narrative and in the metamorphosis of the other, the other woman or the other man, the other daughter or son who is coming and taking on, in the end, the human hope of the species.

24. Gestation for Another,
Paradigm of the Gift

2009

LE DÉBAT: A lot of ink has been spilled already on the subject of gestation for another person. You see it as a further stage in the Women's Liberation Movement (MLF).[1] In what respect?

ANTOINETTE FOUQUE: To me it actually represents a third stage, just as important as the first two: the fight for abortion and the fight for parity.

In this very space, when we first met,[2] I said that during my own pregnancy, in 1964, the process of gestation had set me thinking about the difference between the sexes. Procreation struck me as the key issue to be addressed, politically, in an action that would be not only ideological but above all symbolic. This is what May '68 made possible and particularly effective: engagement in political action in order to transform mentalities, to carry out a "silk" *revolution of the self*,[3] to conquer rights and combat the discriminatory practices that arose, as I saw it, from that kernel of difference. An unprecedented way of articulating between the private stage and political engagement, each questioning the other so that the woman subject could emerge. The possibility of a place where women could be born, politically and historically.

This was the starting point for the MLF as Monique Wittig and I launched it in the wake of May '68 in October. Somewhat idealistically, perhaps, I wanted to see a woman arise, free herself, in every mother, whereas Monique wanted the term "woman" to disappear behind the term "lesbian".

The question of sexual difference, as she posed it from her perspective, has led to today's theorization of the "queer," to sexual indeterminacy. For me the question of the difference between the sexes (and not of sexual difference) finds its defining moment with gestation for another: this act definitively establishes the rock of procreation as the unassailable fact of the reality that there are two sexes.

One of the first aims of this *revolution* was to counter the socialist and feminist tradition of the period between the two world wars, a tradition according to which a woman's emancipation consisted in being integrated into the secular republic, devoting herself to professional life, to teaching or writing, and also to sexuality. This integration to a homosexed model from the angle of an interned difference looked to me like an amputation.

From the outset, I set aside that notion of liberty via sterility in order to connect procreation with liberation. I wagered on liberation via a process of gestation that would be a bearer of identity, thus of liberation from the symbolic alienation inherent in the phallocentric structure. Everything pregnant women say today tends in the same direction, affirming their maternal, procreative, and creative desires, which do not exclude their drives of ambition.

The indexes of fertility and of professional activity on the part of women in France are among the highest in Europe: French women have had the wisdom to try not to sacrifice any aspect of their desire to exist.

And, as I hoped in founding the Women's Liberation Movement, with gestation for another we are seeing that the word *femme*, "woman" has been disengaged from the word *mère*, "mother," for the term *gestatrice* (*gestatrix*, "gestating woman") has emerged. What were first called *mères porteuses*, "childbearing mothers," then *mères de substitution*, "surrogate mothers," had become *femmes porteuses*, "childbearing women," so designated, appropriately, by Nadine Morano.[4] This seems to me to be the culminating point, the last known stage, of the movement that began with the liberation of women in 1968, a movement that transformed the technical advance of contraception into a political act and linked this advance with abortion.

LD: How are these various causes linked, as you see it?

AF: The first major struggle was undertaken to free women from unwanted pregnancies, and I interpreted it not as a right to abort but as a right to procreate, which women do not have as long as they are not free to say "A child if I want one, when I want one." In any case, our slogan was never "No child if I don't want one!" For me abortion was the negative facet of a positive right to procreate, a first step: a seemingly negative right that came by way of the right not to procreate, allowing women to free themselves from thwarted fertility, from enslaved maternity.

We had to go through all the social stages, with Giscard and then the Socialists, to reach the point of a terrible fight over parity, the second struggle, beyond equality. Parity was an opportunity for the *revolution of the symbolic*, an alternative to discontent in a civilization entrenched in war against women.

But, with the arithmetic arrangements that have been adopted, parity seems to me to remain solely quantitative. Certain feminists think that parity is nothing but a tool for achieving equality: with this numerical, anal conception, we shall never proceed to register heterogeneity, difference between the sexes, and the fertility that this difference reflects—we shall not advance toward what I have called *qualitative parity*. There can be no fertility without difference between the sexes. There are sexual differences, yes, but that is not the same thing.

When Spanish prime minister Jose Luis Zapatero draws up a framework law, he applies it: there are equal numbers of men and women ministers in the administration, there is even a woman vice prime minister, which means that she will either deal with different problems or deal with problems differently. When Zapatero selects a woman to head the Defense Ministry, and when that woman is eight months pregnant, this is significant, since pregnancy marks the irreducible difference between one sex and the other. *Qualitative parity*—established on a quantitative basis, with the 30 percent necessary in an assembly for a different discourse to be heard, or, even better, with 50 percent—is a way to advance propositions that take the real of gestation into account and reflect the ethics or the philosophy of the living (*philosophie du vivant*).

Gestation for another is an element that comes with parity. Pregnancy has become political: among all the questions involving women, I draw special attention to that of procreation among women politicians. As the object of a law, gestation is the definitive legitimization of the difference between the sexes, not as inequality but as a supplement to quantitative parity.

Just as parity built on the right to vote—which was granted by de Gaulle but for which women had fought—and gave it a sort of corrective, as a right to be elected, in the same way passive gestation, or negative gestation in abortion, prefigured the affirmative form of the question.

Voluntary interruption of pregnancy liberated the right to procreation,[5] the desire for a child. Parity invented *heterosociality* and political heterogeneity. With gestation for another, the foreclosure of women's bodies as *productive of living beings* has been lifted.

It is a matter of looking very closely at how to think gestation or how to view gestation as a form of thought that may be carried beyond the metaphysical being, beyond the Oedipus complex, beyond the Wailing Wall that seals off the uterus—which remains humanity's organ of culture even as it continues to produce for the structure that keeps it enslaved.

For forty years now, I've been focusing on what the uterine economy might look like. I couldn't follow Lacan, who, in his seminar on psychoses, posits that "there is nevertheless one thing that evades the symbolic tapestry, it's procreation in its essential root—that one being is born from another";[6] and who, wondering "What is a woman?" responds, essentially, "a deranged person," since she is outside the field of the symbolic. The MLF wanted to liberate a woman in every mother, daughter, or sister, in all patriarchal functions.

LD: Where we rediscover the difficulty psychoanalysis has with the woman question . . .

AF: Even before 1968 I questioned the claim, in Lacan or in Freud, that "woman does not exist" and I questioned equality, that is, I raised the question of the difference between the sexes in politics. In psychoanalysis there was only a difference between genders, divided, moreover, into masculine/feminine, active/passive: what active citizen could be a woman? The activity of the feminine became feminism right away, but it did not include the universal particularity that is the ability to be pregnant.

Gestation remains either unnamed or unnamable, as we see in Freud in the process that leads up to *The Origin and Development of Psychoanalysis*. The 1895 "Project for a Scientific Psychology" is basically a gestation of psychoanalysis in which Freud creates his own uterus even while entrusting it to his *alter ego*, Fliess, through transference. Now, the very term *transference* belongs to the order of exchange between an embryo or fetus and a woman. All the words of psychoanalysis speak of gestation without naming it.

Every woman deprived of control over her gestation (at once forbidden and forced, guilty like Eve and subjected to the *diktat* "in pain you shall bring forth children") is from that point on gripped by anxiety, which through transference she transmits *in utero* to the child to be born. Gestation, for millennia, has been a process of hystericization, of the transference of anguish and the anguish of transference. There is a paradox here in the creation of a living being: a repression of the uterus and its closing-off within an economy of law. A male law above the laws, managing gestation as a set of laws vital for the renewal of the species. Whence the transference of anguish from masculine domination to all women.

In the odd text *A Phylogenetic Fantasy: Overview of the Transference Neuroses*, Freud posits that anxiety is the consequence of the climatic environment during the ice age,[7] which supports my position: the world at that point constituted a uterus, an anxiogenic vessel.

We ought to calculate the consequences of the repression of female genitality: the sex organs were obscured, science concerning them was prohibited, and origins were foreclosed, all at the same time. The Enlightenment "shed light" on these simultaneously shameful and sacred parts subject to a taboo—hence the birth of obstetrics. We are familiar with the harmful effects, for both sexes, of the foreclosure of women's genitality; we have seen the ravages of monotheisms and of the male element (*vir*) left alone to represent and affirm humanity.

We ought to see how the foreclosure and the cleavage, the male regression to a *homosexed*, unisex world, are finally a regression to an autoerotic self that, encountering the hostility of the external world, pulls back and withdraws its investment in the object, implementing sameness or a unisex model. This self needs the object only to appease its own drives toward self-preservation.

From that ice age decision ensues the hysteria of women, who are condemned to remain passive or else to become men if they want to exist on the social level.

In a strictly Freudian lineage, and following up on Freud's work on the side of women and thus of genitality, it is indeed a question of lifting the foreclosure. That work still lies ahead of us.

LD: Where can it begin?

AF: The revolution begun by the MLF in October 1968, the longest of revolutions, is twofold: it is science based, with the pill allowing control of fertility; it is humanist, with women's liberation, a development that has permeated all areas of civilization over the last forty years.

In the struggle over abortion, in the early years of the MLF, it was a matter of recognizing what the opponents of gestation for another still do not recognize: the reality of the body, that is, the desire for a child, which, in certain woman, cannot be appeased, even if it can be limited or obstructed. Look at those mothers with large families who keep on wanting one more child.

In his conversations with François Poirié, Emmanuel Levinas cites Jacques Derrida: "The movement of desire can be what it is only paradoxically as the renunciation of desire."[8] This desire is in effect unappeasable, linked to the infinite. "The Infinite," Levinas says, "is produced as Desire— not a Desire that the possession of the Desirable slakes, but the Desire for that Infinite which the desirable arouses rather than satisfies. A desire perfectly disinterested—Goodness."[9] I think it's this charge of desire that women invest in gestation for another, a perfect example of a perfectly disinterested desire, for goodness, which is forgotten in the philosophical gesture that has excluded *hospitality of the flesh* from its reflection. The desire for a child is desire itself, desire for desire.

It is at the heart of this desire that the question of difficulties with pregnancy arises, the most apparent difficulty today being denial. The denial of pregnancy results directly from the foreclosure of the symbolic, of a singular and universal experience that for the moment lacks words and speech; it is interned exclusion , a refusal of full interiority, a continued insistence that "that does not exist."

The fact that pregnancy is a determining element in a woman's life is verified, even in denial: one can only negate an event that cannot be denied. One cannot deny, then, that pregnancy is a very particular situation entailing disruptions of all sorts. It is pregnancy that makes the difference.

The denial of pregnancy is a psychic refusal of pregnancy, a psychic sterility that contravenes physical fertility. When a child is born and then killed in infancy, this infanticide can be read as a refusal to rear the child: here we see the function of the nurturing, child-cultivating, *anthropoculti-vating* mother, with all the diversified—and today often professionalized— functions that the term brings together. This brings to light the enormous work involved in procreation—especially the enormous responsibility.

Today many contemporary women assert that their family lives do not take second place to their career. This is a metamorphosis of the matricial, an affirmation. Here we have the only alternative to the war between the state-centered West, from totalitarianism to democracy, and the market-centered East, the only alternative to the phallocentric system: the genital system that is being announced as an innocent unsurpassable reality. These contemporary women with children illustrate the progressive and efficient articulation between procreation and creation, between the erotic drive and the drive of ambition in *geni(t)ality*.[10]

LD: The desire for a child also leads to gestation without a woman, to the artificial uterus.

AF: I see this rather as the end point of the long repression of women in an extreme technophilic delusion. The threat implicit in the artificial uterus is the creation of a child without a body, without flesh, whereas the promise of gestation for another is that two bodies are better than no body.

Just as philosophers and poets draw on that genitality, so technicians and obstetricians, by intervening in procreation, mean to appropriate for themselves, on the symbolic, economic, and ideological levels, what emerges from procreation without naming the principal actress, the creator of wealth, of living beings. Moreover, through a castrating, feminist body of thought based on various philosophies (queer, anti-Oedipus), they forbid her to bring to light the term *woman* or the woman subject.

In this context of repression by the sciences, by licensed experts, all the phobias are mobilized to prevent woman from existing. This effacement of women, fantasized as all-powerful mothers, is at the origin of misogyny, which has been exacerbated by the advent of the MLF, for every proclamation of, or desire for, independence makes it apparent that there is a war going on—a war of colonization, a war for control of fertility.

Not only has gestation been challenged, mythically, as a competence of women but even thus denied it has served paternal power, the dominating force. The absolute transcendence of the *gestatrix* is the object of all envy. The curse on procreation comes from the principle according to which "what I can't have I destroy": the male destroys gestation by putting it under a curse and perverting it, denaturing the work of civilization. *Uterus envy* guides the androcentrism and the monotheisms that have appropriated the female virtues of childbearing and made them theological virtues. Giving life is the paradigm of the gift, but Marcel Mauss, anthropologist of the gift, does not invoke gestation even once!

When I started the MLF, I used to say that, after the three symbolic blows articulated by Freud (Galileo's discovery that the earth was not the center of the universe, Darwin's discovery that humans are animals like the others, Freud's discovery that we have an unconscious and that consciousness is not the queen of the ego), the fourth narcissistic blow is the recognition that one is born from a woman's body, from thinking flesh. I have called this the *genesic blow*. It is Adam who is born of Eve's body: here is a reversal of Genesis that could not fail to engender terrible resistance. All late-twentieth-century philosophy hinges on this obsession. Texts on hospitality speak—without speaking of it—about what I have called *hospitality of the flesh, the capacity to welcome the other*, the capacity to receive an absolutely foreign body: the ovum and the spermatozoon make an egg that is foreign to a woman and that asks this *gestatrix* to inhibit her biological capacities of rejection and to accept it as a guest.

Pregnancy is the model for every organ transplant that involves inhibiting the capacity to reject. This is why I posit that *gestation is the paradigm of ethics*.

LD: Let's go back to gestation for another person. You didn't have any doubts, as many others did, before you spoke out in favor of this?

AF: My position results from the path my thinking has taken over many years. My mother was in a state of denial during the first five months of her pregnancy until the day her sister said to her: "I'm fourteen years younger than you; I'll bring up your child, let me have it." So, from the fifth month after my conception, I had two mothers, one of flesh, heart, and uterus and another, adoptive. I have always known and accepted this; I offered two bouquets every Mother's Day. If my godmother spoke that way, it was to end the denial of pregnancy, to get my mother to accept it. It was the support of a body and a listening ear: a compassionate body that made a gift of its person, and a backup body for her entire life. If the denial of pregnancy is one side of the coin, gestation for another is precisely its obverse.

When I encountered this question in the early 1980s, gestation was already at the heart of my intellectual commitment and of what I call the *revolution of the symbolic*, so I was favorably disposed to it. I see and understand all the possible missteps and exploitations: but if it is from the starting point of neurosis and lack that one can establish the normal workings of the psyche, one can in the same way envisage all the dangers attached to gestation for another and at the same time the unveiling that this practice constitutes.

The question of surrogate mothers arose around that time, while I was in the United States. We were beginning to see news reports on the practice, which has in fact always existed among humans: a wife adopts a child at its birth, most often pretending to be its mother. I indicated my favorable position right away: a woman must be able to say "yes" or "no," "I want/ don't want to be a mother," and to specify the conditions. I have stressed for a long time that artificial procreation brings to light the sumptuousness of natural procreation, that to recognize the latter is to decolonize the uterus, and that in France the will to prohibit inflicted on women a new dispossession of their bodies.

My reflections have thus quite logically led me to sign the petition for the legalization of gestation for another—the lawyer who originated the petition, Nathalie Boudjerada,[11] is someone I've known for many years. Five years ago I myself had sent Laure Camborieux, the president of the MAIA association for aid to infertile couples, to see Michèle André, then vice president of the Senate.

LD: Gestation for another nevertheless raises the question of service rendered for money, with all the drift toward merchandising to which that can lead.

AF: In reality I view gestation for another as a struggle against prostitution of the uterus. The two are often merged, because many feminists favoring gestation for another are in favor of regulating prostitution.

The uterus, as we have known since Engels's *Origin of the Family, Private Property, and the State*, is the terrain colonized, exploited, looted by androcentrism, the monotheisms, and every androcentric institution. With the free market economy putting profit above all else, we pass to a new status of the enslaved uterus or the purchased, prostituted uterus. We shift from artisanal efforts to an overt industry in the particular form of sexual or procreative tourism, that is, the exploitation of third-world flesh. The production of women's bodies can be purchased for a very low price in the third world or for a very high price in California.

We have to talk about the empire of the dominant group whose members exploit the earth and all its species and the first of the earth's environments, the uterus, a productive environment like all the others. If this environment is under the control of the rich in the richest countries (or of the rich in the poorest countries), we not only experience the commodification of the speaking-thinking living, but also the commodification of gestation, and then the establishment of an ethics committee to control the perverting of ethics itself, to control the transgression of human laws through profit.

There will always be the world of prostitution of the uterus and the world of the gift, of gestation for another. In the capitalist economy it is a matter of liberalization; in the economy of the gift it is a matter of liberation. There will always be a race between women's enslavement and women's liberation. Let me remind you that the MLF, with its slogan "The factory belongs to the workers, the uterus belongs to women, the production of living beings belongs to us," has posited that the uterus belongs to women.

It would seem that gestation for another has always existed, that it has always been practiced in an unofficial or at least unlegislated way. Certain philosophers suggest that we could remain at the artisanal stage. But, in a period of worldwide industrialization, the question turns out to have been already caught up in a speculative economic system that makes human flesh one of its principal resources—gray gold, red gold, sperm banks, organ trafficking, umbilical cord cells . . .

Why say that the donation of an organ has nothing to do with the donation of a child? Why do we find organ donation appropriate? Because it is free. And because it goes from a dead person to a living one. In France, then, we tolerate only gifts from the dead to the living or gifts from one living person to another that do not cause death and do not require work but rather sacrifice. Still, something of a debt is involved—a costly one. In the gift of a child the question of compensation arises: indebtedness or gratitude may remain, but something is different in the cut-up body that led Jean-Luc Nancy say that he had been able to view the organ that saved his life as an intruder.[12]

It will not be a matter of remuneration. We may wonder about the price of this priceless work. How can such work be rewarded? By something beyond money? Compensation brings to the surface the wretchedness of women's true enslavement, even more than slavery itself: it reveals that their production is irreplaceable, that they have a distinctive competence that necessarily partakes of the gift, being free, freely given, a matter of pure gratitude toward the species. They receive nothing in return. Compensation would only be alms.

We are a capitalist country, but one that does not want to give in to the dogma of doctrinaire free market liberalism as the Anglo-Saxon countries have done by and large: even as we posit limits, we press forward with truly alternative thinking, a conception of the gift that goes beyond earlier conceptions. In gestation for another, one woman comes to the aid of another woman. The children thus produced may be the last ones before the artificial uterus comes into play, children of flesh and blood rather than children of a machine, children rooted in a body rather than tomatoes grown without soil.

Up to now, before commercialization, there were altruistic elements, but human genius is in the process of industrializing and dematerializing itself; it is losing not only flesh and origins but the unconscious, prehistory. With gestation for another, there will always be this double economy, but for the first time the economy of the gift that gestation by one woman for another embodies will also be brought to light. It is not an economic question first and foremost; it is a real question that crosses all the layers of human organization, but that has to reach the symbolic function. Recognition of the *genesic function* of women is required if we are to struggle effectively against sexual prostitution and against uterine prostitution, against holding the third world and women's bodies hostage by commodification and free market liberalism.

Today the question is presented to us polemically: one must be for or against without thinking anything through. Thinking solely in legal terms, as libertarians do, will not suffice. Trying to make a judgment in terms of economic factors will not do either. The law proposed in France seeks to give a framework to an underground, extraterritorialized practice and above all to trade in human beings. France is a country of laws, opposed to the commodification of humans. A law on the *production of living beings* will name, limit, and give its full meaning to the gesture of gestation. This recognition would not only lift the denial but would affirm the competence of the *gestatrix*. And, far from the ethics of restriction and prohibition that prevails at present, there would be an affirmative, materialist, liberatory ethics.

LD: Gestation for another also brings up hesitations of a much deeper order having to do with sex roles, the psychic identity of the actors . . .

AF: Yes, precisely what interests me in gestation for another is that there is more than one woman to make gestation circulate. This strikes me as an excellent way to desacralize the patriarchal maternal function and to bring out the difference in competences: the ovum is not a spermatozoon; even if there is some talk of parthenogenesis, the heterogeneity that the spermatozoon brings must be taken into account. Among many women who are opposed to gestation for another, there is the specter of homoparentality—it is not a question of justifying homoparentality "morally" by being "better" parents but of getting this manifest reality recognized—and there is also this disturbing question: does a woman have the right to give a child to another woman?

One of the first laws that followed on the heels of the MLF, in 1970, contemporary with the struggle for abortion rights, was the abolition of the notion of "paternal power." Once parental power is dissociated, we are headed toward fragmentation. The fragmented body: these are the organs from a living body that are being given. An embryo is not a fragment, it is a future! It is, on the contrary, gestation recomposed: everything converges to create a living child.

In gestation for another, the infertility at issue arises indeed from the absence of a uterus in a couple: no uterus is available to proceed with gestation and create the child. Gestation for another then makes it possible for several people to contribute to fertility. Whether the couple in question consists of a man and a woman, two men, or two women is of no importance, since genitality is always at least tripartite: it is plural.

One can imagine an ovum, a spermatozoon, a genitrix, a *gestatrix*, an adoptive mother—or one can say that the genitrix is the mother who will receive a child born to another woman. Matricial filiation is introduced horizontally. It does not simply involve mitochondrial DNA but also the transmission of an embodied unconscious. My body is an inscribed body that remembers and thinks—and gives. It seems to me that what is involved here is not fragmentation but a will to reassemble; rather than a body in pieces, a body plurally conceived and enriched. Rather than one child for two women, two women for one child.

In gestation for another there is a fine idea that topples the matriarch, the positive or negative phantasm of maternal omnipotence; it is an idea of sharing more than of tearing into pieces—a sharing of responsibility and of life. This diversification of functions of the finest occupation in the world is what permits a radical critique of male or female metaphysics. The Diana of the Ephesians is no more fitting than the belief in an omnipotent God, creator of heaven and earth, and of Adam. It is not utero-centrism that is going to cure us of phallocentrism.

Procreation must not be chained to maternity, for placing everything on the mother makes the mother everything. This leads us astray and brings us into a new phallocentrism or into a conservative morality, for, instead of liberating "woman" through procreation, we tie her down with the notion of "mother." Aren't the opponents of gestation for another, in their belief that they are protecting the "mother," ultimately reinforcing patriarchy? The benefits of procreation are alienated when there is naturalization of the maternal function rather than symbolization of matricial activity where flesh would become word, where speech would not be logocentric, and writing would not be semblance. Instead of "woman" bringing about change in the structure of androcentered philosophy or in the Lacanian structure, it would be the unchanged structure that would integrate the woman-as-mother, which has always been the conservative position. The "silk" *revolution of the self* entails liberating a woman from all the roles that have been prescribed heretofore in an effort to thwart women's competence.[13]

Gestation for another leads in this direction. The name of the father is multiplied and exchanged ad infinitum, between the adopter, the genitor, and others. And the body of the mother, nonphallic, is multiplied among several women's bodies. The *foreclosure of the body of the mother* sent women into psychosis; but if we start to think that "mother" is diversified, then there are several women who are liberated. This is where an "I," a woman subject, comes in fully. It is her singularity and her share in universality. It is the adventure common to the greatest number of women, and its extension to gestation for another can only increase the knowledge of all.

I support gestation for another because I am beyond feminism and because I am a psychoanalyst. My thinking about gestation is not totalitarian, that is, not maternalist; it is materialist.

The simple fact of referring to *gestation* reintroduces nonmaternalist materialism in fact. I dream of a woman who is free and whole, with all her competences: brain, uterus, and heart.

If Freud's masterstroke was lifting the repression of the unconscious, that of the women's movement is lifting the foreclosure of the procreating body: not only is it the case that "our bodies belong to us," but "our bodies are here, we exist." Starting from a negative situation, the debate has made it possible to think the historical condition of women. Today, as was true yesterday and will be true tomorrow, we must not remain where we are: we must have the courage to go further. We must work on the function of a woman's body, the uterine function, and the *metaphysiological* unveiling of that function. For the first time, we do not see the uterus in counter-relief, in absentia, as in hysteria, or amputated as in hysterectomy; we see it rather in its necessity, in its vital function.

This is culture; this is civilization: to try to order without repressing, without destroying the burgeoning of culture. There are problems to solve, problems that cannot be solved by a denial of the questions that they raise, a denial that could be the negative response to all the questions.

LD: So for you, then, the essential issues are going to be decided among women?

AF: The childbearing woman comes in where there is no uterus. And she comes in, as it were, through the creation of solidarity, an alliance among women from which both sexes benefit. At this point I see her as an ally, a "comother" (*commère*) who fulfills the role of fairy godmother, who rights the wrongs from which her goddaughter suffers.[14] During this episode a prolonged dialogue between women will be launched.

The coresponsibility is not simply maternal, but matricial, uterine. A different sharing and different compassion come about according to the laws of the living body rather than according to the laws of the mind or of a legal system. It is thus logical that this responsibility should enter into law. One must neither foreclose the childbearing woman in anonymity nor trivialize her gift. There is one more parent, not one less gestation. We need to envisage childbearing in the philosophical sense of the term *bearing*: the sculpturing of a living entity. Between two women homosexuation allows not only the sharing of fertility but a cocreation of a living, speaking being. It is impossible for a woman without a uterus to make a child, and yet it is possible if a *gestatrix* carries the child alongside her, if she does ethical, *poethical* work.

The alliance between women assumes competence and responsibility for the act that has long been viewed as the original sin. Gestation for another is one of the first liberating acts of this gestation without guilt. If the women involved have the possibility of speaking about their pregnancy, they will express their inexpressible jouissance, all anguish surmounted, all hope fulfilled. And this will be the end of the three monotheisms, those murderers of human matter.

LD: You have alluded more than once to the secular stakes that would be attached to gestation for another. What do you mean by that?

AF: Through the pending legislation it is also a question, as I see it, of secularizing maternity, which is still overly sacralized, and of proposing an ethics on the side of "for others"—literally a secular ethics.

Women, artists, and workers—the revolutionary trilogy proposed by Auguste Comte for the transformation of the world—have to be renewed (not abandoned) so as to become women, ecologists, and secular thinkers. By "secularism" I mean women and the secularization of mythologies through metapsychology, depth psychology, a mission that Freud assigns to psychoanalysis. Psychoanalysis has to focus on women, and anthropology on ecology.

Speculation has to give way to the rematerialization of the world, which goes along with secularization, at once a passage from the religious to the scientific (but not necessarily to the technological) and from fantasy to reality (to clinical experience).

Whence the royal road of the psychoanalysis to come, which is gestation, for the analytic scene and creative processes, as well as for the work of the unconscious and the treatment of transference neuroses, early neuroses related to recent experiences (for example, early maturation and pregenital repression in girls).

LD: Do you see women as the actors par excellence in secularization?

AF: The alternative to any discourse, to any metaphysical science, to any master discourse, is an exploration of "Planet Woman"—which is part of Planet Earth. At the 1992 Earth Summit in Rio, Planet Woman—*Planeta Femea*—was the title for the meeting of worldwide women's associations that later organized the UN World Conference on Women in Beijing. There were women from all over the world. It was a matter of saying that, vis-à-vis God, there are women and that women are the locus of secularization. Women are confronting clerics and doctors of Law—doctors of all laws, religious and scientific. The voice of secularism is the collective voice of women.

I said as much at Rio: the uterus is the human being's first environment. Today we see the relation that gestation may have with ecology: How, after the Grenelle de l'environnement,[15] can we fail to see that this environment exists? Contrary to ecology, it is not a matter of man and nature, it is a matter of an intermediary environment that is not nature, that is strictly human, where something is played out involving an environment and a psychic future for the species, of which women, *anthropocultivators*, are the guardians. I do not believe that the earth is a uterus, but I believe, in contrast, that the uterus is both an earth and a world, the soil of civilization, of culture. All phylogenesis relived at the level of ontogenesis: this is *genesics*. Here the process of humanization of the species is endlessly replayed.

The earlier human sciences do not suffice to account for this. We need a new epistemological space; we need to bring a dark continent to light through a discourse that this decentered, ethical, hospitable subject will posit. This is the object of the *feminology* that I have been advocating for years. This science of women, or rather these sciences of women, speak of gestation, from genitality to genius. *Feminology* secularizes; it brings people the knowledge of masters, doctors, clerics, philosophers, authors, all capitalists of meaning, as it liberates what their domination kept enslaved. A politics of civilization has to proceed, today, through women and their humanizing contribution. For our civilization, by putting procreation under a curse, has perverted the human story.

LD: How do you envisage this higher state of civilization?

AF: For me it is summed up in access to the stage of genitality. Envy, which Melanie Klein deemed primordial, has to be transformed into gratitude for women's gift to humanity or into admiration for such an unbelievable thing. Why did Descartes write that admiration is the first of the passions to be formed *in utero*? For my part, I see admiration as opposed, term for term, to envy.

One can also establish an equivalence between faith, hope, and charity with the three keys to thinking offered by Heidegger: "remember, think, and thank." Or one can say that God's primary virtue is mercy and recall that the Hebrew root of this word is the same as that of the word for uterus.

This genitality, which psychoanalysis has been unwilling to theorize, is known. Everywhere in the books of philosophy I read there are traces of the fact that gestation is *the* event. For example, in the Jewish religion it is said that an angel comes to lay a finger on the lips of a newborn child, so that the child will forget everything he or she has already learned, knowledge that the Torah will reimpart. Diderot, in his *Elements of Physiology*, asserts that the child *in utero* already has all the knowledge in the world— Élisabeth de Fontenay calls Diderot a *gynéconome*.[16]

All humanity knows that the newborn is a perfectly equipped male or female human being, created to create, that is, to be a poet, a businessperson, an artist, a doctor, a laborer, an artisan, an engineer—everything that human minds have created and can continue to create—and that women, through gestation and procreation, are going to cultivate still more. We must reach the point of saying that there is a properly human— thus speaking and thinking—structure of the real, for what would be concern for the other, but not in a mothering manner. Women make children, and, ever since *Homo erectus*, have been in culture, have been participating in the creation of human gestures, speech, language.

Our history precedes each of us, comes well ahead of the self. Gestation is the living movement, the permanent invention, of the world and of oneself. The *engram*, that trace in the brain engraved before birth, in which I see an archiwriting, is a programming: there is no past that is not a future. According to Freud, "the individual's mental development repeats the course of human development in an abbreviated form."[17] And humanity circulates with desire. Just as ecology does not respect borders, mitochondrial DNA, also transmitted by women, does not stay confined within them. This means that humanity moves through gestations. It is a generalized diaspora, and women are the traceability of that universal, transhistoric, transcontinental diaspora.

But foreclosure is being reactivated everywhere, endlessly. Every effort is being made to win back the field of gestation—discovered some forty years ago—by enclosing women within a psychotic and schizophrenic programming. This entire field remains unheard.

What would this *gyneconomy* be? It belongs to the order of the absolutely human; it certainly does not belong to the natural order: a woman is a female human, but she is human much more than she is female. What does she weave when she makes a child? What happens during pregnancy, during which intrauterine exchanges occur? We couldn't have surrogate mothers because the whole intrauterine life would be lost? Quite the contrary! Beyond the cultural, symbolic, genetic, genealogical inheritance there is a gift tied to a singular person that will leave traces, at the level of temperament, drives, the creation of a personality. If the bond is maintained (and French law will surely provide for this), one can say that it will enrich the personality of the child to come all the more—and more clues will be available than in the case of an adopted child. This child will benefit from multiple origins, from a sort of interleaving of affects, emotions, resonances. The contribution of the *gestatrix* will be considerable.

Something is happening here that is very important to me, something in which lies, foreclosed, the truth, not just of women but of their procreatures, that is, all human beings, something Freud claims to have found in *The Interpretation of Dreams*: in dreams one sleeps and rediscovers intrauterine life.

Where are we to look for the term *woman* as an absolutely vital element for the humanity of the species in the humanism to come? Woman, for me, would be found in the act of gestation: pregnancy is not merely a state; it even surmounts the opposition between state and act; it is a place of absolute reciprocity, of alterity without alteration. Here is the full performativity of pregnancy: rather than "I write or I die," it is "I give birth; I create." All creators of genius, all poets, say the same thing. Freud writes that, while Martha approaches the end of her pregnancy, he is giving birth to *The Interpretation of Dreams*. Our culture is familiar with this *geni(t)ality*, but marginalizes it, even among men, for it is unacceptable to phallic reason.

Rather than in the forces of the spirit, the *homosexed* Trinity, the Father, the Son, and the Holy Spirit, I believe in the forces of the flesh. Primordial transcendence is a bisexed trinity because it involves mother, child, and flesh. Flesh is the sixth sense, sexed, linked to jouissance rather than to anguish or its spiritualization, hope. It is the primary fleshly transcendence, which is not at all immanence; it is the transformation of a state into an act.

These three words, *Gestation, For, Another,* are magnificent, for they raise ethics to the nth power—or to the power of *g* (gestation, genesics, generosity)—as an absolute value, the human possibility of giving priority to the other over oneself. For the first time what could be called primary ethics and primary philosophy come together, through the mediation of law, to affirm a symbolic order achieved beyond a mercantile and dematerialized civilization. This shift beyond the frivolous represents an opportunity, at last, to think *genesics*, to think differently. All procreation for another is marked with this sign: the gift as interpretation of the world, knowledge, and acknowledgment of others. At the heart of ethics there is ethics itself: giving life.

But one must have the generosity to think such a gift. To love women would be to trust them, to count on their wisdom. The future of the human species lies here, in women as bearers of ethics and in ethics favoring the raising of consciousness on the part of women and of men.

It seems to me that what we have begun in history is this revolution: access to what is always still foreclosed, to *geni(t)ality*, to human genius.

25. Gravida

1980

Here in Quebec we rarely hear a critique of feminism as a simple ambition to share an unchanged power with men. *Gravida* seeks to undertake such a critical approach, among others. This appears indispensable now that feminism has become a major cultural phenomenon.

In the interview that follows, "feminism" must be read as a demand to share in masculine power, or even an ambition to dominate within sites of power, without any radical challenge to that power itself, to its origins or its political and libidinal economies.

Groups of women and some men in Quebec are now working with the ideas of the psychoanalyst Antoinette Fouque.

A women's liberation movement that critiques feminism: does that not warrant a pause for reflection?

Jean Larose

GRAVIDA: Let's begin with the beginnings of the Mouvement de Libération des Femmes in France and of the Psychanalyse et Politique collective.[1]

ANTOINETTE FOUQUE: They are absolutely contemporaneous. In the May '68 movement, which gave rise to the Mouvement de Libération des Femmes, there were two central questions: the question of the authority of the Father and the question of sexuality. Two struggles were going on at the time: one was anti-authoritarian, the other was for sexual liberation. But prior to the women's movement there had been ten years of active anti-imperialist struggles in France and in the world, with the war in Algeria, the independence movements in Sub-Saharan Africa, the war in Vietnam and the groups opposing it.

From the very earliest meetings of what was to be called the MLF (more by the media, as it happens, than by women themselves), in October 1968, and even during the preceding summer, we worked on the self-evident fact that reality is organized around inequality between the sexes, between races, between classes. The inequality between the sexes, which was and still is our principal issue, was either raised in a precritical feminist way that antedated the psychoanalytic revolution—"there is inequality, we want equality"—and in which the question whether equality between two different terms was possible did not even come up; or, if it did, it led to the judgment that psychoanalytic discourse—the only discourse to date that interrogated sexuality—had to be questioned through a critical or postcritical effort to develop it further. Starting with the very earliest meetings of our little group, in October '68, some of us questioned the way the sexual contradiction was inscribed not only in social classes but in the analytic field. The "Psychanalyse et Politique" pairing was already at work. At that point we were trying to work out the dialectics of the economic and the symbolic (Marx and Freud), rather than the dialectics of the anti-imperialist movement and the women's liberation movement; the second process came later.

From October '68 on, we could see the impasses into which the May movement was going to get stuck owing to the unconsciousness that pervaded the political realm. One of my own earliest observations was that expressions of the unconscious were not limited to situations in which there were two interlocutors and did not necessarily require a couch. This may seem a little ridiculous twelve years later, but the Psychanalyse et Politique practice was developed prior to the whole "anti-Oedipus" movement,[2] and it inaugurated what could be characterized as work on the political when the unconscious is not left out of the picture. I was already positing that not only is there something of the unconscious in the political but that there are relations of power and force within the system of hierarchization of the libidinal stages and what constitutes the "reality principle" (a position that is still not accepted, I believe, within institutional psychoanalysis).[3]

GRAVIDA: What is striking for North Americans is the way you use psychoanalysis. Here, we're used to feminists dismissing Freud altogether because of what he wrote about women, whereas you have a totally different relation to psychoanalysis.

AF: It's impossible to posit the contradiction and antagonism between the sexes in a precritical way that doesn't take Freud's discourse into account. We would be condemning ourselves to go back a hundred years in our thinking. We have to recognize, however, that feminists were the ones who unmasked the ideology of masculinity in Freud: in Sexual Politics Kate Millett offered one of the first critiques of the ideology of masculinity underlying Freud's discourse.[4]

GRAVIDA: Yes, but things have played out as though the feminists couldn't get beyond this denunciation.

AF: It's surely more complicated than that. In any case, they haven't used the psychoanalytic instrument to critique the ideology of masculinity and they have maintained a kind of face-off, as if to say "he is masculinist, we are feminists," which is a simple inversion (in fact, the same process of inversion is often found elsewhere in the feminists' positions). The paradox is that the women's movement has not taken the Freudian revolution into account as a condition for the maturation, and perhaps even for the birth, of that movement; it has even envisaged Freud's work in the mode of denegation. In the earliest American texts, even in Millett's, the works of Freud and Marx are addressed negatively, even though they had helped the historical situation to evolve. And then there is the whole question of the hastily forged concept of "patriarchy" to which feminists refer without analyzing their unconscious relation to it.

GRAVIDA: Doesn't the importance of Jung in the United States, as contrasted with Freud, shed some light on the feminists' attitude toward Freud?

AF: About Jung I can only say what everyone knows about him, that he was pursuing a metaphysical deviation. But yes, American feminism is indeed constantly going down blind alleys in the direction of the occult sciences, hypnosis, and pre-Freudianism. Feminism is most often "anti"- or " ante-," pre-Marxist and precritical in terms of the psychoanalytic revolution. And it represses the MLF and the epistemological break this movement has instituted, since feminism starts from and remains wedded to an out-dated humanist philosophy. This attitude, reactionary in its unwilling-ness to acknowledge the discoveries of contemporary thought, often pro-ceeds by substituting an ideal ego for the ideal of the ego, thus remaining at a level of aggressive and anal presymbolization. It's the old story of the musician-assassin. Do you know Dostoevsky's short story? One day a man who sees himself as the world's greatest violinist, without ever having touched a violin, meets the real "greatest violinist in the world." And kills him. Necessarily, since that man was stealing, in reality, his phantasm from him. Here you have the process of paranoia: one has to kill the ideal object with which one identifies oneself so as to take the place of that object phantasmatically. This is Lacan's "Aimée case" or Valérie Solanas's SCUM.[5]

The divergence between feminism and the MLF has been, from the be-ginning, the difference between regression purely and simply experi-enced and regression traversed analytically. Analysis is a way of verbaliz-ing regressive processes, whereas feminism puts them into action. Where Jung is concerned, one can speak of the immaturity of his deviation, of its structure as a libidinal oedipal "immaturation," which is also found in the regressive components of the women's movement, via feminism. The anti-Oedipus, the regressive return, whether denied or acknowledge, to a maternal, preoedipal stage. In fact, this is not what the Women's Move-ment posited. The anti- or anteoedipal, or the prephallic, position is a po-sition advocated in an oppositional move by the proponents of schizo-analysis and a position held by feminists. Some feminists have understood the anti-Oedipus as an antipatriarchal struggle, even as they deny what belongs to the unanalyzed and continually repressed relation to the mother, that is, to prepatriarchal values. Not to think through, analytically, the move beyond the phallic stage seen as the primary genital stage is to find oneself lingering a hundred years behind the times, instead of con-tinuing the Freudian work that stopped with the discovery of the oedipal processes. The process of displacement and maturation—in other words, the analytical process—is continuously replaced by a phantasmatic op-eration of identification, which is then enacted.

GRAVIDA: Is this related to your belief that feminism is historically the last metaphor of patriarchy?

AF: Yes. Just as one can say that "it's the son who makes the mother," one could say that "it's the daughter who makes the father." The maternal inscription is given to a woman by the son who bestows a function on her within patriarchy. There is no mother but the mother of a son. A woman has to have a son, has to bring into the world the being who bears and symbolizes the phallus, if she is to be worthy of figuring honorably in a patriarchal structure. It is much less certain, in contrast, that giving birth to a daughter allows a woman to achieve the prestige of the maternal and its majestic function. Yet it was perhaps Anna Freud, or Lou Salomé, who "made" Freud, who allowed him to attain a paternal function and exit from a certain position as a son dependent on the mother or on a woman taken for the mother. You know that there is a text by Lou Salomé called "Thanks to Freud." In the same vein, the issue of *L'Arc* devoted to Lacan was written exclusively by women from the Freudian school. I think the famous "Name of the Father" can only come historically from this relation of a man to a woman who is not in a position to be his mother and who is going to draw him out of his position as son.[6]

This is why I say that feminism lies within the patriarchal enclosure. The object of feminism is the struggle against the patriarchy, but that struggle "against," at the point where it fails to interrogate its own unconscious motives, where it represses the ambivalence of the relation to the father (ambivalence in its positive aspect)—that struggle is polarized around being "against the father" and very close to the father, without bringing to conscious awareness the daughter's fixation on the father. In fact, it seems to me that what is happening is an identification of the daughter with the father, that is, the daughter "makes" the father: she imitates him and makes him the father, exactly as the son makes the mother a mother, that is, imitates her (putting himself in the position of creation) and gives her her function. Paradoxically, the antipatriarchal struggle is thus also the advent of the symbolic position of the Father; it allows the shift from an unconscious or archaic patriarchy to an assumption of the Name of the Father through the fact that what is advocated at bottom in the counterpatriarchy is access to the paternal identity, to the Name of the Father, and to the phallic position.

GRAVIDA: You're saying that feminism is a fixation of the woman at the phallic phase?

AF: While the chief enemy is presumably the patriarchy, there is a phallic demand, a demand for equality with men in the world as it is, a world in which the reality principle is confused with the principle of inequality between the sexes and still more so with the principle of the absolute primacy of one sex over the other—the other being practically nonexistent.

Lacan established the analytic theory that has predominated over the past twenty years by positing that "the phallus is the signifier of desire." Men and women alike are said to confront this reality principle—which a close look at Freudian theory shows to be a prepubertal reality principle. Historically, the world is stuck in this prepubertal position, for both sexes: jouissance can only come from the phallus, and there is only one sex that stands for both sexes—a position that is called phallocentrism or (in keeping with Derrida's concept) phallogocentrism. The antipatriarchal struggle remains inside this enclosure; thus we witness the paradoxical situation in which the feminists, who think they are struggling against patriarchy, demand the phallus—that is, the Name, individualism (they designate themselves as [female] "individuals," as undivided, nondivided subjects), the Ego, and a share in power on an equal basis with men—without asking to what libidinal phase the history of this struggle is attached. Thus, indeed, if one designates the principal enemy without understanding how that enemy can also be an object of desire or identity and how it can play a role in structuring desire or identity (something that analysis can contribute), one believes one is situating the enemy on the outside and thereby fails to recognize it not only as an internal enemy but as an articulatory component.

It is not a matter of declaring that feminism as a fixation on the father is good or bad, but rather that, from the moment when it fails to recognize the relation of the daughter to the father and the articulatory function of this relation, it represents a fixation, thus a regression. In other words, feminism is a dead end only to the extent that it is an unconscious fixation at the phallic stage, that is, on the aspect of the father-daughter relation that is in play in that phase.

The feminists get out of the self-destructive impasse constituted by the failure to recognize this positive relation to the father only by closing themselves off within political parties, within hyperpatriarchal institutions. In France, even as they denounce patriarchy, the feminists choose to publish with ultracapitalist and patriarchal presses. In other words, a feminist can maintain a conscious discourse against patriarchy and against phallic imperialism, but as long as she does not identify the site where the phallus can be, for her, the signifier of desire, she is in a state of denegation. This persistence in denying the positivity of the relation to the father is the impasse confronting the feminists. Because where there is denegation there is fixation and regression.

But feminism has a strongly positive aspect, as does hysteria. Feminism must not be written off as negative; it is an absolutely necessary phase. This century is feminist, and I believe there is not a single woman today who is not a feminist. But it is one thing to recognize oneself as a feminist, caught up in a process of elaboration, and quite another to stop there and choose feminism as the ultimate state of women's liberation. For the phallic stage and feminism are not the ultimate stage, for women, either in historical or libidinal terms. There is a stage "beyond feminism," because there is a stage "beyond the phallic."

GRAVIDA: You say that there is a stage "beyond feminism and the phallic stage"; couldn't this be rather a question of falling short?

AF: No, it can't be a matter of falling short. And in fact, when there is denegation of that phallic articulation, an anal or oral regression often ensues, with phantasms of matriarchy; or else a fixation, though the latter has the advantage of belonging to its own time. I repeat: this century is feminist; and today, ultimately, to articulate a phallic phase well is to traverse the century on the side of the privileged few. Just as, in the class struggle, there are the proletariat and the bourgeoisie, and then the immense majority belonging to the lower bourgeoisie, people who belong economically to the proletariat but ideologically or symbolically choose bourgeois power, one could say that the feminists are "lower [female] phallocrats." When I said this, a dozen years ago, they went for the jugular, and yet . . . What's more, I wonder if it isn't the women's struggle that is going to bring back to light the desire that the exploited may have for the exploiter. That would make it possible to do some real work on the master-slave dialectic; Lacan does this, but it could be done on a massive historical scale. In fact, in the struggle women are undertaking, we see the desire that women can have for the phallus, that is, for their principal enemy, whereas it is much more complex to speak of the masochism of the working class or of colonized peoples or of the desire that the colonized may have for the colonizer, that a black may have for the "Great White." But it's high time to talk about this; otherwise I don't see how we can account for the mechanisms of colonization, especially the aftereffects of decolonization.

GRAVIDA: "Articulate a phallic phase well," you say. But this isn't easy for a woman.

AF: That's right; if one doesn't want to remain fixed in a regressive and antioedipal posture, it's obvious that the structuring of the phallic phase is extremely important. In Freudian theory the phallic phase has to be traversed and surpassed, except for women, who have to regress and fall short. But Freud also said that one never gives up a desire. The situation of regression in which he places women is the very situation that produces hysteria, that is, a fixation at the phallic stage.[7] So you can say "hysteria" or "feminism" in 1980: it's the same thing. It's the insistent fixation on the phallic phase, through a threat of regression dictated by the primacy of the phallus. And to fixate on the phallus is to renounce being women. So one has to articulate both the phallic phase and its surpassing—and its surpassing for men too. For them, fixation at the phallic stage is priapism or Don Juanism; this is where capitalist society is stuck.

One could also speak of the priapism of the feminists who are in a permanent state of erection. Feminism is hysteria enacted in a phallic positivity. In feminism there is thus the danger of losing a difference. In hysteria, prior to feminism, this difference is maintained, in alternation, in the "I want"/"I don't want." At the beginning of the Movement, women were raising questions about the ontological value of negation: from what positive space is the refusal organized? On what positive foundation does the negation rest? For, in the case of the hysteric, one tends not to hear what she is saying yes to when she is saying no. Some claim that this positivity of hysteria, in its refusal of the phallic, which I stress, is a regression to the uterus and that by recognizing this I am reducing women to uteruses. Others say that, in any case, for the time being, women have to acquire rights without worrying about this difference. I believe that this way of thinking is absolutely antimaterialist because there is precisely this self-evident, paradoxical fact that, in the phallic phase, a woman is being developed and a woman is being lost. It is obvious that now, today, this difference must be put to work; we must not wait until tomorrow. This century is feminist, but we have to think critically about and beyond feminism, which, failing to think the difference, reinforces the patriarchal enclosure. The Women's Movement is situated beyond feminism. Here, moreover, is the fundamental break.

The fixation at the phallic stage has effects on erotic practices as well as on clinical analyses; this is completely obvious in statements by feminists or hysterics, for example. This fixation induces a whole series of erotic practices that are manifestly related to frigidity: for example, the refusal of penetration. In the Movement's early days, there was a call for an absolute refusal of penetration.

GRAVIDA: Isn't there a connection, nevertheless, with the fight against rape?

AF: Yes, the fight against rape is one of the struggles the Movement has taken up, has been working on in fact since 1970: how does the structure of rape fit into the libidinal economy? We noticed very early on that its structure was similar to that of castration. Rape, for a daughter, would be the structural equivalent of castration, for a son. There would be no legitimization, no practically introjectable identity for the daughter, without rape, that is, without "paternal trauma," as Michèle Montrelay would say; Françoise Dolto speaks of "gentle rape," consensual rape, something like the father's stamp on the daughter's body. And, with regard to hysteria, Freud first believed that, when a hysteric said that she had been raped, there had been a rape. Later, he claimed that the report of rape was a fantasy, almost a "primal fantasy," and this Freudian position has been maintained, whereas rape is still very often a reality in such cases. This is to say that, while castration does not exist in reality for sons, rape really does exist for daughters.

In Jewish culture the boy's body is actually marked and the girl's is not. Where is the marking for the girl? Michel de Certeau is almost the only one who has really worked on the marking of the body through the signifier, through the articulation between the real and the symbolic, thus on the relation of the law to the body.[8] And that law, for women, is most often imposed in a completely savage and barbarian manner.

And, confronting Freud, there are the feminists for whom rape exists only when it is real. They do not recognize its phantasmatic dimension, still less its symbolic dimension. In fact, they have taken up the question of rape again, several years after we did, but solely in the courtroom context, demanding that the law recognize the existence of rape so as to punish rapists.

GRAVIDA: In the face of an assertion such as Georges Bataille's that "women basically want to be raped," feminists say simply "no, that's wrong, that's unacceptable." They respond with a kind of passion that denies the possibility there could be something to think about here.

AF: Freud "battled," if I may put it that way, between "she wants" and "she doesn't want." But be careful: a woman does not want rape. Where a woman desires jouissance in relation to penetration, what she encounters in reality is rape. I believe that this is a structuring fantasy of the *female libido*—I am deliberately not saying "feminine" to avoid a generic opposition between "femininity" and "masculinity" within a monologic Logos. But, where there is a certain type of desire in a woman, rape is imposed on her, that is, penetration by physical force—and, by the way, rape is not only practiced on women. This issue allows us to illustrate the feminist fixation at the phallic stage, in relation to the refusal of penetration of which I spoke earlier. But this refusal is accompanied by a denegation of the symbolic function and of questions about early seduction as a primal fantasy. Preserving the integrity of what is inside the body, denying the existence of the vagina, fixating on the clitoris . . . In the United States there have always been arguments about vaginal orgasms versus clitoral orgasms. This is important, because these are points of conflict that are in fact points of repression.

GRAVIDA: It's very important, this relation between points of conflict and points of repression. And not only in feminism; in left-wing politics, as well.

AF: There is the indication of a point of conflict, but at the same time the impossibility of thinking it, owing to the repression of the unconscious. Each conflictual theme at the sexual level is immediately transformed into a fetish, through a process that derives from pervertization or psychotization. The refusal to allow penetration is the very definition of frigidity . . .

GRAVIDA: What's more, women drag men all the way into it.

AF: Men, poor guys, they simply don't get it. The point where frigidity becomes a major point of conflict may be an important moment. In Spain women have refused penetration by the penis, but not in homosexual practice, nor with an artificial penis. A sort of vaginal strike, in the perspective of the fight against rape. This is not uninteresting. For the time being, women are saying no, collectively, to the phallus. Instead of an isolated "no," they have set up an organized, intentional frigidity; it cannot be said to be really conscious, even though it is conscious by virtue of the repression of the unconscious. But women feel that there's a real question to be addressed here. In frigidity there is a defensive reaction toward the phallus that is positive, but there is also the deprivation of a whole anal cluster. This female clitoral, phallic level refers back to a sort of oral mastery, but it completely censors the relation with the anal and the vaginal. In refusing penetration, women are depriving themselves of the occasion to capture the penis, which is a moment in a heterosexual relation. In other words, the refusal of penetration is positive from the standpoint of phallic structuring, but the phallic structure in this case is immediately referred back regressively to a pre-anal stage, through its fixation on the oral, and it even rules out capturing the phallus of the other. There is something in penetration that is arrayed on the side of mastery for the woman (consider the male phantasms of the toothed vagina). Although the vagina is not a sphincter, there is nevertheless a certain element of mastery, of capture. Mastery is structured at the anal level. If one deprives oneself of vaginal penetration, one is also foregoing the capture of the penis, which is one of the fundamental moments in feminine genital maturation. The paradox is that the feminists are depriving themselves in this way of the relation to mastery that they need in their feminism. As a result, they have a mastery that is purely a truncated erection. They remain most often in a process of identifying with the father, rather than in a process of introjecting the anal penis.

GRAVIDA: It takes place completely in phantasms.

AF: It takes place phantasmatically through identification: women mimic the father instead of becoming the father. When women unleash a campaign in support of a law against rape, they are, as daughters, bringing the Father into existence. The extreme leftists have criticized the feminists who appealed to the judge, calling for repression. But in fact that repressive law is not unrelated to the symbolic law: it puts men in a position where they can become men and stop being little boys, stop avenging themselves with respect to their mother's bodies on the bodies of other women. And this is where the daughter *acts as* the father. She lays down the law to the little brother who wanted to rape her, or to the big brother. She appeals to something that is experienced as the Father and that she wants to put in a symbolic position. At bottom, in acting as the father, she brings to maturity, pulls toward maturity a little boy fixated at the anal stage (assuming that the structure of rape is recognized as anal). She enables an exit from the mother-son problematic by placing herself, as mediator, between two men, the son and the father. And this is the feminist function: a certain advent of a "higher patriarchy," one might say, in fact—what Lacan calls the Name of the Father. That is to say that she founds the symbolic law of the Father. As a matter of fact, this was Athena's role, to found the new Law. Feminists are modernists, in a way.

GRAVIDA: How can one think beyond feminism? How can a woman get beyond the phallic stage without simply rejecting it?

AF: According to Freudian theory, the Oedipus complex that constitutes "reality" would be succeeded by a genital phase (which Freud does not develop very fully), and the Oedipus complex would be resolved, for males, by the recognition of castration. Thus the whole question is that a man gives up his phallic fixation, his erectile fixation; or, if he fails to give it up, he regresses toward an anal phallic stage. Ultimately, if, in the terminology of the phallic period, phallic is opposed to castrated, then castration applies to both men and women. We could say that the phallic stage is the stage of primal genitality. Obviously, if the phallus is deemed to be the ultimate phase, the only possibility that remains is to regress and devote oneself to the anal, or to the interior of the body experienced as anal; moreover, in the equivalence "penis-feces-child-gift" Freud indicates this anal regression starting from the phallic stage.

But thinking beyond the phallic stage . . . Perhaps this entails thinking in relation to what happens when the erection is over in a man's body. Or what happens in a woman's body. The clitoris is not, as Freud called it, an "atrophied penis." For there to be atrophy, there has to have been existence, then muscular regression. Regarding the clitoris, I would be more inclined to speak of the advent of an "age of the cut penis." We talk about cut stone; I don't see why we shouldn't talk about the cut penis.

The penis has several functions: urination, sexual pleasure, and reproduction. Whereas in a woman these functions are separated: she has a more elaborate, tripartite genital apparatus (clitoris-vagina-uterus), each part having a specific function; and if diversification is recognized as an evolutionary process, without venturing into biologism we can say that the female genital apparatus is more highly evolved than that of the male, and that this allows us to read the relativity of the phallic function at the genital stage. This is a hypothesis, of course. And here I should like to say that I still consider as hypotheses the principal points that I am setting forth in this interview, since hypotheses leave room for both prudence and boldness. But these intuitions, if they are to be thought and expressed, have to pass through the constraint of phallocentric language at the risk of getting lost or getting stuck there, immobilized. So I reserve the possibility of changing my mind. We are at the very beginning of a process of acquiring knowledge, with all the risks that that entails. And the assertive form is only the effect of the enormous difficulty Phallogocentrism has in thinking beyond the Phallus; Phallogocentrism and Culture, speculative and specular, organized around a mirror: what does not appear in a mirror is considered as nonexistent. In other words, a female sex organ does not exist: the girl child does not know the vagina and still less the uterus. Now, a woman's sex begins beyond the mirror, by no means before. Nor does it begin behind—there is no behind except in a problematics of the mirror.

GRAVIDA: But isn't this "age of the cut penis" beyond the phallic stage?

AF: Supposing that we remain at the strictly phallic stage: the phallic equivalent for men is the penis, and for women it is the clitoris. I don't see why we would speak of atrophy for the clitoris. That is reductive. It's humiliating. It's like an illness. Whereas it is not the same organ. There is in fact a "beyond" of the phallic stage that does not belong to the order of castration, it has to do with elaborating something else. The reality of the drives—the physical aspect of psychic phenomena, the articulation between the somatic and the psychic—passes, for women, through this stage. It is not utopian; it is a physical and symbolic reality. Feminism is a historic moment of demanding equality (I am proceeding by analogy, but this is no worse an approach than any other), just as one could demand, at the phallic stage, the symbolic equality of the penis and the clitoris, because, after all, if it comes down to comparing one form of jouissance to another, no one can say whether that of the clitoris is inferior to that of the penis. Thus, in the phallic phase, equality is demanded and tolerated between one organ—the penis—and the other—the clitoris, since both are caught up in the phallic phase.

GRAVIDA: In fact, there are women more or less everywhere who have claimed the clitoris as the source of women's jouissance.

AF: Yes, and who, in order to articulate that claim, have repressed, pushed ahead, what is beyond, that is, women's multifaceted sex organ (which has at least three components). And some women—the ones we were talking about earlier—even absolutely refused vaginal penetration (they were said to tolerate anal penetration) in order to establish that claim. And this isn't ridiculous. It's ridiculous when it isn't understood. But it has a basis. As long as the girl's jouissance in clitoral masturbation is not symbolized as equivalent to the boy's jouissance in penile masturbation, we won't get there. But, by fixating on this equivalence, feminism adds grist to the mill of phallocentrism, if it does not question the phallic stage itself.

GRAVIDA: But can we go further?

AF: It isn't that we can go further: we are further! One really has to call on all the forces of censorship, repression, denegation, ignorance not to observe that we have gone further, as soon as we are in the period of puberty; and even before, even in the phallic period. There is no reason why a girl child should not know that she has a genital apparatus that is very different from a boy's, one that has effects with which she is familiar. And I think the boy child knows this too. And so, here, the question concerns the symbolic existence of the vagina and the uterus in the boy. Because in a woman there is no doubt about it whatsoever. Symbolization follows this route. It isn't a question of reducing symbolization to anatomy, it is a question of thinking the symbolic reality of a woman's sex organ, which is tripartite (clitoris-vagina-uterus). At that point, if this is a symbolic reality, why not in a man? After all, the recognition of an organ for creating and producing living beings exists among creative men, in a symbolic manner. A (male) poet is a uterine being, one might say, a man endowed with a symbolic uterus. He recognizes in himself the faculty of producing the living (le vivant).[9]

GRAVIDA: At this point we are much further along than the phallic stage, then?

AF: No. We are not much further along; we are in the process of elaborating the following phase of the phallic stage, that is, the genital phase.

GRAVIDA: It is as though you were saying that, for men, the problem is symbolizing the vagina and the uterus.

AF: It is a problem for both sexes to exit from hysteria, that is, from the refusal to symbolize the uterus. In hysteria the uterus is everywhere, except where it is, that is, in its symbolic function. We've known about the "displaced uterus," the "wandering womb," ever since the Middle Ages, and we're familiar with all the effects of false pregnancy in men . . . Freud's master stroke was to have detected hysteria in men as well as in women. It is obvious that, once symbolization is achieved, just as phallic symbolization occurs for both sexes, there is no reason why symbolization of the uterus, as the space for production of living beings, should not also occur for both sexes. We already have examples of that symbolization: male poets, creators of living productions. This would be the truly genital stage, beyond the phallic stage, a stage of sexual differentiation. For there to be difference, there must be at least two sexes.

The question, then, concerns the paths along which this symbolization is elaborated. The girl child, we were saying, knows about her vagina, but every effort is made to make her forget it—and this is even more the case for her knowledge of her uterus. It's something that is constantly censored, forbidden, covered up. The vagina is accepted only as isomorphic with the anus. Since a man has an organ to be penetrated, he tolerates the vagina. But the uterus is another matter, because he doesn't have one. In fact, this is the poetic martyrdom of the man who feels that he does have a uterus, who is aware of something like that faculty for creation in his body. This is Mallarmé, it's Rilke . . .

GRAVIDA: If only poets are involved, that means almost nobody. Poets are exceptions. So how can the uterus win the right to exist politically?

AF: It would be better to say "the right to speak," or "the right to be inscribed," or "the right to be symbolized." For example, one could point out that the phallic phase for a man is accomplished through identification with the father, through homosexuality and through love for the father as the ego ideal. So it is hardly extraordinary if, for a woman, symbolization, that is, the passage from identification to identity, a narcissistic assumption, the elaboration of a symbolizable uterus, can come about only between two women. Just as something of the phallic phase is elaborated for the boy in the choice of the father as ego ideal. Now, we notice that the incestuous oedipal structure (we learn this from reflecting on the structure of rape) is reserved for the mother-son couple, with variations on this couple: mother-son, father-daughter, infinite reversals and reduplications of roles. In the mother-daughter relation it is not a matter of incest, unless the daughter plays the son's role. The mother-daughter relation cannot be pinned down by this determination, and it inscribes, as it were, something to do with being a woman. This is to say that the mother releases herself from the fact that she is in relation with the daughter. Freud has a lot to say about the mother-son relation, calling it "the most perfect, the most marvelous" relation, while the mother-daughter relation is "the most devastating." Devastating, because its positivity is not revealed in its difference, in what it brings into play in addition: libidinal difference when a relation between two women is at stake, even if at the outset they are mother and daughter. It is from this relation, between two women, outside of the patriarchy, that "woman" comes about, real, imaginary, and symbolic.

As a matter of fact, "nonmixity" was the distinguishing feature of the Women's Liberation Movement at its birth: a form of conditioning for the appearance of difference between the sexes, a "way out," a way of taking on the process of exclusion of difference by phallogocentrism. We are excluded from a system of speech that asserts that "there is only one libido, it is phallic." We are exiting from that enclosure where we are, as Derrida would say, "interned excluded." A first gesture: externment, if one can call it that, of the internment, a taking into account and an interrogation of the exclusion. Nonmixity of the Women's Liberation Movement, outside the enclosure. Madwomen at liberty, but mad outside, that is, mad because outside-the-law, since such is the law: "there is only one libido, and it is phallic." And, starting from there, a questioning of that difference.

And so homosexuality, de facto, female; one could say symbolic homosexuality or ideological or political. And, from that starting point, a questioning of homosexuality at an analytic level. The feminists refuse to analyze homosexuality, but they nevertheless live it and affirm it as subversive from the outset. In fact, they have dismissed that question with "lesbianism," which is in itself an ideologization. One might say that there is an equivalence between the way Freud brings the unconscious to light on the basis of hysteric neurosis and the way one can bring to light, today, the specificity of a libido other than the phallic, the maturation of the phallic process in genitality, on the basis of female homosexuality. Lou Salomé asked herself: "Woman, what is there between you and me?" Women today are asking themselves this question on a massive scale, and my way of answering is to say that between two women there emerges *production of the living*, sexual difference, the other—the other by asserting each other's identity through the other.

The norm would have it that the boy's assertion of his identity through the father as an ego ideal is desexualized and that the sexual object remains the mother. We may wonder what the situation is for women, whether that relation has to remain desexualized, that is, idealized, or whether, owing to the fact of what is to be symbolized—the uterus—, it is precisely the body that is in question and whether this assertion of identity passes through an erotic relation. In this choice by a woman of the other woman as an ego ideal, if the body is repressed at the outset, one risks finding oneself back in phallic symbolization, in a regression from the phallic to the anal, in a problematic of the partial object.

In practical terms something incredible happens: what is called female homosexuality is most often phallic, which will lead us to talk about the relation between feminism and lesbianism. But we must first posit that it is impossible to separate out what, in 1970 when we worked on the question of homosexuality, I called libido 2, designating in this way a libido other than the phallic libido, without freeing ourselves from the Freudian and Lacanian assertion that "there is only one libido, and it is phallic."

I don't characterize this other libido as feminine. In fact, the terms masculine and feminine designate a gender difference within a monosexed, monologic, phallic language. The Derridean concept of phallogo-centrism brings out the absolute complicity between the Phallus and the Logos in the Western conceptual system. Masculine and feminine are both phallic: masculine = phallus plus, and feminine = phallus minus. What is in question then is not a difference between the sexes but a differ-ence in gender, a localization within the phallogocentric system of a posi-tion with respect to the phallus. Thus, in the same way, I very quickly de-termined that femininity is transvestism. We know, for example, that feminine fashion is the work of homosexuals who see themselves as women and project their visions on women. And, moreover, one can say of a man that he is feminine and of a woman that she is masculine. We find this difference in gender again in political language, with the couple macho-feminist. This other libido could be called a *uterine libido*, to refer to another body, a body sexed differently, a woman's body.

The libidinal difference, in my opinion, can only emerge through a questioning of female homosexuality, for both sexes. The symbolization of the uterus, of a space where the living is produced, can only be questioned from the starting point of female homosexuality, for men and women alike, in just the same way that the phallic phase applies to both sexes.

But what is a man poet? What is a man who works with his body? What is the production of a man's body, that is, a body endowed with language? What we encounter with Rilke, with Lautréamont, with every (man) poet, is a theoretical postulate according to which every man is in relation with the uterine, with the production of the living, of course symbolizable, the model of which, in the real, is making a child.

As there is "foreclosure of the Name of the Father" in male paranoia, there is, in female paranoia, *foreclosure of the body of the mother* (I created this formula with reference to Lacan's, obviously, but in order to desig-nate something about which Lacan precisely does not speak; this is the other slope of the Lacanian work.) Then the question of the relation of the son to the matricial arises, and the question of the specificity of the rela-tion between the daughter and the matricial, the *mise en abyme* of the uterus: a woman engenders a woman who engenders a woman who, and so on, and the question of what emerges from this, for both sexes, on the side of the production of the living. We would then go through a process of geni-tal maturation, that is, to reach a poetic humanity that recognizes its ca-pacity to separate the phallic from the anal and to give the phallic access, by setting it into relation with another genitality, access to production of the living. This production is always tripartite: a phallus, a uterus, and the product, the production. At the level of the real, it is a man and a woman who make a child. But elsewhere? It would be a creative, genitalized society. It's utopian and it's not utopian; it's something like a project, a political project.

GRAVIDA: Isn't there a need to pursue the question of why this appears owing to female homosexuality?

AF: I said that the Movement had positioned itself from the moment of its birth through externment, starting from an "interned exclusion," to go back to the Derridean concept; the emergence of a difference is produced by extraction from the One in which the difference is interned. To separate out a difference between libidos is not exactly to separate out a difference between the sexes. The elaboration of a libido other than phallic puts into play the question of the repression of the body, its imperialization by the sex organ. Perhaps there is only one symbolizable sex and it is the phallus. But there is not just one libido. The uterus does not belong to the order of sex, it belongs to the order of the extension of sex to a system of production of the living in the body and through the body. This is a very different matter; it goes beyond the notion of sex in genital maturation. I think this is very important, because, when we speak of bisexuality, we do not exit from the empire of sex, we do not exit from the empire of the signifier or from the empire of the sign. The masculine-feminine opposition endlessly refers to the empire of the sign. In writing, I don't believe anyone anywhere has yet achieved a system for producing texts that effectively challenges the empire of the sign over the body. I believe that the system of production of writing is marked by that system of exploitation of the body by the sign, by the signifier. I think there is a struggle to be undertaken here, not against writing but against the current system for producing writing, which is a narcissistic system, no matter what anyone says, a system that refers to something on the order of the phallus, the One, and the exploitation of the body by the One, the exploitation of difference by Sameness. Here again, Michel de Certeau's work is interesting. In Lacan, in contrast, there is an imperialism of the signifier and an absolute unawareness of the importance of the political in the unconscious, that is, of the power relations between structures. The relation between the oral and the anal is not just any relation, nor is the relation between the oral and the phallic. History shows, for example, the repression of all oral cultures.

So what is the situation of the oral, in terms of the oral-written opposition, and then, in libidinal terms, the oral-phallic opposition? In hysteria, we witness a constant deployment of the oral, which keeps coming back, and of oral conflict. How is the oral dealt with, for example, in the Lacanian "real-imaginary-symbolic" structure? When Lacan arrives at the Borromean rings, he says clearly that there are relations among these three terms. Simple relations? No, political relations. It is obvious that the real is dealt with by the symbolic. A question of dealing/trafficking: in bodies, in (male and female) slaves. The body is dealt with by the signifier. Here is where the articulation between psychoanalysis and politics lies. There is power in the structuring of the unconscious. It is not linear, it is dialectical, and this dialectics of the libidinal stages does not come about without bringing into play the master-slave, dominant-dominated relation. Which is not necessarily the man-woman relation. The question is not whether one has a penis or not; the question is what the phallus imperializes. The feminist position says: "He has it, so we're going to cut it off and take it away from him!"

Here is where we can come back to the relation between feminism and lesbianism. In lesbianism, there is an equivalent for everything I have said about feminism: a strictly phallic between-two-women and a fixation on the phallic stage, with regression to a very primary, very oral homosexuality. And then there is another homosexuality, beyond the phallic phase and its oedipal reality principle, a homosexuality that can be called tertiary, or genital, between two women. Many women in the MLF have had heterosexual experiences that can be characterized as "normal," "satisfying," that is, without frigidity in the phallic system, with orgasms and the capacity for pleasure shared with a man. These women often also have children; in other words, they have fully realized their heterosexuality, as sexuality is understood today in the phallic system. And when these women encounter another female body, they say that the encounter constitutes an extension, an amplification, a surpassing of the hetero type of jouissance, not a regression; this is what is absolutely extraordinary!

GRAVIDA: This constitutes a political situation in the broadest sense.

AF: Yes. That the MLF, homosexed, is not regressive, does not refer back to something about the mother, to something before or beneath patriarchy, but to a surpassing of history as it is being played out—this is what is not accepted by the phallic monopoly, by phallic imperialism. It is intolerable for a certain number of men who are not themselves "yearning for a uterus."

GRAVIDA: Right now the repression of the phallic is generalized, in the feminist manner, both among women and among men who identify with the feminists or who are taking up their demands on their own behalf. "Phallic" and "imperialism of the phallus" are completely confused with one another. Can't we imagine that no particular libidinal stage has primacy over the others?

AF: What must be challenged is the crushing of the pregenital stages by the primacy of the phallus, that is, an unsuccessful integration, a repression or a censoring of the oral and the anal and then the primacy of the phallic as the ultimate genital stage, whereas it is only the primary genital stage or even, for certain authors, a pregenital stage or a moment of articulation between the secondary structure and a tertiary structure. For example, it is obvious that right now the phallic stage, historically, is completely caught up in the anal stage. One only has to see, in New York, the skyscrapers literally standing in shit; the lower part of the city is absolutely anal. And this is not a metaphor, it is a reality. If the phallic cannot think its own surpassing, it regresses.

GRAVIDA: But how can one think the passage from the phallic to the genital, when the phallic, as soon as it is imperialist—and in our experience, it almost always is—forbids that passage? Do we have to go through a castration first?

AF: I think, first, that castration is an anal phantasm. The idea that the penis could be detached from the body is a reduction of the penile organ to the fecal "stick," that is, to something that detaches and falls away from the body. Now, it is not true that the penis detaches from the body. It is either in an erect state or in a flaccid state, but it does not fall off. At the genital level things happen very differently. When, after an erection, the penis returns to its ordinary position, there is neither loss nor castration, there is a quite different reality that men have to envisage.

GRAVIDA: This is to say that the passage from the phallic to the genital is also a passage from a phantasmatic mode to something else?

AF: To a materialist mode! In the pregenital stages we are dealing with the pleasure principle. We are perhaps also dealing with a reality principle that, for the time being, is entirely organized around the "Oedipus complex" for the man. However, as a reality principle it is incomplete, because there are several realities: an oedipal reality for the man and another, not strictly oedipal, for the woman; the two realities are organized around different genital equipment. And then there is surely a principle of revolution or of creation, of differentiated elaboration—I don't know what to call it—beyond these realities . . . The primary stage is related to the pleasure principle and the secondary stage to the reality principle (which is incomplete, because as soon as there are two sexes there is more than one reality). And then, as I see it, there is a tertiary principle, related to genitality, and this one would be a principle of production of the living.

In the Freudian schema of the pleasure principle that is said to govern the primary, pregenital stages, we are dealing with what Freud calls free energy and what he calls an identity of perception; this principle is followed by the reality principle, an already secondary stage, with bound energy and an identity of thought. The finally tertiary stage that I am proposing would be a principle of genitality, transformation, production of the living: this is the stage of the one with the other, of "being with" and no longer the other reduced to the same. And here we would have an identity—it sounds paradoxical—"of differentiation," or a differentiated identity, which is a contradiction in terms; it cannot be thought. A double possibility of symbolization, for the two sexes, differentiated. And here we would be dealing with a managed, or unbound, energy. We are no longer in the free energy of the primary stage (to which it is not a matter of returning in order to avoid the secondary stage), nor are we in the bound energy of the secondary, phallic stage, which bundles together all the pregenital drives. (*Faisceau*, the French word for "bundle," is related to the Italian *fascio* ["bundle," hence "group" or "association"] from which the word *fascism* is derived; this was the emblem of power for the Romans and also for the French Vichy government, with the sheaf of wheat.)

So can we get beyond this bundle to something that is unbound energy, that is, freed (not "free"), in other words an energy that recognizes gestation, time to understand, as in analysis, and time to create? And this would no longer belong to the order of ejaculation, orgasm, flashes, lightning bolts, or ec-stasy. It would mean situating oneself outside, setting up another space, a three-dimensional space where there would be time for gestation. If we take a child as representative of the production of the living, we know that it takes a certain time for him or her to be made, to be "made with." We would be at the stage of an unbound, managed energy that is redistributed. I once heard a biologist say that most miscarriages are abortions owing to a selection operated by the uterus, a powerful sifting out of everything that does not suit it. The uterus is in the end an extraordinary machine for organizing, sorting, setting up, managing life. I believe that there is actually a passage from a stage that could perhaps be called pederastic (in Villon and Verlaine we find phantasms of anal childbirth) to a genital stage, a time for the production of the living. Moreover, this demand for time also comes up in ecology, in the movements of these last few years, on the new left.

GRAVIDA: Isn't this passage from the flash, the instantaneous, ecstasy, to time also the passage from phantasm (instantaneous realization) to thought?

AF: And the passage from the "auto-"—since phantasms govern all auto-eroticism—to "being with the other" or "doing/making with the other" or "seeing with the other." I think this is the dimension of the "with."

GRAVIDA: This may be the point of greatest difficulty at the social level. Take America, for example: it's really the land of the instantaneous, the thing that happens of its own accord, autoconception . . .

AF: And the land of orgasms as well. That phallic punctuality, which is the event, after which everything would dissolve . . . it isn't real. After orgasm everything doesn't dissolve. Moreover, it's in a phallic economy that the man, and now the woman, after orgasm, will pick up a cigarette. There's depression here of the paranoid type, it's obvious . . .

GRAVIDA: If we want to think this through politically, we can also make a social projection. What would a society that is no longer phallic but genital look like—if we can put the question that way?

AF: It would be a society that has differentiated realities productive of the living rather than just objects and waste products. A society that could be called "communist," but one we haven't seen. Today we have societies that are mired in an absolutely passive anality, with a hyperphallicity. In Latin America, for example, we see skyscrapers and slums side by side. Chinese society, Maoist and post-Maoist, in contrast, has an economy that profits from the benefits of anality, from its positive sides, to the utmost. For example, they use waste products to the point of complete elimination. Which is a form of ecology. A genital society, on the side of the *production of the living*, would be a society that would move beyond treating the other as an anal object, that is, as waste, with all that follows from such treatment: torture, degradation, fetishization, idealization. It would be a society of the dialectic of the one and the other, or the other and the other. The production of the living is tripartite: it includes the third party as a living product. The model of the third party is the child, a living-speaking being.

In the story of castration complex and in Freud's "penis-feces-child" equation, the child is reduced on the one hand to a penis, thus to an organ that remains attached to the body, and on the other hand to feces, thus to wastes that are detached from the body but that are lifeless. Whereas the child is, without question, detached from the body of the woman who has made it, but it is alive. In contrast, the penis is reduced to feces, to the fecal "stick": but if the penis is cut off, it never gets hard. In the film by Marco Ferreri, *La dernière femme* (The last woman), a man castrates himself and the cut-off penis remains erect. A phantasm! This film presents a man who is involved with a feminist and who believes he has to cut off his penis in order to respond to her desire . . . In this struggle to have it, why wouldn't women use the same weapons? And from the moment when men decreed that women were castrated, shouldn't women castrate men too? All's fair within the "phallic circus" . . . And yet when a woman says that beyond her heterosexual experience an experience with another woman completely enlarges her libidinal field, this can't be thought of as regressive. It isn't utopian; in fact, it's something beyond.

GRAVIDA: In your practice the transformation of society first comes through transformation . . .

AF: Through transformation of the structures of production, above all. Through economic independence. We have a publishing house that is absolutely independent economically, where the money that comes in—which is always from capitalist sources (since in this world all money is capitalized in some sense)—is decapitalized, if I can put it this way: it is spent without making new capital; it doesn't function in the system of added value and the accumulation of capital.

GRAVIDA: Do you think you'll always be able to avoid the question of power?

AF: But we don't have to avoid the question of power, or power itself; it's the abuse of power that's dangerous. From the political standpoint, we are in a position of absolute independence, and that's why we have given the MLF an official status. In 1968 it was unthinkable to create a formal association. In 1979 it was indispensable to do so, in my opinion, because the process of repression was such that the movement risked being completely wiped out. But most women didn't understand this. They thought something was being taken away from them, whereas we were giving them something. It may have looked like a provocation with respect to all the women involved in the struggle; but in 1979 the feminists had already long since abandoned the word *liberation*. MLF was becoming a slanderous term. We had entered the period of major repression with the International Year of the Woman (1975) and then the creation of a Secretariat for the Condition of Women and the reinternment of our victories. Reforms are necessary, but they presuppose a paralysis of the movement. This paradox is difficult, but it has to be borne.

Thus, in October 1979, we who had never given up the acronym MLF—it is found in our texts, our newspapers, and especially in the books we published—thought that it was necessary, even urgent, to give the Movement a minimal anchoring. The legislation adopted in 1901 allowing the formation of associations governs political parties as well as fun-loving bowlers' associations; this was the supplest form that could lend itself to our movement—neither an organization nor a party but a form that we invented. Yes, a movement is the specific form of revolutionary art that defeats the totalitarianism of omnipotent politics. In 1979 there was a risk that the MLF would be wiped out. We were in great danger. Prime Minister Michel Rocard was talking about "incorporating" women. Out of the question to let him do it. Out of the question, too, to delegate as our representatives some party leader, some woman creator of yet another political trend, some woman theorist who was an institution in and of herself. And then, under the impetus of contradictions that had become divisions, the Movement was at risk of splintering, self-destruction, sterility. It was time to reconnect. So we created this association to bring about a symbolic liaison and a historical inscription. It was not a publishing house that seized possession of an acronym; it was a movement that had created, one after another, a publishing house, a monthly magazine, a weekly newspaper, and this association. But a large number of women, in the phallic stage where they were, experienced these developments as an abuse of power. People fight over an object, there is only one, and everybody wants it. Except that the Movement is not an object, and it is not a phallus. And we have to prove this, that is, to make it. To make it other. It is not certain that women today can think beyond the problematics of having it or not having it.

GRAVIDA: Could you describe your practice? On the militant level. There are the books, the weekly publications . . .

AF: There is a great deal of agitation, mobilization, explanation, political consciousness-raising . . . No one has said that we'll always refuse to stake out a position in the play of elections, but such positioning can't be reduced to a reinternment of a women's movement within a system that, in the short or the long run, has to stifle and diminish it. It isn't a question of passing from the situation of internal exclusion to a position of externment—which we have done—only to reintern ourselves once again within unchanged structures. I think that the leap outside the system is something important; it raises the question of how to think about externment from a phallogocentric enclosure instituted by the patriarchy, and then how that externment could avoid being a ghetto. It is obvious that our externment is fertile, active. For example, it is out of the question today that a woman from the MLF could present herself as a candidate in the presidential election (May 1981). Women in the various parties are going to do this. But it is not out of the question that the Movement could constitute itself as a political force and need to stake out its position. Exactly as it was indispensable, as I said before, to create an association under the 1901 law.[10]

GRAVIDA: Everything you say can be translated for men. The feminists are the ones who are keeping you from being heard by men.

AF: They have done this deliberately. But I believe that it also comes from men's immaturity. As support for their castration, they need erect feminists, priapism on the part of women. I have men in analysis who say to me: "I want to see her hard" or "to have her/it hard." In other words, they'll refer to a girl who is hysterical, hard, with a hard-on and erect, because she guarantees their castration. Men's fixation at the phallic stage is what imposes that position on women. We might say, *mutatis mutandis*, that men are the ones who want women to be feminists. This is why I say that feminism is one of the last pillars of patriarchy. The feminists' fixation on the father makes feminism the last historically known metaphor for patriarchy.

GRAVIDA: Still, there is a possibility for certain men . . .

AF: It would be among the men who are in relation with the body, male poets, men with a nonhyperphallocentric libidinal structure. But the Don Juan/feminist couple sends them back into psychosis. We recently held an open meeting, at the Maison de la Chimie (Chemistry house); the men present expressed a desire to have the meetings continue. They understand, there's something that touches them, but it may still take years.

They cannot yet articulate it, because these questions are powerfully repressed. Most of the time men are reduced to nonspeech, as are all those with a libidinal structure such that it cannot speak, because it is mortgaged by phallic abuse. They also have all the defense mechanisms on the order of obsessionality, paranoid contiguity . . . There are cases of impotence or pseudo-impotence, such as premature ejaculation, with the need to identify with a feminist or a hysteric, a woman who is hard. All Pavese's writing has to do with this, Bataille's too. With Pavese it remained absolutely at the zero degree of literary utterances, beneath perversion, at the level of psychosis: no perversion, blank writing, completely made of what is flagrant and naked, of nothing at the level of nothing, that is, the thing. And it ended in suicide. And the scansion indeed came from premature ejaculation, anal nonmastery and what lay "beneath" or "behind," the delegation of the anal phallic to the woman, with the man remaining at the oral phallic stage, in a fluttering . . . It seems to me that only men who are highly developed in their thinking can envisage practical paths. But who might they be, given that this work constantly threatens the privilege of the hypernarcissistic intellectual? For intellectuals and writers, it is a question of detachment. Writing does not tolerate constant contamination or alteration, and this type of critical work leads to the loss of privilege for writing itself. Writing nonetheless has countless other privileges to gain if it allows itself to be altered and changes its system of production—but one cannot explain to an owner what he stands to gain from the revolution.

GRAVIDA: Still, one could explain to a man what he stands to gain from the women's revolution.

AF: He would have to ask himself what his own interest is in this type of work. With feminism it would be the advent of the Father, that is, the completion of the patriarchy, men no longer being sons dependent on a Mother. You can see the damage done by that regressive position in a film such as Fellini's *City of Women*, which we might call the city without women, the polity of the son, the polity of the oral-anal phantasms of an elderly newborn stuck in a sort of sordid, putrefied placenta. What a man has to gain from feminism, in fact, is the advent of the father and the opportunity to situate himself somewhere as an adult in a patriarchal system; this is not nothing. And then, later on, in relation to the shift from feminism to a liberation movement, he can become a man, that is, he can encounter women, encounter the difference between the sexes and be in relation, himself, with his own difference. A world without women is a world without men. For the time being, we are in a world without women, in a mother-son world and, to a limited extent, a father-daughter world.

GRAVIDA: How do you imagine men relating to your movement in practical terms?

AF: It can only be a relation of analytic work, of elaborating genitality: that is, work on resistance or nonresistance to castration, on the notion of castration as an anal phantasm; work on the material reality of the body and on what passes for the body in the phallic system; analytic work, then, or simply hystericization of the subject.

GRAVIDA: Hystericization of the subject?

AF: Yes. The analytic work involves taking into consideration that there is an other, thus that there is an unconscious, that there is a pregenital stage, and then also another sex. Hysteria can be said to be the rejection of the uterus and, at the same time, its recognition. Unconscious recognition in denegation. In other words, the male hysteric knows something about the uterus. This knowledge is unaware of itself, but it is expressed in various ways . . . Beyond the phallic and its imperializing function of bundling, there is what is unbound. Liberation. The word *liberation* comes to designate not the free energy of the pleasure principle but acquisition of a freedom. An active freedom, not a state-of-freedom; freedom in action. So it is obvious that this necessarily privileges everything that is different and everything that is oppressed, not only in the structures of class and race but also in the libidinal structures.

The libidinal stages are highly hierarchized, and the primacy of the phallus is established by a crushing of the pregenital, thus of the oral structure or a certain anal structure. A man who lacks integration, or who has only a fragile phallic integration, and who confronts a massive surge of women into the phallic system, may find himself tipping into schizophrenia or paranoia, that is, into regressive psychotic stages. This is why feminism is a danger; if it does not think through its struggle in the right place, it will bring grist to the mill of capital, of imperialism and phallocracy—as can be seen everywhere in institutional structures. In the last analysis, Margaret Thatcher is the pinnacle of feminism . . . And who pays the price? The oppressed of all sorts.

GRAVIDA: You really think that there's a possibility of moving ahead, of progress for humanity?

AF: I don't think in terms of "progress." I think in terms of revolution and of repeated, ongoing, achronological shifts, progress being only what allows revolution. For example, Freudian theory is progress, to the extent that it allows the conceptualization of regression. After all, bringing the Oedipus complex to light is what has allowed work on the pregenital, which in turn allows us to venture into something obscure. Here is where we have dialectics. Progress, for me, has meaning only as a cross-section of the revolutionary spiral. In this sense, we might say that the MLF is a seeming regression that is actually an advance.

GRAVIDA: A regression?

AF: Yes, you know, people tend to accuse us of reverting to matriarchy, to something prephallic: "women among themselves who haven't found any men, who need a good fucking." And even the legal challenges the feminists brought against us were trials to see whether we had successfully integrated our phallic phase, to see whether we weren't operating underneath the law of society. They lost them all. What the Women's Movement is bringing about is not a regression, nor is it a "leap forward"; it is a leap outside the nineteenth-century patriarchal enclosure in quest of a true heterosexuality.

Notes

FOREWORD

1. Vienna Declaration and Programme of Action adopted by the World Conference on Human Rights in Vienna on 25 June 1993, section 1, article 19, www.ohchr.org/EN/ProfessionalInterest/Pages/Vienna.aspx (accessed December 16, 2013).

PREFACE TO THE FIRST EDITION

The prefaces, the acknowledgments, and the first twenty-two chapters are from Antoinette Fouque, *Il y a deux sexes: Essais de féminologie*, revised and augmented edition (Paris: Gallimard, 2004).

1. See chapter 2, p. 32.
2. See chapter 1, p. 8.
3. For the significance of these two dates, see chapter 1, pp. 1–2, and chapter 19, pp. 152–53. —TRANS.

PREFACE TO THE SECOND EDITION

1. The Mouvement de Libération des Femmes, or Women's Liberation Movement, often referred to by its acronym MLF, was founded in October 1968. —TRANS.

2. Psychanalyse et Politique (Psychoanalysis and Politics), known informally as Psych et Po, was founded by Antoinette Fouque at the beginning of the Movement. —TRANS.

3. See chapter 2, pp. 25–26. In French, this term plays on the similarity between the words génialité, "genius," and génitalité, "genitality." —TRANS.

4. As Serge Leclaire put it in Rompre les charmes (Paris: InterÉditions, 1981), 233–34.

5. Chapters 20–22, plus "Tant qu'il y aura des femmes," which has not been included in the present English-language edition; see Antoinette Fouque, Il y a deux sexes (Paris: Gallimard, 2004), pp. 273–80. —TRANS.

6. Comparable to the Velvet Revolution once advocated by Vaclav Havel in the hope that love and peace might replace hatred and war.

   The French révolution de soi(e) is a revolution of the self (soi), nonviolent and as soft as silk (soie). —TRANS.

7. See chapter 3, p. 53.

8. It should be noted that the French word libéralisme strongly connotes giving free rein to market forces. —TRANS.

9. See chapter 19, p. 175.

10. The law of May 4, 2002, allowing the transmission of the mother's surname has been revised, its scope limited, and its application postponed.

11. See the appeal made by Elle to President Chirac on "women's rights and the Islamic veil": "Elle s'engage!" Elle, December 8, 2003, p. 9.

12. "Spare us the complaint about the slippery slope toward communitarianism," wrote Michel Rocard. L'Express, June 20, 1996.

    The French term communautarisme is often used pejoratively to designate a form of ethnocentrism that places a higher value on the ethnic or minority group than on the individual or the larger society. —TRANS.

13. Article 75 of the 1958 Constitution.

14. As early as 1989, the Alliance des Femmes pour la Démocratisation (the Women's Alliance for Democratization, a nonprofit cultural-political organization founded by Antoinette Fouque in 1989), which had already voiced its support for the struggle of Algerian women against the Family Code on several occasions, held public forums in Paris and Marseille in which the

absence of women from public debate on the veil was stressed: "In the debate between secularism and fundamentalism, the discussion of the veil has left women out" (assemblies held on November 22 at the Institut Océanographique in Paris and on December 8 at the Maison des Associations in Marseille). See also Michel Fize, *Les pièges de la mixité scolaire* (Paris: Presses de la Renaissance, 2003).

15. Instituted on November 9, 1999, the Pacte civil de solidarité, or PACS, offers nonmarried couples, particularly same-sex couples, many of the legal rights (in the realms of taxation, welfare, and inheritance, for example) enjoyed by married couples. —Trans.

16. "La bande à mono," as Jean-François Josselin dubbed them in a facetious article in *Le Nouvel Observateur*, July 6, 1995.

    The term is an allusion to Bande à Bonnot or Bonnot Gang, the designation given an anarchist group famous in the years prior to World War I for its politically motivated holdups, and to monotheism, monarchy, and monosexuality. —Trans.

17. For a discussion of backlash, see chapter 2, p. 26. Susan Faludi has analyzed the way the exclusion of women was engineered in the U.S. following the initial victories of the women's movement; see Susan Faludi, *Backlash: The Undeclared War Against Women* (New York: Vintage, 1993).

18. The need for this neologism was impressed upon me by the reality of the massacres of women reported day after day by the Observatoire de la Misogynie (Observatory of Misogyny) that I founded at the same time as the Alliance des femmes pour la démocratie, in 1989.

19. Amartya Sen, "One Hundred Million Women Are Missing," *New York Review of Books* 37, no. 20 (December 20, 1990): 61–66; see chapter 19.

20. Amartya Sen, "The Many Faces of Gender Inequality: When Misogyny Becomes a Health Problem," *New Republic* 225, no. 12 (September 17, 2001): 40 (35–40).

21. Reference to Primo Levi's *If This Is a Man*; see chapter 21, "If This Is a Woman."

22. *Paris Match*, November 13–19, 2003; *Marianne*, January 12–18, 2004.

23. On October 9 I addressed a letter to Blandine Kriegel, special assistant to the president of the republic, to denounce this misogynist crime and to try to come up with ways to ensure that similar crimes will not be committed in the future; see chapter 22.

24. Michèle Fitoussi, "Sohane tuée par le machisme!" *Elle*, October 21, 2002, p. 24.

25. François Corbara, "Brûlée vive par son compagnon," *Le Parisien*, October 1, 2003, p. 16.

26. "Chronologie," *Le Monde*, December 28, 2003.

27. A number of the texts in this volume aim to increase public attention to the growing feminization of poverty in France, in Europe, and around the world; see especially chapter 19.

28. "La précarité des familles monoparentales s'enracine," *Le Parisien*, November 5, 2003.

29. Sen, "More Than One Hundred Million Women," p. 61.

30. INED, October 2003.

31. See Viviane Forrester, *The Economic Horror* (Cambridge: Polity, 1999).

32. The Harkis were Algerians who fought on the French side in the Algerian struggle for independence. The word rhymes with *marquis*, a reference to the Marquis de Sade —TRANS.

33. See chapter 2, pp. 31-32.

34. See chapter 3, p 42.

35. Psychanalyse et Politique (MLF), leaflet issued in 1970.

36. Friedrich Engels, "The Origin of the Family, Private Property and the State," in Karl Marx and Friedrich Engels, *Collected Works* (London: Lawrence and Wishart, 1990), 26:129–276. But the "determining factor in history," which Engels considers to be "the production and reproduction of immediate life" (p. 131) as well as the distinction he makes between "the production of means of subsistence" and "the production of human beings themselves, the propagation of the species" (p. 132) were to remain dead letters (see chapter 12).

37. Sigmund Freud, "A Difficulty on the Path of Psycho-Analysis," *The Standard Edition of the Complete Psychological Works of Sigmund Freud*, ed. James Strachey (London: Hogarth, 1955), 17:135–43.

38. See chapter 1, pp. 4–5.

39. See chapter 3, p. 41.

40. Denis Diderot, *Éléments de Physiologie*, ed. Paolo Quintili (Paris: Champion, 2004); Denis Diderot and Jean d'Alembert, *Encyclopédie, ou Dictionnaire raisonné des sciences, des arts et des métiers*, 10 vols. (Paris: Imprimerie nationale, 1950 [1751]).

41. See chapter 5.

42. Sigmund Freud, *A Phylogenetic Fantasy: Overview of the Transference Neuroses* (London: Belknap Press of Harvard University Press, 1987) and "Moses and Monotheism," in *The Standard Edition of the Complete Psychological Works of Sigmund Freud*, ed. James Strachey (London: Hogarth, 1964), 23:3–137.

43. Jean-Pierre Dupuy, *Le sacrifice et l'envie: Le libéralisme aux prises avec la justice sociale* (Paris: Calmann-Lévy, 1992).

44. The French term *production de vivant* has been translated as "production of living beings" when it refers to the real (production of children) and as "production of the living" when it refers to the symbolic (production in the realms of art, ideas, politics, and so on), though sometimes the real and the symbolic overlap.

45. Nancy Folbre, *De la différence des sexes en économie politique* (Paris: Des femmes, 1997).

46. Jean-Joseph Goux, "Numismatiques," *Tel Quel*, no. 35 (Fall 1968): 64–89, and no. 36 (Winter 1969): 54–75, *Économie et symbolique* (Paris: Seuil, 1973).

47. Gilles Lipovetsky, *La troisième femme, permanence et révolution du féminin* (Paris: Gallimard, 1997); see also Fouque, "Tant qu'il y aura des femmes," p. 273.

48. Jacques Lacan, "The Hysteric's Question (II): What Is a Woman?" in *The Seminar of Jacques Lacan*, book 3, *The Psychoses, 1955–1956*, trans. Russell Grigg (New York: Norton, 1993), p. 179.

49. The available English translations of Euripedes do not refer to "the race of women." Cf. Euripides, *Medea*, in *Euripides I: The Complete Greek Tragedies*, ed. David Greene and Richard Lattimore (Chicago: University of Chicago Press, 1983): "It is the thoughts of men that are deceitful, / Their pledges that are loose. / Story shall now turn my condition to a fair one, / Women are paid their due" (415–418, p. 73); "It would have been better far for men / To have got their children in some other way, and women / Not to have existed. Then life would have been good" (573–575, p. 77). —TRANS.

50. In book 1, chapter 4 of *The Politics*, Aristotle describes the slave as a "living instrument." Aristotle, *The Politics*, ed. Stephen Everson (Cambridge: Cambridge University Press, 1988), book 1, chapter 4, 1253b:25–30, p. 5.

51. For Freud, there are three unsustainable positions, three impossible tasks: governing, educating, and analyzing.

52. The French *un retour de femme* is an untranslatable pun on the expression *retour de flamme*, meaning either "sudden burst of flames" or "sudden rekindling of passion," using the word *femme* in place of *flamme*, as well as a play on the expression *retour du refoulé* ("return of the repressed"). —TRANS.

53. See chapter 3.

54. See chapter 21, p. 190.

55. See chapter 19, pp. 154–55. Twelve exceptional women from five continents received trophies from the Alliance des Femmes: twelve exceptional French women presented each of the honorees with a jewel designed by Sonia Delaunay. The event brought together political figures, journalists, mathematicians, philosophers, creative artists, athletes, and actresses, including

Simone Veil, Elena Bonner, Danielle Mitterrand, Ela Bhatt, Edith Cresson, Kanitha Wichiencharoen, Françoise Giroud, Yvonne Choquet Bruhat, Blandine Kriegel, Charlotte Perriand, Sonia Rykiel, Michèle André, Albertina Sisulu, Jeannie Longo, and Arielle Dombasle. *Alliance des femmes 8 Mars: Journée internationale des femmes 1990* (Des femmes, France-U.S.A., bilingual edition, 1992). On the topic of women's strength, see also Françoise Barret-Ducrocq and Evelyne Pisier, *Femmes en tête* (Paris: Flammarion, 1997).

56. VSD, December 31, 2004.

57. See Blandine Grosjean, "Liberté, égalité, maternité," *Libération*, April 29, 2003, pp. 2–4.

58. In a declaration adopted by the Assemblée générale in November 1967. —TRANS.

59. Adopted in December 1965, effective January 1969. —TRANS.

60. See chapter 16, p. 144.

61. Jean-Claude Michea, *Impasse Adam Smith* (Paris: Climats, 1992); Hans Jonas, *The Imperative of Responsibility* (Chicago: University of Chicago Press, 1985); René Frydman, *Lettre à une mère* (Paris: L'Iconoclaste, 2003).

62. Luca and Francesco Cavalli-Sforza, *The Great Human Diasporas: The History of Diversity and Evolution* (Reading, MA: Addison-Wesley, 1995), v (dedication).

63. See chapter 3, p. 41.

64. Cf. Marcel Gauchet, *La condition historique* (Paris: Stock, 2003).

65. Cf. Peter Brown, *The Making of Late Antiquity* (Cambridge: Harvard University Press, 1993).

66. See chapter 3, p. 48.

67. The word *délivrance* in French refers both to childbirth and to deliverance in the sense of freedom or release. —TRANS.

68. Erri de Luca, *Le contraire de un* (Paris: Gallimard, 2004), back cover.

1. OUR MOVEMENT IS IRREVERSIBLE

Text delivered as the opening paper at the États généraux des femmes, an assembly held on March 8, 1989, at the Sorbonne on the occasion of International Women's Day, in the year of the bicentennial of the French Revolution. See *États Généraux des femmes* (Paris: Des femmes, 1990): 9–21.

1. See the second preface, this volume, note 1.

2. Mouvement pour la Liberté de l'Avortement et de la Contraception (Movement for freedom of abortion and contraception), a feminist association founded in France in April 1973. —TRANS.

3. Choisir la Cause des Femmes (Choose the cause of women), an association formed in April 1971 to denounce the criminalization of abortion. —TRANS.
4. The law legalizing abortion under certain conditions was presented to the National Assembly by Minister of Health Simone Veil in November 1974 and adopted in January 1975. —TRANS.
5. The French antiracist slogan "Touche pas à mon pote!" was created in the mid-1980s in a campaign by SOS Racisme to support the integration of young foreigners, especially those of North African origin. —TRANS.
6. Gabriel Riquet de Mirabeau, speech to the National Assembly, July 21, 1789, in *Collection complète des travaux de M. Mirabeau l'aîné, à l'Assemblée*, ed. Étienne Méjean (Paris: Veuve Lejay, 1791), p. 61.
7. Ernest Renan, "Réponse au discours de réception de M. Pasteur (27 avril 1882)," *Œuvres complètes*, 10 vols. (Paris: Calmann-Lévy, 1947–1961), 1:774.
8. This term combines the French words *phallisme* ("phallism" or, more commonly, "phallicism," the worship of the phallus) and *laïcité* ("secularism," with a special emphasis on the separation of church and state). —TRANS.
9. The Algerian Code de la Famille, adopted in 1984, set forth legislation governing familial relations in terms often drawn from Islamic law. —TRANS.
10. In April and again in November 1989 the National Organization for Women organized mass protests in Washington, DC, in defense of women's reproductive rights. —TRANS.
11. Preamble, paragraph 7, www.un.org/womenwatch/daw/cedaw/text/econcention.htm#intro (accessed September 21, 2103).
12. In 1989 we were already engaged in long-standing debates about parity as a means and/or as a goal of true political equality. That year in particular we had tried an active approach: the Women's Alliance for Democracy had presented two lists of candidates—the majority of them women—in the March 12 municipal elections (Paris, sixth district, and Marseille, fourth district). In 1992 I created the Club Parité 2000 (Parity Club 2000), which presented a list in the March 22 Bouches-du-Rhône regional elections.
13. I use the term *gyneconomy* in reference and in deference to Élisabeth de Fontenay's brilliant text, "Diderot gynéconome," published in *Digraphe* (1976): 29–50, and incorporated for the most part in her *Diderot, Reason and Resonance*, trans. Jeffrey Mehlman (New York: Braziller 1982 [1981]).

2. WOMEN IN MOVEMENTS

This text brings together interviews conducted by Pierre Nora and Marcel Gauchet between October 1989 and February 1990, published in April 1990 by Gallimard in the bimonthly magazine *Le Débat*, no. 59, pp. 122–37.

1. See the second preface, this volume, note 2. —TRANS.
2. Or "to talk nonsense," "bullshit." —TRANS.
3. Adélaïde Fouque was the founding mother of the Rougon-Macquart family to which Zola devoted a cycle of twenty novels (1852–1870). —TRANS.
4. Le Seuil was the publishing house that brought out the works of France's intellectual avant-garde (Lacan, Barthes, Derrida, and others). The journal of literary and social theory *Tel Quel* was also published by Le Seuil.
5. The École Normale Supérieure, or Normale Sup, was created at the end of the nineteenth century as an elite state institution of higher education specializing in the training of future academics and scholars; its students are known as *normaliens*. —TRANS.
6. Université Paris VIII was founded as an experimental academic centre in Vincennes in 1969. It moved to Saint-Denis in 1980. —TRANS.
7. A French feminist writer; several of her novels became best sellers in the 1950s and 1960s. —TRANS.
8. To be able to keep on thinking "differently," I had to say no to Simone de Beauvoir and to all the other women who brandished her as their intellectual authority in the name of feminism.

    Les femmes s'entêtent can be translated as "Women put their feet down," or "The Headstrong Women," but it is also a pun on *les femmes sans tête*, or "headless," that is to say, "leaderless women." —TRANS.
9. A group of feminists from the women's movement was organized in the fall of 1970 around the pamphlet titled *For a Revolutionary Feminist Movement*.
10. The École Freudienne (Freudian School) was founded by Lacan in 1964 and dissolved by him in 1980 shortly before he died.
11. The Centre Hospitalier Sainte-Anne is a psychiatric hospital in Paris. —TRANS.
12. *Le torchon brûle* was the first newspaper published by the Women's Movement (six issues between 1971 and 1973). The title can be translated as "The dishcloth is burning," but also as "There is a running battle" or a "flare-up." *Un torchon* is also a dismissive term for a newspaper (cf. the English "rag"). —TRANS.

13. In 1971, as a protest against the criminalization of abortion, at the initiative of the MLF and a journalist from *Le Nouvel Observateur*, 343 women, including a number of celebrities, signed a petition declaring that they had had abortions. The petition appeared in the national press. —TRANS.

14. Even if we had to wait until 1982 for abortion to be reimbursed by the national health insurance system, thus making it effectively free for most women.

    The law that authorized abortion in 1975 bears the name of Simone Veil, minister of health in the Giscard d'Estaing administration, who defended the law before the French government. —TRANS.

15. Left-wing writer François Maspero started his own publishing house in 1959; it became Éditions de la Découverte in 1983. —TRANS.

16. Hélène Cixous, *Dedans* (Paris: Grasset, 1969); in English as *Inside*, trans. Carol Barko (New York: Schocken, 1986).

17. See, among other documents, reports on the UNESCO General Conference, twenty-fifth session (Paris, October 17–November 16, 1989), and on the annual meeting of the UN Committee to Eliminate Discrimination Against Women (New York, January 22–February 2, 1990). For newspaper coverage, see "Égalité professionelle, pas de passe-droit pour les femmes," *Les Échos*, August 21, 1989; "Participation des femmes à la vie parlementaire: Un recul général," *Profession politique*, December 18, 1989; "Un bilan des plans d'égalité professionnelle," *Le Monde*, October 19, 1989; "La formation des femmes reste en plan," *Libération*, March 8, 1990; "Les statistiques de la honte," *Le Monde*, January 29, 1991.

18. A widely influential French Marxist and philosopher, Louis Althusser strangled his wife in a fit of madness. —TRANS.

19. An autodidact interested in psychoanalytic issues, Daniel Karlin produced and cohosted (with Tony Lainé) a weekly television show about the sex lives of the French titled *L'amour en France*. It aired during the 1988–89 season. The reference here is to an occasion when Karlin declared his phantasmatic identification with a man who had killed his (female) lover. —TRANS.

20. The neologism *filse* is composed from *fils* (son) and the feminine ending "-e"; a *filse* is a daughter who identifies herself as a son. —TRANS.

21. A terrorist group, founded in the early seventies, similar to other European commandos (such as the Italian Red Brigades or the German Red Army Faction), who proclaimed their affiliation with the far left. —TRANS.

22. The author writes *hommosexuée*, doubling the "m" to invoke the word *homme*, "man." —TRANS.

23. Jacques Lacan, "The Mirror Stage as Formative of the Function of the I as Revealed in Psychoanalytic Experience," in *Écrits: A Selection*, trans. Alan Sheridan (New York: Norton, 1977).

24. Albert O. Hirschman, *The Passions and the Interests: Political Arguments for Capitalism Before Its Triumph* (Princeton: Princeton University Press, 1977).

25. Bernard Pivot was the creator and host of the influential literary television program *Apostrophes*, which ran from the late 1970s until 1990. Antoinette Fouque plays on his surname to comment on his pivotal role. —TRANS.

26. See Otto Fenichel, "The Symbolic Equation: Girl = Phallus," in *The Psychoanalytic Quarterly* 18 (1949): 303–24.

27. Georges Devereux, *Baubo, la vulve mythique* (Paris: Godefroy, 1983).

28. The *Bébête Show* was a televised series popular in the 1980s that featured puppet caricatures of political figures. "Marchy" and "Pencassine" were derogatory feminized representations of Georges Marchais, head of the French Communist Party from 1972 to 1994, and Jean-Marie Le Pen, founder of the far-right Front National party. —TRANS.

29. See the second preface, this volume, note 14.

3. THERE ARE TWO SEXES

This text is based on a lecture given at a colloquium titled "Lectures de la différence sexuelle" (Readings of sexual difference) organized in October 1990 by the Collège international de philosophie at the initiative of the Centre de recherches en études féminines (Center for research in women's studies) at Paris VIII. The proceedings were published as *Colloque de la différence sexuelle* (Paris: Des femmes, 1994); "Il y a deux sexes" appears on pp. 283–317.

1. The DES (Diplôme d'études supérieures) was a degree required of teachers in the higher education system who were preparing to take the *agrégation*, a competitive examination for prospective university professors. —TRANS.

2. *Jouissance*, referring to an intense, orgasmic sensation, is sometimes translated as "enjoyment" or "pleasure," but neither English term captures the meaning adequately; thus the French term will be retained throughout. —TRANS.

3. See chapter 2, note 20.

4. In modern French the word *femelle* is generally reserved for discussions of plant and animal life. —TRANS.

5. Earlier this year, in Diderot's *Éléments de Physiologie*, ed. Paolo Quintili (Paris: Champion, 2004), under the heading "Raison," I found a lovely definition of anthropoculture: "Reason, or man's instinct, is determined by his/its organization, and by the tendencies, tastes, and aptitudes that the mother communicates to the child, who for nine months is one with her."

6. Ever since I formulated the concept of *uterus envy*, which appeared in 1970 in a leaflet that set forth a research program for Psychanalyse et Politique, I have never stopped trying to work out its political and psychoanalytical implications. This theoretical advance has recently been taken up in part by contemporary anthropology.

7. René Frydman and Julien Cohen-Solal, *Ma grossesse, mon enfant: Le livre de la femme enceinte* (Paris: Odile Jacob, 1989).

8. In French, a *non-lieu*, which denotes the verdict in a case that is dismissed, carries the offensive connotation that the criminal act has "not taken place," never happened, and is in this sense a negation of the victim's experience of the crime. —TRANS.

9. A subscription television channel premiered in France in 1984, supplementing the five free public channels. —TRANS.

10. See chapter 2, note 22.

11. An allusion to a well-known book by philosopher and Marxist critic Guy Debord, *La société du spectacle* (1967), in English as *The Society of the Spectacle*, trans. Donald Nicholson-Smith (New York: Zone, 1994). —TRANS.

12. Preamble to the Constitution of 27 October 1946, articles 1–3, http://legisla tionline.org/download/action/download/id/1601/file/6b1891a9a33272f1c7f8 a8d0142e.htm/preview (accessed December 16, 2013).

13. An allusion to the fact that the words inscribed on the pediments of city halls in France are *Liberté, Égalité, Fraternité*. —TRANS.

14. See chapter 5, p. 60.

15. Robert Antelme, *The Human Race*, trans. Jeffrey Haigh and Annie Mahler (Marlboro, VT: Marlboro, 1992), p. 111.

16. For example, students in an all-female group would be called *étudiantes*; however, if even one male were to join them the masculine term *étudiants* would be used for the whole group. —TRANS.

17. *Reconnaissance*, a French synonym for gratitude, can be broken into morphemes roughly translatable as "rebirth together." —TRANS.

18. Paul Celan, *Poèmes* (Paris: Mercure de France, 1986).

19. Emmanuel Levinas, *Proper Names*, trans. Michael B. Smith (Stanford: Stanford University Press, 1996 [1975]), pp. 38–39.

4. Does Psychoanalysis Have an Answer for Women?

Interview with Emile Malet, "La psychanalyse a-t-elle réponse à tout?" in *Passages* 37 (April 1991): 16–17.

1. Paul Celan, Bremen Prize speech, in *Collected Prose*, trans. Rosemarie Waldrop (Manchester: Carcanet, 1986), p. 13.

2. See Martin Heidegger, *What Is Called Thinking?* trans. Fred D. Wieck and J. Glenn Gray (New York: Harper and Row, 1968), p. 163.

5. The Plague of Misogyny

First published in the proceedings of a conference titled "Three Days on Racism," organized in June 1991 by the monthly magazine *Passages* and the Maison des Sciences de l'Homme; reprinted in Michel Wieviorka, ed., *Racisme et modernité* (Paris: La Découverte, 1993): 289–97.

1. *Dictionnaire Quillet de la langue française* (Paris: Quillet, 1975).

2. *Dictionnaire usuel illustré*, ed. Henri Flammarion, Charles-Henri Flammarion, Guy Rocaut, and Christian Rocaut-Quillet (Paris: Quillet-Flammarion, 1980).

3. See chapter 2, note 13.

4. The woman Lacan called a "brilliant tripe butcher." *Écrits: The First Complete Edition in English*, trans. Bruce Fink with Héloïse Fink and Russell Grigg (New York: Norton, 2006, p. 632, cf. p. 374. See Melanie Klein, *Envy and Gratitude and Other Works 1946–1963* (London: Virago, 1988).

5. Florence Arthaud is a champion sailor who broke the record for a solitary crossing of the Atlantic in 1990. Edith Cresson, a politician, was the first (and so far the only) woman to serve as prime minister of France, under François Mitterrand, from May 15, 1991, to April 2, 1992. —TRANS.

6. See chapter 2, note 17. The women in the Jospin government broke with this practice and insisted on being called Madame la Ministre. They had the support of the prime minister, who made this the general practice with a decree (March 6, 1998) recommending the feminization of occupational names, functions, ranks, and titles in all regulations and official documents published by the state and the establishment of a commission on terminology. In his preface to *Femme, j'écris ton nom*, ed. Annie Becquer et al. (Paris: La Documentation française, 1999), Lionel Jospin wrote: "Parity has its place in our language" (p. 6).

7. I established the Observatoire de la misogynie (Observatory of Misogyny) in 1989, at the same time as the Alliance des femmes pour la démocratisa-

tion (Women's Alliance for Democratization). The Observatoire records threats to women's lives and dignity, ensures that the laws are applied, promotes solidarity, suggests ways of fighting discrimination, and in this way promotes the democratization of society.

8. The *banlieues* are suburban rings around major French cities. —TRANS.
9. In 1982 Gisèle Halimi pushed through a law stipulating that "lists of candidates cannot include more than 75 percent individuals of the same sex." The law was repealed by the Constitutional Council on November 18, 1982, on the grounds that article 3 of the Constitution provides for equal voting rights for all citizens.

6. AND IF WE WERE TO SPEAK OF WOMEN'S POWERLESSNESS?

Published in *Passages* 40 (September 1991): 28–29, in the special issue "Les femmes aiment-elles le pouvoir?" (Do women like power?).

1. See Jean-Claude Chesnais, "Les trois revanches," *Le Débat* 60 (May–August 1990): 99–101.
2. The press had a field day with crime this summer, turning several women criminals into stars so that at least in this field we might see some equality. A mirage, as always, when it is a question of equality between men and women: according to the Ministry of Justice statistics on crime in France published by *Le Nouvel Observateur*, June 6–12, 1991, p. 102, more than 88 percent of murderers are men.
3. The Confédération générale des cadres (General Confederation of Cadres) is a trade union for middle management. —TRANS.
4. See *Elle* (French edition), August 5, 1991.

7. "IT IS NOT POWER THAT CORRUPTS BUT FEAR"

This essay was published in *Passages* 43 (December 1991): 12–13. The title is a quotation from Aung San Suu Kyi, *Freedom from Fear and Other Writings* (New York: Penguin, 1991), p. 180. Aung San Suu Kyi was awarded the Nobel Peace Prize in 1991.

1. Aung San Suu Kyi, *Freedom from Fear and Other Writings* (New York: Penguin, 1991).
2. Aung San Suu Kyi, *Aung San of Burma: A Biographical Portrait* (Edinburgh: Kiscadale, 1991).
3. Preface, *Freedom from Fear*, pp. xvi–xvii.

4. Václav Havel, *Václav Havel or Living in Truth: Twenty-two Essays Published on the Occasion of the Award of the Erasmus Prize to Václav Havel*, ed. Jan Vladislav (London: Faber and Faber, 1986), p. 5.

5. Dominique Lecourt, *Contre la peur* (Paris: Hachette, 1990).

6. *Le Monde*, October 19, 1991.

7. Jean-Pierre Clerc, "Nul ne sait où Mme Suu Kyi est détenue en Birmanie," *Le Monde*, October 19, 1991.

8. MY FREUD, MY FATHER

First published in *Passages* 46 (April 1992): 27–28.

1. See Elisabeth Roudinesco, *La bataille de cent ans: Histoire de la psychanalyse en France* (Paris: Seuil, 1986), p. 430.

2. Paris: Gallimard 1964 (c. 1946).

3. See chapter 2, note 20.

4. Yesterday, Antigone, today, "queer Anna," unquestionably less than ever me. See Isabelle Mangou, "Queer Anna," in *L'Unebévue, revue de psychanalyse* 19 (Winter 2001–Spring 2002): 9–42.

5. See Jacques Lacan, *On Feminine Sexuality: The Limits of Love and Language; Encore 1972–1973*, ed. Jacques-Alain Miller, trans. Bruce Fink (New York: Norton, 1999).

6. Jacques Lacan, *Ecrits: The First Complete Edition in English*, trans. Bruce Fink with Héloïse Fink and Russell Grigg (New York: Norton, 2006).

9. FROM LIBERATION TO DEMOCRATIZATION

Text in support of Antoinette Fouque, "Une expérience du mouvement des femmes en France, 1968–199," doctoral thesis submitted to the Université de Paris VIII, July 1, 1992. The jury consisted of Hélène Cixous (chair), Francine Demichel, André Demichel, Francine du Sorbier, and James Y. Siegel.

1. Sigmund Freud, "New Introductory Lectures on Psychoanalysis," in *The Standard Edition of the Complete Psychological Works of Sigmund Freud*, ed. James Strachey (London: Hogarth, 1964), 22:80.

2. Monique Wittig, *Les Guérillères*, trans. David Le Vay (New York: Avon, 1971 [1969]).

3. Des femmes.

4. See chapter 2, note 18.

5. See Thomas Laqueur, *Making Sex: Body and Gender from the Greeks to Freud* (Cambridge: Harvard University Press, 1990).

10. Our Editorial Policy Is a Poethics

First published in Françoise Barret-Ducrocq, ed., *Traduire l'Europe* (Paris: Payot, 1992), pp. 142–46.

1. See the second preface, this volume, note 14.
2. "But language—the performance of a language system—is neither reactionary nor progressive; it is quite simply fascist; for fascism does not prevent speech, it compels speech." Roland Barthes, "Inaugural Lecture," trans. Richard Howard, in *A Barthes Reader*, ed. Susan Sontag (New York: Hill and Wang, 1982), p. 461.
3. "Profession . . . traductrice?" *Des femmes en mouvements*, April 4, 1978, pp. 74–76.
4. Excerpts from a lecture given at Hofstra University in 1985 and from an interview with Jean-Pierre Salgas published in *La Quinzaine littéraire* (December 1, 1986).
5. *Childhood*, trans. Barbara Wright in consultation with the author, preface by Alice Kaplan (Chicago: University of Chicago Press, 2013); *Tropisms*, trans. Maria Jolas (New York: Braziller, 1967).
6. Marcel Proust, *In Search of Lost Time*, vol. 1, *Swann's Way*, the C. K. Moncrieff translation edited and annotated by William C. Carter (New Haven: Yale University Press), p. 47. *François le Champi* is a novel by George Sand first published in periodical form in 1847–48, in book form in 1850.

11. Dialogue with Isabelle Huppert

First published in *Cahiers du cinéma* 477 (March 1994): 36–47; this special issue was designed and edited by the actress.

1. Trans. Barbara Wright, in consultation with the author, pref. Alice Kaplan (Chicago: University of Chicago Press, 2013).
2. In Claudel's play *La ville* (Paris: Mercure de France, 1970), a female character defines herself as "the promise that cannot be kept."

12. Recognitions

Excerpt from a request for accreditation to supervise research submitted to Université de Paris VIII on March 9, 1994; jury members were Hélène Cixous, Francine Demichel (chair), André Demichel, Jean-Pierre Gastaud, and Blandine Kriegel.

1. Cf. Montaigne, "On Experience," in *The Essays of Michel de Montaigne*, ed. and trans. M. A. Screech (London: Allan Lane, Penguin, 1991), book 3, pp. 1207–1269.

2. Cf. Saint Augustine, *Confessions*, trans. R. S. Pine-Coffin (Penguin: Harmondsworth, 1961), 4:4.

3. See chapter 2, note 11.

4. See the second preface, this volume, note 1.

5. Ibid., note 2.

6. Answer to an inquiry about "experience," *Mise en page* 1 (May 1972), cited in Philippe Lacoue-Labarthe, *Poetry as Experience*, trans. Andrea Tarnowski (Stanford: Stanford University Press, 1999), p. 128, note 15.

7. Hannah Arendt, *The Human Condition* (Chicago: University of Chicago Press, 1958).

8. *N'être fille*, "not to be a girl," is a homophone for *naître fille*, "to be born a girl"; it introduces a note of negativity and hints at the deprecatory *n'être que fille*, "to be merely a girl."

9. An anastrophe is a figure of speech in which the normal order of syntactic elements is reversed or disrupted.

10. Alain Rey, ed., *Dictionnaire historique de la langue française* (Paris: Dictionnaires Le Robert, 1992).

11. Henri Ey, Paul Bernard, and Charles Brisset, eds., *Manuel de Psychiatrie* (Paris: Masson et Cie, 1960).

12. Jean Laplanche and Jean-Bertrand Pontalis, *The Language of Psychoanalysis*, trans. Donald Nicholson-Smith (New York: Norton, 1973), pp. 166–69.

13. Jacques Lacan, "The Hysteric's Question (II): What Is a Woman?" in *The Seminar of Jacques Lacan, Book III, The Psychoses, 1955–1956*, trans. Russell Grigg (New York: Norton, 1993), pp. 179–80.

14. Discussion following a paper read by André Green to Claude Lévi-Strauss's seminar on identity: André Green, *Atome de parenté et relations oedipiennes* (Paris: Grasset, 1977), p. 100.

15. André Green, "La réserve de l'incréable," in *Créativite et/ou symptôme*, ed. Nicos Nicolaïdis, Elsa Schmidt-Kitsikis, and Antonio Andreoli (Paris: Clancier-Guénaud, 1982); reprinted in André Green, *La déliaison. Psychanalyse, anthropoculture et littérature* (Paris: Belles Lettres, 1992), pp. 313–40.

16. Arendt, *The Human Condition*, pp. 8–11.

17. Diplôme d'études approfondies, a degree in advanced studies roughly equivalent to a masters degree in the United States. —TRANS.

18. Work at the legal level resulted, for example, in a letter to UN Secretary General Boutros Boutros-Ghali putting forward the view that the rapes in the former Yugoslavia should be considered not simply as "war crimes" but as "crimes against humanity" and should be punished accordingly. This position was defended at a Human Rights Conference held last June; it will be defended again at future UN conferences on population and especially at the conference on women to be held in September 1995.

13. WARTIME RAPES

First published as "Les viols en ex-Yougoslavie sont désormais reconnus comme des crimes contre l'humanité," *Passages* 61 (April 1994): 34–35.

1. In the UN Security Council's resolution 827 (May 25, 1993), which defines the competence of the Tribunal, rapes committed for "political, racial, or religious reasons" are considered to be "crimes against humanity."
2. A European public cultural television channel targeting French and German audiences in particular. —TRANS.
3. See chapter 12, p. 117–18.
4. The Nazis sterilized Jewish women in the camps and also organized *Lebensborn* (Himmler, 1935; the word might be translated as "fountains of life") in order to produce a "pure Aryan race" that would rule the world "for a thousand years." These *Lebensborn* centers took in women (blond, blue-eyed women in good health) and SS personnel for the purpose of making babies. The centers took care of the pregnant women and their children. After a few months the children were handed over to adoptive Nazi families. It is estimated that twenty-five thousand babies were born in the *Lebensborn* between 1936 and 1945.

14. RELIGION, WOMEN, DEMOCRACY

Presented at a conference titled "Europe et Migrations" organized by the journal *Passages*, March 18–19, 1994, during a round-table discussion on churches, mosques and secularism.

1. Jules Ferry, "De l'égalité de l'éducation," speech given in Paris on April 10, 1870, in *Discours et opinions de Jules Ferry*, ed. Paul Robiquet (Paris: Armand Colin, 1893), 1:305.
2. The word *man* does not appear in the title of the standard English translation. —TRANS.

3. Ayatollah Ruhollah Khomeini, who later became Iran's supreme leader, spent a period of exile in Neauphle-le-Château, a small town in north central France, in 1978–79. —TRANS.

4. Emmanuel Levinas, "It Is Indispensable for Us Westerners to Adopt the Perspective of a Promising Time." Interview, *Le Monde*, June 2, 1992.

5. See chapter 13, p. 124.

6. Bruno Étienne makes the same point in "Les femmes et les intégrismes: Des définitions à l'exemple musulman," *Après-demain* 330 (January 1991): 19–20, 25. *Après-demain* is a journal published by the Ligue des droits de l'homme (League for Human Rights). See www.fondation-seligmann.org/ApresDe main/AD330/330_3618.pdf (accessed December 2, 2013).

7. Georges Bernanos (1888–1948) was a French Catholic writer whose novels include *Under the Sun of Satan*, *Diary of a Country Priest*, and *Dialogues of the Carmelites*. —TRANS.

8. Albert Memmi said as much in remarkable terms at the time of the "headscarf affair": "Portrait de femme sous le monothéisme," *Libération*, January 12, 1990.

9. See chapter 5, note 8, and chapter 12, p. 120.

10. The Parc de la Villette is a park and cultural complex on the northeast edge of Paris. —TRANS.

11. Despite an article published in *Libération* in late 1993 denouncing Nasrin's plight, and despite the information campaign launched by the Alliance des femmes pour la démocratie, the defenders of human rights remained silent for a long time. In July 1994 Nasrin sent me an alarming fax: "I am in great danger. The fundamentalists could kill me at any moment. Save me, I beg you." While the Alliance des femmes alerted public opinion and held daily demonstrations outside the Bangladeshi Embassy throughout the month of July, I repeatedly contacted the Ministry for Foreign Affairs and the Presidency of the Republic, set up a defense committee on behalf of the writer, sent two lawyers to Dacca to make sure she was safe, and put her name forward for the European Parliament's Sakharov Prize. With the exception of the few who demonstrated alongside us in July, the democratic intellectuals took a long time to rouse themselves to action. They eventually did so, and at that point the media stepped up in support.

12. "Beur Chicks"; the designation *Beurs* refers to French-born children of North African immigrant parents. —TRANS.

13. Christian Baudelot and Roger Establet, *Allez les filles!* (Paris: Seuil, 1993).

14. The Falloux law, adopted in 1850, in effect authorized Catholic instruction in public primary and secondary schools. —TRANS.

15. See François-Georges Dreyfus, *Histoire de la démocratie chrétienne en France, de Chateaubriand à Raymond Barre* (Paris: Albin Michel, 1988).

16. Alain Finkielkraut, "Voiles: La sainte alliance des clergés," *Le Monde*, October 25, 1989.

17. *Contrat d'insertion professionnelle*: a short-term employment contract for job seekers under age twenty-six. —TRANS.

18. *Salaire minimum interprofessionnel de croissance*: minimum wage. —TRANS.

19. *Revenu minimum d'insertion*: income support for unemployed people of working age who have no other employment benefits. —TRANS.

20. See "Le retour de l'ordre moral," in Antoinette Fouque, *Il y a deux sexes* (Paris: Gallimard, 2004), pp. 203–8.

15. Our Bodies Belong to Us

This dialogue with Taslima Nasrin first appeared in *Passages* 62 (June 1994): 44–45. Taslima Nasrin is a Bangladeshi doctor and writer. She is living under a fatwa because she has denounced Islam's oppression of women in a collection of articles. Thanks to the international mobilization in which the Alliance des femmes pour la démocratie (Women's Alliance for Democracy) played a part, she was able to leave her country and travel to Paris. She now teaches at Harvard.

1. Taslima Nasrin, *Femmes, manifestez-vous!* (Paris: Des femmes, 1994).

2. The United Nations held an International Conference on Population and Development in Cairo in September 1994.

3. See chapter 1, note 9.

4. See chapter 2, note 14.

16. Homage to Serge Leclaire

Text read at an event honoring Serge Leclaire's memory organized by his wife and children on October 23, 1994.

1. Serge Leclaire, *Rompre les charmes: Recueil pour des enchantés de la psychanalyse* (Paris: InterÉditions, 1981).

2. "Quocirca et absentes adsunt . . . et, quod difficilius dictu est, mortui vivunt": epigraph in Jacques Derrida, *Politics of Friendship*, trans. George Collins (London: Verso, 1997), p. vi.

280 17. HOW TO DEMOCRATIZE PSYCHOANALYSIS?

17. How to Democratize Psychoanalysis?

Excerpted from an interview with Vanina Micheli-Rechtman, "Comment démocratiser la psychanalyse?" *Passages* 65 (November 1994): 48–51.

1. See the second preface, this volume, note 2.
2. The French construction paraphrased here, *ne . . . que*, is normally translated as "only." But these terms are also near homophones of French nouns, *noeud*, "knot," and *queue*, "tail": both are familiar terms for "penis." —TRANS.
3. See the second preface, this volume, note 1.
4. See chapter 9, p. 85.
5. See chapter 2, note 20.
6. I now call it *libido creandi*. See the second preface, this volume p. xxx.
7. This phrase designating a dance sequence for two people can also be read as "not two," or "no two." —TRANS.
8. In Serge Leclaire, "Un soulèvement de questions: Le mouvement analytique animé par Jacques Lacan," *Cahiers confrontation* 3 (1980): 69–76, reprinted in *Rompre les charmes: Recueil pour des enchantés de la psychanalyse* (Paris: InterÉditions, 1981), pp. 199–210.
9. Ibid., p. 76.

18. Democracy and Its Discontents

First published in *Profession politique* 149 (February 1995): 2.

1. Articulated in two complementary texts in which Freud set forth a program for modernity that is more contemporary than ever: Sigmund Freud, "The Future of an Illusion" and "Civilization and Its Discontents," in *The Standard Edition of the Complete Psychological Works of Sigmund Freud*, ed. James Strachey (London: Hogarth, 1961), 21:3–56 and 59–145; citations from pp. 42, 29, and 79.
2. Gilles Kepel, *The Revenge of God: The Resurgence of Islam, Christianity, and Judaism in the Modern World*, trans. Alan Braley (University Park: Pennsylvania State University Press, 1994 [1991]).
3. Monseigneur Gaillot served as bishop of Evreux from 1982 to 1995, when he was removed from the post by papal decree after expressing controversial positions on social, political, and religious topics, including abortion. —TRANS.
4. See chapter 1, note 9.

5. As a woman journalist emphasized in *L'Express* on January 12, 1995, referring to one of M. Balladur's first proposals for dealing with youth unemployment. Édouard Balladur was prime minister under François Mitterrand from March 29, 1993, to May 10, 1995. —TRANS.
6. Philippe de Villiers and Charles Pasqua are right-wing politicians noted among other things for expressing anti-Islamic sentiments. —TRANS.
7. A reference to then President François Mitterrand. —TRANS.

19. TOMORROW, PARITY

An abridged version of this text was presented on March 8, 1995, at the World Summit for Social Development in Copenhagen, in the context of a roundtable discussion titled "Bridging the Gender Gap: Open Dialogue Between Parliamentarians and Civil Society." The roundtable was set up by two nongovernmental organizations: Parliamentarians for Global Action (PGA) and Women's Environment and Development Organization (WEDO).

1. See the second preface, this volume, note 1.
2. A founder of the modern Russian women's movement. —TRANS.
3. Jacques Delors was president of the European Commission from 1985 to 1995. —TRANS.
4. Universal Declaration of Human Rights, Preamble and article 2, http://publications.ossrea.net/index.php?option=com_content&view=article&id=75:universal-declaration-human-rights-1948-&catid=16:other-instruments&Itemid=55 (accessed December 16, 2013).
5. Fourth Geneva Convention, August 12, 1949, article 27, www.icrc.org/ihl/WebART/380-600032?OpenDocument (accessed December 16, 2013).
6. www.un.org/womenwatch/daw/cedaw/text/econvention.htm (accessed December 16, 2013).
7. The explicit goal of UNCED was to "lay the foundation of a world association between developing countries and industrialized countries, based on common needs and interests, to secure the future of the planet" (Maurice Strong, secretary general of the Rio Conference).
8. Vienna Declaration and Programme of Action adopted by the World Conference on Human Rights in Vienna on June 25, 1993, www.ohchr.org/EN/ProfessionalInterest/Pages/Vienna.aspx (accessed December 16, 2013).
9. www.unhchr.ch/huridocda/huridoca.nsf/%28Symbol%29/A.RES.48.104.En (accessed December 16, 2013).

10. Along with two other militant women from the (French) Women's Alliance and Rosiska Darcy de Oliveira from Terra femina, I had met with Mr. Fall in early 1993, before the Vienna Conference. We spoke to him about the action the alliance was carrying out in solidarity with raped women from the former Yugoslavia and we drew his attention to the importance of women's rights.

11. Forty-Seventh World Health Assembly, agenda item 19, "Maternal and Child Health and Family Planning: Traditional Practices Harmful to the Health of Women and Children," WHA47.10, May 10, 1994, http://whqlibdoc.who.int /wholis/3/WHA47_R10_eng.pdf (accessed December 8, 2013).

12. For comments on the danger of this notion of equity, see this chapter, p. 165.

13. UNFPA Master Plans for Development, "Programme of Action of the International Conference on Population and Development," chapter 2, principle 4, www.unfpa.org/public/cache/offonce/home/sitemap/icpd/International-Conference-on-Population-and-Development/ICPD-Programme;jsessionid =59AB6ECA018C77EFDEC536003FD60547.jahia02#ch2 (accessed December 8, 2013).

14. Statute of the Council of Europe, 5 May 1949, http://conventions.coe.int /Treaty/en/Treaties/Html/001.htm (accessed December 3, 2013).

15. www.conventions.coe.int/Treaty/en/Treaties/Html/005.htm (accessed December 3, 2013).

16. Maastricht Treaty, Agreement on Social Policy, article 6, section 3,www .cvce.eu/obj/treaty_on_european_union_maastricht_7_february_1992-en-2c2f2b85–14bb-4488–9ded-13f3cd04de05.html (accessed December 3, 2013).

17. To pursue higher education without their husband's consent, however, married women had to wait for the law of 1938 that abolishing their "civil incapacity."

18. The schools known as *grandes écoles* in France are prestigious public or private institutions of higher education specializing in a wide variety of fields (engineering, education, business, agriculture, veterinary science, and many others). Students are admitted on the basis of highly competitive examinations, typically after several years of preparatory study. —TRANS.

19. The École Normale Supérieure de Sèvres was founded under the Third Republic at a time when there was still separate schooling for girls.

20. See the second preface, this volume, note 2.

21. The prohibition of abortion under the 1810 penal code was followed by the prohibition of contraception in 1920. In 1942, under the Vichy regime, abortion was a state crime punished by death. It was only in 1967 that the Neuwirth law authorized contraception.

22. The Maison de la Mutualité was owned by a regional nonprofit insurance federation; its conference facilities were regularly rented to outside users for political meetings. —TRANS.

23. With Gisèle Halimi and the association Choisir, during the famous Aix trial.

    In early 1978 two men went on trial on charges of having repeatedly raped two teenage girls several years earlier. Attorney Gisèle Halimi represented the girls, with the support of feminist organizations such as Choisir (Choose). The case drew national attention and triggered both widespread outrage at the attacks and a vociferous backlash against the feminists. —TRANS.

24. In the European Union the poor are defined as those whose income is less than half the average income of the population as a whole; in poor countries the poor live on one dollar a day. To try to reduce this great gap, Gustave Speth, administrator of the United Nations Development Program, has invented the Human Development Index (HDI), using the criteria of life expectancy, educational level, and buying power; these make it possible to come a little closer to the realities of life, especially in poor countries. See *Démographie et pauvreté* 8 (February 1995).

25. It is interesting to note, too, that women own only 1 percent of the world's wealth.

26. Of 100 million children aged six to eleven who do not go to school, 70 percent are girls.

27. *Human Development Report* 1994, published by the UN Department of Information (http://hdr.undp.org/en/media/hdr_1994_en_contents.pdf) in preparation for the Copenhagen World Summit for Social Development, March 6–12, 1995.

28. If one applies to the world population as a whole the ratio of 1.05 women for each man found in developed countries, 100 million women are lacking in the overall census; see Amartya Sen, "More Than 100 Million Women Are Missing," *New York Review of Books,* December 20, 1990, and *On Ethics and Economics* (Oxfordshire: Blackwell, 1987).

29. *Asiaweek,* Hong Kong.

30. "Women's Action," *Equality Now* (March 1995).

31. In the United States, according to a survey carried out at the request of the federal government, more than 12 million women appear to have been raped at least once; 61 percent of the victims were under eighteen years old at the time of the rape, and three out of ten were not yet eleven. In 80

percent of the cases the rapist was known to the victim. Only 16 percent of these attacks were reported. *Newsweek*, July 1990; Observatoire de la Misogynie.

32. Figures cited by the Chinese minister of public safety, probably on the low side.

33. Particularly by the Zenska group Tresnjevka, from Croatia-Zagreb.

34. According to the latest report from Amnesty International, women represent more than 80 percent of refugees or displaced persons.

35. Along with death threats against those who do not wear the headscarf, there are sometimes threats of reprisals from the other side against those who do.

36. The Family Code was promulgated in 1984 in spite of massive protest from women's associations.

    See chapter 1, note 9. —TRANS.

37. Koudil received an award for her work on behalf of human rights in 1994 in recognition of the courage she showed by producing the film.

38. The victim was Louisa Lardjoune; see Nicole Penicaut and Emmanuèle Peyret, "Une femme sur sept serait victime de violences conjugales." *Libération*, March 2, 1995.

39. As I make the final corrections to this text, I can say with relief that the term *equity* is not mentioned in the draft platform for the Beijing Conference as discussed during the last preparatory meeting in New York.

40. Lissy Gröner, report on the poverty of women in Europe for the European Parliament's Committee on Women's Rights, February 10, 1994.

41. In the Brandenburg region the number of sterilizations has grown tenfold in two years: from 827 in 1991 to 8,224 in 1993.

42. The law of July 1, 1972, followed France's ratification of the United Nations' International Convention on the Elimination of All Forms of Racial Discrimination on July 28, 1971, a convention that took effect in 1969, http://treaties.un.org/Pages/ViewDetails.aspx?src=TREATY&mtdsg_no=IV-2&chapter=4&lang=en&clang=_en (accessed December 2, 2013).

43. *Libération*, March 2, 1995.

44. "L'Hebdo," Canal Plus, March 4, 1995.

45. In 1988, 89,082 boys and 119,597 girls received baccalaureate degrees. Christian Baudelot and Roger Establet, *Allez les filles* (Paris: Seuil, 1988), p. 29.

46. In France the term *laïcité* refers to the principle of separation between the secular and the religious sectors of society: the state holds no religious power and churches no political power. —TRANS.

47. The rate of activity varies with age, however; the highest rate, 78 percent, is among women aged twenty-five to twenty-nine. INSEE (National Institute of Statistics and Economic Studies), *Les femmes, contours et caractères*, February 1995.

48. According to a survey by the Caisse d'allocations familiales (Bureau of family allowances) in Yvelines (a department west of Paris) carried out in December 1993 and released on February 25, 1995, by INSEE.

49. See Antoinette Fouque, "Le retour de l'ordre moral," *Il y a deux sexes*, rev. ed. (Paris: Gallimard, 2004), pp. 203–15.

50. *Info Matin*, March 2, 1995, p. 15.

51. Of 3 million unemployed, 1.7 million are women. Young unemployed women constitute such a large majority that INSEE, in *Données sociales 1993* (an annual statistical report on the French workforce), noted that "the typical unemployed person is a young woman without a diploma who has just lost a temporary position in the administration of a business."

52. Statement by Michel Giraud, minister of labor, cited in "Le chômage confirme sa reprise," *Libération*, November 3, 1994.

53. Christiane Cordero, *Le travail des femmes* (Paris: Le Monde, 1995).
    Île-de-France is the administrative region immediately surrounding Paris. —TRANS.

54. The ratios of women's membership in French political institutions in 1995 were as follows: 5.6 percent in the National Assembly, 5 percent in the Senate, 12.6 percent in regional councils, 5.1 percent in general councils, 17.1 percent in municipal councils, 5.4 percent among mayors, and a total of 3 women ministers.

55. In this section I shall focus primarily on political parity between the sexes, that is, equal representation of men and women in political institutions.

56. See chapter 2, note 22.

57. The text of our 1973 poster read as follows: "We are women; we are not voting. The workers vote for the bosses, the blacks vote for the whites, women vote for men . . . " For its part, the association Choisir planned to present "one hundred women for women" at the 1978 legislative elections; because of the difficulties they encountered the number of candidates was reduced to forty-four. They were all eliminated in the first round, but Gisèle Halimi, president of the association, won 4.3 percent of the votes.

58. On March 8, 1981, as the various feminist tendencies were scattered among minor lists, I issued the MLF appeal to vote for François Mitterrand in the first round, without any illusions, but in the hope of contributing to the

maturation process of the left. Our posters read: "Let the heart speak: no candidate for women. Let reason speak: François Mitterrand in the first round." In the subsequent legislative election we supported women wherever they were candidates with this slogan: "To the left of the left, women."

59. In the 1989 local elections, many women expressed a desire to propose lists of women candidates. Some did so, for example Annie Dubourgel in Tanninges, Maria-Andréa Pélegrin in Violès, and Nicole Tournebise in Sarreguemines; Tournebise was elected.

Bouches-du-Rhône is the department that includes Marseille. —TRANS.

60. Shortly before the 1981 presidential elections, and probably with women voters in mind, the right-wing government put a bill through that set the representation of each sex on electoral lists at a minimum of 20 percent. This was the first time there was a quota. Under pressure from Gisèle Halimi, the proposal of a 25 percent quota was adopted again by the left and supported almost unanimously by Parliament. However, the amendment was invalidated by the Constitutional Council on November 18, 1982.

61. www.conseil-constitutionnel.fr/conseil-constitutionnel/root/bank_mm /anglais/cst3.pdf (accessed October 26, 2013).

62. Claudette Apprill, an expert serving on the Steering Committee for Equality Between Women and Men (CDEG) in "Les apports du Conseil de l'Europe au concept de parité" (The contributions of the Council of Europe to the concept of parity), an article published in September 1994 in Belgium in a handbook, *Women's Studies*, put out by the Belgian services of scientific, technical, and cultural affairs, claimed that she had invented the concept of "parity-based democracy." Under the heading "La démocratie paritaire, quarante ans d'activité du Conseil de l'Europe" (Parity-based democracy, forty years of activity by the Council of Europe), the CDEG organized a study group on parity in November 1989. The first part of the Belgian handbook contains interesting articles on parity, especially Éliane Vogel-Polsky's article "Les impasses de l'égalité, ou pourquoi les outils juridiques visant à l'égalité des femmes et des hommes doivent être repensés en termes de parité" (The impasses of equality, or why legal means aiming at equality between women and men must be rethought in terms of parity"). See *Women's studies: Manuel de ressources*, ed. Point d'appui, U.L.B. (Brussels: Services fédéraux des affaires scientifiques, techniques et culturelles, 1994).

63. The manifesto called for the adoption of "an organic law containing a straightforward statement requiring that the assemblies elected at the sub-

national and national levels be composed of as many women as men." *Le Monde*, November 10, 1993.

64. I met with Michel Rocard as early as March 1993 to try to convince him to observe parity on the Socialist Party list. I had not expected him to choose a form of parity that excluded all the feminists of his party.

65. See chapter 2, note 20.

66. Originally, the English word *gender* designated the masculine and feminine genders, as *genre* does in French; in theoretical feminist texts, however, it tends more and more to replace the word *sex*. Thus Western feminism markedly rejects any reference to biological reality to assert the exclusively cultural and historical (and therefore transformable) character of sexual difference.

67. "Mourir à Ankara pour délit d'opinion," *Libération*, September 9, 1994.

20. WOMEN AND EUROPE

This text was written in my capacity as member of the European Parliament for the First Conference of Parliamentary Committees on equal opportunities in the fifteen member states and the European Parliament (Brussels, May 23, 1997). The text was revised for the negotiations over the Amsterdam Treaty and published in *Lettre de la Députée* 3 (third quarter, 1997): 1–2.

1. A ruling of the European Court of Justice in 1995 invalidating a local German law that, given equal qualifications, gave priority to women candidates for recruitment and promotion in civil service positions, www.senat.fr/rap/r96–293/r96–2932.html (accessed December 6, 2013).

2. See the Bourlanges-Martin report, May 1995, www.europarl.europa.eu/igc1996/fiches/fiche12_en.htm (accessed December 16, 2013).

3. See the Dury-Maij-Wegen report, March 5, 1996, www.helsinki.fi/science/xantippa/wle/wle13.html (accessed December 6, 2013).

21. IF THIS IS A WOMAN

Excerpted from Antoinette Fouque, "Si c'est une femme," *Informations Sociales* 80, "Regards vers le XXIe siècle" (fourth quarter, 1999): 38–50.

1. Primo Levi, *If This Is a Man* and *The Truce*, trans. Stuart Woolf (London: Vintage, 1996), p. 17.

2. In Belgium a so-called prostitutes' defense committee has introduced training schemes for prostitutes (legislation governing prostitution, accounting,

commercial management, and sexual techniques). In the Netherlands, thirty-seven pimps organized a demonstration calling for the abolition of new regulations restricting the opening hours of prostitutes' windows and demanding government compensation for loss of earnings. *Marianne* 127, (September 27, 1999).

3. Amartya Sen, "One Hundred Million Women Are Missing," *New York Review of Books* 37, no. 20 (December 20, 1990): 61–66.

4. Developed in 1990 and published by the United Nations Development Program, the Human Development Index takes into account life expectancy, literacy, percentage of children in school, and share of salaried income.

5. Sen, "One Hundred Million Women Are Missing," p. 66.

6. UNICEF, the State of the World's Children, 1996, www.unicef.org/sowc96 /contents.htm?470,238 (accessed October 26, 2013.).

7. Girl children who are infibulated (as are almost 90 percent of girls born in Sudan) are in immediate danger of death after the operation or from the infections that often result from it. As for the survivors, they will suffer for the rest of their lives from the irreversible lesions caused by these mutilations. United Nations Population Fund reports for 1995 and 1997.

8. See chapter 19, p. 167. According to a study carried out in five countries (the United States, South Africa, Thailand, Turkey, and Zambia), 58 percent of women who prostitute themselves were victims of childhood sexual abuse. Melissa Farley, Isin Baral, Merab Kiremire, and Ufuk Sezgin, "Prostitution in Five Countries: Violence and Post-Traumatic Stress Disorder," *Feminism and Psychology* 8, no. 4 (November 1998): 405–26.

9. And one hundred fifty million remain seriously handicapped for life. Three hundred million women who do not wish to have more children lack access to contraceptives. Seventy thousand die each year as the result of an abortion.

10. An anonymous midwife quoted by Peter Adamson in "A Failure of Imagination," *The Progress of Nations 1996*, UNICEF, www.unicef.org/pon96/womfail .htm (accessed December 9, 2013).

11. In Kosovo and Albania, the Code of Leke Dukagjani, which has been in force since the fifteenth century in some regions, condemns women who have been raped to silence, confinement to the home, or even suicide. Gordana Igric, Institute for War and Peace, in *Le Courrier des Balkans* (June 18, 1999).

12. Figure for 1990; Observatoire de la misogynie.

13. *Libération*, April 10, 1999, citing the Russian daily *Vremia*. A UNICEF report published September 21, 1999, stresses that the "transition" to capitalism in the former USSR and the countries of Eastern Europe "is building

upon, rather than levelling, existing inequalities," and that "violence against women, including domestic violence, was more prevalent under Communism than previously assumed . . . [and] "is now on the rise." UNICEF Press Release, September 22, 1999, www.unicef-irc.org/files/doc uments/d-3054-UNICEF-report-provides-fi.pdf (accessed November 16, 2013).

14. NTM (Nique ta mère, "Fuck your mother") is a French rap-graffiti group. Lio is the stage name of a Portuguese-born Belgian singer who became an activist in the defense of battered women after being beaten by her lover, a French singer, in the late 1990s. —TRANS.

15. The GDI measures achievement in the same basic capabilities as the HDI does, but takes note of inequality in achievement between men and women. The GDI figures, in which equality is indexed at 1, show the relative standing of females to males as, at best, 0.939 in Canada and, at worst, 0.155 in Sierra Leone.

16. Three-quarters of the children who do not have access to primary education are girls. See the annual report of the UN Development Program for 1997.

17. The directive on parental leave (1996), in the name of a purported "reconciliation of work and family life," is weighted most heavily on the family side and ends up with triple precariousness for women. The second directive, on part-time work (1997), claims that such work is to the benefit of women, whereas the European Commission itself recognizes that part-time work serves entirely to increase the competitive position of businesses. The employment guidelines adopted at the Luxemburg Employment Summit in 1997—when thirteen of the fifteen countries in the Union had left-wing or social-democratic governments—openly defended the principles of employability and flexibility, whose negative effects on the professional rights of women are known.

See *La Lettre de votre Députée* (The newsletter from your [female] deputy), published during my mandate as member of the European Parliament: no. 4 (fourth quarter, 1977), and nos. 5 and 6 (fourth quarter, 1998).

18. On one occasion a woman cabin crew member left her baby at home in a basket in the bathtub because she could not find anyone to take care of the child. She was distraught when she learned that the flight that should have brought her home was postponed. That was in 1991, but there is still no crèche at Roissy for flight crews. The unpredictable hours crew members work are off-putting for qualified nursery staff. And yet the forty-five thousand people employed at Roissy have a total of five thousand children under

age three. Anne Fairise, "La cruelle inadaptation des systèmes de garde," *Libération*, August 30, 1999.

19. Only 52 percent of mothers of two children, including at least one under the age of three, were economically active in 1997, as against 63.5 percent in 1994. Françoise Battagliola, "Les trajectoires d'emploi des jeunes mères de famille," *Recherches et prévisions*, no. 52 (Paris: Caisse Nationale des Allocations Familiales, June 1998).

20. The Gender Empowerment Measure (GEM), which has been calculated for forty countries on the basis of the number of women in parliament, senior management and leadership positions, and women's share of salaried income, reveals that there is no equality—indexed as 1—in any country. In 1997 it did not reach 0.8 percent in Norway, which was the most advanced country, and was below 0.2 in Mauritania. The average for the countries analyzed is 0.4.

21. "Women are men, just like other men . . . ": such is the philosophy of a journalist writing in *Libération*. François Wenz-Dumas, "Hommes-femmes: L'égalité par la mixité" (*Libération*, September 2, 1999) discovers behind the latest report submitted to the prime minister by Socialist Party deputy Catherine Génisson. According to Génisson, we must above all avoid any specific measures that might favor women and encourage the recruitment of men in sectors where the vast majority of workers are women.

22. A French racing cyclist who won the world championship thirteen times.

23. The American feminist economist Nancy Folbre has looked at the disproportionate share of nonmarket labor that is assumed by women. Nancy Folbre, *De la différence des sexes en économie politique* (Paris: Des femmes, 1997).

24. See chapter 2, note 22.

25. See the second preface, this volume, notes 1 and 2.

22. THEY'RE BURNING A WOMAN

Excerpt from a letter sent by Antoinette Fouque in her capacity as chair of the Alliance des femmes pour la démocratie to Blandine Kriegel in her capacity as an official representative of the presidency of the republic.

1. The recent attack on Bertrand Delanoë reminds us of the need to include this phrase.

    Delanoë, the openly gay Socialist mayor of Paris, was stabbed at a public event on October 2, 2002, by a man who allegedly claimed to hate politicians, Socialists, and homosexuals. The mayor's injuries were not life threatening, though he remained hospitalized for about two weeks. —TRANS.

2. Excerpt from a speech by Jacques Chirac to the plenary session of the World Summit on Sustainable Development, Johannesburg, September 2, 2002, http://discours.vie-publique.fr/notices/027000247.html (accessed December 18, 2013).

23. WHAT IS A WOMAN?

Testimony published in *Génération MLF: 1968–2008* (Paris: Des femmes–Antoinette Fouque, 2008), reprinted in Antoinette Fouque, *Génésique: Féminologie III* (Paris: Des femmes, 2012), pp. 89–115.

1. See the second preface, this volume, note 1.
2. See chapter 2, note 11.
3. See chapter 3, note 1.
4. See chapter 3, note 2.
5. Jacques Lacan, "The Hysteric's Question (II): What is a Woman?" in *The Seminar of Jacques Lacan*, book 3, *The Psychoses, 1955–1956*, trans. Russell Grigg (New York: Norton, 1993), p. 179.
6. Jacques Rancière, *La nuit des prolétaires* (Paris: Fayard, 1981), in English as *The Nights of Labor: The Workers' Dream in Nineteenth-Century France*, trans. John Drury (Philadelphia: Temple University Press, 1989).
7. See the second preface, this volume, note 2, and this chapter, pp. 202–3.
8. Monique Wittig, *Les Guérillères*, trans. David Le Vay (New York: Avon, 1971 [1969]).
9. See chapter 2, note 13.
10. See the second preface, this volume, note 6.
11. *Libération*, September 14, 2008.
12. Blandine Grosjean, "Liberté, activité, maternité," *Libération*, April 29, 2003.
13. This is confirmed by the evocative title of the September 14, 2008, article in *Libération*: "Génération Benoît XVI" (The generation of Benedict XVI).
14. *Génération MLF: 1968–2008*, ed. Antoinette Fouque (Paris: Des femmes, 2008).
15. See the second preface, this volume, note 15.
16. See chapter 12, note 8.
17. George Sand, *Story of My Life: The Autobiography of George Sand*, ed. Thelma Jurgrau, group trans. (Albany: State University Press of New York, 1991), part 1, chapter 14, p. 271.

24. GESTATION FOR ANOTHER

Excerpted from an interview with Marcel Gauchet, first published as "Les enjeux de la gestation pour autrui," *Le Débat* 157 (November–December 2009): 145–57; reprinted in Antoinette Fouque, *Génésique: Féminologie III* (Paris: Des femmes, 2012), pp. 15–39.

1. See the second preface, this volume, note 1.
2. Pierre Nora and Marcel Gauchet interviewed Antoinette Fouque in October 1989 and February 1990; the interviews were published in April 1990 in *Le Débat* 59 and appear in this volume as "Women in Movements—Yesterday, Today, Tomorrow" (chapter 2).
3. See the second preface, this volume, note 6. —TRANS.
4. Nadine Morano served as secretary of state for family under Prime Minister François Fillon in 2008–2009.
5. In French abortion is described in legal terms as *interruption volontaire de grossesse* or IVG.
6. Jacques Lacan, "The Hysteric's Question (II): What Is a Woman?" in *The Seminar of Jacques Lacan*, book 3, *The Psychoses, 1955–1956*, trans. Russell Grigg (New York: Norton, 1993), p. 179.
7. Sigmund Freud, *A Phylogenetic Fantasy: Overview of the Transference Neuroses*, trans. Axel Hoffer and Peter T. Hoffer (London: Belknap Press of Harvard University Press, 1987), pp. 13–14.
8. Jacques Derrida, *Writing and Difference*, trans. Alan Bass (Chicago: University of Chicago Press, 1978), p. 93, cited in François Poirié, *Emmanuel Levinas: Essai et entretiens* (Arles: Actes Sud, 1996), p. 29.
9. Emmanuel Levinas, *Totality and Infinity: An Essay on Exteriority*, trans. Alphonso Lingis (The Hague: Martinus Nijhoff, 1979), p. 50; cited in Poirié, *Emmanuel Levinas*, p. 29.
10. For the play on words, see the second preface, this volume, note 3. —TRANS.
11. She initiated the appeal of March 28, 2009, in favor of legalizing gestation for another in France.
12. Jean-Luc Nancy, *L'intrus* (Paris: Galilée, 2000). Nancy had a heart transplant in the early 1990s.
13. See the second preface, this volume, note 6. —TRANS.
14. *Commère* is an archaic French word for "godmother." —TRANS.
15. The multiparty Grenelle agreements signed in May 1968 have come to serve as a reference for other open debates in France that bring together representatives from all sectors (government, business, professional associations,

NGOs), with the goal of establishing public policy on specific issues. The *Grenelle de l'environnement* process began in September 2007 and led in 2008 to the adoption of the law known as Grenelle 1. —TRANS.

16. Élisabeth de Fontenay, *Diderot ou le matérialisme enchanté* (Paris: Grasset, 1981).
17. Sigmund Freud, "Leonardo da Vinci and a Memory of His Childhood," in *The Standard Edition of the Complete Psychological Works of Sigmund Freud,* ed. James Strachey (London: Hogarth, 1964 [1957]), 11:97.

25. GRAVIDA

Interview with Antoinette Fouque conducted by Jean Larose in 1980, published in two parts in the first two issues of the Canadian journal *Gravida* (Fall 1983): 22–42, (Winter 1984): 55–74, reprinted in Antoinette Fouque, *Gravidanza: Féminologie II* (Paris: Des femmes, 2007): 67–108. This text is added to the collection to highlight Antoinette Fouque's psychoanalytic analysis of feminism.

1. See the second preface, this volume, notes 1 and 2.
2. See Gilles Deleuze and Félix Guattari, *Anti-Oedipus: Capitalism and Schizophrenia,* trans. Robert Hurley, Mark Seem, and Helen R. Lane (New York: Viking, 1977 [1972]).
3. According to Freud, the conflict between the pleasure principle and the reality principle also corresponds to the psychic conflict between the ego and the repressed. The sexual maturation of the subject and the subject's access to what Freud calls "complete object-love," as well as the gradual constitution of that libidinal object, thus arise from submission to the reality principle just as much as the recognition of what is real or unreal in the external world does. This comes down to saying that access to reality and control of the appetite for jouissance do not come simply through the recognition of material reality but above all through the traversal of the oedipal dialectic, which is governed by the law of the father and by the "final" completion of castration. This is what makes it possible to speak of a principle of phallic, or phallogocentric, reality, based on a particular economic organization of the libidinal stages. Human access to "reality" is no more "natural" than any other component of the human. It is attained by way of the symbolic law. It can thus be analyzed, challenged, worked over, transformed. See Sigmund Freud, "Instincts and Their Vicissitudes," in *The Standard Edition of the Complete Psychological Works of Sigmund Freud,* ed. James Strachey (London: Hogarth, 1957), 14:109–40, and "Beyond the Pleasure Principle," in *The Standard Edition*

of the Complete Psychological Works of Sigmund Freud, ed. James Strachey (London: Hogarth, 1955), 18:3–64.

4. Kate Millett, *Sexual Politics* (New York: Doubleday, 1970).

5. See Jacques Lacan, "Le cas Aimée," in *De la psychose paranoïaque dans ses rapports avec la personnalité* (Paris: Seuil, 1975); and Valerie Solanas, *Society for Cutting Up Men, Manifesto* (1968), published as SCUM *Manifesto* (London: Verso, 2004). Solanas is also known for her attempt to kill Andy Warhol.

6. "Even when in fact it is represented by a single person, the paternal function concentrates in itself both imaginary and real relations, always more or less inadequate to the symbolic relation that essentially constitutes it. It is in the *name of the father* that we must recognize the support of the symbolic function which, from the dawn of history, has identified his person with the figure of the law." Jacques Lacan, "The Function and Field of Speech and Language in Psychoanalysis," in *Écrits: A Selection*, trans. Alan Sheridan (New York: Norton, 1977), p. 74.

7. Sigmund Freud and Joseph Breuer, *Studies in Hysteria*, trans. Nicola Luckhurst (London: Penguin, 2004); Sigmund Freud, "Femininity," in *New Introductory Lectures in Psychoanalysis*, ed. and trans. James Strachey (New York: Norton, 1965).

8. Among other texts, see Michel de Certeau, *The Writing of History*, trans. Tom Conley (New York: Columbia University Press, 1988).

9. See the second preface, this volume, p. xxviii, note 44.

10. For that very presidential election, held on March 8, 1981, it was the talk of the town: the MLF issued a strong appeal for voters to support Mitterrand in the first round.

Biographical Notes

Born October 1, 1936, in Marseille, to Alexis Grugnardi and Vincente Bonavita

Completed elementary and high school studies at the Lycée Longchamp, in Marseille; obtained a bachelor's degree in modern literature at the University of Aix-en-Provence

Married René Fouque in 1959

Obtained a secondary teaching diploma in modern literature; taught and obtained a postbachelor's degree in modern literature at the University of Paris-Sorbonne

Employed as literary critic and translator at *Cahiers du Sud* and the *Quinzaine littéraire*, as well as manuscript reader at Éditions du Seuil

Gave birth to daughter Vincente in 1964

Participated in Roland Barthes's seminar in the École Pratique des Hautes Études and prepared master's in advanced studies with Barthes (dissertation on the avant-garde)

Participated in Jacques Lacan's seminar; began psychoanalytical training with Lacan in 1968

Co-founded the Mouvement de Libération des Femmes (MLF) in October 1968 and created the Psychanalyse et Politique research group

Founded and directed:

- the Éditions Des femmes (1973), the first women's publishing house in Europe
- the Des femmes bookstores (1974 in Paris, 1976 in Marseille, 1977 in Lyon) and the Des femmes gallery (1980)
- *Le Quotidien des femmes* (newspaper, 1975), *Des femmes en mouvements* (monthly, then weekly magazine, 1977–1982)
- the Institut d'Enseignement et de Recherches en Sciences des Femmes and the Collège de Féminologie (1978, a field developed to consider the specific experience of women in the elaboration of knowledge)
- the Alliance des Femmes pour la Démocratie (AFD, 1989)
- the Observatoire de la Misogynie (1989)
- the Club Parité 2000 (1990)
- the Espace Des femmes (an art gallery and a venue for encounters and discussions dedicated to women's creation, 2007)

Earned doctorate in political science at Université de Paris VIII in 1992

Served in European Parliament. 1994 to 1999; vice chair of the Committee on Women's Rights; member of the Committees on Foreign Affairs and Civil Liberties

Headed the Alliance Française of San Diego, California, 1985–1988

Headed the international sector of the Women's International Center, 1985–1988

Represented France and the European Union at the United Nations Conferences of Cairo (1994), Beijing (1995), and Istanbul (1996); participated as president of the AFD in those of Rio (1992), Vienna (1993), and Copenhagen (1995), working for the full integration of women's rights into human rights

Served on L'Observatoire de la Parité entre les femmes et les hommes (created by President Jacques Chirac in 1995, with the purpose of conducting an institutional follow-up of questions on parity), 2002–2010

Defended women in danger throughout the world, including

Eva Forest (imprisoned by Franco's regime in Spain, 1975)

Tatiana Mamonova, Julia Voznesenskaya, and the authors of *Women and Russia* (dissidents fighting for women's liberation in the USSR, 1980)

Aung San Suu Kyi, whom she met in 1995 in Rangoon, after publishing her book *Se libérer de la peur (Freedom from Fear)* in 1991

Leyla Zana (Kurd deputy imprisoned by the Turkish government, 1994)

Taslima Nasrin (victim of an Islamic fatwa in Bangladesh, 1994)

Bulgarian nurses (who risked the death sentence in Libya, 2006)

Antoinette Fouque died on February 20, 2014

PUBLICATIONS

Il y a deux sexes (Paris: Gallimard, 1995; 2d ed. Gallimard 2004)

Gravidanza: Essais de féminologie 2 (Paris: Des femmes, 2007)

Génération MLF: 1968–2008 (ed.) (Paris: Des femmes, 2008)

Qui êtes-vous Antoinette Fouque? interviews with Christophe Bourseiller (Paris: Bourin, 2009)

Génésique: Essais de féminologie 3 (Paris: Des femmes, 2012)

Le Dictionnaire universel des créatrices (coeditor), a pioneering encyclopedic work sponsored by UNESCO that highlights forty centuries of women's creation on all continents and in every field of human history, the arts, culture, science and technology (Paris: Des femmes, 2013)

Index

WEDO, *see* Women's Environment and Development Organization
WHO, *see* World Health Organization
Wilson, Bob, 100, 104
Wittig, Monique, xix, 10–11, 16, 196, 200, 201–2, 206; on difference, 216; *Les Guérillères*, 86, 201–2
Woman giving birth to a woman (*l'enfante femme*), 211
Women's Alliance for Democratization (Alliance des femmes pour la démocratisation), 9, 262n14, 273n7
Women's Alliance for Democracy (Alliance des femmes pour la démocratie), 89, 171, 267n14, 279, 296; honorees, 265n55
Women's capacity to welcome the other, 49, 53, 58, 104, 116, 222
Women's Environment and Development Organization (WEDO), 281
Women's International Center, 296
Women's Liberation Movement (Mouvement de Libération des Femmes), xi, xix, 262n1, 296; activism, 256–57; assertion of a sexed identity by, 211; commitments, xxxi; dynamics, 9; evolution, 24–25, 213–14; feminism and, 207, 236, 257; fight against rape and, 161–62, 241; first public

demonstration, 83–84, 205; as genesic event, 196; gestation for another and, 215–16; going public, 17–18; history, 195, 200–213, 234–35; Lacan and, 206; legal work, 87; May '68 and, 27–28, 201–2, 216; men and, 257–59; as a movement of civilization, 5, 24, 32, 208, 213; naming, 15; nonmixity of, 203, 247–48; origins of, 10–11; psychoanalysis and, 143–44; role of, 3–4; struggles, 3, 5–6, 9, 21, 161, 175, 217, 220, 226, 256; *see also* Psychanalyse et Politique
Woolf, Virginia, 4, 95, 103–4
Workforce, 160, 168–69; discrimination, 180, 186–87; equality in, 71–72; night, 71–72; part-time, 289n17; *see also* Unemployment
World Health Organization (WHO), 158
World Summit for Social Development in Copenhagen, 281
Writing, 23, 48, 86, 91; female compared to feminine, 22, 39, 93; *see also* Language

Zana, Leyla
Zapatero, Jose Luis, 217
Zetkin, Clara, 1, 152